EZEKIEL
A Commentary in the Wesleyan Tradition

*New Beacon Bible Commentary

EZEKIEL
A Commentary in the Wesleyan Tradition

Brad E. Kelle

BEACON HILL PRESS
OF KANSAS CITY

Copyright 2013
by Beacon Hill Press of Kansas City

ISBN 978-0-8341-2945-0

Printed in the United States of America

Cover Design: J.R. Caines
Interior Design: Sharon Page

Unless otherwise indicated all Scripture quotations are from the *Holy Bible, New International Version*® (NIV®). Copyright © 1973, 1978, 1984 by Biblica, Inc.™ Used by permission of Zondervan. All rights reserved worldwide. www.zondervan.com.

King James Version (KJV).

The following copyrighted versions of the Bible are used by permission.

The Holy Bible, English Standard Version (ESV), copyright © 2001 by Crossway Bibles, a division of Good News Publishers. All rights reserved.

The *Hebrew-English Tanakh* (JPS), © 2000 by The Jewish Publication Society. All rights reserved.

The *New American Standard Bible*® (NASB®), © copyright The Lockman Foundation 1960, 1962, 1963, 1971, 1972, 1973, 1975, 1977, 1995.

The *New King James Version* (NKJV). Copyright © 1979, 1980, 1982 Thomas Nelson, Inc.

The *Holy Bible, New Living Translation* (NLT), copyright 1996, 2004. Used by permission of Tyndale House Publishers, Inc., Carol Stream, IL 60188. All rights reserved.

The *New Revised Standard Version* (NRSV) of the Bible, copyright 1989 by the Division of Christian Education of the National Council of the Churches of Christ in the USA. All rights reserved.

Library of Congress Cataloging-in-Publication Data

Kelle, Brad E., 1973-
  Ezekiel / Brad E. Kelle.
    p. cm. — (New Beacon Bible commentary)
  Includes bibliographical references.
  ISBN 978-0-8341-2945-0 (pbk.)
  1. Bible. O.T. Ezekiel—Commentaries. I. Title.
  BS1545.53.K45 2013
  224'.407—dc23

2012044461

DEDICATION

To the generations of Scripture readers before and after me:

To my father, Gene Kelle, lifelong learner (and Sunday school teacher!)
from whom I received a legacy of excitement for reading
(and teaching) the texts of Scripture

and

To my son, Grayson, with whom I have already shared
so many moments finding new meanings (and new questions!)
in these ancient texts

COMMENTARY EDITORS

General Editors

Alex Varughese
  Ph.D., Drew University
  Professor of Biblical Literature
  Mount Vernon Nazarene University
  Mount Vernon, Ohio

Roger Hahn
  Ph.D., Duke University
  Dean of the Faculty
  Professor of New Testament
  Nazarene Theological Seminary
  Kansas City, Missouri

George Lyons
  Ph.D., Emory University
  Professor of New Testament
  Northwest Nazarene University
  Nampa, Idaho

Section Editors

Joseph Coleson
  Ph.D., Brandeis University
  Professor of Old Testament
  Nazarene Theological Seminary
  Kansas City, Missouri

Robert Branson
  Ph.D., Boston University
  Professor of Biblical Literature
    Emeritus
  Olivet Nazarene University
  Bourbonnais, Illinois

Alex Varughese
  Ph.D., Drew University
  Professor of Biblical Literature
  Mount Vernon Nazarene University
  Mount Vernon, Ohio

Jim Edlin
  Ph.D., Southern Baptist Theological
    Seminary
  Professor of Biblical Literature and
    Languages
  Chair, Division of Religion and
    Philosophy
  MidAmerica Nazarene University
  Olathe, Kansas

Kent Brower
  Ph.D., The University of Manchester
  Vice Principal
  Senior Lecturer in Biblical Studies
  Nazarene Theological College
  Manchester, England

George Lyons
  Ph.D., Emory University
  Professor of New Testament
  Northwest Nazarene University
  Nampa, Idaho

CONTENTS

General Editors' Preface	11
Acknowledgments	13
Abbreviations	14
Bibliography	17
INTRODUCTION	21
A. Overview	22
B. The Historical Background of the Prophet and the Book	23
1. Judean History and the Fall of Jerusalem	24
2. The Date Sequence in Ezekiel	26
C. The Prophet and His Audience	28
1. The Exilic Community and the Nature of Exile	28
2. The Trauma of Exile	30
3. Ezekiel, the Priest-Prophet in Exile	32
a. Ezekiel and His Location	33
b. Ezekiel the Priest	34
c. Ezekiel the Priest *and* Prophet	35
D. The Book and Its Audience	37
1. Origins and Composition of the Book of Ezekiel	37
2. Literary and Rhetorical Features	39
a. Language, Style, and Genre	40
b. Visions, Metaphors, and Symbolic Actions	42
c. Traditions in the Book of Ezekiel	43
3. Outline and Movement of the Book	45
E. Ezekiel's Theology	49
1. Ezekiel's Alternative Plot Line for the Trauma of Exile	49
2. The Theology of Debate and Politics	51
a. A Prophet in Debate	52
b. A God in Debate	53
c. The Politics of Debate	54
3. Ezekiel's Priestly Theology	55
4. The Theology of Holiness: Judgment and Restoration	57
a. Holiness and Judgment	57
b. Holiness and Restoration	58
COMMENTARY	63
I. First Vision of God's Presence: Ezekiel's Commissioning (Ezekiel 1—3)	63
A. Superscription(s) (1:1-3)	68
B. Visionary Context of Commissioning: Part I (1:4-28)	69

C. Ezekiel's Commissioning as a Prophet (2:1-7)	73
D. Ingesting the Trauma of the People (2:8—3:15)	75
E. Ezekiel's Commissioning as a Watchman (3:16-21)	78
F. Visionary Context of Commissioning: Part 2 (3:22-23)	79
G. Transition: Instructions for Symbolic Acts (3:24-27)	80

II. Acts and Oracles of Judgment (Ezekiel 4—7) — 85
   A. Five Symbolic Acts (4:1—5:4) — 89
   B. Explanatory Oracles (5:5—7:27) — 96
      1. On Jerusalem (5:5-17) — 96
      2. On the Mountains of Israel (6:1-14) — 100
      3. On the Land of Israel (7:1-27) — 102

III. Second Vision of God's Presence: God Leaves the Temple (Ezekiel 8—11) — 111
   A. Introduction: Visionary Movement to Jerusalem (8:1-4) — 117
   B. First Vision Couplet (8:5—9:11) — 121
      1. Four Scenes of Abomination in the Temple (8:5-18) — 121
      2. The Executioners in Jerusalem (9:1-11) — 127
   C. Second Vision Couplet (10:1—11:23) — 132
      1. Yahweh's Glory Begins to Depart the Temple (10:1-22) — 132
      2. Interruption 1: Judgment on Wicked Officials (11:1-13) — 135
      3. Interruption 2: Promise of Restoration for the Exiles (11:14-21) — 138
      4. Yahweh's Glory Departs the City (11:22-23) — 142
   D. Conclusion: Visionary Return to the Exiles (11:24-25) — 143

IV. Acts and Oracles of Judgment (Ezekiel 12—24) — 149
   A. Part 1: Acts and Oracles of Siege, Exile, and Intercession (12:1—14:23) — 153
      1. Symbolic Acts of Siege and Exile (12:1-28) — 156
      2. Explanatory Oracle: Lack of True Prophets (13:1-23) — 165
         a. Condemnation of Male Prophets (13:1-16) — 166
         b. Condemnation of Female Prophets (13:17-23) — 169
      3. Explanatory Oracle: Lack of True Intercession (14:1-23) — 171
         a. No Intercession for the Sinful (14:1-11) — 171
         b. No Intercession by the Righteous (14:12-23) — 174
   B. Part 2: Metaphorical Discourses (15:1—17:24) — 179
      1. The Useless Vine (15:1-8) — 183
      2. The Faithless Bride (16:1-63) — 185
         a. Introduction (16:1-3a) — 186
         b. Accusations Against Jerusalem (16:3b-34) — 187
         c. Yahweh's Judgment Against Jerusalem (16:35-43) — 192
         d. Renewed Accusations Against Jerusalem (16:44-52) — 194
         e. Oracle of Restoration (16:53-58) — 195
         f. Covenant Renewal with Jerusalem (16:59-63) — 196
      3. The Two Eagles and the Vine (17:1-24) — 198

	C. Part 3: Oracles of Judgment and Lament (18:1—19:14)	205
	1. Retribution and Judgment (18:1-32)	207
	2. Lament over Jerusalem (19:1-14)	214
	D. Part 4: Israel's History of Sin/Rebellion (20:1-49)	216
	1. Introduction (20:1-4)	216
	2. Historical Rehearsal (20:5-29)	217
	3. Application to the Exiles' Present and Future (20:30-44)	219
	4. Oracle of Destruction Against the Negev (20:45-49)	221
	E. Part 5: Metaphorical Discourses and Symbolic Acts (21:1—24:27)	223
	1. The Sword of God (21:1-32)	226
	2. Jerusalem, the Bloody City (22:1-31)	229
	3. The Two Wives of God (23:1-49)	231
	4. The Boiling Pot (24:1-14)	238
	5. Symbolic Act: Ezekiel's Muteness (Beginning of Siege) (24:15-27)	239
V.	The Oracles Against the Nations (Ezekiel 25—32)	245
	A. Oracles Against Surrounding States (25:1-17)	252
	B. Oracles Against Tyre (26:1—28:19)	253
	1. Oracle Against the City of Tyre (26:1-21)	253
	2. Lamentation over Tyre (27:1-36)	256
	3. Oracle Against the King of Tyre (28:1-10)	256
	4. Lamentation over the King of Tyre (28:11-19)	257
	C. Oracle Against Sidon (28:20-24)	258
	D. Future Blessing on Israel (28:25-26)	259
	E. Oracles Against Egypt (29:1—32:32)	259
	1. Proclamation Against Egypt (29:1-21)	261
	2. Lamentation over Egypt (30:1-19)	263
	3. Proclamation Against Pharaoh (30:20—31:18)	263
	4. Lamentation over Pharaoh and Egypt (32:1-16)	265
	5. Funeral Dirge over Egypt (32:17-32)	265
VI.	Preparatory Oracles of Restoration: The Transformation of Israel (Ezekiel 33—37)	273
	A. Ending of the Siege: Ezekiel's New Commission (33:1-33)	277
	B. Metaphorical Discourse: False and True Shepherds (34:1-31)	283
	C. Metaphorical Discourses: Judgment on Mount Seir (Edom) and Restoration for the Mountains of Israel (35:1—36:15)	289
	1. Judgment on Mount Seir (Edom) (35:1-15)	290
	2. Restoration for the Mountains of Israel (36:1-15)	292
	D. Oracle of Transformation for Israel (36:16-38)	293
	E. Vision of the Valley of Bones (37:1-14)	300
	F. Symbolic Act and Oracle of Restoration for Israel (37:15-28)	301
VII.	Preparatory Oracles of Restoration: The Defeat of Gog and the Final Vindication of God (Ezekiel 38—39)	307

      A. Gog's Invasion (38:1-16) — 312
      B. Proclamation of Divine Judgment on Gog (38:17-23) — 315
      C. Gog's Destruction (39:1-10) — 317
      D. Gog's Burial (39:11-20) — 318
      E. Coda: The Final Vindication of Yahweh (39:21-29) — 320

VIII. Third Vision of God's Presence: The Return to a New Temple, Land, and City (Ezekiel 40—48) — 325
      A. The New Temple (40:1—42:20) — 330
      B. Vision of the Return of Yahweh's Presence (43:1-11) — 335
      C. The Torah of the New Temple (43:12—46:24) — 336
      D. The New Land (47:1—48:29) — 343
      E. The New Jerusalem (48:30-35) — 346

GENERAL EDITORS' PREFACE

The purpose of the New Beacon Bible Commentary is to make available to pastors and students in the twenty-first century a biblical commentary that reflects the best scholarship in the Wesleyan theological tradition. The commentary project aims to make this scholarship accessible to a wider audience to assist them in their understanding and proclamation of Scripture as God's Word.

Writers of the volumes in this series not only are scholars within the Wesleyan theological tradition and experts in their field but also have special interest in the books assigned to them. Their task is to communicate clearly the critical consensus and the full range of other credible voices who have commented on the Scriptures. Though scholarship and scholarly contribution to the understanding of the Scriptures are key concerns of this series, it is not intended as an academic dialogue within the scholarly community. Commentators of this series constantly aim to demonstrate in their work the significance of the Bible as the church's book and the contemporary relevance and application of the biblical message. The project's overall goal is to make available to the church and for her service the fruits of the labors of scholars who are committed to their Christian faith.

The *New International Version* (NIV) is the reference version of the Bible used in this series; however, the focus of exegetical study and comments is the biblical text in its original language. When the commentary uses the NIV, it is printed in bold. The text printed in bold italics is the translation of the author. Commentators also refer to other translations where the text may be difficult or ambiguous.

The structure and organization of the commentaries in this series seeks to facilitate the study of the biblical text in a systematic and methodical way. Study of each biblical book begins with an ***Introduction*** section that gives an overview of authorship, date, provenance, audience, occasion, purpose, sociological/cultural issues, textual history, literary features, hermeneutical issues, and theological themes necessary to understand the book. This section also includes a brief outline of the book and a list of general works and standard commentaries.

The commentary section for each biblical book follows the outline of the book presented in the introduction. In some volumes, readers will find section ***overviews*** of large portions of scripture with general comments on their overall literary structure and other literary features. A consistent feature of the commentary is the paragraph-by-paragraph study of biblical texts. This section has three parts: **Behind the Text**, **In the Text**, and **From the Text**.

The goal of the **Behind the Text** section is to provide the reader with all the relevant information necessary to understand the text. This includes specific historical situations reflected in the text, the literary context of the text, sociological and cultural issues, and literary features of the text.

In the Text explores what the text says, following its verse-by-verse structure. This section includes a discussion of grammatical details, word studies, and the connectedness of the text to other biblical books/passages or other parts of the book being studied (the canonical relationship). This section provides transliterations of key words in Hebrew and Greek and their literal meanings. The goal here is to explain what the author would have meant and/or what the audience would have understood as the meaning of the text. This is the largest section of the commentary.

The **From the Text** section examines the text in relation to the following areas: theological significance, intertextuality, the history of interpretation, use of the Old Testament scriptures in the New Testament, interpretation in later church history, actualization, and application.

The commentary provides **sidebars** on topics of interest that are important but not necessarily part of an explanation of the biblical text. These topics are informational items and may cover archaeological, historical, literary, cultural, and theological matters that have relevance to the biblical text. Occasionally, longer detailed discussions of special topics are included as **excurses**.

We offer this series with our hope and prayer that readers will find it a valuable resource for their understanding of God's Word and an indispensable tool for their critical engagement with the biblical texts.

Roger Hahn, Centennial Initiative General Editor
Alex Varughese, General Editor (Old Testament)
George Lyons, General Editor (New Testament)

ACKNOWLEDGMENTS

The completion of a commentary, even one in a series with clearly defined goals and a specific focus, is not the work of one person but so many. Several different colleagues and friends have helped shape this work and offered support throughout the process. I am grateful to my current colleagues in the School of Theology and Christian Ministry at Point Loma Nazarene University for ongoing conversation and for bearing with my seemingly endless desire to chat about some new element of Ezekiel that had arrested my attention on any given day. PLNU supported my work on this commentary through several research grants and fellowships from the Wesleyan Center for Twenty-First Century Studies. Thanks are also due to Alex Varughese for his fine editorial work on the manuscript (and seemingly endless patience with missed deadlines!). I am, of course, most indebted to my wife, Dee, and our now twelve-year-old son, Grayson. As always, they patiently endured my preoccupation with the writing of yet another book, never demanding for themselves but always allowing me the time and space without which the work could not have been completed. I hope that the small contribution of this commentary will lead them to find themselves as I do—captured by the words of this ancient prophetic text and drawn toward the love and mystery of a holy God.

ABBREVIATIONS

With a few exceptions, these abbreviations follow those in *The SBL Handbook of Style* (Alexander 1999).

General

A.D.	anno Domini (precedes date) (equivalent to C.E.)
B.C.	before Christ (follows date) (equivalent to B.C.E.)
B.C.E.	before the Common Era
C.E.	Common Era
cf.	compare
ch	chapter
chs	chapters
e.g.	*exempli gratia*, for example
esp.	especially
etc.	*et cetera*, and the rest
f(f).	and the following one(s)
fem.	feminine
Gk.	Greek
Heb.	Hebrew
i.e.	*id est.*, that is
ktl.	*kai ta loipa* (Gk.: etc.)
lit.	literally
LXX	Septuagint
masc.	masculine
MS	manuscript
MSS	manuscripts
MT	Masoretic Text (of the OT)
n.	note
n.d.	no date
n.p.	no place; no publisher; no page
nn.	notes
NT	New Testament
OAN	oracles against the nations
OT	Old Testament
passim	here and there
pl.	plural
Q	Qumran
Repr.	Reprint(ed)
sg.	singular
s.v.	*sub verbo*, under the word
v	verse
vs.	versus
vv	verses

Modern Edition of the Bible

BHS	Biblia Hebraica Stuttgartensia

Modern English Versions

ESV	English Standard Version
JPS	Hebrew-Jewish Tanakh
KJV	King James Version
NASB	New American Standard Bible
NIV	New International Version (1984 ed.)
NKJV	New King James Version
NLT	New Living Translation
NRSV	New Revised Standard Version

Print Conventions for Translations

Bold font	NIV (bold without quotation marks in the text under study; elsewhere in the regular font, with quotation marks and no further identification)
Bold italic font	Author's translation (without quotation marks)

Behind the Text: Literary or historical background information average readers might not know from reading the biblical text alone
In the Text: Comments on the biblical text, words, phrases, grammar, and so forth
From the Text: The use of the text by later interpreters, contemporary relevance, theological and ethical implications of the text, with particular emphasis on Wesleyan concerns

Ancient Sources

Old Testament

Gen	Genesis	Dan	Daniel	**New Testament**	
Exod	Exodus	Hos	Hosea	Matt	Matthew
Lev	Leviticus	Joel	Joel	Mark	Mark
Num	Numbers	Amos	Amos	Luke	Luke
Deut	Deuteronomy	Obad	Obadiah	John	John
Josh	Joshua	Jonah	Jonah	Acts	Acts
Judg	Judges	Mic	Micah	Rom	Romans
Ruth	Ruth	Nah	Nahum	1—2 Cor	1—2 Corinthians
1—2 Sam	1—2 Samuel	Hab	Habakkuk		
1—2 Kgs	1—2 Kings	Zeph	Zephaniah	Gal	Galatians
1—2 Chr	1—2 Chronicles	Hag	Haggai	Eph	Ephesians
Ezra	Ezra	Zech	Zechariah	Phil	Philippians
Neh	Nehemiah	Mal	Malachi	Col	Colossians
Esth	Esther			1—2 Thess	1—2 Thessalonians
Job	Job			1—2 Tim	1—2 Timothy
Ps/Pss	Psalm/Psalms			Titus	Titus
Prov	Proverbs			Phlm	Philemon
Eccl	Ecclesiastes			Heb	Hebrews
Song	Song of Songs / Song of Solomon			Jas	James
				1—2 Pet	1—2 Peter
				1—2—3 John	1—2—3 John
Isa	Isaiah			Jude	Jude
Jer	Jeremiah			Rev	Revelation
Lam	Lamentations				
Ezek	Ezekiel				

(Note: Chapter and verse numbering in the MT and LXX often differ compared to those in English Bibles. To avoid confusion, all biblical references follow the chapter and verse numbering in English translations, even when the text in the MT and LXX is under discussion.)

Secondary Sources: Journals, Periodicals, Major Reference Works, and Series

AB	Anchor Bible
AnBib	Analecta biblica
ANET	*Ancient Near Eastern Texts Relating to the Old Testament*. Edited by J. B. Pritchard. 3d ed. Princeton, 1969.
AOTC	Abingdon Old Testament Commentaries
ARAB	*Ancient Records of Assyria and Babylonia*. Daniel David Luckenbill. 2 vols. Chicago, 1926-27.
BZAW	Beihefte zur Zeitschrift für die alttestamentliche Wissenschaft
CBOTS	Coniectanea Biblica Old Testament Series
COS	*The Context of Scripture*. Edited by W. W. Hallo. 3 vols. Leiden, 1997—2003.
CurBS	*Currents in Research: Biblical Studies*
FCB	Feminist Companion to the Bible
FOTL	Forms of the Old Testament Literature
HSM	Harvard Semitic Monographs
HUCA	*Hebrew Union College Annual*
ICC	International Critical Commentary
Int	*Interpretation*
JBL	Journal of Biblical Literature
JSOTSup	Journal for the Study of the Old Testament: Supplement Series
LHBOTS	Library of Hebrew Bible/Old Testament Studies
NCBC	New Century Bible Commentary
NIB	*The New Interpreter's Bible*
NIBCOT	New International Biblical Commentary on the Old Testament
NICOT	New International Commentary on the Old Testament
OTG	Old Testament Guides
OTL	Old Testament Library

SBLABib	Society of Biblical Literature Academia Biblica
SBLDS	Society of Biblical Literature Dissertation Series
SBLSymS	Society of Biblical Literature Symposium Series
SBT	Studies in Biblical Theology
SSN	Studia semitica neerlandica
VTSup	Supplements to Vetus Testamentum
WBC	Word Biblical Commentary

Apocrypha

Bar	Baruch
Add Dan	Additions to Daniel
Pr Azar	Prayer of Azariah
Bel	Bel and the Dragon
Sg Three	Song of the Three Young Men
Sus	Susanna
1—2 Esd	1—2 Esdras
Add Esth	Additions to Esther
Ep Jer	Epistle of Jeremiah
Jdt	Judith
1—2 Macc	1—2 Maccabees
3—4 Macc	3—4 Maccabees
Pr Man	Prayer of Manasseh
Ps 151	Psalm 151
Sir	Sirach/Ecclesiasticus
Tob	Tobit
Wis	Wisdom of Solomon

Greek	Letter	English	Hebrew/Aramaic	Letter	English
α	alpha	a	א	alef	ʾ
β	bēta	b	ב	bet	b
γ	gamma	g	ג	gimel	g
γ	gamma nasal	n (before γ, κ, ξ, χ)	ד	dalet	d
δ	delta	d	ה	he	h
ε	epsilon	e	ו	vav	v or w
ζ	zēta	z	ז	zayin	z
η	ēta	ē	ח	khet	ḥ
θ	thēta	th	ט	tet	ṭ
ι	iōta	i	י	yod	y
κ	kappa	k	ך/כ	kaf	k
λ	lambda	l	ל	lamed	l
μ	mu	m	ם/מ	mem	m
ν	nu	n	ן/נ	nun	n
ξ	xi	x	ס	samek	s̄
ο	omicron	o	ע	ayin	ʿ
π	pi	p	ף/פ	pe	p; f (spirant)
ρ	rhō	r	ץ/צ	tsade	ṣ
ρ	initial rhō	rh	ק	qof	q
σ/ς	sigma	s	ר	resh	r
τ	tau	t	שׂ	sin	ś
υ	upsilon	y	שׁ	shin	š
υ	upsilon	u (in diphthongs: au, eu, ēu, ou, ui)	ת	tav	t; th (spirant)
φ	phi	ph			
χ	chi	ch			
ψ	psi	ps			
ω	ōmega	ō			
ʿ	rough breathing	h (before initial vowels or diphthongs)			

BIBLIOGRAPHY

Abma, Richtsje. 1999. *Bonds of Love: Methodic Studies of Prophetic Texts with Marriage Imagery (Isaiah 50:1-3 and 54:1-10, Hosea 1—3, Jeremiah 2—3)*. SSN 40. Assen: Van Gorcum.
Allen, Jon G. 1995. *Coping with Trauma: A Guide to Self-Understanding*. Washington, D.C.: American Psychiatric Press.
Allen, Leslie C. 1990. *Ezekiel 20—48*. WBC 29. Dallas: Word Books.
———. 1994. *Ezekiel 1—19*. WBC 28. Dallas: Word Books.
Antze, Paul, and Michael Lambek, eds. 1996. *Tense Past: Cultural Essays in Trauma and Memory*. New York: Routledge.
Barton, John. 1990. History and Rhetoric in the Prophets. Pages 51-64 in *The Bible as Rhetoric: Studies in Biblical Persuasion and Credibility*. Edited by M. Warner. Warwick Studies in Philosophy and Literature. London: Routledge.
Baumann, Gerline. 2003. *Love and Violence: Marriage as Metaphor for the Relationship between YHWH and Israel in the Prophetic Books*. Collegeville, Minn.: Liturgical Press.
Betts, Terry J. 2005. *Ezekiel the Priest: A Custodian of Tôrâ*. Studies in Biblical Literature 74. New York: Peter Lang.
Blenkinsopp, Joseph. 1990. *Ezekiel*. Int. Louisville, Ky.: John Knox.
Block, Daniel I. 1997. *The Book of Ezekiel Chapters 1—24*. NICOT. Grand Rapids: Eerdmans.
———. 1998. *The Book of Ezekiel Chapters 25—48*. NICOT. Grand Rapids: Eerdmans.
Boadt, Lawrence. 1992. Ezekiel, Book of. Pages 711-22 in vol. 2 of the *Anchor Bible Dictionary*. Edited by David Noel Freedman. 6 vols. New York: Doubleday.
Booth, Wayne G. 1979. Metaphor as Rhetoric: The Problem of Evaluation. Pages 47-70 in *On Metaphor*. Edited by S. Sacks. Chicago: University of Chicago Press.
Bowen, Nancy R. 1999. The Daughters of Your People: Female Prophets in Ezekiel 13:17-23. *JBL* 118:417-33.
———. 2010. *Ezekiel*. AOTC. Nashville: Abingdon.
Brueggemann, Walter. 1986. *Hopeful Imagination: Prophetic Voices in Exile*. Philadelphia: Fortress.
———. 2008. *Old Testament Theology: An Introduction*. Library of Biblical Theology. Nashville: Abingdon.
Calvin, John. 1948. *Commentaries on the First Twenty Chapters of the Book of the Prophet Ezekiel*. Translated by Thomas Myers. 2 vols. Grand Rapids: Eerdmans.
Carley, Keith W. 1974. *Ezekiel among the Prophets: A Study of Ezekiel's Place in Prophetic Tradition*. SBT 2/31. Naperville, Ill.: Allenson.
Caruth, Cathy. 1996. *Unclaimed Experience: Trauma, Narrative, and History*. Baltimore: Johns Hopkins University Press.
Carvalho, Corrine L. 2010. *The Book of Ezekiel: Question by Question*. Question by Question Bible Study Commentary. New York: Paulist.
Casson, David S. 2004. The Mountain Shall Be Most Holy: Metaphoric Mountains in Ezekiel's Rhetoric. PhD diss. Emory University.
Christman, Angela Russell. 2005. *"What Did Ezekiel See?" Christian Exegesis of Ezekiel's Vision of the Chariot from Irenaeus to Gregory the Great*. Bible in Ancient Christianity 4. Leiden: Brill.
Clements, Ronald E. 1996. *Ezekiel*. Westminster Bible Companion. Louisville, Ky.: Westminster John Knox.
Cody, Aelred. 1969. *A History of the Old Testament Priesthood*. AnBib 35. Rome: Pontifical Biblical Institute.
Cook, Stephen L., and Corrine Patton, eds. 2004. *Ezekiel's Hierarchical World: Wrestling with a Tiered Reality*. SBLSymS 31. Atlanta: Society of Biblical Literature.
Cooke, G. A. 1937. *A Critical and Exegetical Commentary on the Book of Ezekiel*. 2 vols. ICC. New York: Charles Scribner's Sons.
Cross, Frank Moore. 1973. *Canaanite Myth and Hebrew Epic: Essays in the History of the Religion of Israel*. Cambridge: Harvard University Press.
Darr, Katheryn Pfisterer. 1994. Ezekiel among the Critics. *CurBS* 2:9-24.
———. 2001. The Book of Ezekiel. Pages 1073-1607 in vol. 6 of *NIB*. 12 vols. Nashville: Abingdon.

Davis, Ellen F. 1989. *Swallowing the Scroll: Textuality and the Dynamics of Discourse in Ezekiel's Prophecy.* Bible and Literature Series 21. Sheffield: Almond.

Dijk-Hemmes, Fokkelien van. 1995. The Metaphorization of Women in Prophetic Speech: An Analysis of Ezekiel 23. Pages 244-55 in *A Feminist Companion to the Latter Prophets.* Edited by Athalya Brenner. FCB 8. Sheffield: Sheffield Academic Press.

Driver, S. R. 1891. *An Introduction to the Literature of the Old Testament.* The International Theological Library 1. New York: C. Scribner.

Duguid, Iain M. 1994. *Ezekiel and the Leaders of Israel.* VTSup 56. Leiden: Brill.

Durlesser, James A. 2006. *The Metaphorical Narratives in the Book of Ezekiel.* Lewiston, N.Y.: Edwin Mellen.

Eichrodt, Walther. 1970. *Ezekiel.* OTL. London: SCM.

Figley, Charles R. 1985. From Victim to Survivor: Social Responsibility in the Wake of Catastrophe. Pages 398-415 in *Trauma and Its Wake: The Study and Treatment of Post-Traumatic Stress Disorder.* Edited by Charles R. Figley. New York: Brunner/Mazel.

Figley, Charles R., and Rolf J. Kleber. 1995. Beyond the "Victim": Secondary Traumatic Stress. Pages 78-95 in *Beyond Trauma: Cultural and Societal Dynamics.* Edited by Rolf J. Kleber, Charles R. Figley, Berthold P. R. Gersons. The Plenum Series on Stress and Coping. New York: Plenum.

Fischer, O. R. 1939. The Unity of the Book of Ezekiel. PhD diss. Boston University.

Fox, Michael. 1980. The Rhetoric of Ezekiel's Vision of the Valley of the Bones. *HUCA* 51:1-15.

Friebel, K. G. 1999. *Jeremiah's and Ezekiel's Sign-Acts.* JSOTSup 283. Sheffield: Sheffield Academic Press.

Gafney, Wilda C. 2008. *Daughters of Miriam: Women Prophets in Ancient Israel.* Minneapolis: Fortress.

Galambush, Julie. 1992. *Jerusalem in the Book of Ezekiel: The City as Yahweh's Wife.* SBLDS 130. Atlanta: Scholars Press.

_____. 2004. God's Land and Mine: Creation as Property in the Book of Ezekiel. Pages 91-108 in *Ezekiel's Hierarchical World: Wrestling with a Tiered Reality.* Edited by Stephen L. Cook and Corrine Patton. SBLSymS 31. Atlanta: Society of Biblical Literature.

_____. 2006. Necessary Enemies: Nebuchadnezzar, YHWH, and Gog in Ezekiel 38—39. Pages 254-67 in *Israel's Prophets and Israel's Past: Essays on the Relationship of the Prophetic Texts and Israelite History in Honor of John H. Hayes.* Edited by Brad E. Kelle and Megan Bishop Moore. LHBOTS 446. New York: T&T Clark.

Garber, David G., Jr. 2004. Traumatizing Ezekiel, the Exilic Prophet. Pages 215-35 in *Psychology and the Bible: A New Way to Read the Scriptures Volume 2: From Genesis to Apocalyptic Vision.* Edited by J. Harold Ellens and Wayne G. Rollins. Praeger Perspectives: Psychology, Religion, and Spirituality. Westport, Conn.: Praeger.

_____. 2007 (November 19). "I Went in Bitterness": Theological Implications of a Trauma Theory Reading of Ezekiel. Paper presented at the annual meeting of the Society of Biblical Literature. Washington, D.C.

Geller, Jay. 2000. Trauma. Pages 261-67 in *Handbook of Postmodern Biblical Interpretation.* Edited by A. K. M. Adam. St. Louis: Chalice.

Gowan, Donald E. 1985. *Ezekiel.* Knox Preaching Guides. Atlanta: John Knox.

Greathouse, William, and H. Ray Dunning. 1982. *An Introduction to Wesleyan Theology.* Kansas City: Beacon Hill Press of Kansas City.

Greenberg, Moshe. 1983. *Ezekiel 1—20: A New Translation with Introduction and Commentary.* AB 22. Garden City, N.Y.: Doubleday.

_____. 1997. *Ezekiel 21—37: A New Translation with Introduction and Commentary.* AB 22A. New York: Doubleday.

Habel, Norman C., ed. 2001. *The Earth Story in the Psalms and the Prophets.* Earth Bible 4. Sheffield: Sheffield Academic Press.

_____. 2004. The Silence of the Lands: The Ecojustice Implications of Ezekiel's Judgment Oracles. Pages 127-40 in *Ezekiel's Hierarchical World: Wrestling with a Tiered Reality.* Edited by Stephen L. Cook and Corrine Patton. SBLSymS 31. Atlanta: Society of Biblical Literature.

Hahn, Scott W., and John S. Bergsma. 2004. What Laws Were "Not Good"? A Canonical Approach to the Problem of Ezekiel 20:25-26. *JBL* 123:201-18.

Halperin, D. J. 1993. *Seeking Ezekiel: Text and Psychology.* University Park, Pa.: Pennsylvania State University Press.

Hals, Ronald M. 1989. *Ezekiel.* FOTL 19. Grand Rapids: Eerdmans.

Hasel, Michael G. 2005. *Military Practice and Polemic: Israel's Laws of Warfare in Near Eastern Perspective.* Berrien Springs, Mich.: Andrews University Press.

Hayes, John H., and Paul K. Hooker. 1988. *A New Chronology of the Kings of Israel and Judah and Its Implications for Biblical History and Literature*. Atlanta: John Knox.

Herman, Judith. 1997. *Trauma and Recovery: The Aftermath of Violence—from Domestic Abuse to Political Terror*. 2nd ed. New York: Basic Books.

Herntrich, Volkmar. 1933. *Ezekiel Probleme*. BZAW 61. Geissen: Töppelmann.

Jenson, Robert W. 2009. *Ezekiel*. Brazos Theological Commentary on the Bible. Grand Rapids: Brazos.

Joyce, Paul. 1989. *Divine Initiative and Human Response in Ezekiel*. JSOTSup 51. Sheffield: JSOT Press.

———. 2007. *Ezekiel: A Commentary*. LHBOTS 482. New York: T&T Clark.

Kamionkowski, S. Tamar. 2003. *Gender Reversal and Cosmic Chaos: A Study on the Book of Ezekiel*. JSOTSup 368. Sheffield: Sheffield Academic Press.

Kelle, Brad E. 2005. *Hosea 2: Metaphor and Rhetoric in Historical Perspective*. SBLABib 20. Atlanta: Society of Biblical Literature.

———. 2007. *Ancient Israel at War 853-586 B.C*. Essential Histories 67. Oxford: Osprey.

———. 2008. "Wartime Rhetoric: Prophetic Metaphorization of Cities as Female." Pages 95-111 in *Writing and Reading War: Rhetoric, Gender, and Ethics in Biblical and Modern Contexts*. Edited by Brad E. Kelle and Frank Ritchel Ames. SBLSymS 42. Atlanta: Society of Biblical Literature.

Kenny, Michael G. 1996. Trauma, Time, Illness, and Culture: An Anthropological Approach to Traumatic Memory. Pages 151-71 in Paul Antze and Michael Lambek, eds. *Tense Past: Cultural Essays in Trauma and Memory*. New York: Routledge.

Kohn, Risa Levitt. 2002. *A New Heart and a New Soul: Ezekiel, the Exile and the Torah*. JSOTSup 358. London: Continuum.

Kutsko, John F. 2000. *Between Heaven and Earth: Divine Presence and Absence in the Book of Ezekiel*. Biblical and Judaic Studies from the University of California, San Diego 7. Winona Lake, Ind.: Eisenbrauns.

Lakoff, George, and Mark Johnson. 1980. *Metaphors We Live By*. Chicago: University of Chicago Press.

Lapsley, Jacqueline E. 2000a. *Can These Bones Live? The Problem of the Moral Self in the Book of Ezekiel*. BZAW 301. Berlin: Walter de Gruyter.

———. 2000b. Shame and Self-Knowledge: The Positive Role of Shame in Ezekiel's View of the Moral Self. Pages 143-73 in *The Book of Ezekiel: Theological and Anthropological Perspectives*. Edited by Margaret S. Odell and John T. Strong. SBLSymS 9. Atlanta: Society of Biblical Literature.

Levenson, Jon D. 1976. *Theology of the Program of Restoration of Ezekiel 40—48*. HSM 10. Missoula, Mont.: Scholars Press.

———. 1985. *Sinai and Zion: An Entry into the Jewish Bible*. New Voices in Biblical Studies. San Francisco: Harper and Row.

Lieb, Michael. 1998. *Children of Ezekiel: Aliens, UFOs, the Crisis of Race, and the Advent of End Time*. Durham, N.C.: Duke University Press.

Lyons, Michael A. 2009. *From Law to Prophecy: Ezekiel's Use of the Holiness Code*. LHBOTS 507. New York: T&T Clark.

Matties, Gordon H. 1990. *Ezekiel 18 and the Rhetoric of Moral Discourse*. SBLDS 126. Atlanta: Scholars Press.

McKeating, Henry. 1983. Repr. 1995. *Ezekiel*. OTG. Sheffield: Sheffield Academic Press.

Meyers, Carol. 1992. Cherubim. Pages 899-900 in vol. 1 of the *Anchor Bible Dictionary*. Edited by David Noel Freedman. 6 vols. New York: Doubleday.

Milgrom, Jacob. 1991. *Leviticus 1—16: A New Translation with Introduction and Commentary*. AB 3. New York: Doubleday.

Miller, Patrick D. 2000. *The Religion of Ancient Israel*. Library of Ancient Israel. London: SPCK.

Mol, Jurrien. 2009. *Collective and Individual Responsibility: A Description of Corporate Personality in Ezekiel 18—20*. SSN 53. Leiden: Brill.

Moore, Megan Bishop, and Brad E. Kelle. 2011. *Biblical History and Israel's Past: The Changing Study of the Bible and History*. Grand Rapids: Eerdmans.

Moughtin-Mumby, Sharon. 2008. *Sexual and Marital Metaphors in Hosea, Jeremiah, Isaiah, and Ezekiel*. Oxford Theological Monographs. Oxford: Oxford University Press.

Newsom, Carol A. 1984. A Maker of Metaphors: Ezekiel's Oracles Against Tyre. *Int* 38:151-64.

Odell, Margaret S. 2005. *Ezekiel*. Smyth and Helwys Bible Commentary. Macon, Ga.: Smyth and Helwys.

O'Rourke, Marjorie Boyle. 2001. The Law of the Heart: The Death of a Fool (1 Samuel 25). *JBL* 120:401-27.

Petersen, David L. 2002. *The Prophetic Literature: An Introduction.* Louisville, Ky.: Westminster John Knox.

Renz, Thomas. 1999. *The Rhetorical Function of the Book of Ezekiel.* VTSup 76. Leiden: Brill.

Schmitt, John J. 2004. Psychoanalyzing Ezekiel. Pages 185-201 in *Psychology and the Bible: A New Way to Read the Scriptures, Volume 2: From Genesis to Apocalyptic Vision.* Edited by J. Harold Ellens and Wayne G. Rollins. Praeger Perspectives: Psychology, Religion, and Spirituality. Westport, Conn.: Praeger.

Smith-Christopher, Daniel L. 1997. Reassessing the Historical and Sociological Impact of the Babylonian Exile (597/587-539 BCE). Pages 7-36 in *Exile: Old Testament, Jewish, and Christian Conceptions.* Edited by James M. Scott. Supplements to the Journal for the Study of Judaism 56. Leiden: Brill.

_____. 1999. Ezekiel on Fanon's Couch: A Postcolonialist Dialogue with David Halperin's *Seeking Ezekiel.* Pages 108-44 in *Peace and Justice Shall Embrace: Power and Theopolitics in the Bible.* Edited by Ted Grimsrud and Loren L. Johns. Telford, Pa.: Pandora.

Stevenson, Kalinda Rose. 1996. *Vision of Transformation: The Territorial Rhetoric of Ezekiel 40—48.* SBLDS 154. Atlanta: Scholars Press.

Strong, John T. 2000. God's *Kābôd:* The Presence of Yahweh in the Book of Ezekiel. Pages 69-95 in *The Book of Ezekiel: Theological and Anthropological Perspectives.* Edited by Margaret S. Odell and John T. Strong. SBLSymS 9. Atlanta: Society of Biblical Literature.

Sweeney, Marvin A. 2001. *Ezekiel: Zadokite Priest and Visionary Prophet of the Exile.* Occasional Papers 41. The Institute for Antiquity and Christianity. Claremont, Calif.: Institute for Antiquity and Christianity.

_____. 2005. *The Prophetic Literature.* Interpreting Biblical Texts Series. Nashville: Abingdon.

Tooman, William A., and Michael A. Lyons, eds. 2010. *Transforming Visions: Transformations of Text, Tradition, and Theology in Ezekiel.* Princeton Theological Monograph Series. Eugene, Oreg.: Pickwick.

Tsevat, M. 1959. The Neo-Assyrian and Neo-Babylonian Vassal Oaths and the Prophet Ezekiel. *JBL* 78:199-204.

Tuell, Steven S. 1992. *The Law of the Temple in Ezekiel 40—48.* HSM 49. Atlanta: Scholars Press.

_____. 2000. Divine Presence and Absence in Ezekiel's Prophecy. Pages 97-116 in *The Book of Ezekiel: Theological and Anthropological Perspectives.* Edited by Margaret S. Odell and John T. Strong. SBLSymS 9. Atlanta: Society of Biblical Literature.

_____. 2009. *Ezekiel.* NIBCOT. Peabody, Mass.: Hendrickson.

Viberg, Ake. 2007. *Prophets in Action: An Analysis of Prophetic Symbolic Acts in the Old Testament.* CBOTS 55. Stockholm: Almqvist and Wiksell.

Wesley, John. 1971. *A Plain Account of Christian Perfection.* Repr. Kansas City: Beacon Hill Press of Kansas City.

_____. 1975. *Explanatory Notes upon the Old Testament.* 3 vols. Salem, Ohio: Schmul.

Wevers, John W. 1969. *Ezekiel.* NCBC. Grand Rapids: Eerdmans.

Yee, Gail A. 2003. *Poor Banished Children of Eve: Woman as Evil in the Hebrew Bible.* Minneapolis: Fortress.

Zimmerli, Walther. 1979. *Ezekiel 1: A Commentary on the Book of the Prophet Ezekiel.* Hermeneia. Philadelphia: Fortress.

_____. 1982. *I Am Yahweh.* Edited by Walter Brueggemann. Atlanta: John Knox.

_____. 1983. *Ezekiel 2: A Commentary on the Book of the Prophet Ezekiel.* Hermeneia. Philadelphia: Fortress.

INTRODUCTION

And I said, Ah Lord Yahweh! They say of me,
"Is he not always speaking in metaphors?" (Ezek 20:49).

"There is much in this book which is very mysterious,
especially in the beginning and latter end of it"
(Wesley 1975, 2281).

For readers from the Wesleyan theological tradition, the book of Ezekiel presents an interesting dilemma. On the one hand, to engage this theological document is to step into a mad world of bizarre imagery, exotic visions, and graphic language. The book teems with visions that are esoteric, cosmic, and surreal, and with images that portray doom, violence, and sex. Even the talk of restoration and hope, like that of judgment and destruction, appears in categories foreign to most contemporary readers—"priestly" categories that emphasize the temple, priests, cleanness/purity, and defilement/contamination and are similar to traditions found in OT books such as Exodus and Leviticus. Within ancient Judaism, there was a tradition that forbade Jews under the age of thirty from reading the beginning and ending of the book (Block 1997, 44), and Christians have similarly struggled to find in Ezekiel the kinds of connections with the gospel of Christ afforded by books such as Isaiah and Micah.

On the other hand, John Wesley, while recognizing the book's strangeness (see opening quotation), heralded Ezekiel as a crucial voice for the theology of holiness. He saw Ezek 36:25-38, for example, as one of the clearest portraits of sanctification in the OT, with v 26 yielding the picture of a "sanctified heart, in which the almighty grace of God is victorious, and turns it from all sin to God" (Wesley 1975, 2385). Indeed, the emphasis on God's holiness and its implications for God's people is a dominant characteristic of Ezekiel. The book's theology is grounded in the conviction that God is holy, with an uncompromising sovereignty and freedom. For Ezekiel, this divine holiness results in judgment upon God's people, even as it alone provides the hopeful possibility of an alternative future.

This commentary attempts a fresh engagement with Ezekiel and its challenges in dialogue with the Wesleyan theological tradition. There is no attempt in this introduction or in the commentary that follows to address every critical issue in the interpretation of the book. Ezekiel study on the whole remains indebted to the three seminal commentaries by Walther Zimmerli (1979; 1983), Moshe Greenberg (1983; 1997), and Daniel Block (1997; 1998), which comprehensively handle the book's critical issues in their various ways. The reader is encouraged to consult these commentaries, as well as the host of other recent works listed in the bibliography that provide a variety of approaches to Ezekiel. The aim of this volume is to offer a distinctive engagement with the theological dynamics of the book for readers from the Wesleyan theological tradition, with a special eye to Ezekiel's use of OT priestly theology to respond to the trauma associated with the Babylonian exile.

A. Overview

How should we approach this strange prophet and foreign, yet important, book? That process begins by entering into the world of Ezekiel and the book that bears his name. The book is a presentation of the words, actions, and visions of a Jerusalemite priest, who was deported with other Judeans to Babylonia in 597 B.C. After nearly five years in exile, he experienced visions of Yahweh that commissioned him to serve as a prophet and later other visions that showed him abominations in the Jerusalem temple and Yahweh's abandonment of it. Through symbolic actions and spoken oracles, Ezekiel proclaimed a message of judgment and destruction for Jerusalem until its fall in 586 B.C., followed by subsequent messages of hope and restoration based on Yahweh's holiness. Finally, about fourteen years after Jerusalem's destruction, the prophet again experienced visions of Yahweh that revealed a plan for a restored temple, city, and people.

On the one hand, then, this book testifies to the experiences of Ezekiel and his immediate audience. Simultaneously, it represents a purposefully crafted collection of materials designed to be a theological document read by generations of exiles attempting to understand their past and present. Hence, the best entryway into the world of the prophet and the book is precisely the very human experiences of Ezekiel, his immediate audience, and the subsequent generations of his people.

The Humanity of the Biblical Writers

Some interpreters, such as the sixteenth-century Reformer John Calvin, shied away from the human dimension of the book of Ezekiel. Calvin denied that any part of the book came from Ezekiel's own experience, rhetoric, or style, but every single utterance, including the bizarre visions and graphic metaphors, were of direct divine origin, having been given by the Holy Spirit's unfettered acting upon the prophet's mind (Calvin 1948, ix-xx). In this view, "inspiration" is virtually dictation, rather than the Spirit's broad and cooperative guidance of a human being's formulations, and the human experiences of Ezekiel and his audience are largely insignificant for understanding the book. By contrast, the Wesleyan tradition features a more dynamic view of inspiration that appreciates the full participation of the human writers, including the impact of their particular contexts and experiences, and highlights the act of cooperation between God and humans that gave rise to the biblical texts.

B. The Historical Background of the Prophet and the Book

> "The end has come! The end has come!
> It has roused itself against you.
> It has come!" (Ezek 7:6).

The smell of destruction and death lingers over the words of the book of Ezekiel, and all subsequent readers, even those now separated by thousands of years, find themselves drawn back into the experiences of a community of exiles. The opening verses of Ezekiel locate the beginning of the prophet's ministry in "the fifth year of the exile of King Jehoiachin" (593 B.C.; 1:2). With this statement, the book informs its readers of the intimate connection between Ezekiel's preaching and the larger historical developments that led to the traumatic events of Jerusalem's destruction and the people's exile. The opening locates Ezekiel and his audience in one of the most turbulent periods in the history of the ancient Near East, and the reference to exile reminds readers that the kingdom of Judah, even before the beginning of Ezekiel's prophetic activity, was enmeshed in a web of shifting political powers and had already experienced the traumatic realities of war, vassalage, and conquest.

1. Judean History and the Fall of Jerusalem

In order to understand these experiences and how they impact the book of Ezekiel, we must see them in the light of certain historical events that unfolded across the ancient Near East during the seventh and sixth centuries B.C. For nearly two hundred years before this period, the Assyrian Empire had dominated the smaller kingdoms in Syria-Palestine, including Israel and Judah. Between the ninth and seventh centuries, several of the kingdoms made various attempts to throw off the Assyrian yoke, and in response the Assyrians subjected significant parts of the ancient Near East to destruction, deportation, and provincialization. The northern kingdom of Israel, for example, suffered destruction at the hands of the Assyrians near the end of the eighth century. Although Judah became involved in some unsuccessful rebellions against Assyria and suffered some punitive actions (see, for example, 2 Kgs 18—19), it was primarily a submissive vassal throughout the period of Assyria's greatest power in the seventh century.

The rise of the Babylonians in 626 B.C., however, marked the beginning of a turbulent period when dominance of the ancient Near East shifted away from the Assyrians. Throughout the last part of the seventh century, Judah and its neighbors were caught in a vortex of competing powers as the Assyrians, Egyptians, Babylonians, and Medes vied for dominance. If the prophet Ezekiel was thirty years old at the beginning of his ministry (see commentary on 1:1), then he was born during this period of struggle that marked the transition from Assyrian to Babylonian domination.

As Assyria gradually lost its grip on Syria-Palestine, Egypt exerted increasing dominance over the area and positioned itself as the successor to Assyrian control. When the Babylonians and Medes conquered the Assyrian capital of Nineveh in 612 B.C. and pushed the remnants of the Assyrian army to Harran in northern Syria, the Egyptian pharaoh, Neco II, marched northward to support the Assyrians. On the way, for reasons that are unknown, he killed King Josiah of Judah at Megiddo (2 Kgs 23; cf. 2 Chr 35). The Babylonians and Medes ultimately dealt the final blow to the Assyrians at Haran around 609 B.C. and forced the Egyptians to withdraw. On his way home, Pharaoh Neco established Egyptian control of Syria-Palestine up to the area of Carchemish and placed a new king named Jehoiakim on the throne in Jerusalem as an Egyptian vassal (2 Kgs 23:34-35).

The decisive turning point for the history of Judah and its neighbors came a few years later at the battle of Carchemish in 605 B.C. At that time, the Babylonians, led by their newly crowned emperor Nebuchadnezzar II, defeated the Egyptians and gained control of all of Syria-Palestine. Soon after, Jehoiakim officially switched Judah's loyalty from Egypt to Babylonia, but this loyalty would be short-lived. Just four years later, around 601 B.C., Nebuchadnezzar suffered an unexpected defeat while attempting to invade Egypt. Upon this defeat, rebellion broke out against Babylonia across Syria-Palestine, and Jehoiakim withheld Judah's tribute payment in a sign of open defiance (2 Kgs 24:1).

The Babylonian response came in the form of a campaign by Nebuchadnezzar against Jerusalem that began in 598 B.C. Although there are differing biblical traditions about what happened to Jehoiakim, it appears that he died in office while the Babylonians were still en route to Jerusalem (see 2 Kgs 24:6; cf. 2 Chr 36:6). His eighteen-year-old son, Jehoiachin, inherited both his father's throne and ill-fated rebellion (2 Kgs 24:6). When Nebuchadnezzar arrived and laid siege to Jerusalem, Jehoiachin surrendered without resistance. Babylonian records indicate that they took the city on March 15 or 16, 597 B.C. Likely because Jehoiachin was not personally responsible for the revolt and immediately surrendered, Nebuchadnezzar did not destroy Jerusalem. Rather, he deported Jehoiachin, along with the "upper crust" of Jerusalem's religious, political, and social leaders, into exile in Babylonia, and appointed Zedekiah king in Jerusalem as a Babylonian vassal (2 Kgs 24:17).

The Babylonian Capture of Jerusalem

The chronicles of ancient Babylonia preserve the record of King Nebuchadnezzar II's initial capture of Jerusalem in 597 B.C.: "Year 7 [598-597], month Kislev [December-January]: the king of Akkad moved his army in Hatti land [west], laid siege to the city of Judah [Jerusalem] and on the second day of the month Adar [March 15 or 16] he captured the city and seized its king. He appointed in it a king of his liking, took heavy booty from it and sent it to Babylon" (ANET 564).

The choice of Zedekiah proved disastrous for Judah and Jerusalem. In the decade after 597 B.C., the region continued to be torn between Babylonian and Egyptian attempts at dominance. Throughout this time, biblical texts depict Zedekiah as a weak, vacillating ruler who floundered amid competing pro-Babylonian and pro-Egyptian policy advisers. Just a few years after 597, Zedekiah apparently hosted a conference in Jerusalem with officials from Edom, Moab, Ammon, Tyre, and Sidon in order to coordinate a rebellion in the west (ca. 593 B.C.; see Jer 27:1-3). The revolt never materialized, and Judean representatives, perhaps including Zedekiah himself, went to Babylon shortly after to confirm their loyalty (Jer 51:59).

In 592 B.C., however, Pharaoh Psammetichus II, who had come to the Egyptian throne in 595, won a sweeping victory against Ethiopia and celebrated by embarking on a victory tour of Syria-Palestine. Likely as a result of this Egyptian resurgence, coupled with anticipation of direct Egyptian help, Zedekiah rebelled openly against Babylonian sovereignty in the late 590s or early 580s.

In the late fall of 589 B.C., Nebuchadnezzar set out from Babylon, and by January of 587 B.C. he had placed Jerusalem under siege (2 Kgs 25:1-2). While the territory of Judah was devastated (Jer 34:7; 44:2; Lam 2:2-5), Jerusalem itself withstood the siege for about eighteen months but finally fell in the summer of 586 B.C. (2 Kgs 25; Jer 21:3-7; 39; 52:4-5; Ezek 24:1-2). Unlike in 597 B.C., this time the Babylonian treatment of Jerusalem was severe. Zedekiah was taken before Nebuchadnezzar at Riblah where his sons were killed in front of him, his eyes were put out, and he was sent to Babylonia in chains (2 Kgs 25:7).

Within a month, the Babylonians burned Jerusalem's temple, palace, and houses and broke down the city walls. Several of the city's important religious and political leaders were executed (2 Kgs 25:18-21), and most of Jerusalem's inhabitants were exiled to Babylonia. We do not know how many people died during the siege and destruction of Jerusalem. Although life went on for the groups of people who remained in the land of Judah (see 2 Kgs 25; Jer 40) and later generations of exiles would receive the opportunity to return home under Persian rule (ca. 539 B.C.; 2 Chr 36:22-23; Ezra 1:1-8; 6:3-5), these events of the first two decades of the sixth century provided the decisive force that shaped much of the theological reflection that has been preserved in biblical books like Ezekiel.

The ministry of the prophet Ezekiel, as well as the book that bears his name, fit into and reflect the events surrounding Jerusalem's destruction and exile. Ezekiel was a priest (at least in training) of the Jerusalem temple who was taken into exile to Babylonia after the first capture of Jerusalem in 597 B.C. The date given for his initial commissioning vision in Ezek 1:2, for example, corresponds to the time of Zedekiah's plans for revolt against Babylonia (ca. 593 B.C.). For nearly ten years between the Babylonians' first capture of Jerusalem in 597 and the city's final destruction in 586, Ezekiel carried out a ministry among his fellow exiles (and would continue to do so after the destruction). He sought to interpret theologically their present condition, as well as the events unfolding under Zedekiah back in Jerusalem.

2. The Date Sequence in Ezekiel

One particular literary feature of Ezekiel illustrates well the book's close connection to the historical events surrounding Jerusalem's destruction and exile: the so-called date sequence. Fourteen precisely dated passages are spread throughout the length of the book. While several prophetic books contain oracles that are dated by year (e.g., Jer 25:1; 26:1; 27:1) or by month (e.g., Jer 28:1; 36:9; 41:1), nearly all of the dates in Ezekiel follow a formula that provides a year, month, and even day for the particular passage. The dates span the period from 593 to 571 B.C., and, with two exceptions (29:1, 17), they appear in chronological order. The fact that Ezekiel's dates occur in such a series also distinguishes them from those in other prophetic books (but cf. Haggai and Zech 1—8). The sequence of dates in the book is as follows (Greenberg 1983, 8):

1:2	fifth year, x month, fifth day (593)
3:16	one week later (593)
8:1	sixth year, sixth month, fifth day (Sept. 592)
20:1	seventh year, fifth month, tenth day (Aug. 591)
24:1	ninth year, tenth month, tenth day (Jan. 588)
26:1	eleventh year, x month, first day (Mar./Apr. 587-586)
29:1	tenth year, tenth month, twelfth day (Jan. 587)
29:17	twenty-seventh year, first month, first day (Apr. 571)
30:20	eleventh year, first month, seventh day (Apr. 587)
31:1	eleventh year, third month, first day (June 587)
32:1	twelfth year, twelfth month, first day (Mar. 585)
32:17	twelfth year, x month (LXX: first month), fifteenth day (Apr.? 585)
33:21	twelfth year, tenth month, fifth day (Jan. 585)
40:1	twenty-fifth year, first or seventh month, tenth day (Apr. or Oct. 573)

Because half of the dates are in the section of oracles against the nations (chs 25—32), which also contains the dates that break the chronological order, scholars debate whether the series of fourteen dates in the book may have originally existed as two independent series of seven dates each. Other debated issues include whether the dates themselves are original to the prophet or were added by later editors (see Eichrodt 1970, 18; Boadt 1992, 713; Cooke 1937, xix), and how much of the material following each date is governed by that date (see Wevers 1969, 2; McKeating 1995, 69).

In spite of these uncertainties, two significant observations should be made about the date sequence in Ezekiel. First, the year listed in each date is that of the exile of King Jehoiachin, which began in 597 B.C. (see 1:2) and in which Ezekiel himself was deported. In a subtle way, then, these dates express Ezekiel's conviction that King Zedekiah and those remaining in Jerusalem after 597 B.C. represent a condemned leadership and an empty hope for the future of Judah. By contrast, even the form of the book's historical references underscore Ezekiel's belief that any possible future plot line for Judah's story lies not with those remaining in Jerusalem after the first deportation but with those who now find themselves living in exile.

Second, the majority of the dated oracles cluster around the years 587-585 B.C., the years immediately preceding, during, and following the final destruction of Jerusalem in 586 B.C. For Ezekiel's preaching, this event, and the developments surrounding it, form the focal point of Yahweh's past, present, and future actions with the Judean people.

C. The Prophet and His Audience

> "During the daytime, while they watch, bring out your belongings packed for exile. Then in the evening, while they are watching, go out like those who go into exile" (Ezek 12:4).

1. The Exilic Community and the Nature of Exile

One of the complicating factors in engaging Ezekiel and his audience is that different parts of the book seem to have different audiences in view. The immediate audience of Ezekiel's words, for example, was the community living in exile in the early years of the sixth century B.C. On another level, however, the book as a whole likely took its final shape during the time of the second generation of Babylonian exiles, and portions of the book seem to address the needs of that later group (see Renz 1999; Darr 2001). This audience was somewhat removed from the destruction of Jerusalem and possessed a knowledge not shared by Ezekiel's original audience, namely, that the prophet had been correct about what Yahweh was going to do. Accordingly, some scholars suggest that we should read the book of Ezekiel as a carefully crafted rhetorical composition, created out of the prophet's preaching by later editors and designed to persuade the second generation of exiles to adopt Ezekiel's theological perspectives about the past and future (Renz 1999; Darr 2001; see D.1 Origins and Composition of the Book of Ezekiel). On still another level, the present canonical book addresses us as contemporary readers who read the book within a canon of sacred Scripture. Nonetheless, the book invites each of these audiences to identify in some way with the experiences of the exilic community.

According to 2 Kgs 24:14-16, those who went into exile with Ezekiel in 597 B.C. totaled ten thousand people and included King Jehoiachin, members of the royal family, government officials, trained soldiers, smiths, artisans, and the leading elite of the land. References in other biblical books suggest that the upper strata of religious leaders such as priests and prophets were also part of the deportation. In short, Ezekiel's primary audience was Jerusalem's social, political, and religious elite, who now found themselves living as refugees in the land of their conqueror. The OT provides very little information about the situation of these exiles. Jehoiachin and other royal officials were apparently imprisoned but later released (2 Kgs 25:27-30). Babylonian records continue to refer to Jehoiachin as king of Judah after 597 and indicate that he and his sons received rations from royal supplies (*ANET* 398). The Babylonians likely incorporated exiled military personnel into the Babylonian army and put exiled smiths and artisans to work on imperial building projects (Darr 2001, 1081).

The majority of the deportees settled at Tel Abib near the Kebar canal (Ezek 1:1). Although the location of this canal is uncertain, it appears to be on the Euphrates near the city of Nippur, about twenty miles south of Babylon. Hence, the Babylonians did not follow the earlier practice of the Assyrians and forced deported peoples to intermix with the population as a whole. Rather, they settled exiled groups according to their origin and ethnicity and allowed them some limited self-governance. The designation "Tel," which means "mound" or "ruin," in the name of the Judean exiles' location also suggests that the Babylonians settled deported populations into devastated areas of the empire in need of revitalization, particularly those regions between Assyria and Babylonia that had been depleted during wars between the two empires.

Perhaps the most significant question for understanding Ezekiel's audience, however, concerns the nature of their life in exile. Scholars remain divided over exactly what Ezekiel and his fellow deportees experienced and how those experiences affected them physically, socially, and psychologically. The majority of interpreters conclude that, while some deportees surely experienced imprisonment and conscription, the exiles should not be thought of as slaves or prisoners of war in the modern sense (see Darr 2001; Block 1997). The available evidence suggests that the exiles were not only permitted to live together and maintain their ethnic and social identity, but they were also able to participate in the economic activities of the empire and continue religious practices like circumcision and Sabbath (see Isa 56:2-4; 58:13). Overall, the exiles served as something like land tenants to the Babylonian king, who provided needed labor, revenue, and military service.

Even so, several recent scholars have rightly emphasized that contemporary readers must not overlook the life-altering physical, psychological, social, and even theological effects associated with the exile (see Smith-Christopher 1997 and 1999; Garber 2004). While the exiles may not have been subject to enslavement, the captures of Jerusalem in 597 and 586 B.C., along with the subsequent deportations, constituted a series of events that caused a severe disruption for both individuals and the life of the community. Ezekiel's audience, who had formerly been members of Jerusalem's social, religious, and political elite, had lived through months and years in which they experienced the military siege and conquest of their city, the killing of friends and family members, the loss of social status and possessions, and the forced separation from their ancestral kin and land. Additionally, the final destruction of Jerusalem in 586 B.C. involved the tearing down of the temple, the seeming end of the Davidic dynasty, and the loss of the promised land, all of which served as the major symbols of the people's theological identity. In effect, those who had once been Yahweh's chosen people in the world now lived as refugees of imperial conquest in a foreign land.

2. The Trauma of Exile

It is in light of these historical events that one of the most recent trends in Ezekiel scholarship provides a significant lens for understanding the nature of the book and its theological message. The contemporary study of the phenomenon known as "trauma" gives a helpful window into the nature of the historical experiences described above and the needs that they created in the prophet's audience (see Bowen 2010; Smith-Christopher 1997, 1999; Garber 2004; Schmitt 2004). In modern study, the term "trauma" is a way of designating certain kinds of effects that some experiences have on those who endure them. By definition, trauma occurs when the experience of one or more catastrophic events produces a variety of responses that continually disrupt normal life and result in both conscious and unconscious ways of continually reliving the event in an unhealthy manner (Caruth 1996, 11). Such "traumatic" experiences can be physical, psychological, social, or economic: terror, death, disaster, helplessness, oppression, warfare, and more (Geller 2000, 261; Allen 1995, 4). Importantly for the book of Ezekiel, such trauma can result not only from the direct experience of catastrophic events but also from the indirect experience of merely witnessing or hearing a report of an event (so-called secondary trauma; Figley and Kleber 1995, 78-95; Smith-Christopher 1999, 139-43). Additionally, trauma can be experienced at both personal and communal levels, disrupting the coherence of individual lives but also destabilizing a group's identity and understanding (Herman 1997).

The experiences of destruction and deportation described above, which form the context of the book of Ezekiel, were "traumatic" for the prophet's audience because they were physically, psychologically, socially, and theologically destabilizing and disruptive for their lives as individuals and as a people. The Judean exiles experienced firsthand the Babylonian capture of Jerusalem in 597 B.C., with its subsequent deportation of the "upper crust" of Judean society, and even though separated geographically, these first exiles also indirectly experienced the ultimate destruction of Jerusalem and its temple, as well as the deaths or deportations of thousands of additional Judean men, women, and children, a little more than a decade later in 586 B.C. Even later generations, who matured after the time of these events, found themselves born into a situation of ongoing displacement and a life of exile. These experiences were more than a series of defeats of an army and captures of a city. They signified the loss of a divinely promised land, the destruction of a temple that represented Yahweh's presence in their midst, the end of a royal dynasty supposedly divinely established in perpetuity, and the apparent defeat of the very God on whose word the whole thing rested. Such conquest, colonization, and exile meant the individual and communal experience of trauma, with all of its terror, shame, helplessness, and disruption to life.

Ezekiel, too, experienced these traumatic events, being deported from his homeland, losing access to the temple for which he had trained as a priest, taking up forced residence in an unclean land, and witnessing the death of fellow priests and citizens. Yet Yahweh called Ezekiel out of the midst of these experiences to offer a divine word to his people in a way that will be discussed further below. The key to that divine word, however, lies in what is perhaps the most significant element of understanding trauma, namely, the particular effect that traumatic events have on those who, like Ezekiel's audience of exiles, experience them directly or indirectly. At the most important level, what makes an event traumatic is that it creates what is called a "disruption" or "missed" experience (see Figley and Kleber 1995, 78-95; Bowen 2010, xvi-xvii). That is, traumatic experiences refuse to be integrated in a coherent way into the narrative (or conceptual framework) of a person's or community's life, so the victim is unable to make sense out of the experience within the normal categories of his or her life story. The trauma exists as a force that remains outside the recognizable narrative of life and is unable to be coherently understood or articulated. The traumatized person or group may thus be unable to comprehend what has happened, why, and to what effect, leaving them in a state of denial or silence concerning their experience yet continually finding that the trauma intrudes into their life in ways that are often not fully conscious or controllable (factors recently identified by modern medicine as post-traumatic stress disorder).

As a result, the experience of traumatic events has the effect of leaving trauma sufferers like Ezekiel's audience in need of a way to "emplot" (i.e., to place within a narrative plot or framework) such experiences within the story of their life and thereby make them able to be comprehended, endured, and perhaps surpassed (see Antze and Lambek 1996, xvi). People need a way to "narrativize" the trauma by reweaving their story in such a way that it incorporates the traumatic experience into a larger narrative plot of history and gives a new vision of the past, present, and possible future. In other words, trauma sufferers like Ezekiel's audience need to receive a new story that links the past, present, and future together in new and meaningful ways (Kenny 1996, 161; Herman 1997, 2-3). As we will see, the divine message through the prophet Ezekiel provides the people with a new plot line in which to understand their overall story and the place of the trauma of destruction and exile within it. For Ezekiel, however, this response is not some form of psychological therapy, but a deeply theological articulation that calls the people to understand all the events of their past, present, and future in light of the larger work of Yahweh's holiness in the world (see the further explanation of the prophet's response in the section Ezekiel's Theology below).

3. Ezekiel, the Priest-Prophet in Exile

For many readers, the strangeness of some of Ezekiel's actions reported in the book has been a starting point for efforts to understand this historical prophet. The book contains numerous descriptions of Ezekiel's seemingly weird behaviors, such as eating food cooked over dung, lying bound and naked, remaining mute, cutting off his hair, and refusing to mourn the death of his wife. The book also relates the prophet's narrative descriptions of visionary travels, strange creatures, sexual imagery, and graphic violence. Accordingly, some interpreters in the twentieth century have suggested that Ezekiel may have suffered from some sort of mental disorder (see most recently Halperin 1993). Such psychological interpretations of Ezekiel have ranged from catalepsy, epilepsy, and schizophrenia to a suppressed rage against women caused by childhood neglect and abuse.

Most scholars today reject such attempts to diagnose Ezekiel with psychological disorders (see Schmitt 2004). At one level, making modern diagnoses of an ancient person to whom we have access only through a literary text is inherently problematic. Most importantly, Ezekiel's actions, though strange, also make sense within the rhetorical context of the prophet and book. Many of the eccentric actions, for example, are symbolic acts designed to convey particular messages, have similarities to the actions of earlier Israelite prophets like Elijah (Blenkinsopp 1990, 9), or represent understandable actions for Zadokite priests (Sweeney 2001, 19). Most importantly, however, such psychological interpretations analyze Ezekiel's experience without paying sufficient attention to the traumatic social and political events surrounding the final years of the kingdom of Judah (Smith-Christopher 1999, 134). Ezekiel's strange behavior is best explained not by psychological diagnoses but by careful attention to his location and identity, as well as to the ways those things were shaped by the experience of exile.

a. Ezekiel and His Location

The book's superscription in 1:2-3 indicates that Ezekiel was a priest, or at least a priest in training, at the Jerusalem temple when he was deported to Babylonia in 597 B.C. Unlike many other prophetic books, however, the book of Ezekiel gives virtually no other third-person biographical information but presents nearly every text in the prophet's own first-person narration. Hence, much less is known about Ezekiel than, say, Jeremiah. Additionally, no information is available for Ezekiel outside of the book. If Ezekiel was thirty years old at the time of his commissioning (see commentary on 1:1), then he was born around the time of the religious reform of King Josiah of Judah in the 620s B.C. (see 2 Kgs 22—23). He apparently had a house in the exilic community in Tel Abib, where elders of the people visited him on at least three occasions. He also had a wife who died around the time of the final siege of Jerusalem in 588 B.C. (24:15-18), although her name and the names of any children remain unknown.

According to the dates given in the book, Ezekiel was active from 593 to 571 B.C., a time span that overlapped that of the prophet Jeremiah. Unlike Jeremiah, who preached in Judah and eventually resided in Egypt, Ezekiel's entire prophetic career took place in Babylonia. This location of Ezekiel's ministry has often been a point of debate among interpreters (see McKeating 1995, 35-38; Renz 1999, 32-37). Although the book's superscription locates Ezekiel in Babylonia (see also 3:11, 15; 8:1-3; 11:24; 33:21; 40:1), much of the prophet's speeches and visions demonstrate detailed familiarity with and express the highest levels of concern over activities unfolding in Jerusalem between 597 and 586 B.C. Consequently, some scholars have suggested that Ezekiel's entire career was spent in Jerusalem and the book's Babylonian setting represents a later editorial framework (e.g., Herntrich 1933). Others concluded that Ezekiel moved back and forth between the two locations throughout his ministry (e.g., Fischer 1939).

There is, however, no significant evidence for disputing Ezekiel's Babylonian location, and the focus on affairs in Jerusalem are at home within the prophet's rhetorical context (Greenberg 1983, 15-17; Darr 2001, 1087; Renz 1999, 38). Since Ezekiel and his fellow deportees had been members of Jerusalem's elite before their deportation, they would have been familiar with and concerned about the state of the city and its inhabitants. Biblical texts such as Jer 29 show that there was significant correspondence and close contact between the deportees and those who remained in Jerusalem after 597 B.C.

Elements of the book's language and imagery, such as references to clay tablets and mud-brick walls, also bear similarities to elements of the Babylonian environment, and certain literary motifs in the book have connections with Babylonian literature.

b. Ezekiel the Priest

Perhaps the most distinguishing feature of Ezekiel's identity, the feature without which one cannot truly understand the visions, acts, and oracles that make up the book, is his vocation as a priest (Ezek 1:3; see Sweeney 2001). Various texts in the book indicate that Ezekiel was a member of the particular priestly line of the Zadokites, the dominant priestly group in Jerusalem in the years leading up to the exile (see 40:46; 43:19; 44:15; 48:11). While other OT prophets were also priests of various lines (e.g., Jeremiah [Levite], Zechariah [Zadokite]), the elements of priestly belief and practice hold a much more prominent place in Ezekiel. While early twentieth-century biblical scholarship often judged these priestly aspects to be later additions to Ezekiel's authentic preaching, such a distinction cannot be maintained, and the prominence of Ezekiel's priestly identity means that readers must interpret a large number of his words and actions through the lens of priestly thought and practice (see Sweeney 2001, 2005; Betts 2005).

Priests in Ancient Israel and the Origins of the Zadokites

Priests in ancient Israel, as elsewhere throughout the ancient Near East, were a particular class of religious functionaries, often related through genealogical lines, who had charge of maintaining the religious order and practices of the community. The biblical texts indicate that the primary tasks of the priesthood before the exile consisted of overseeing the sanctuary, officiating sacrifices and ceremonies, giving oracles from Yahweh, and teaching Torah (priestly instruction) concerning ritual cleanness and moral action (see Deut 33:8-10).

The precise history and nature of the priesthood in ancient Israel are extremely difficult to uncover (see Betts 2005; Cody 1969; Levenson 1985; Miller 2000). Any such discussion is bound up with the debate over the dating of the priestly materials in the Pentateuch, especially Exodus, Leviticus, and Numbers. Additionally, different biblical texts present varying views of the status of and relationship among the major priestly lines of the Levites, Aaronides, and Zadokites. In broad strokes, the biblical texts, with the primary exception of Deuteronomy, present the Aaronides and/or Zadokites as the dominant priestly line, with the Levites in a subservient role. In the primary biblical picture, this situation, particularly the dominance of the Zadokites in Jerusalem, pertains from the time of David and Solomon (2 Sam 8:17; 1 Kgs 2). It is unclear, however, precisely when the texts that give this picture emerged. Some scholars have suggested that the Zadokites indeed became dominant in Jerusalem quite early, and the equality of all the priestly groups reflected in the book of Deuteronomy was a temporary aberration in Judah's history (but cf. Duguid 1994, 80-84). Others have concluded that the texts in Leviticus and Numbers that show the Zadokites as dominant over the Levites are only exilic or postexilic in their origin and retroject that situation back into premonarchic and monarchic times. In any case, the status of the Zadokites as the dominant priestly group in Jerusalem is clearly envisioned in Ezekiel (e.g., Ezek 44) and was likely operative in the preceding era as well (Miller 2000, 171-72).

The specific origins of the Zadokite line are similarly debated. Taking its cue from the stories of David in 2 Sam 8, the long-standing view has been that Zadok was originally a non-Israelite priest at Jerusalem who was incorporated into the traditional Israelite priestly lines (see Zimmerli 1983, 457). In light of some more obscure OT texts like 1 Chr 6:8-12 and 16:39, however, some scholars suggest that Zadok was an Israelite priest at Gibeon whom David brought to Jerusalem, while others conclude that he was simply an Aaronide priest in Hebron in Judah (Cross 1973, 211-14). Whatever the Zadokites' precise origins, they were the priestly group whose members were carried into exile by Nebuchadnezzar in 597 B.C. (see 1 Chr 6:15).

More will be said about priestly theology below, but throughout the book Ezekiel's specific experiences and actions have a distinctively priestly character. His commissioning vision in chs 1—3, for example, has many points of contact with the priestly ordination rituals in Lev 8—9 (see Sweeney 2001, 4) and may have taken place when he was thirty years old, the specified age for priests to begin service in the temple (Num 4:23; cf. Num 8:24). Ezekiel often uses legal and priestly terms in his messages to his audience (e.g., Ezek 12—14) and focuses the content of his message on ritual, civil, and moral instruction similar to that found in priestly texts such as Lev 18—20 (e.g., Ezek 18). The visions of restoration clearly display the conviction that Israel's hope for the future lies in a community fully conformed to the priestly ideals of ritual purity and divine holiness and led by the guiding authority of the Zadokite priests (see chs 40—48).

c. Ezekiel the Priest and Prophet

While considering the person of Ezekiel, however, we must remember that not only does he possess an explicit and pervasive priestly identity, but he is also a prophet who stands in the long tradition of figures like Amos, Hosea, Micah, and Isaiah. Far from being simply, or even primarily, predictors of the future, particularly the distant future, prophets in cultures throughout the ancient Near East were divine spokespersons who spoke an authoritative message from a deity concerning social, religious, and political issues of their day, and often functioned within societal institutions like the royal government. Similarly, prophets in ancient Israel were something akin to rhetorical orators, who spoke carefully crafted speeches or engaged in symbolic actions in order to provide a word from Yahweh, often introduced with the so-called messenger formula ("Thus says the LORD"). These words aimed to persuade an audience of the proper interpretation of contemporary events or the true call of Yahweh upon the community's belief and practice (see Kelle 2005).

The intersection of these two identities, priest and prophet, has given rise to debate over how best to understand Ezekiel as he is depicted in the book. Which identity was dominant for him? Should we conceive of Ezekiel as a priestly prophet or a prophetic priest? One trend among interpreters has understood Ezekiel primarily as a prophet shaped in some ways by priestly perspectives. Clearly, Ezekiel fulfills common roles of the prophets by receiving repeated commands to "say" (e.g., 6:2-3; 13:2; 36:1), offering authoritative words from Yahweh, reporting divine visions, and engaging in symbolic acts before the people. Conversely, he performs few of the most typical priestly tasks, such as administering Sabbath and circumcision. The identity of prophet also fits well with the book's tone of argumentation and debate, in which Ezekiel attempts to persuade his fellow exiles to understand events and institutions in a particular way (see Darr 2001; Renz 1999).

Other recent interpreters, however, have noted the predominance of priestly elements in the book and have come to view Ezekiel as primarily a priest shaped in some ways by prophetic practices (see Sweeney 2001; Betts 2005). Throughout the book, priestly theological emphases on Yahweh's holiness and the separation of clean and unclean dominate Ezekiel's language, while a focus on the temple and its status characterizes his visions. Several passages have Ezekiel employing specifically priestly terminology in lengthy discussions of legal and ritual practices (see ch 22). Additionally, many of Ezekiel's actions are strange for a prophet. He remains silent for five years after his calling (3:25-27; 33:21-22), and the book never describes him as preaching in any public location (see 3:24-25), although he is consulted by the elders of the exiles at his house.

In light of the book's indications of both priestly and prophetic practices, it seems unwise to emphasize one identity to the exclusion of the other and better to think of Ezekiel as a priest-prophet. Evidence from across the ancient Near East shows that there was no strict dichotomy between prophets and priests in societies like ancient Israel, and the OT presents other figures such as Moses and Jeremiah as both priest and prophet.

The priestly part of Ezekiel's identity has seemingly been overlooked by many readers, perhaps because they have failed to realize the ways that the exile changed the priestly office. There is much debate about the nature of priests and their functions during and after the exile, and, as mentioned above, Ezekiel himself does not engage in many traditional priestly functions. Yet, scholars have shown that the typical priestly office even before the Exile included the task of teaching divine law/instruction (*torah*) to the people, and that this teaching involved not simply ritual matters of clean versus unclean but moral and ethical instruction (Betts 2005, 1-26; contra Cody 1969, 119). With the deportations from Jerusalem after 597 B.C., this task of teaching became the predominant priestly duty, and Ezekiel offers just such instruction on ritual, moral, and ethical matters throughout the book (e.g., the connections between Ezekiel's teaching in 18:2-3 and the priestly instructions of Lev 18—20). What makes Ezekiel truly a priest-prophet, however, is that he often casts such priestly teaching in the form of prophetic oracles, visions, and sign-acts.

D. The Book and Its Audience

> "Therefore say to them, 'This is what the Sovereign LORD says: None of my words will be delayed any longer; whatever I say will be fulfilled, declares the Sovereign LORD'" (Ezek 12:28).

The canonical book that bears the name of Ezekiel emerged out of the historical, social, and theological situation of the priest-prophet and his audience. The complex process that produced this book, however, makes it difficult to ascertain the exact relationship between the historical Ezekiel of the sixth century and the words of the literary composition that now appears in our Bibles. Gaining some insight into this process of composition and formation can illuminate the significance of some of the elements of the book and allow a deeper engagement with the power of the book's theological discourse.

I. Origins and Composition of the Book of Ezekiel

The study of the origins of the book of Ezekiel has revolved around the question of whether the book consists primarily of Ezekiel's own words and actions or primarily of the work of later writers and editors. Within the history of this study, views have ranged from seeing Ezekiel as responsible for virtually everything in the book, including the process of committing the elements to writing, to identifying a core of Ezekiel's words supplemented by his later followers, to restricting Ezekiel's original words to just a few fragments or even relegating Ezekiel to a pseudonymous figure (Block 1997, 18-19; see also McKeating 1995; Darr 1994). Before 1900, scholars largely understood the book of Ezekiel to be a unified composition from the sixth-century prophet, with no major later additions (see Driver 1891). Between 1900 and 1950, however, the tide of Ezekiel study changed, and the book was no longer regarded as the unified product of a single person but as a composite collection with many major editorial additions (see Cooke 1937). In accordance with the views of biblical literature at the time, Ezekiel scholars often saw a strict opposition between the book's poetic/prophetic and legal/priestly elements, as well as between the judgment and restoration messages, with the poetic and judgment aspects representing the original essence of Ezekiel's message. Some scholars of this era went so far as to attribute only about one hundred fifty verses of the book to Ezekiel himself. In the years following 1950, however, a relative consensus has emerged that sees the book's content and arrangement as predominantly the work of Ezekiel, who was indeed a priest-prophet living among the exiles in Babylonia in the years after 597 B.C., with some additions by later editors/compilers.

This consensus takes two forms, represented by two of the classic commentaries on Ezekiel. One form sees the core of the book as essentially the work of Ezekiel but with later revisions, expansions, and additions by a "school" of his disciples in the years following his death (Zimmerli 1979, 1983). The school may have been active even into the postexilic period after 538 B.C. and seemingly had close connections to the so-called priestly portions of the Pentateuch in Leviticus and Numbers. This approach may help explain some portions of the book that seem to contain a basic oracle, followed by a passage that updates the original oracle and then a passage that ties the two together (Allen 1994, xxv). The second form, however, sees virtually the entire book as a unified composition that reflects the purposeful design of a single individual who provided both the content and arrangement of the work (Greenberg 1983, 1997). Since the book's acts and oracles fit within the chronology and context of the sixth century, this view maintains that there is no reason to deny that Ezekiel was the individual responsible for nearly every part of the present canonical book. Emerging from this emphasis on the unity of Ezekiel is the recent notion that the book took its final shape specifically as a rhetorical composition directed to the *second* generation of exiles, namely, those who had grown up in Babylonia in the years after Ezekiel's generation. Seen in this way, the book as a whole is designed to present a unified argument to the second generation that aims to convince them of how to understand their past, present, and future with Yahweh (see Renz 1999; Darr 2001).

Also emerging from this emphasis on the book's unity is the suggestion that Ezekiel was primarily a writer rather than a speaker and that the contents of the book were written from the beginning, possibly without ever having been spoken in public (see Davis 1989). This view allows that Ezekiel himself may have used written messages from the very start or that Ezekiel may have given some oral proclamations that were occasional and disconnected and that received their first coherence when written down by either Ezekiel or his later followers. Note that the book has a comparatively greater presence of autobiographical passages and complex narrative units, rarely reports Ezekiel's actual public proclamation of any oracles, and describes Ezekiel's occasional inability to speak at all. Additionally, because the exile represented a time of transition from a predominantly oral culture to an increasingly literary culture, Ezekiel may have initially written his messages but used traditional elements of oral prophecy to do so. This combination would explain the book's inclusion of both literary elements, such as complex metaphorical narratives, and more traditionally oral genres, such as divine speeches introduced by the messenger formula ("Thus says the LORD . . .").

This commentary takes a middle-ground approach that neither attributes the bulk of the book to the work of later editors whose additions need to be set apart, nor discounts the possibility that later editors may have occasionally supplemented Ezekiel's original messages in order to show their continuing relevance for later generations. Similarly, there was no strict separation between oral and written discourse in the ancient context, and Ezekiel himself may have used both. Nonetheless, the book's constant references for Ezekiel to "say," as well as the prevalent indicators of dialogue and debate with specific audiences and the performance quality of the prophet's symbolic acts, suggest that Ezekiel's original ministry likely took the typical prophetic form of oral proclamation and symbolic acts designed to persuade an audience (Darr 2001, 1087; Blenkinsopp 1990, 6). This does not exclude the possibility that some of these proclamations may have been written down or arranged shortly after their delivery, perhaps by Ezekiel himself (e.g., chs 25—32), or that some of the more elaborate vision reports and metaphorical discourses may have been written from the beginning (e.g., chs 40–48). The book as a whole seems to have been completed before the end of the exile in 538 B.C., since it does not contain any references to the return from exile or the issues of the postexilic community (Darr 2001, 1088; Allen 1994, xxv).

This balanced and integrative approach encourages interpreters to pay increased attention to the book's literary characteristics, such as metaphorical narratives and gender imagery (see Durlesser 2006; Galambush 1992), even as it urges them to engage the book as it presents itself to us: the words and actions of a sixth-century priest-prophet attempting to interpret the trauma experienced by the exilic community and open the possibility of a new future with God.

2. Literary and Rhetorical Features

The book of Ezekiel shares many literary features with the other OT prophetic books, yet because of Ezekiel's priestly identity and exilic context, the book is unique in several ways. When one sees this book as the product of Ezekiel's narrative act of imagination, which seeks to reenvision Israel's story in the past, present, and future, these literary features serve as rhetorical devices that aim to persuade all readers of the book to reimagine their identity and practice (see Renz 1999, 131-227).

a. Language, Style, and Genre

The language of the book of Ezekiel is often imagistic, metaphorical, and reflective of abnormal experiences. Readers encounter not only complex grammar and ambiguous wording but also sexual and fecal language (e.g., chs 6; 16; 23). The book's elaborate metaphorical discourses and strange visions also have much in common with the apocalyptic imagery of books like Daniel and Zechariah. Within this strangeness, however, key phrases and sentences occur repeatedly throughout the book to teach its readers a new language and introduce them to the narrative world in which Ezekiel shapes his interpretation of Israel's past, present, and future (Wevers 1969, 1). Some of the language of Ezekiel's narrative world includes "Son of man" (2:1); "the word of the LORD came to me" (3:16); "the hand of the Sovereign LORD came upon me" (8:1); "the Spirit of the LORD" (37:1); "the glory [$k\bar{a}b\hat{o}d$] of the LORD" (3:23); "detestable practices" ($t\hat{o}\,\!^{\varsigma}\bar{e}b\hat{o}t$) (5:11); "you will know that I am the LORD" (20:44).

As we learn the theological language of Ezekiel, its uniqueness becomes increasingly apparent. The book is missing several of the prominent theological terms that appear elsewhere in the OT. For example, missing are references to the "love" of/for God, which are so prominent in Deuteronomy, and the language of "praise" so frequent in the Psalms. In their place is a unique vocabulary that features some one hundred thirty words not appearing elsewhere in the OT and uses words in distinctive ways (e.g., "idols," $gill\hat{u}l\bar{\imath}m$) (Zimmerli 1979, 22-23).

The Hebrew Text of Ezekiel

One of the long-standing methods of biblical study is text criticism, the quest to establish the most original and reliable Hebrew version of a particular passage. The large number of textual notes that appear in modern biblical translations of Ezekiel illustrates that the Hebrew text of the book has many otherwise unknown words and unclear grammatical constructions that appear to be the results of errors and modifications in the process of copying and editing. Additionally, the wording of the book seems to have been influenced at several points by Aramaic, the official diplomatic language of the Babylonian and Persian Empires in which Ezekiel and his successors lived (Block 1997, 40-41).

Since no significant manuscripts of Ezekiel are usable from the Dead Sea Scrolls, the current Hebrew text of Ezekiel (the Masoretic Text) is the only complete Hebrew version of the book and should be the focus of contemporary interpretation. The Septuagint, the ancient Greek translation of the OT dating from the third century B.C., provides the other significant version of Ezekiel. The Greek version, however, differs in many places from the Hebrew text, leading some scholars to suggest that the Hebrew text was further expanded after the Septuagint translation was made or that the Greek translation is based on a different Hebrew version of Ezekiel that is no longer in existence (for the classic text-critical commentary on Ezekiel, see Cooke 1937).

Alongside the peculiar language of Ezekiel, the book's style is distinctive among the OT prophets. Whereas most of the prophetic books, with the possible exceptions of Jeremiah and Jonah, are primarily poetry, Ezekiel's style is predominantly narrative and autobiographical. Even though most of the book's words are presented as the words of Yahweh, the text nearly always includes a first-person ("I style") comment that Ezekiel is the one reporting Yahweh's words (e.g., 2:1; 3:1; Zimmerli 1979, 24).

The primary genres found in the book of Ezekiel are those of the prophetic and priestly literature (for a full summary, see Bowen 2010, xii-xiv). As noted above, Ezekiel contains many of the typical genres of the prophetic literature, such as messenger speeches, laments, and oracles of judgment, woe, and salvation (see 6:8-10; 13:1-16; 19:1-14), as well as a number of genres associated with the priestly literature, such as didactic and legal sayings that teach divine instructions (see 14:12-23; 20:1-44). Through the use of these genres, particular patterns are visible in the book that help to form the theological argument. For example, many oracles in the book fall into a three-part pattern in which the longest part (part A) introduces a theme, a second, briefer part (part B) introduces a related theme, and a concluding coda brings together elements of both themes (Greenberg 1983, 25; e.g., 38:1-23; 39:1-20; 39:21-29 [coda]).

For understanding the rhetorical act of theological interpretation that Ezekiel undertakes with his traumatized exilic audience, however, the book's most significant genres are those associated with argument and persuasion. The book contains many examples of the "disputation speech," a genre in which Ezekiel quotes the arguments of his audience, either his fellow exiles or those back in Jerusalem, and responds with counterarguments (e.g., 12:21-28; 18:1-32). Similarly, Ezekiel repeatedly relays Yahweh's words using the genre of the "proof saying," which describes divine actions of judgment undertaken to persuade the people to acknowledge Yahweh's sovereignty and normally concludes with the declaration that "you will know that I am the Lord" (e.g.,

12:17-20). These genres support the conclusion that much of the book originated as argument aimed to alter the belief and practice of Ezekiel's exilic audience (Darr 2001, 1087).

b. Visions, Metaphors, and Symbolic Actions

Three specific literary genres play significant roles in Ezekiel's theological construction and thus deserve special attention: vision reports, metaphorical discourses, and symbolic actions.

First, a major feature of Ezekiel's ministry presented in the book is the experience of visions in which the prophet himself participates in the vision and offers a report of it. As mentioned above, the book itself revolves around three major visions in chs 1—3, 8—11, and 40—48. While other prophets experience visions and give reports (e.g., Isa 6; Amos 7—9), Ezekiel goes beyond merely reporting the content and significance of the vision to offering elaborate descriptions of the vision's elements and their corresponding effect on his person. Moreover, Ezekiel's vision reports contain bizarre and evocative language rarely equaled among the prophets (see McKeating 1995, 13-18). Such language includes consistent references to "the hand of the LORD" coming upon Ezekiel as the agent that transports him through various visionary travels (e.g., 1:3; 8:1; 37:1; 40:1; see also Elijah in 1 Kgs 18:46 and 2 Kgs 2:16).

Second, Ezekiel's heavy use of metaphorical discourses also distinguishes this book among the OT prophets (e.g., chs 15—17; 23; 34; see Durlesser 2006). The book contains about a dozen metaphorical narratives, and Ezekiel's metaphors are extended, elaborate, and complex, with some narratives being nearly fifty or more verses long (see chs 16; 23). This use of metaphor is not merely decorative but functions as a key part of the prophet's attempt to persuade his audience. Metaphors have the power to construct new worlds of understanding and reshape current perspectives. Ezekiel uses his metaphors not only to reason with his audience but also to open new ways of perceiving the realities of their past, present, and future, realities including exile and the destruction of Jerusalem.

Third, Ezekiel makes heavy use of the prophetic practice of performing symbolic actions or sign acts, deeds that physically signify a prophetic message (see 4:1—5:17). Such acts are not magic but something more akin to street theater: acts of nonverbal rhetoric, usually followed by an explanatory oracle, designed to persuade in specific social and historical contexts (see Friebel 1999). They normally feature a command to execute the act, a report of the execution, and a description of the audience that witnesses the act. In keeping with Ezekiel's overall cast as the prophet's first-person report of Yahweh's words to him, however, the book typically gives only Yahweh's command to perform the action and rarely a report of the actual execution or a description of the audience.

Ezekiel's Symbolic Actions

Symbolic actions or "enacted prophecies" (McKeating 1995, 19), acts that physically signify a prophet's message, are important parts of the activity of several OT prophets, especially Jeremiah (see Jer 27; 28). Scholars are divided over the exact number of Ezekiel's symbolic actions, yet the acts appear in clusters around certain visions or oracles:

3:1-3	eating a scroll
3:24-27	Ezekiel shut in his house
4:1-3	a model of Jerusalem
4:4-8	Ezekiel lies on left then right side
4:9-17	eating the food of exile
5:1-17	Ezekiel shaves his head
12:1-11	the baggage of an exile
12:17-20	eating food with trembling
21:6-7	groaning before the people
21:18-24	a signpost in the road
24:1-14	a cooking pot
24:15-24	Ezekiel commanded not to mourn wife's death
37:15-28	the joining of two sticks

In comparison to the symbolic acts in other prophets, Ezekiel's acts, like his metaphors, are more numerous and elaborate. Ezekiel often takes something that is merely a metaphor in another prophetic book and performs it as a literal action (cf. Jer 15:16 with Ezek 3:1-3). In the midst of the people's condition of "blindness" and "deafness" (12:1-2), living in an environment saturated by the words of false prophets (13:1-23), Ezekiel's seemingly bizarre acts may have provided a way for his message to rise above the noise and capture the attention of his exilic audience.

c. Traditions in the Book of Ezekiel

Ezekiel's identity as a Zadokite priest of the Jerusalem temple who was deported to Babylonia in 597 B.C. manifests itself in a concern over the ritual categories of unclean, clean, and holy as they relate to Yahweh's presence in the temple, as well as in the performance of the priestly tasks of teaching the divine law and offering civil and moral instruction. These priestly elements raise the issue of what ancient oral and written traditions may underlie and illuminate various passages in the book. It is not in keeping with the aims of this commentary series to explore issues of sources and editing in depth (see Kohn 2002; Kutsko 2000; Zimmerli 1979, 41-52). We should, however, note some of the ways that Ezekiel makes use of the traditions that also appear elsewhere in the OT. As we will see, Ezekiel is an "imaginative practitioner" of Israel's traditions, who, at times, freely modifies and even challenges them from the vantage point of his identity and context (Brueggemann 1986, 59).

The most long-standing area of study in this regard has been the possible relationship between Ezekiel and two sections of the Pentateuch: the so-called Priestly Code or P (Exod 19—40; Lev 1—16; Numbers) and Holiness Code or H (Lev 17—26). Similar to what one sees in Ezekiel, P has a special emphasis on holiness associated with sacred space and personnel, emphasizing the construction of the tabernacle, preservation of sacred space, and the importance of the priests (e.g., Exod 25—40; Lev 1—16; cf. Ezek 40—48). H expands this notion of holiness into an ideal for the whole community, which is lived out through proper social relations (e.g., Lev 19; 26). Both of these codes represent the kind of priestly characteristics one observes in Ezekiel, especially the notion that Yahweh's presence dwells in a sanctuary that must be protected from human defilement.

Because of such similarities and Ezekiel's priestly vocation, scholars have suggested a variety of possible relationships between the book of Ezekiel and these traditions: (1) that Ezekiel drew from P and H, which were already in existence by his day; (2) that Ezekiel preceded and contributed to the content of these codes that came into existence after his day; (3) that there was no direct dependence but Ezekiel simply drew from the heritage of priestly thought that also gave birth to these codes (for full discussion, see Lyons 2009; Kohn 2002; Zimmerli 1979, 46-52). Regardless of one's conclusion about such chronological issues, P and H provide some of the thought-world that underlies Ezekiel's rhetorical imagination, and one can see the violation of laws that appear in these codes standing behind Ezekiel's interpretation of the people's exile. Yet Ezekiel tailors and modifies his priestly conceptions for the situation in which he works, at times echoing the language of such codes and at other times synthesizing, adapting, and even reversing such language in a new vision of the past, present, and future. On the whole, Ezekiel seems most heavily indebted to H, working with it freely in the ways just noted, yet transforming the legal materials into prophetic words that accuse past and present generations, interpret disaster as judgment, give instructions for behavior, offer hope for restoration, and more (Lyons 2009).

Also important, however, are Ezekiel's connections with other OT prophetic traditions (see Carley 1974). Some elements of Ezekiel's visions, such as references to "the hand of the LORD" and the activity of the Spirit, echo the language and imagery of the narratives of Elijah (cf. 1 Kgs 18:12, 46; 2 Kgs 2:15). Several of Ezekiel's metaphors likewise seem to draw upon and deliberately expand those found in other prophets. The imagery for Jerusalem and Samaria in Ezek 16 and 23, for example, resembles the earlier prophetic marriage metaphors of Hos 1—3 and Jer 2—3.

Ezekiel seems to have special connections with the preaching of Jeremiah, even while adapting it to his own perspective and context. Ezekiel's act of eating a scroll, for example, develops the similar imagery of Jer 15:16, and both prophets cast their visions of future restoration in the language of Yahweh's granting the people a "new heart" (cf. Ezek 36:26-27; Jer 24:7; 31:33; 32:39). Jeremiah and Ezekiel thus represent two prophets, both of whom were also priests (see Jer 1:1), who proclaimed Yahweh's word to the people during the final years of Judah and its subsequent exile. Both shared the similar message that the Babylonians are Yahweh's appointed instrument of judgment, all rebellious political alliances against them are futile, and the future of Israel lies with those who have suffered the trauma of exile. Yet the relationship between them highlights Ezekiel's distinctiveness: while Jeremiah was primarily a poetic preacher, raised among the subordinate class of Levite priests in the rural Judean town of Anathoth and active from about thirty years before the exile, Ezekiel came from the privileged Zadokite class of priests in Jerusalem and began his ministry only after experiencing the trauma of exile for himself (Clements 1996, 5).

3. Outline and Movement of the Book

The book of Ezekiel in its final form is tightly structured and well-organized, and several organizational patterns are apparent. The first observable pattern is that the book divides into two major thematic sections: Chapters 1—24 predominantly contain the prophet's messages of judgment, while chs 33—48 consist primarily of preaching about restoration. Between these two major blocks is a transitional section (ch 24—33) focused on the fall of Jerusalem: Chapter 24 describes the beginning of the siege of Jerusalem; chs 25—32 contain oracles against a variety of foreign nations; and ch 33 reports the conclusion of the siege and the fall of the city. Several symmetrical parallels link the judgment and restoration sections together (e.g., Ezekiel as a watchman in 3:16-21 and 33:1-9; addresses to the mountains of Israel in 6:1-10 and 36:1-15). The division between the judgment and restoration portions of the book is not rigid, however, since chs 1—24 also contain some passages of restoration (e.g., 16:53-62; 17:22-24) and chs 33—48 contain some announcements of judgment (e.g., 34:1-10).

The thematic pattern of the book occurs within a second organizational scheme that is chronological. Specific date references attached to several passages give the book an overall chronological movement from 593 B.C. in chs

1—3, through the fall of Jerusalem in 586 B.C. in ch 33, to 573 B.C. in chs 40—48. Most of Ezekiel's preaching of judgment leads up to the fall of Jerusalem in 586 B.C., with the primary chapters of restoration dating after that event. Thus, the book's plot movement from judgment to restoration unfolds sequentially over the first two decades of the sixth century.

Perhaps the book's most theologically significant organizational pattern revolves around the visions experienced by Ezekiel. The book contains three major visions that reveal a three-part movement of Yahweh's presence ("glory," Heb., *kābôd*). Chapters 1—3 constitute Ezekiel's commissioning vision in which Yahweh's presence appears among the exiles in Babylonia. Chapters 8—11 form a second vision in which the prophet sees Yahweh's presence leave the temple in Jerusalem. Finally, chs 40—48 are a vision of a new temple in which Yahweh's glory returns to take up residence again in the midst of a restored people.

Each of these three major visions is connected to a series of prophetic acts and oracles that sets forth the vision's meaning. This series of acts and oracles follows each of the first two visions but precedes the third, so that the final vision of the return of Yahweh's presence provides the climax to the entire book.

As we will see, the three-part, visionary movement of Yahweh's presence is a window into the theology of Ezekiel. These visions work together with the prophet's acts and oracles to offer a unique theological interpretation of the plot line of Israel's story. The decline, fall, and restoration of Judah are inextricably linked with the presence, absence, and return of a holy God among the people (Blenkinsopp 1990, 6).

The book may be outlined as follows:

    I. First Vision of God's Presence: Ezekiel's Commissioning (chs 1—3)
        A. Superscription (1:1-3)
        B. Visionary Context of Commissioning: Part 1 (1:4-28)
        C. Ezekiel's Commissioning as a Prophet (2:1-7)
        D. Ingesting the Trauma of the People (2:8—3:15)
        C'. Ezekiel's Commissioning as a Watchman (3:16-21)
        B'. Visionary Context of Commissioning: Part 2 (3:22-23)
        A'. Transition: Instructions for Symbolic Acts (3:24-27)
    II. Acts and Oracles of Judgment (chs 4—7)
        A. Five Symbolic Acts (4:1—5:4)
        B. Explanatory Oracles (5:5—7:27)
            1. On Jerusalem (5:5-17)
            2. On the Mountains of Israel (6:1-14)
            3. On the Land of Israel (7:1-27)

III. Second Vision of God's Presence: God Leaves the Temple (chs 8—11)
   A. Introduction: Visionary Movement to Jerusalem (8:1-4)
   B. First Vision Couplet (8:5—9:11)
      1. Four Scenes of Abomination in the Temple (8:5-18)
      2. The Executioners in Jerusalem (9:1-11)
   C. Second Vision Couplet (10:1—11:23)
      1. Yahweh's Glory Begins to Depart the Temple (10:1-22)
      2. Interruption 1: Judgment on Wicked Officials (11:1-13)
      3. Interruption 2: Promise of Restoration for the Exiles (11:14-21)
      4. Yahweh's Glory Departs the City (11:22-23)
   D. Conclusion: Visionary Return to the Exiles (11:24-25)

IV. Acts and Oracles of Judgment (chs 12—24)
   A. Part 1: Acts and Oracles of Siege, Exile, and Intercession (12:1—14:23)
      1. Symbolic Acts of Siege and Exile (12:1-28)
      2. Explanatory Oracle: Lack of True Prophets (13:1-23)
      3. Explanatory Oracle: Lack of True Intercession (14:1-23)
   B. Part 2: Metaphorical Discourses (15:1—17:24)
      1. The Useless Vine (15:1-8)
      2. The Faithless Bride (16:1-63)
      3. The Two Eagles and the Vine (17:1-24)
   C. Part 3: Oracles of Judgment and Lament (18:1—19:14)
      1. Retribution and Judgment (18:1-32)
      2. Lament over Jerusalem (19:1-14)
   D. Part 4: Israel's History of Sin/Rebellion (20:1-49)
   E. Part 5: Metaphorical Discourses and Symbolic Acts (21:1—24:27)
      1. The Sword of God (21:1-32)
      2. Jerusalem, the Bloody City (22:1-31)
      3. The Two Wives of God (23:1-49)
      4. The Boiling Pot (24:1-14)
      5. Symbolic Act: Ezekiel's Muteness (Beginning of Siege) (24:15-27)

V. The Oracles Against the Nations (chs 25—32)
   A. Oracles Against Surrounding States (25:1-17)
      1. Oracle Against Ammon (25:1-7)
      2. Oracle Against Moab (25:8-11)
      3. Oracle Against Edom (25:12-14)

    4. Oracle Against Philistia (25:15-17)
   B. Oracles Against Tyre (26:1—28:19)
    1. Oracle Against the City of Tyre (26:1-21)
    2. Lamentation over Tyre (27:1-36)
    3. Oracle Against the King of Tyre (28:1-10)
    4. Lamentation over the King of Tyre (28:11-19)
   C. Oracle Against Sidon (28:20-24)
   D. Future Blessing on Israel (28:25-26)
   E. Oracles Against Egypt (29:1—32:32)
    1. Proclamation Against Egypt (29:1-21)
    2. Lamentation over Egypt (30:1-19)
    3. Proclamation Against Pharaoh (30:20—31:18)
    4. Lamentation over Pharaoh and Egypt (32:1-16)
    5. Funeral Dirge over Egypt (32:17-32)
VI. Preparatory Oracles of Restoration: The Transformation of Israel (chs 33—37)
   A. Ending of the Siege: Ezekiel's New Commission (33:1-33)
   B. Metaphorical Discourse: False and True Shepherds (34:1-31)
   C. Metaphorical Discourses: Judgment on Mount Seir (Edom) and Restoration for the Mountains of Israel (35:1—36:15)
    1. Judgment on Mount Seir (Edom) (35:1-15)
    2. Restoration for the Mountains of Israel (36:1-15)
   D. Oracle of Transformation for Israel (36:16-38)
   E. Vision of the Valley of Bones (37:1-14)
   F. Symbolic Act and Oracle of Restoration for Israel (37:15-28)
VII. Preparatory Oracles of Restoration: The Defeat of Gog and the Final Vindication of God (chs 38—39)
   A. Gog's Invasion (38:1-16)
   B. Proclamation of Divine Judgment on Gog (38:17-23)
   C. Gog's Destruction (39:1-10)
   D. Gog's Burial (39:11-20)
   E. Coda: The Final Vindication of Yahweh (39:21-29)
VIII. Third Vision of God's Presence: The Return to a New Temple, Land, and City (chs 40—48)
   A. The New Temple (40:1—42:20)
   B. Vision of the Return of Yahweh's Presence (43:1-11)
   C. The Torah of the New Temple (43:12—46:24)
   D. The New Land (47:1—48:29)
   E. The New Jerusalem (48:30-35)

E. Ezekiel's Theology

"Then the nations will know that I the LORD make Israel holy,
when my sanctuary is among them forever" (Ezek 37:28).

Whether one approaches the message of Ezekiel by focusing on the historical prophet in the sixth century B.C., the literary composition that was completed and read by the second generation of exiles, or the present canonical form of the book that appears in modern Bibles, several central theological convictions underlie the narrative imagination at work in these texts (see Darr 2001, 1085). First, Ezekiel proclaims Yahweh's sovereignty over all of history and the kingdoms that exist within it. Second, part of that sovereignty is a divine plan for Israel that includes destruction and exile as part of a larger work that Yahweh is doing. Hence, Ezekiel asserts, these events are not the result of the power of the Babylonians or the weakness of Israel's God, but are purposeful outworkings of Yahweh's own plan and part of his ongoing covenant with Israel. Third, Ezekiel declares that Yahweh does not act on a whim; rather, his actions are fully justified by the people's sinfulness that has so often gone unrecognized. Fourth, however, Yahweh's own holiness opens the possibility that the divine plan includes a restoration beyond judgment; there is a vision of the future because Yahweh remains committed to his covenant with and plan for Israel. These central theological convictions come into special focus—and allow us to see Ezekiel's theological message most clearly—in relationship to the traumatic nature of the Babylonian exile.

Wesley on Ezekiel

In keeping with the interpretive practices of the eighteenth century, John Wesley, while not hostile to historical and linguistic study, typically interpreted Ezekiel in figurative and christological ways. For example, he saw the "face of Jesus Christ" in the "figure like that of a man" in Ezek 1:26 (Wesley 1975, 2282), and he identified the new Davidic ruler in 37:22 as a "type" of the Messiah (Wesley 1975, 2389). Wesley also followed the practice of interpreting the text in relation to the theological categories of his day. Hence, for Wesley, Ezekiel's assertion that the people sinned even before coming out of Egypt (see chs 16; 23) is a clear illustration of original sin: "in the day that we were born, we were shapen in iniquity" (Wesley 1975, 2318).

I. Ezekiel's Alternative Plot Line for the Trauma of Exile

In the previous discussion of Ezekiel's audience and the experience of exile, we noted the importance of the concept of trauma for understanding the context and character of Ezekiel's theological message to his people (see

The Trauma of Exile above). As noted above, a central facet of understanding an experience such as the exile as a traumatic event is that it constitutes an experience that refuses to be integrated in a coherent way into the narrative (or conceptual framework) of a person's or community's life, leaving them unable to comprehend what has happened, why, and to what effect. Ezekiel speaks to an audience of exiles who need a way to "narrativize" their trauma by reweaving their story so that it incorporates the traumatic experience into a larger narrative plot of history that gives a new vision of the past, present, and possible future. In the face of this need, Yahweh speaks through the prophet Ezekiel and offers an alternative theological plot line for the people and their story defined in terms of Yahweh's holiness.

The book of Ezekiel preserves the visions, acts, and oracles given to this prophet in order to give a new understanding of the people's past, present, and future. Ezekiel is engaged in a powerful act of narrative imagination: the book's visions, acts, and oracles take the story of Judah's past—a story of traumatic destruction and exile that seemingly refuses to be integrated into the people's collective life in an understandable way—and reinterpret it in light of Yahweh's holiness and the people's continual disregard of it. Specifically, the categories and conceptions of the priestly theological tradition of ancient Israel provide the resources for Ezekiel to narrate a different plot line into Israel's past story that calls the people to understand the what, how, and why of their past and present in a different light. Ezekiel uses priestly categories related to Yahweh's holiness to declare that Judah's past sufferings and present situation are not the result of the power of Babylonia or the defeat of their God, but they are the outworkings of Yahweh's own sovereignty and holiness in relation to his people. Simultaneously, this new narrative plot line of the past and present permits Ezekiel to open the possibility of a new plot line for the future of Judah's story. This new plot line for the future goes beyond what the people can imagine from their old understanding of the past and present. Yahweh's holiness, which required the judgments of destruction and exile (see below), also contains an unforeseen surplus that will grant Judah a future plot line of restoration to faithfulness before Yahweh and reconnection to their communal identity.

Ezekiel's Trauma

The important acknowledgment of the humanity of the biblical writers within the Wesleyan theological tradition (see sidebar above, "The Humanity of the Biblical Writers") reminds readers of the book of Ezekiel to recognize that the prophet himself shared in and was affected by the experience of the trauma of destruction and exile. Clearly, one should reject the attempts made by some earlier scholars to diagnose Ezekiel as suffering from some sort of psychological dysfunction (see most recently, Halperin 1993). Yet taking the prophet's humanity seriously allows readers to acknowledge that Ezekiel himself felt the effects of trauma and, importantly, that his experience of destruction and deportation and his efforts to articulate that experience may partially explain some of the most difficult and troubling language, conceptions, and imagery that appear in the book. For example, just as the verbalizing of trauma is often difficult and must rely on a variety of images, metaphors, and symbols rather than one uniform account (Garber 2004, 221; Geller 2000, 261-62), the book of Ezekiel contains multiple impressionistic images with metaphors and symbols, which give expression to experiences that remain somewhat elusive. Ezekiel is also known not only for repeated references to destruction and imprisonment but also for strange actions, such as confinement to his house and shaving his head (see Smith-Christopher 1997). Additionally, the book contains several passages that feature a problematic use of female imagery and sexual violence, as well as frequent pictures of God's wrath and his destruction of the wicked, which modern readers may find as portrayals of violence in the book. An appreciation of the nature and effects of trauma may help explain these elements as reflecting some of Ezekiel's own experiences of terror, violence, shame, and displacement (see Kamionkowski 2003).

The book of Ezekiel, then, represents an inspired exercise of the prophet's narrative imagination by which he reinterprets the story of Israel's past, present, and future in light of Yahweh's holiness, as understood by the conceptual framework of priestly theology. Readers of this book are invited to enter Ezekiel's narrative world, a theological world that enabled its audience to endure destruction and exile, with all of the accompanying religious and social trauma, by affirming a divine holiness that did not fail in the past and will not fail in the future.

What remains, then, is to explore the specific ways in which Ezekiel responds theologically to the people's need using priestly theology and thus renarrates their trauma into the alternative plot line of divine holiness.

2. The Theology of Debate and Politics

The first specific way in which Ezekiel addresses the people's trauma with a new plot line of Yahweh's holiness appears in his responses to contemporary beliefs and sociopolitical happenings of his time. The book's visions, acts, and oracles illustrate how Ezekiel communicated his theological convictions by contesting the standard beliefs of his day and by giving theological interpretations of historical events and political realities.

The theology of the book of Ezekiel is, at its heart, a theology of debate. Witness the frequent use of the genres of the disputation oracle (i.e., argument and counterargument; see ch 18) and proof saying ("Then you will know that

I am the LORD") described above. Ezekiel aims to convince his audience that Yahweh has set into motion a divine plan that includes the destruction of Jerusalem on account of the people's abominations and that allows for a restoration only after such destruction has occurred.

a. A Prophet in Debate

As Daniel Block observes (1997, 7-8; see also Darr 2001, 1075-76), Ezekiel debates and challenges each of the major pillars of the orthodox theological belief dominant in his day. These pillars included the belief that Yahweh had chosen the Israelites and assured them of blessing with the Sinai covenant, granted them the land of Canaan as an inheritance, promised unconditional support for the Davidic dynasty in Jerusalem, and vowed never to allow the destruction of Jerusalem or its temple.

Ezekiel's visions, acts, and oracles contain direct challenges to each of these orthodox beliefs. Ezekiel declares that Israel has nullified its blessings by violating its covenant obligations from the very beginning, violations that also nullify their right to the promised land. Moreover, the kings of the Davidic dynasty themselves have openly rebelled against Yahweh, effectively canceling any unconditional commitment to them. Most importantly, Ezekiel uses ideas of the priestly tradition in ancient Israel (see below) to assert that Yahweh has removed his presence from the polluted Jerusalem temple and thereby allowed for its destruction (Darr 2001, 1084).

When we place these assertions into Ezekiel's context, the rhetorical aim of his debate becomes clear. His audience of exiles stands in a transitional stage between the old Israel, which is under judgment, and whatever new Israel Yahweh may reveal for the future. Especially throughout the first half of the book, a number of Ezekiel's visions and metaphors represent old Israel as the city of old Jerusalem, variously depicted as an unfaithful wife, a prostitute, a murderous entity, etc. Especially in the latter part of the book, however, Ezekiel represents the future restored Israel with the symbol of a new temple and city, meticulously described in every detail in the book's final vision (chs 40—48).

Rhetorically, therefore, Ezekiel calls his audience to choose between two cities and what they represent. By describing their participation in Israel's history of rebellion, Ezekiel identifies his audience as citizens of old Jerusalem, yet he calls them to disassociate from that past by recognizing divine judgment upon it (Renz 1999, 92-93). So complete is this disassociation that Ezekiel never offers a positive word about those who remain in Jerusalem with King Zedekiah between 597 and 586 B.C. In contrast with this past, Ezekiel presents Yahweh's vision of a new future in which citizenship is available to all who make this radical break with their past identity. As we will see, however, the new city and temple are not simply a restoration to an original state. In his climactic vision of restoration (chs 40—48), for example, the prophet never uses the traditional designation of "Zion" to refer to the new city. Rather, for Ezekiel, the new city represents a truly new, spiritually different people made possible only through Yahweh's holiness (Renz 1999, 230).

Covenant in Ezekiel

The covenant theology of the OT shapes significant parts of Ezekiel's proclamations of both judgment and restoration. The typical covenant formula ("I will be your God, and you will be my people"), as well as references to "judgments" and "ordinances," appear throughout the book (see 11:20; 14:11; 36:28; 37:23). Judgment is required because of the people's historic disregard of the requirements of the covenant, and this judgment is often described in language similar to that of the covenant curses from Lev 26 and Deut 28. Rather than marking the dissolution of the covenant, however, such judgments are a part of the covenant itself and thus represent the continuation of that relationship. Moreover, covenant texts like Lev 26, which contain punishments for violating the covenant, also contain words of hope that promise restoration within the bounds of the relationship (Block 1997, 48-55).

b. A God in Debate

Several rhetorical features in the book indicate that it is not merely Ezekiel but Yahweh himself entering into theological debate with the people. Virtually every element in the book, although occasionally introduced by Ezekiel, takes the form of direct words and actions of Yahweh (Zimmerli 1979, 24). In contrast to other prophetic books, which frequently distinguish between the prophet's words and divine speech (e.g., Amos 3:1-2), Ezekiel's persona is nearly completely subsumed beneath a dominant divine emphasis. The book as a whole reads like a monologue by Yahweh that Ezekiel simply recounts. On two occasions (3:26-27; 24:27), for example, Yahweh renders Ezekiel mute for a period of time until "I speak to you . . . [and] open your mouth" (3:27). Unlike the false prophets, who speak freely "out of their own imagination" (13:2), Ezekiel can speak only when Yahweh enables him and provides a message. Similarly, several passages in the book describe Ezekiel as being coercively transported from place to place by the hand or Spirit of Yahweh (3:14; 8:3; 11:1, 24; 37:1; 40:1; 43:5). These kinds of features, combined with the near-total presentation of the book's words as Yahweh's first-person monologue, turn Ezekiel into a kind of passive narrator who simply relates what Yahweh says and does, while Yahweh stands as the book's main character and primary speaker/actor/debater.

A characteristic feature of the book that further emphasizes divine participation in debate is Yahweh's repeated use of the designation "son of man" for Ezekiel. Outside of the introduction in 1:2, the book addresses Ezekiel by his name only once (24:24), but uses "son of man" ninety-three times. The phrase appears as a title in the OT only in the book of Daniel (see Dan 7:13), where it designates a divine figure in the midst of human beings (Block 1997, 30). It has the opposite function in Ezekiel. In the Hebrew idiom, to be a "son of man" is simply to be one of the species of human (see Num 23:19), hence the NRSV's translation, "mortal." The repeated use of this designation for Ezekiel emphasizes his mortality and creaturehood in comparison to Yahweh, who is often designated with the double title "Sovereign LORD" (*'ădōnāy yahweh*; see 37:3).

Perhaps the feature that most reveals this divine emphasis is the repeated use of the recognition formula, "you/they will know that I am the LORD," at the conclusion of virtually every major activity in the book. The formula does not simply say, "you will know me," but focuses on the divine name: "you will know that I am Yahweh." The Hebrew verb normally translated "to know" may also be read in this context as "to recognize." Hence, the formula emphasizes that nearly every activity in the book is about the self-revelation of Yahweh's name and the ways it represents his saving acts throughout history (see Zimmerli 1982). In Ezekiel's context, where Yahweh's name and reputation have been impugned by his people and called into question by the exile, the divine words and actions have the goal of persuading the people to recognize once more who Yahweh is and what that means for the past, present, and future.

c. The Politics of Debate

Perhaps the primary way in which Ezekiel engages in a theology of debate is by consistently giving theological interpretations to historical and political events, interpretations that reflect his understanding of Yahweh's will and plan over against that of the orthodox beliefs of his audience. It is not unusual for Ezekiel to assign a theological meaning to actions of political leaders or the making and breaking of treaty alliances, describing them as either in accordance with or in violation of Yahweh's will. In keeping with the common practice of ancient prophets, Ezekiel takes what appear to be contingencies of history—who wins or loses a battle, what tactical decisions are made, etc.—and assigns them a religious meaning within a larger divine plan (see Barton 1990).

Such a practice was at home in the ancient world, where a kingdom's political treaties were sworn in the name of its God and understood to be that God's own treaty (see Tsevat 1959). Accordingly, the breaking of a treaty sworn in a deity's name, if not done according to the deity's will, constituted the sin of apostasy. Ezekiel sees Judah's rebellions against Babylonia as the breaking of a divinely sanctioned treaty (see ch 17) and an action that lies outside of Yahweh's will for the people. Throughout the book, he invests the actions of Judah, Babylonia, Egypt, and others with theological significance and thus calls his audience to understand them within the context of his overall theological convictions.

3. Ezekiel's Priestly Theology

The central way in which Ezekiel responds to the trauma of destruction and exile—indeed, the most essential content of his response—emerges from OT priestly theology. Readers have long noted that one of the most distinctive features of Ezekiel is that his thinking and language take the form of priestly theology and terminology similar to the books of Exodus and Leviticus. It is from this perspective that Ezekiel debates other beliefs, interprets historical and political events, and constructs an alternative plot line for understanding his people's past, present, and future.

A primary aspect of priestly theology is the notion that all of life divides into the realms of unclean, clean, and holy (see Lev 10:10). Special care must be taken to guard against the "defilement" or "pollution" of what is clean and holy and to "purify" or "cleanse" that which has become unclean (see Lev 1—12). The other primary element of priestly theology, which explains the importance of distinguishing among unclean, clean, and holy, is the conviction that Yahweh's presence dwells in the temple in the midst of the community. For priestly theology, then, the people's sins are not simply transgressions against Yahweh but agents of pollution that create an increasing level of defilement or uncleanness on the temple and endanger the dwelling of Yahweh's presence in the midst of the community (see Lev 12). Given that Yahweh is holy, and that holiness must be kept separate from uncleanness, continued acts of sin will defile the temple and cause Yahweh to withdraw his presence, thus leading to destruction.

This aspect of Ezekiel's theology is most readily recognized through his use of distinctive priestly language. For example, the sins mentioned in the book are similar to those in other prophets, yet Ezekiel adds the dimension of cultic/ritual concerns, such as Sabbath keeping and purity regulations (McKeating 1995, 86). Passages like ch 36 interpret the people's sinful history as a series of acts that polluted the land, rendering it unclean and leading Yahweh to expel its inhabitants (see 36:17-18; Lev 18:24-30). Most significantly, Ezekiel repeatedly refers to the people's wrongful actions with the Hebrew word *tô'ēbôt* ("detestable things" [NIV]; "abominations" [NRSV]), a priestly term that gives their actions a ritual interpretation and indicates that they serve to pollute the temple where Yahweh's presence must dwell in holiness (see Lev 18:26).

The primary concern of the book of Ezekiel, then, is the presence of Yahweh in the midst of the people, especially as it is connected to the status of the temple and the city of Jerusalem that houses the temple (Galambush 1992, 127). In Ezekiel especially, and in the priestly literature more broadly, this presence of Yahweh in the temple is represented by the Hebrew word *kābôd*, often translated "glory." This term appears around two hundred times in the OT and plays an especially prominent role as the representation of Yahweh's presence among the people in the wilderness tabernacle (Exod 26; 29; 40). In comparison to some traditions in the Psalms and Isaiah, which appear to understand Yahweh himself as sitting enthroned in the temple, as well as the tradition represented by Deuteronomy, which sees only the name of Yahweh as resting upon the temple, the priestly traditions in Exodus and Leviticus envision "glory" as the visible manifestation of Yahweh's splendor or presence that dwells in the holy of holies as long as it remains undefiled by the pollution caused by human sin (see Strong 2000; Tuell 2000; Kutsko 2000).

This notion of the "glory/presence of Yahweh" plays a key role throughout Ezekiel, appearing nearly twenty times in the book. Ezekiel consistently emphasizes that the sins of Judah have polluted the dwelling place of Yahweh's *kābôd* in Jerusalem and jeopardized the divine presence in the community. For Ezekiel, however, the *kābôd* is not the fixed presence in the temple that one sees in the priestly tradition in general but is a mobile presence that can leave Jerusalem and appear in other lands (cf. Num 14; 16). As outlined above, three major visions of Yahweh's *kābôd* employ these priestly perspectives to carry the theology of the book. In the opening vision of chs 1—3, Yahweh's glory/presence appears to Ezekiel among the exiles in Babylonia. The second major vision in chs 8—11 depicts Yahweh's presence leaving the polluted temple in Jerusalem as a prelude to the destruction of the city. In the book's final vision (chs 40—48), however, the future restoration of the people is symbolized through the return of Yahweh's *kābôd* to a purified land and temple.

In order to express his theological convictions about Yahweh's plan and Judah's fate, Ezekiel employs the priestly conception of the *kābôd* as a symbol of both judgment and hope (Kutsko 2000, 79). The withdrawal of Yahweh's presence from the temple symbolizes the defiling consequences of the people's sinful actions. Simultaneously, however, especially for Ezekiel's fellow exiles who had experienced defeat and deportation in 597 B.C., the mobility of the divine glory/presence symbolizes that Yahweh has not been defeated by the power of foreign conquerors but is present in the land of exile and willing to return to a purified temple.

4. The Theology of Holiness: Judgment and Restoration

Alongside notions of purity and the divine presence, the dimension of priestly theology that allows Ezekiel to imagine a new version of Israel's past and present is the holiness of Yahweh. For Ezekiel, holiness means more than that Yahweh represents the realm of the holy and must dwell in the midst of a city and people undefiled by impurity. Yahweh's holiness also means that he possesses a name, reputation, and authority that set him apart. To be holy is to be sovereign over and distinct from all human affairs. Holiness is incomparability in power and integrity. Whereas Jeremiah stresses divine pathos and the ability of humans to struggle with and intimately engage Yahweh, for Ezekiel, Yahweh's holiness means that he is not readily accessible, near, or trivial, but sovereign, separate, and free (Brueggemann 1986, 53). This notion of holiness as a name and reputation set apart to a distinctive status is what gives rise to Ezekiel's preaching of judgment and restoration.

a. Holiness and Judgment

We have observed that one of Ezekiel's primary concerns is to reinterpret the traumatic events of destruction and exile in ways that give them meaning as part of Yahweh's sovereign plan for Israel. Since Ezekiel begins his preaching after the first deportation of Judeans in 597 B.C. and continues through the years leading up to and immediately following the final destruction of Jerusalem in 586 B.C., the majority of his preaching of judgment before 586 aims to convince his hearers that the ultimate destruction of Jerusalem and its accompanying exile are both certain and justified. Especially in the first half of the book (chs 1—24), unlike prophets such as Hosea and Jeremiah, Ezekiel does not call those remaining in Jerusalem to repentance in the hopes of avoiding judgment but tries to explain that the judgment is a necessity in light of Yahweh's holiness and the people's impurities. His talk of judgment focuses largely on the political rulers in Jerusalem between 597 and 586 B.C. and the ways in which their sinful religious practices and political alliances constitute both rebellion against Yahweh and "abominations" that defile his dwelling in the community. Ezekiel acts like a judge who delivers a guilty verdict on these rulers (22:2; 23:36) and interprets Nebuchadnezzar and the Babylonian army as instruments of divine punishment (21:23; 23:22-24; 24:14; see Allen 1990, xxiii).

In a unique move among the voices of the OT, however, Ezekiel extends this theology of judgment back to the very beginning of Israel's history. In several lengthy passages (see chs 16; 20; 23), Ezekiel reinterprets the entire history of Israel as a history of sin and rebellion and even traces that condition of sinfulness back to the people's life before they came out of Egypt. In contrast to prophets like Isaiah, Jeremiah, and Hosea, who envision Israel as having had a positive beginning with Yahweh followed by steady decline, the full sweep of the people's history in Ezekiel's eyes is a consistent inability to be faithful (Zimmerli 1979, 57). Throughout the book, for example, the prophet's primary designation for Israel is "rebellious house" (*bêt měrî*; see 2:5; 3:9, 26-27; 12:2-3). This rebellious character, along with its contaminating effects, necessitates radical action by Yahweh in the form of judgment.

Ezekiel's theology of holiness, then, provides a ready way to proclaim judgment and explain the trauma of destruction and exile. From the perspective of Ezekiel's priestly theology, Israel's rebellious actions of the past and present have defiled the required holiness of Yahweh's temple and forced him to withdraw his presence from the community (see chs 8—11). The presence of a holy God cannot dwell in the midst of uncleanness, but the withdrawal of that presence virtually guarantees the destruction of the city. Moreover, Ezekiel proclaims, Yahweh is purposefully carrying out the destruction of the old, defiled sanctuary in order to replace it with a new, pure house in which his presence can again dwell among the people (see chs 40—48).

b. Holiness and Restoration

In a surprising twist, the concept of holiness provides Ezekiel not only with an explanation for judgment but also with the basis for promises of restoration. As noted above, Yahweh's holiness means not only that he must remain separate from impurity but also that he possesses a name, reputation, and authority that set him apart. Although a strange concept to most contemporary readers, in Ezekiel's ancient cultural context, because Yahweh was first and foremost the God of Israel, his name and reputation depended upon that people's actions and status. Certainly the people's impure worship and rebellious actions profaned Yahweh's holiness by defiling his temple and land. Yet, the fact that Yahweh's land had been destroyed and his people sent into exile equally impugned his holiness. In Ezekiel's context, the defeat of a god's land and people was most readily understood as a demonstration of the weakness of that god and of his defeat by the god of the conquering enemy. Hence, although Ezekiel proclaimed that the events of Israel's history unfolded according to a divine plan, Yahweh had "lost face" in the eyes of the nations through Judah's destruction and exile (Allen 1990, xxii). Judah's present condition meant that Yahweh's name, reputation, and sovereignty were in need of vindication if all nations were to "know" or "acknowledge" who he was (see 36:20; 39:27-28).

Thus, rather than sharing Jeremiah's vision that restoration is possible because Yahweh is motivated by a deep compassion for his people (see Jer 31:20), Ezekiel's theology of restoration understands any possible future for Israel as only a by-product of Yahweh's concern for his own holiness and reputation. Yahweh must act to resanctify his name in the eyes of the nations and, as a result, Israel has the possibility of a return from exile and a new life in a restored land (e.g., 20:41-42; 36:16-32). On several occasions, for example, Ezekiel identifies "jealousy" or "zeal" (Heb., *qin'â*) as the motivation for Yahweh's actions, a term that designates passionate concern for one's name and reputation, rather than simple envy (e.g., 39:25; Block 1997, 13).

From this starting point, the major element of the restoration proclaimed by Ezekiel is the exiles' return to the land of Israel, which will itself receive renewed blessings of fertility and be where Yahweh will again dwell in the midst of the people. The prophet often uses the language of a new exodus to depict this divine regathering of the exiles and their reentry into a renewed land (see 11:16-17; 20:41-42; 34:11-15; 36:24-28; 37:12-14, 21). Other elements of Ezekiel's vision of restoration fall into place within this primary arc of return to the land. Yahweh will unify the nation under one shepherd from the Davidic line (34:23-24; 37:22-25), ensure that the people live in prosperity and security (34:25-29; 36:29-30; 38:1—39:29), and dwell within a new temple in the community (chs 40—48). Ezekiel's dominant theological concern with holiness and the vindication of Yahweh's name, however, gives this vision of restoration a unique shape. In Ezekiel's priestly theology, Yahweh's holiness demands that he cannot dwell among that which is unclean, but Ezekiel interprets the people's past religious and political sins as having rendered them and the land unclean. As a result of these convictions, the climax of Ezekiel's vision is that, before vindication and restoration can occur, there must be a transformation of the people so that they can return to a cleansed land and live in the presence of a holy God.

It is at this point that Ezekiel's theology stands the most apart from other prophetic voices in the OT and yet offers a special treasure to readers from the Wesleyan and holiness traditions. Some recent work on Ezekiel has observed that the prophet's preaching of judgment and restoration connects in significant ways to the perennial issue of the nature of the human person and the capacity of the moral self (see Lapsley 2000a). This issue has typically taken the form of questions about the relationship between character and actions: do actions determine one's moral character or does one's character determine his or her actions? What constitutes a moral person, changed actions or a changed character?

Throughout the majority of the OT, especially in Deuteronomy and in Ezekiel's own contemporary, Jeremiah, the dominant moral understanding is that human beings are capable of obedient actions and the problem of sin is simply the problem of a perverted will. The people have the ability to live in faithfulness to Yahweh yet choose not to do so. Hence, for Jeremiah, the promise of restoration after the exile takes the form of a call for the people to repent from their past actions and choose to do good (Jer 31:18-22). Jeremiah describes the divine act that brings restoration as Yahweh's placing his law directly in the people's minds and hearts, so that they will better know how they ought to act (see Jer 31:31-34). In Ezekiel's theology of restoration, however, there is a different conviction at work. As Ezekiel looks back over the entire history of his people, a history that he saw as consisting of nothing other than sin from its inception (ch 20), he apparently concludes that human beings are essentially incapable of living and acting for the good. The ways he talks about judgment and the language he uses for restoration consistently reveal that, for Ezekiel, it is not simply a matter of will; there is a flawed character that prevents humans from living morally. Hence, it is not enough for Yahweh to reveal the law more directly or to call for repentance more strongly because the people do not "possess the right moral equipment to exercise the moral will at all" (Lapsley 2000a, 10). Human beings have a character and condition that make it impossible for them to live faithfully in the presence of a holy God.

This view of the human condition leads to the central conviction of Ezekiel's theology of restoration: in order for restoration to occur and for the people to have a future with Yahweh, there must first be a transformation of the people's character that will enable them to live in holiness. Thus, at the heart of the prophet's restoration message is the proclamation that Yahweh will first undertake an act of re-creation: through the work of the Spirit, Yahweh will affect an inward transformation of the people that will give them the ability to live a life of obedience. In Ezekiel's language, Yahweh "will remove the heart of stone" that has made the people incapable of choosing the good and will give them "a new heart" and "a new spirit" from which right actions of holy living follow (see 11:19-20; 36:26). Once the Spirit has converted the people's divided heart into one that is wholly attuned to Yahweh's will, they will be able to live faithfully with Yahweh's presence in their midst and Yahweh's holiness will be vindicated and displayed through them.

By prioritizing this work of inner transformation that makes wholehearted obedience possible, Ezekiel thus shifts the source of morality and faithfulness from human capacity to a divine gift. Additionally, unlike other OT conceptions, Ezekiel makes human morality primarily about identity and knowledge rather than behavior and actions (Lapsley 2000a, 6). Yahweh first gives the people a transformed identity and then calls them to gain knowledge of their new identity and the God who provided it. Perhaps this is the reason for the book's repeated emphasis that Yahweh's various actions will cause the people to "know that I am the LORD." As the people come to know/acknowledge their new identity given by the Spirit, actions of holy living will result.

The full context of the book's final chapters suggests that Ezekiel's strong language describes the miraculous replacement of an incapable human capacity with an identity and knowledge that enable, and even perhaps predispose, persons to live according to the divine will (Lapsley 2000a, 182). Surely such a proclamation of salvation, which places all the emphasis on the free and gracious activity of Yahweh and admits that Israel has nothing to warrant or affect redemption, embodies the trauma experienced by Ezekiel and his audience. This kind of restoration is uniquely suited to those who have lost the ability to generate life for themselves and who lack the resources to imagine a possible future.

There is much in this conception that resonates with readers from the Wesleyan tradition. John Wesley himself saw in this prophetic language (especially 36:25-38) an image of holiness that envisions God's Spirit re-creating the human heart and character in order to enable a life of undivided love and loyalty before a holy God (see commentary on ch 36). Yet, for Ezekiel, this re-creation serves as the key element in a larger process of restoration. Once Yahweh finishes the act of inward transformation and creates a people inclined to obedience, this new community characterized by wholehearted faithfulness can once again live successfully in the land and allow Yahweh's presence to return to dwell in their midst. Thus, the book of Ezekiel ends with a vision of Yahweh's "glory" returning to dwell among a cleansed people (chs 40—48) and with a statement that testifies to a transformation achieved: "And the name of the city from that time on will be: THE LORD IS THERE" (48:35).

COMMENTARY

I. FIRST VISION OF GOD'S PRESENCE: EZEKIEL'S COMMISSIONING (EZEKIEL 1—3)

BEHIND THE TEXT

The book of Ezekiel opens with the first of three major visions of the glory/presence (*kābôd*) of Yahweh (see chs 1—3; 8—11; 40—48). This opening visionary experience in chs 1—3 contains within it Ezekiel's commissioning as a prophet and forms one of the most complex and difficult sections in the book. While living among the exiles in Babylonia, Ezekiel witnesses a storm cloud arriving from the north, which reveals the likeness of four living creatures within it, each with four faces, four wings, human bodies, and calves' feet. Wheels within other wheels move in tandem below the creatures. Above the creatures is a domelike structure that separates them from an exalted throne upon which sits what appears to be a human figure clothed with fire. Ezekiel proclaims that this scene is "the appearance of the likeness of the glory of the LORD" (1:28), and chs 2—3 go on to place Yahweh's personal commissioning of Ezekiel within this visionary context.

Ezekiel's Wheel in Music and Art

The imagery and descriptions of Ezekiel's vision in ch 1 have inspired a number of works of art and music, including the traditional spiritual "Ezekiel Saw de Wheel," performed in different versions by a number of musicians, and artistic renderings by the English poet and painter William Blake (1757—1827). See Christopher Rowland, *"Wheels within Wheels": William Blake and the Ezekiel's Merkabah in Text and Image* (The Père Marquette Lecture in Theology; Milwaukee, Wis.: Marquette University Press, 2007).

Because this vision and commissioning is characterized by a complex structure, moments of repetition, and parallels with passages elsewhere in the book, scholars often conclude that it developed out of a long process of editing and expansion by Ezekiel's later followers (see Zimmerli 1979, 124; but cf. Greenberg 1983, 42-59). The superscription in 1:1-3, for example, with its alternation between autobiographical and biographical comments, seems to reveal the fruits of such editing. The superscription as it now stands, however, provides three key pieces of background information for Ezekiel and his ministry: date, location, and vocation.

First, the opening verse of the book dates Ezekiel's initial commissioning vision to "the thirtieth year, in the fourth month on the fifth day." Subsequently, v 2 adds the chronological indicator of "the fifth year of the exile of King Jehoiachin." Based on the ancient Judean calendar, the fourth month (Tammuz) in v 1 and the fifth year of Jehoiachin's exile in v 2 would yield a likely date of July 31, 593 B.C. (Block 1997, 83). Although perhaps the result of a later editorial addition, the date reference in v 2 is likely meant to clarify the time indicated by v 1. The "thirtieth year" in v 1 remains mysterious, however, because no further specification is given. Most scholars view the date as a reference to Ezekiel's age at the time of his commissioning, a view suggested by the NIV's text note that proposes reading "*my* thirtieth year." The designation may also refer, perhaps simultaneously, to the thirtieth year since the religious reform undertaken in Judah by King Josiah, which began around 623 B.C. and focused on centralizing the worship of Yahweh in a cleansed Jerusalem temple (see 2 Kgs 22—23; Sweeney 2005, 129; Hayes and Hooker 1988, 86-88).

If the thirtieth year in Ezek 1:1 refers to Ezekiel's age at the time of his commissioning, the vision in ch 1 occurred during what would have been a significant transitional moment in the life of an ancient Judean priest like Ezekiel. According to the priestly regulations, the age of thirty marked the time at which Levitical priests began their official service in the Jerusalem temple (Num 4:3, 23, 30; cf. Num 8:23-25). Additionally, if Ezek 1:1 refers to Ezekiel's thirtieth year, then the date of his final vision in 40:1 corresponded to his fiftieth year, the time at which Levites are mandated to retire from temple service (see Num 4:3; 8:25). Seen in this way, the moment identified as the beginning point of Ezekiel's ministry represented a turning point in his life that underscored his sense of displacement and no doubt exacerbated his experience of trauma. At the time when he should have moved to the highest levels of purity and service in the temple, he instead found himself among refugees in an impure, foreign land (Odell 2005, 16). Even so, precisely during the time when this displaced priest would have spent twenty years in service in the Jerusalem temple, Yahweh used him to live among and speak to Judean exiles in a desolate region of the Babylonian Empire.

The superscription's placement of Ezekiel's initial commissioning vision in 593 B.C. also coincides with significant political events in Jerusalem and alerts the reader to the theo-political dimensions of Ezekiel's message. Around this time, King Zedekiah, whom the Babylonians had placed on the throne in Jerusalem after the city's first capture in 597, convened a meeting of emissaries from the kingdoms of Moab, Ammon, Edom, Tyre, and Sidon, apparently to plot a rebellion against Babylonia (Jer 27—28). Such a rebellion failed to materialize, and Zedekiah was eventually brought to Babylon, likely to reaffirm his loyalty to Nebuchadnezzar (Jer 51:59). Against this background, Ezekiel's use of King Jehoiachin, Zedekiah's predecessor, as the reference point for the dates given throughout the book has a certain rhetorical significance. In the face of a king back in Jerusalem who continued to engage in political activities that were outside of Yahweh's will, Ezekiel implicitly identified the exiled Jehoiachin as the true king of Judah, who was in exile as part of the outworking of a larger divine plan.

The second piece of background information provided by the book's superscription locates Ezekiel geographically "among the exiles" (v 1) and "by the Kebar River in the land of the Babylonians [lit., Chaldeans]" (v 3). These statements identify Ezekiel as one of the deportees taken from Jerusalem into exile to Babylonia after the first capture of Jerusalem just four years earlier in 597 B.C. and remind readers that his ministry to come will be shaped by and attempt to deal with the experiences of such dislocation. Although earlier generations of scholars suggested that this Babylonian setting for Ezekiel's ministry may be only a later editorial addition or that Ezekiel moved back and forth between Babylonia and Jerusalem, there is no significant reason to doubt that he received his commissioning and carried out his ministry among the Judean deportees.

The more specific location of Ezekiel and his community of exiled Judeans "by the Kebar River" refers to a canal located near the ancient city of Nippur. This city, which sat on the Euphrates River about twenty miles south of Babylon, had played significant roles in previous wars between Assyria and Babylonia and, at times, represented a last Assyrian holdout against emerging Babylonian power (Block 1997, 84). Hence, in keeping with general Babylonian practice, Ezekiel and his fellow Judean deportees were apparently settled into one of the most war-torn areas of the empire, no doubt with the implicit goal of revitalizing the area for the sake of the imperial agenda.

The superscription's final piece of background information is given only in passing but provides, in this commentary's view, the most vital item for understanding Ezekiel's identity and the book's theological discourse. Verse 3 identifies Ezekiel as "the priest, the son of Buzi." Although the Hebrew is unclear as to whether "the priest" designates Ezekiel or his father, either case locates Ezekiel as a member of the priestly line in Jerusalem. As discussed earlier, the elements of priestly experience and the perspectives of priestly theology provide the dominant lens through which Ezekiel interprets his commissioning vision and undertakes his prophetic ministry.

The effort to understand the possible traditions and genres that stand behind the unusual imagery of Ezekiel's commissioning vision forms a final background consideration for chs 1—3. The imagery in ch 1 contains a mixture of elements known from biblical and ancient Near Eastern sources. Within the biblical literature, the vision's form and imagery bear resemblances to both OT "storm theophanies" and "throne theophanies." The OT storm theophany is a scene in which clouds, lightning, brightness, and thunder mark the manifestation of the presence of Yahweh (Odell 2005, 19; Zimmerli 1979, 119). In Ps 18, for example, smoke, fire, and clouds accompany Yahweh's manifestation, which occurs with flying creatures (see also Exod 15; Pss 29; 97; 104). Throne theophanies in the OT describe visionary manifestations of Yahweh's presence accompanied by a divine throne and creaturely attendants (see Isa 6). Such representations appear not only in biblical texts that depict Yahweh as riding on the clouds but also in various Ugaritic and Assyrian texts that portray deities as cloud riders or winged disks.

There are no exact parallels to the four-headed flying creatures described in Ezek 1 in either biblical or ancient Near Eastern sources, but there are numerous examples in Mesopotamian iconography and artwork of various winged human figures with animal heads (see Block 1997, 98). In such representations, the creatures often serve as pedestals for the images of gods and thus as indications of their exaltation (Greenberg 1983, 56). Ezekiel's vision may similarly serve to reaffirm the sovereignty of Israel's God by making such creatures attendants to Yahweh's throne.

Alongside elements of storm and throne theophanies, Ezekiel's vision depicts Yahweh's sovereignty by providing a look into the heavenly throne room using imagery that reflects the decor and layout of Assyrian royal palaces known from throughout ancient history (Odell 2005, 21-22). Assyrian throne rooms were decorated with ornate carvings and representations of creatures, humans, thrones, etc. Additionally, just as Ezekiel reports first seeing only a "likeness" (*dĕmût*; 1:28) of Yahweh's glory, so the layout of Assyrian throne rooms was such that one entered to face initially a visual representation of the Assyrian king in a triumphant depiction before turning a ninety-degree angle to enter the actual presence of the king. In the same way that the features of these Assyrian palaces served to assert the power of the Assyrian king, Ezekiel's use of this well-known royal layout functions rhetorically to enhance the depiction of Yahweh as the enthroned sovereign in the midst of a foreign land.

Ezekiel and the Early Christian Interpreters

Early Christian interpreters and patristic writers offered a variety of perspectives on Ezekiel's opening vision that differ from those of modern biblical scholarship. Rather than focusing on questions of grammar and history, early Christian interpreters like Irenaeus explored the theological question of what this text says to the church about the triune God who was revealed in Jesus Christ. Because such interpreters operated with a conviction that the OT and NT formed a unity in Christ, they attempted to understand Ezekiel by using intertextual comparisons with other biblical passages. More importantly, they interpreted the Ezekiel texts with an eye toward how these scriptures illuminate the moral or virtuous life, as they are read by and practiced within the community of faith (see Christman 2005, 2-4).

Perhaps most important for highlighting Ezekiel's priestly identity and theology, however, is the recognition that much of the imagery of the opening vision finds parallels in the OT's priestly traditions concerning Yahweh's glory/presence (*kābôd*) and the Jerusalem temple. Depictions of the divine presence at Sinai, for example, describe the *kābôd* of Yahweh in the midst of fire, cloud, and light (Exod 19; 24; 40). Note also the reference to the "pavement" (*rāqîaʿ*; cf. Ezek 1:22) under Yahweh's feet in the priestly description of Exod 24:10. The radiant imagery of the creatures and throne can also be compared with depictions of the ark of Yahweh and its accompanying cherubim in the Jerusalem temple. In fact, Ezek 10:9-14 later identifies the four creatures from ch 1 with the cherubim in the temple (cf. Exod 25:17-22; 1 Kgs 6:23-28).

As noted above, instances of repetition and disjointedness that occur throughout the overall vision and commissioning in chs 1—3 have led some commentators to see these chapters as a composite of several originally distinct visions and encounters (e.g., Zimmerli 1979, 94). On balance, however, chs 1—3 stand as a unified composition (see Block 1997, 77). The apparent break at 3:15, where the vision seemingly ends with Ezekiel being returned to the Kebar River, is only a pause for a seven-day period of seclusion. The vision immediately picks up again in 3:16, and the chronological reference ("At the end of seven days") joins the subsequent commissioning of Ezekiel as a "watchman" (3:16-21) with his preceding commissioning as a prophet (2:1-7). As a whole, then, Ezekiel's opening vision follows a ringlike structure, with the prophet's ingesting of a scroll of "lament and mourning and woe" (2:10) at its center:

    A. Superscription (1:1-3)
    B. Visionary Context of Commissioning: Part 1 (1:4-28)
    C. Ezekiel's Commissioning as a Prophet (2:1-7)
    D. Ingesting the Trauma of the People (2:8—3:15)
    C'. Ezekiel's Commissioning as a Watchman (3:16-21)
    B'. Visionary Context of Commissioning: Part 2 (3:22-23)
    A'. Transition: Instructions for Symbolic Acts (3:24-27)

IN THE TEXT

A. Superscription(s) (1:1-3)

■ 1-3 Ezekiel's commissioning vision in chs 1—3 opens with three verses that introduce the prophet and his situation and serve as a superscription for the book as a whole. When compared with the superscriptions of other prophetic books (cf. Hos 1:1; Amos 1:1; Mic 1:1), Ezek 1:1-3 is unusual. Rather than the typical third person report of an editor/compiler (e.g., "the word of the LORD that came to Hosea" [Hos 1:1]), Ezek 1:1 begins with the first person speech of Ezekiel himself. Abruptly, however, vv 2-3 switch to third person description. Since v 4 then returns to Ezekiel's first person report to relate the vision of the divine throne, the third person description in vv 2-3 may represent a later addition, perhaps to clarify the unspecified reference to the **thirtieth year** in v 1.

Ezekiel's first person speech in v 1 introduces the book's characteristic autobiographical style. The name **Ezekiel** (v 2) occurs elsewhere in the book only in 24:24, and most passages are presented as the words of Yahweh in first person. Throughout the book, Ezekiel the prophet recedes behind an emphasis on divine speech and action. The opening three verses also introduce two characteristic phrases in the theological language of Ezekiel's narrative world: **the word of the LORD came to Ezekiel,** and **the hand of the LORD was upon him** (v 3). Both phrases underscore Yahweh's predominance in the book's visions, acts, and oracles. The **hand of the LORD,** which also serves as the opening marker for the book's other major visions (8:1; 37:1; 40:1), may be related to the prophetic traditions of Elijah and Elisha, in which Yahweh's hand enables prophets to do extraordinary things. It characteristically brings Ezekiel into a supernatural, visionary experience of Yahweh's presence.

As noted above, the superscription provides the reader with three major pieces of background information: Ezekiel's date in the turbulent political period of 593 B.C., location among the exiles in the southwestern region of Babylonia, and vocation as a Zadokite priest-in-training, who, likely in this very year, should have assumed his priestly duties at the temple in Jerusalem (see Behind the Text). Verses 1-3 also prepare us for the first vision of Yahweh's presence in chs 1—3 with Ezekiel's statement, **the heavens were opened and I saw visions of God** (v 1). The first phrase (**the heavens were opened**) implies that Ezekiel was given the ability to see directly into the heavenly throne room (cf. Rev 4:1-2). Moreover, Ezekiel's opening statement labels the entire commissioning vision that follows in chs 1—3 as **visions of God** (*marĕôt ʾĕlōhîm*). The Hebrew construction here is probably better understood as a general designation (***divine visions***), and the plural **visions** may be a plural of emphasis indicating a single, yet direct and defining encounter with the divine presence (Odell 2005, 13; Block 1997, 85; Greenberg 1983, 41).

B. Visionary Context of Commissioning: Part I (1:4-28)

■ **4** Ezekiel's vision of Yahweh's presence begins in v 4, and this vision provides the context for his commissioning as a prophet in chs 2—3. Often referred to as the "chariot" ("Merkabah" from the Hebrew) vision, Ezekiel's report describes the appearance among the exiles in Babylonia of a mobile divine throne, which is accompanied by heavenly attendants and upon which a representation of Yahweh's presence rests. The imagery contains a mixture of elements known from biblical and ancient Near Eastern sources, including OT "storm theophanies" and "throne theophanies," as well as ancient Mesopotamian iconography of various winged human figures with animal heads and the internal designs of Assyrian royal palaces (see Behind the Text). These elements combine to give a picture of sovereignty. In a historical context where Yahweh's people had been conquered and his own sovereignty as a deity was in question in the eyes of some, the text visually represents Yahweh as sitting enthroned as a king, even in the very place of the people's exile.

As a means of drawing the reader into this portrait of Yahweh's sovereignty, the vision in ch 1 steadily directs the reader's gaze upward from the creatures, who are described first and from bottom to top (vv 5-14), to the expanse over their heads (v 22), to the throne above the expanse (v 26), and finally to the kingly figure seated on the throne (vv 26-28).

■ **5-14** The vision begins with the appearance of a strong wind out of the north and a cloud of fire, within which stand **what looked like four living creatures** (v 5). The creatures, whose four faces combined human and animal features and accompanying multidimensional wheels (see vv 15-21), are representative of the bizarre and sometimes obscure imagery that characterizes the entire vision. The four heads of Ezekiel's creatures who accompany Yahweh's throne may represent the four lords of creation: the eagle as the lord of the air, the lion as the lord of the wild animals, the ox as the lord of the domesticated animals, and the human as the lord of all creation. The vision's imagery reaffirms Yahweh's sovereignty by depicting the most powerful beings of creation as mere attendants to his divine throne.

The Spirit in Ezekiel

In the context of Ezekiel's description of the four living creatures in 1:4-14, v 12 contains the book's first reference to the Spirit (*rûaḥ*), an entity that will play a prominent role in several sections of the book. Here, the Spirit serves as an animating force that moves the creatures. It will play a similar role for Ezekiel in other passages (e.g., 1:20; 2:2; 3:24). Yet the *rûaḥ* plays a variety of roles in the book, and it is difficult to discern how they relate to one another (cf. 1:4; 3:12, 14; 36:27; 37:1, 9, 14).

Along with the depiction of divine sovereignty through the creatures, there is a large amount of priestly and temple imagery spread throughout the vision (Sweeney 2005, 134). The **burnished bronze** in v 7, for example, resembles the imagery of the ark of the covenant overlaid with gold and later replaced with bronze (1 Kgs 14:25-28; 2 Kgs 18:14-16), while the **coals of fire** in Ezek 1:13 are similar to the burning incense altars in the tabernacle (Exod 30:1-10). Such parallels no doubt reflect Ezekiel's own priestly identity and frame of reference, but also make the point that the God who appears to Ezekiel in this foreign land is indeed Israel's own God whose presence is manifest in the Jerusalem temple.

Perhaps the most noteworthy feature that runs throughout Ezekiel's description of his vision is the repeated use of indirect language. In describing virtually every element of the vision, the language and imagery remain opaque, never offering a direct or precise description of any entity but prefacing almost every reference with such words as "like," "as" (*kaʾăšer*), "likeness" (*dĕmût*), and "appearance" (*marĕʾēh*). Ezekiel describes only **what looked like** [*dĕmût*] **four living creatures** (v 5), something "like [*kaʾăšer*] a wheel intersecting a wheel" (v 16), "what looked like [*dĕmût*] a throne" (v 26), etc. (for such language, see 1:5, 10, 13, 14, 16, 22, 24, 26, 27, 28). He seems unable to express things in their actual essence but only in relationship to analogous concepts and entities (Block 1997, 90). Commentators often understand this indirect language as representing Ezekiel's sense of Yahweh's holiness; that is, he is reticent to describe or disclose fully the things he sees, for they are too holy (Darr 2001, 1109; cf. Odell 2005, 30). Yet, the recurring use of indirect descriptions may also relate to the dimensions of trauma that characterize the prophet and the book. Traumatic experiences, such as the destruction and deportation experienced by Ezekiel and his audience, are often "missed," or partially comprehended, and thus may be difficult to articulate fully or directly. Additionally, Ezekiel's own unexpected experience of seeing Yahweh's holiness in an unclean land may have added another traumatic element that generated his indirect language.

■ **15-21** Following the description of the creatures, vv 15-21, which are often seen as a later addition (e.g., Zimmerli 1979, 105; but cf. Darr 2001, 1116), break the steady upward movement of the vision's viewpoint in order to describe the wheels that accompany the four living creatures. One wheel, apparently with another wheel somehow inside and a rim **full of eyes** (v 18), accompanies each creature and moves the creature around much like the wheels of a chariot. It remains difficult to envision precisely what Ezekiel describes here, whether two wheels intersecting at right angles, concentric circles, or other combinations. The **eyes** in the rims of the wheels may be round semiprecious stones (Odell 2005, 28) or actual eyes that represent Yahweh's watchfulness over the earth (Greenberg 1983, 58). In any case, the description of chariot-like wheels accompanying the four living creatures is likely another example of priestly imagery, as it may reflect the furnishings of the Jerusalem temple that included wheeled cult stands with animal carvings on the sides (see 1 Kgs 7:27-37; Odell 2005, 28).

■ **22-28** With the description of **what looked like an expanse** (v 22) above the heads of the four creatures, vv 22-25 resume the upward movement of the reader's gaze. The Hebrew word for **expanse** (*rāqîaʿ*) literally denotes a "glassy dome." The same word appears in Gen 1:6 as the item that God uses to separate the chaotic waters in creation. Here, the **expanse** seems to serve as a platform upon which the divine throne sits, yet it also provides a clear line of demarcation between the creatures who attend the throne and the Sovereign One who sits enthroned above their heads. As we follow Ezekiel's gaze above the heads of the four living creatures to the platform that they support, a focus on visual sights gives way to Ezekiel's description of sound (vv 24-25). A deafening sound accompanies the movement of the creatures and their throne-chariot: **like the roar of rushing waters, like the voice of the Almighty, like the tumult of an army** (v 24).

Suddenly, however, the deafening noise turns to silence, as the flying creatures come to a stop and fold their wings. In that moment of silence, Ezekiel hears a voice speak from above the glassy platform (v 25). Only now does he lift his eyes further and describe what is above the **expanse**. As expected, the language is indirect, even more so than previously: **what looked like [*dĕmût*] a throne**, with one seated upon it who was a **figure [*dĕmût*; lit., *likeness*] like that [*kĕmarĕʾēh*] of a man** (v 26). Literally, the verse describes the sight as *the likeness of a throne* with one seated upon it who has the *likeness of the appearance of a man.* The figure has a shining radiance and is consumed in flames below the waist. Upon viewing this figure (lit., *likeness*) of a human, the final verse of the chapter (v 28) provides the long-awaited explanation of the sights that Ezekiel has been seeing. Ezekiel identifies the figure sitting on the throne high above the earth with the key term that represents the presence of Yahweh in the book but with language that is indirect in the extreme: **This was the appearance [*marĕʾēh*] of the likeness [*dĕmût*] of the glory [*kĕbôd*] of the LORD** (v 28). The priestly traditions within which Ezekiel stood envisioned the *kābôd* ("glory") as the visible manifestation of Yahweh's splendor or presence that dwells in the holy of holies as long as it remains undefiled by the pollution caused by human sin. This term (*kābôd*) appears around two hundred times in the OT and plays an especially prominent role as the representation of the presence of Yahweh among the people in the wilderness tabernacle (Exod 16; 29; 40). Against the backdrop of the priestly tradition, Ezek 1:28 declares that Ezekiel finds himself before the most direct manifestation of the presence of Israel's God, even though he stands on the soil of a foreign land and in the wake of his own people's defilement of the central dwelling place of Yahweh's presence in the Jerusalem temple. Overwhelmed (and perhaps shocked) by the experience, Ezekiel's only response is to fall prostrate.

New Testament and Early Christian Appropriations of Ezekiel's Chariot Vision

The language and imagery of the vision in Ezek 1 appear in the writings and artwork of the early Christians in the NT and beyond. The portrayal of the heavenly throne in Rev 4:2-8, for example, draws on a number of OT visions, including Ezekiel's, and contains about a dozen expressions taken directly from Ezek 1:1-27 (Block 1997, 110-11). The iconography of early Christians similarly identified Christ with the "appearance of the likeness of the glory of the LORD" from Ezek 1:28 (Odell 2005, 33).

This opening vision in ch 1 not only provides the context for Ezekiel's commissioning that follows (chs 2—3) but also holds powerful theological significance for the traumatized community of exiles who had suffered the dismantling of their most precious religious conceptions. From Ezekiel's priestly perspective, Yahweh is inseparably linked to the Jerusalem temple in the land of Israel, a location to which this community of deportees has now lost all access. Yet here in the opening vision, the very *kābôd* of Yahweh thought to be restricted to the Jerusalem temple, appears free and mobile, even coming to be in the midst of a foreign, unclean land. By hearing the report of this vision, Ezekiel's traumatized community experiences the presence of Yahweh come to them in the midst of their exile. Additionally, the text implicitly signals Yahweh's abandonment of the rebellious people remaining in Judah under Zedekiah in favor of the exiles with whom Judah's future lies (see chs 8—11). Still, the opening vision is not just a statement of divine freedom and mobility; its imagery of elements of nature and all the classes of living creatures (see 1:1-5, 10) is ultimately a visual representation of Yahweh's sovereignty over the entire cosmos. In the end, for Ezekiel, this sovereignty of Yahweh turns out to be the sole source of hope that can provide an alternative plot line for Israel's future after exile.

C. Ezekiel's Commissioning as a Prophet (2:1-7)

The opening of ch 2 relates Yahweh's first actual words to Ezekiel in the book, forming a direct continuation of the final phrase of ch 1 ("and I heard the voice of one speaking" [v 28]). Out of the visionary context of the divine presence in ch 1, Yahweh speaks from the throne in 2:1-7 in order to commission Ezekiel as a prophet who will speak to the disobedient Israelites. The divine speech, which begins with the Spirit once again acting as an animating agent to lift Ezekiel to his feet (cf. 1:12; 3:12), has several elements of typical OT call scenes (e.g., the use of the verb "to send" [2:3-4]; the admonition not to **be afraid** [v 6]). Yet, in keeping with the heavy divine emphasis throughout the book and in contrast to many of the prophetic call narratives elsewhere, Ezekiel does not resist the call or offer a response of any kind (see Isa 6; 1 Kgs 22); the scene is dominated by Yahweh's words and actions.

1:22— 2:2

■ **1-2** The first words of Yahweh to Ezekiel in v 1 introduce the primary designation used for the prophet throughout the book: **son of man** (Heb., *ben 'ādām*). The phrase occurs ninety-three times in the book. In the context of Ezekiel, the phrase should not be read as a title (contra NIV). The phrase appears as a title in the OT only in the book of Daniel (see Dan 7:13), where it designates a divine figure in the midst of human beings (Block 1997, 30). In referring to Ezekiel, it has the opposite function in this book. In the Hebrew idiom, to be a **son of man** is simply to be one of the species of human (see Num 23:19; see "son of Israel" for "Israelite"); hence, the NRSV translates correctly, "mortal." The repeated use of this designation for Ezekiel emphasizes his mortality and creaturehood in comparison to Yahweh, who is often designated with the double title "Sovereign LORD" (see 37:3) and has just been portrayed as the king of the cosmos in the opening vision of ch 1. Indeed, nearly every activity in the book is presented as the direct words and actions of Yahweh, while Ezekiel's persona is virtually subsumed beneath this divine emphasis. This heightened acknowledgment of Yahweh's sovereignty answered a sense of powerlessness among Ezekiel's audience, created by the experiences of destruction and exile.

■ **3-7** Against this backdrop of Yahweh's sovereignty, vv 3-5 provide the essence of Ezekiel's call: **I am sending you . . . say to them . . . they will know.** Here at the outset (v 3) and throughout the book, Ezekiel uses the name *Israel* to refer to the exiles and other Judeans. Such a designation is surprising, as the name more strictly designates the northern kingdom with its capital in Samaria that was destroyed centuries earlier in 722 B.C. By using such a name, Ezekiel evokes the tradition of an ideal, unified kingdom living in proper relationship to Yahweh. Yet, the further description of *Israel* as **a rebellious nation** in v 3 is actually plural in the Hebrew text ("rebellious nations"). The reason for this plural designation remains debated. The reference may be to the multiple kingdoms that had allied with King Zedekiah of Judah to plot a rebellion against Babylonia at the time of Ezekiel's call in 593 B.C. (see Behind the Text). Or, the reference may be a recognition of the fact that two Judean communities existed after the first deportation of 597 B.C., namely, the exiles in Babylonia, and Zedekiah and those remaining in the land of Judah. Alternatively, the plural "nations" may refer to the entire history of the peoples of Israel and Judah as a rebellion, joining with the second half of v 3 to extend Israel's rebellion back to the entirety of its existence in the land: **they and their fathers have been in revolt against me to this very day** (note how 37:22 envisions a restoration of Israel and Judah as a single "nation"). Thus, Ezekiel begins already to renarrate the entire history of the people of Israel as a history of rebellion (see ch 20).

Verse 5 then introduces one of Ezekiel's main titles for the people: **rebellious house** (*bêt mĕrî*; see also vv 6, 7, 8). Occurring fourteen times in the book, the title again recasts the entire history and character of Israel as one of rebellion. Moreover, the language has both religious and political resonances (Odell 2005, 43). The verb "to rebel" (*mārad*) is a common term in ancient Near Eastern and biblical texts for the rebellion of a vassal against a political overlord (e.g., Gen 14:4; 2 Kgs 18:7, 20). Such a reference is fitting, given King Zedekiah's involvement in plans for rebellion against Babylonia at this time. Simultaneously, since Ezek 1 has established a vision of Yahweh as the enthroned king of all creation, Ezekiel's designation depicts Israel as a rebellious vassal to the divine king (see 17:15) and virtually equates Zedekiah's budding rebellion against Babylonia with rebellion against Yahweh.

Given the proven rebelliousness of Israel, Yahweh attaches a special dimension to Ezekiel's call: he is to preach **whether they listen or fail to listen** (v 5). Ezekiel's successful fulfillment of his divine commission does not depend on the response of the people but only upon his own faithfulness to the task (see also 3:16-21; see Isa 6:9-13). Such preaching will, however, cause the people to **know** [or, *acknowledge*] **that a prophet has been among them** (v 5). Ezekiel's message will show those people who will soon experience divine judgment through the destruction and exile of 586 B.C. that Yahweh had provided them with warnings. In this way, the book of Ezekiel begins to address the trauma of those who have experienced and will experience destruction. While such destructions could be perceived as signs of the weakness and defeat of their God, Ezekiel's message renarrates them as part of Yahweh's own sovereign plan to restore the holiness of the people and land.

Ezekiel and the Call Experience

The stories of several prophets and other important leaders in the OT include accounts of their call experience. These "call narratives" typically take two forms: (1) a process of dialogue with Yahweh in which the prophet initially resists or refuses the divine call, or (2) a powerful experience of Yahweh's presence that overwhelms the prophet so that he or she offers no resistance to the divine charge. Most interpreters view Ezekiel's call as one of the second type, since he experiences an overwhelming vision of Yahweh's presence that leaves him with no room to resist (Zimmerli 1979, 99). More recently, however, other commentators have suggested that Ezekiel's call must be understood in light of the whole of chs 1—3 and that Ezekiel's actions of sitting silently, being bound, etc., indicate that he was resistant to the call (Block 1997, 78). In any case, the presence of more than one type of call in the OT texts reminds contemporary readers that their own call experiences may be of many different, even unpredictable types, and that calls often include an extended process of dialogue in which a person can raise questions and receive responses and assurances from God.

D. Ingesting the Trauma of the People (2:8—3:15)

■ **2:8—3:3** Between Ezekiel's commissioning as a *prophet* in 2:1-7 and his commissioning as a *watchman* that follows in 3:16-21, the strange scene of Yahweh giving Ezekiel a scroll to eat (2:8—3:15) stands at the center of the entire unit of chs 1—3. Ezekiel sees a scroll with writing on its front and back, eats the scroll, and discovers that it tastes **as sweet as honey** (3:3). The text immediately alerts the reader to the magnitude of the scroll's contents, as scrolls in the ancient world normally have writing on only one side, while Ezekiel's scroll is overflowing with words on the front and back. In contrast with the obstinacy of the **rebellious house,** Ezekiel is to obey without resistance Yahweh's command to eat. In fact, the prophet remains passive throughout the encounter, as the verb in 3:2 (**he gave me the scroll to eat**) is a causative form in Hebrew, literally reading, **he fed me.**

The scene is similar to the call of Jeremiah, in which Yahweh claims to have placed his words in the prophet's mouth (Jer 1:9-10), as well as to a later passage, in which Jeremiah refers to eating words of suffering sent by Yahweh (Jer 15:16). For Jeremiah, however, the image remains only symbolic and metaphorical. Ezekiel literalizes the symbol, with Yahweh actually force-feeding him the scroll itself. The text seems to present this event only as part of the vision that Ezekiel is experiencing (see 2:9), but this kind of blurring of the line between vision and literal act is characteristic of Ezekiel's visionary reports throughout the book (Block 1997, 125).

Ezekiel's description of the words on the scroll labels them as **words of lament and mourning and woe** (2:10). Hence, most commentators take the scroll to contain the content of Ezekiel's prophetic message, that is, the words that he should speak to the Israelites (see Darr 2001, 1125). Others take the whole scene as simply a test of obedience that Yahweh gives to Ezekiel after his initial call in 2:1-7, not directly related to the actual content of his message (see Odell 2005, 44). The scroll's contents of **lament and mourning and woe,** however, more readily represent responses to a message rather than the message itself (see Zimmerli 1979, 135). Seen in this way, Yahweh gives Ezekiel a firsthand experience of the traumatic nature of the events that will befall the people of Israel and around which his preaching will revolve. Ezekiel ingests the trauma of the people into his own being. The prophet's assertion that the taste of such experiences was **sweet as honey** (3:3) does not attribute pleasantness to the people's trauma but likely resembles language found in the psalms that describes Yahweh's word as "sweeter than honey" (Pss 19:10; 119:103) and thereby indicates that the trauma to come upon the people is part of the divine word to Israel (Zimmerli 1979, 136).

In conjunction with the possibility that Ezekiel experienced his call at the very time in which he would have begun his service as a priest at the Jerusalem temple (see 1:1), the scene of ingesting the people's trauma at the midpoint of his call is similar to the ritual for the ordination of priests in Lev 8—9, where the priests eat the sin offering in order to take on the people's guilt and provide forgiveness for it. The priests identify with the people in their sin for the sake of Yahweh's larger purpose of forgiveness. Likewise, Ezekiel here identifies in a most personal way with the people's trauma for the larger purpose of speaking Yahweh's message to them.

■ **4-11** Following the eating of the scroll, Yahweh again commands Ezekiel to go and speak his words to the Israelites (3:4-11; see 2:1-7). Ironically, Yahweh tells Ezekiel that his own people will be less receptive to the divine message than a foreign people of **obscure speech and difficult language** (3:5; cf. the receptivity of the foreign sailors and Ninevites in the book of Jonah). Against the backdrop of the portrayal of Yahweh as a cosmic, sovereign ruler in ch 1, it is Yahweh's own people (subjects) who are the most unwilling to listen to him (Odell 2005, 45). The people's defiance has nothing to do with Ezekiel but results from the fact that they are **hardened and obstinate** (v 7) to Yahweh (see Yahweh's words to Samuel at the people's demand for a king in 1 Sam 8:7). Literally, Ezek 3:7 describes the people as having "a hard forehead and a stubborn heart" (so NRSV), thus depicting both an external and internal hardness. To meet the challenge of the people's hardness, however, Yahweh equips Ezekiel with a corresponding hardness, which even surpasses that of the people: **I will make your forehead like the hardest stone** (v 9).

Verses 4-11 also explicitly reiterate the central theme of the direct and dominant role played by Yahweh in Ezekiel's ministry. Ezekiel is repeatedly said to be speaking the very words of Yahweh and only when Yahweh opens the prophet's mouth to do so. This idea is implied here by Yahweh's force-feeding of the scroll and made explicit by Yahweh's statements that Ezekiel will **speak my words . . . all the words I speak to you** (vv 4, 10). As earlier in 2:7, Ezekiel is to speak these words to the people, regardless of **whether they listen or fail to listen** (v 11).

Yahweh's instructions in vv 4-11 also give a fuller picture of Ezekiel's audience. Upon reading the initial commissioning of 2:1-7, one might conclude that the sole focus of Ezekiel's message is the rebellious group that remains in the land of Judah under Zedekiah (see 2:3, 7). But the instructions in 3:11 link the exiles in Ezekiel's own Babylonian community to the "rebellious house" that was mentioned previously (see 2:6). Yahweh instructs Ezekiel to address the exiles with the same messenger formula (**This is what the Sovereign LORD says**) with which he is to address the group mentioned earlier (cf. 2:4; 3:11) and to preach to both groups in the same manner: **whether they listen or fail to listen** (3:11; see 2:7). The book as a whole maintains this tension, in which the exiles with Ezekiel in Babylonia are the focus of Yahweh's future plans for restoration but also bear some responsibility for what has happened to Judah. Even so, the prophet calls them to break with the old Israel through a return to faithfulness toward Yahweh.

■ **12-15** Following Yahweh's instructions (vv 4-11), vv 12-15 abruptly return to the imagery of the wheeled throne carried by the living creatures, thus reminding the reader what he or she has nearly forgotten, namely, that Ezekiel's commissioning takes place in the visionary context of the appearance of the glory of Yahweh at the Kebar River. As if startling Ezekiel (and the readers!) awake, the prophet hears the noise of wings and wheels as the chariot throne begins to move once again (cf. 1:24-25). Although one can read 3:12 as a doxology that praises the **glory of the LORD** (**May the glory of the LORD be praised in his dwelling place**), the Hebrew phrase is likely better read as a description of the rising of the glory from the place where it had come to rest before Ezekiel ("as the glory of the LORD rose from its place" [NRSV]; see Zimmerli 1979, 94). As the glory of Yahweh begins to move, the Spirit returns Ezekiel to the exiles in Tel Abib, although the text never indicated that he left them.

Upon his arrival back among the exiles, Ezekiel describes his reaction to the visionary experience in harsh terms: **I went in bitterness and in the anger of my spirit** (v 14). Moreover, following the initial call to be a prophet and the symbolic ingesting of the people's trauma, Ezekiel sits **overwhelmed** (v 15; "stunned" [NRSV]; lit., ***desolate, devastated***) for a period of seven days. Some interpreters have taken this as a sign of Ezekiel's resistance to his call (Block 1997, 138, 141), while others say it represents his feelings of despair about his mission (Greenberg 1983, 90). It is perhaps better to see this momentary pause in Ezekiel's overall commissioning in chs 1—3 as reflecting the practices for the ordination of priests described in Lev 8—9 (Odell 2005, 47; Darr 2001, 1111). In the midst of the priestly ordination process, the priests being ordained have a seven-day period of seclusion in the sanctuary prior to the completion of their ordination in order to mark the transition from their former life to their future life (Lev 8:33-36). Whatever the interpretation, Ezekiel's silence and awe reemphasize the fact that Ezekiel will speak only when Yahweh opens his mouth and provides the words (see Ezek 3:10).

E. Ezekiel's Commissioning as a Watchman (3:16-21)

The story of Ezekiel's eating the scroll in 2:8—3:15 stands at the center of his commissioning vision in chs 1—3. Ezekiel receives a commission to be a prophet (2:1-7), ingests the trauma of the people, endures a seven-day interlude of desolation (2:8—3:15), and then proceeds to the remainder of his commissioning in 3:16-21. Some commentators suggest that the commissioning in these verses is a later addition to the text, as the designation of Ezekiel as a "watchman" appears in a developed form later in 33:1-9 (so Zimmerli 1979, 154). As in 2:1-7, Ezekiel again receives a call to speak Yahweh's message to the house of Israel, and the text reiterates the book's consistent emphasis on divine initiative and activity, as Ezekiel will speak when he hears a word from Yahweh (3:17).

■ **16-21** Here, Yahweh specifically commissions Ezekiel to be a **watchman** (v 17) or "sentinel" (NRSV; Heb., *ṣōpeh*). In the ancient world, the **watchman** was a lookout who served to warn of an approaching enemy (see 2 Sam 13:34; 2 Kgs 9:17; Jer 6:17; Hos 9:8; Mic 7:4). Revisiting a theme of Ezekiel's commissioning as a prophet in 2:1-7, 3:18-21 elaborates on the demand that Ezekiel must be faithful to warn no matter the audience's response. It is up to the people, both the wicked and the righteous, to respond to the sentinel's warning; Ezekiel's only charge is to sound the warning. But these verses develop the importance of this charge in a far greater way than the commissioning in 2:1-7. So important is the sentinel's duty to speak the message of warning faithfully that Yahweh's speech in vv 18-21 makes Ezekiel's life dependent upon it. If Ezekiel fails to speak Yahweh's warning and the people remain in their wickedness or turn from their righteousness, Ezekiel himself will be held **accountable** for their blood (vv 18, 20). These divine instructions offer a lasting reflection on the seriousness of a divine call and the measure of its success. The success of such a call to service is not measured by the nature or amount of the people's response but by the servant's faithfulness in proclaiming the message. Even so, the faithful execution of the duty to which one is called is not a light matter of vocational choice but a life-or-death charge in which the servant is held responsible for the lives put into his or her care.

These divine instructions to Ezekiel have a legal style characterized by hypothetical scenarios, which reflects that of priestly legal texts in Leviticus (see Block 1997, 142). Here is another aspect of Ezekiel's priestly identity, that is, his charge to take on the primary role of teaching divine instruction (*tôrāh*), one of the main tasks of priests in the exile. Yet there remains a deep irony in this commissioning. The text does not state the identity of the enemy about whom Ezekiel, as a **watchman,** is to warn the people, but it implies that the same God who appoints the watchman is the very One who is coming against the people as an enemy in the destruction that will occur in 586 B.C. In fact, Yahweh's statement in v 17 to **give them warning from me** could be translated as a command to *give them warning against me* (see Darr 2001, 1134).

F. Visionary Context of Commissioning: Part 2 (3:22-23)

The traditional view of the structure of chs 1—3 sees 3:21 as the ending of the opening vision/commissioning and 3:22—5:5 as the next major section of the book that focuses on Ezekiel's symbolic acts (e.g., Sweeney 2005, 136-

37). In the same way that 1:4-28 provided the visionary context for Ezekiel's commissioning as a prophet in 2:1-7, however, 3:22-23 may be seen as a return to that visionary context following Ezekiel's commissioning as a watchman in 3:16-21 and preceding additional instructions given to him by Yahweh in 3:24-27 (see outline above). Verses 24-27 reveal the content of the vision in vv 22-23 and provide the transition to the beginning of Ezekiel's public demonstrations through symbolic acts (4:1—5:4).

■ **22-23** As at the beginning of the initial vision by the Kebar River (1:3), in 3:22 the **hand of the LORD** comes upon Ezekiel and causes him to move to the geographical location of a **plain,** presumably the flood plain beside the Kebar River where the first vision took place. In one simple descriptive sentence, Ezekiel relates that he once again encounters the glory/presence (*kābôd*) of Yahweh that had appeared to him at the first: **And the glory of the LORD was standing there, like the glory I had seen by the Kebar River** (v 23). Even though Ezekiel gives only an abbreviated summary statement of this encounter, he evokes the memory of the full vision of Yahweh's presence in ch 1 and imports all of that imagery into this scene (see Block 1997, 153). Just as before, the experience of the divine presence is overwhelming, and Ezekiel falls prostrate (see 1:28).

G. Transition: Instructions for Symbolic Acts (3:24-27)

Because vv 24-27 switch from Ezekiel's visionary and commissioning encounter with Yahweh to instructions for symbolic acts (see commentary on 4:1—5:4), some commentators see these verses as a later addition or the beginning of a new section of the book. Yet, these verses that appear to inaugurate the start of Ezekiel's public ministry remain inextricably connected to the preceding visionary encounter in 1:1—3:23. Verses 24-27 provide the content of what Yahweh says to Ezekiel when the glory/presence appears to him in the plain and simultaneously provides the bridge to the next chapter by relating the divine instructions for the first of Ezekiel's symbolic actions. As is characteristic of all the symbolic actions in the book, the text provides only the instructions for the act; no report of the action or the audience's response is given (see also the instructions in 4:1—5:4). Additionally, here and throughout the following section, Yahweh begins several sets of instructions with the book's common designation that emphasizes Ezekiel's mortality, **And you, son of man** (v 25; "mortal" [NRSV]; see also 4:1; 5:1).

■ **24-27** Similar to the transition from the initial vision to Yahweh's address to Ezekiel in 2:2, **the Spirit** in v 24 raises the prophet from his prostrate position to be addressed by the divine words. Yet, Yahweh's instructions to Ezekiel in the plain are a strange way to begin a prophetic ministry. Yahweh instructs Ezekiel to seclude himself within his house. Moreover, the prophet will be bound with ropes to restrict his movement, and have his tongue stick to the roof of his mouth so that he cannot speak to the people about their sins. The interpretation of these symbolic acts hangs on the translation of the verses. It is unclear whether the verbal clause here is active (**you . . . they will tie with ropes**) or passive ("cords shall be placed on you" [NRSV]). The Hebrew verb form (from the root meaning, "to put, place") can support either translation, and the Greek translation of the OT reads the verb as a passive. The majority of commentators take the verb as active (**they will tie**) and understand the verse as Yahweh's prediction that Ezekiel's audience will actively oppose his message and ministry (so Zimmerli 1979, 160; Greenberg 1983, 102). Yet, throughout the book, there are no reports of such resistance or hostile actions by Ezekiel's audience. The exiles often seek Ezekiel's guidance and make inquiries of him (e.g., 8:1; 14:1; 20:1; 33:30-33; see Block 1997, 155). Additionally, many of the prophet's symbolic actions reflect the events and effects of warfare, destruction, and exile (e.g., 4:1-3, 9-17).

Seen in this light, the actions in 3:25-26 are best translated as passive constructions ("cords shall be placed on you, and you shall be bound with them" [NRSV]), not describing resistance by a specific group but perhaps serving as symbols of the past experiences of siege, defeat, and deportation that Ezekiel and his fellow exiles had experienced in the capture of Jerusalem in 597 B.C., as well as signs of what the people who remained in the land of Judah would eventually experience by Yahweh's judgment in the final destruction of Jerusalem to come in 586 B.C. (see also Odell 2005, 57). Thus, in order to begin the public presentation of Yahweh's message to the people, the divine voice speaks again out of the visionary context and instructs Ezekiel himself to symbolize the trauma that the people of Judah will endure as they are transformed into prisoners of war and deportees of a foreign empire.

The only clear active statement in Yahweh's instructions in vv 25-26 is the statement that Yahweh will render Ezekiel unable to speak for a time (v 26). The Hebrew verb is causative and first person: **I will *cause* your tongue *to cling* to the roof of your mouth**. The difficulty involved in reconciling this action with Yahweh's preceding commission to warn the people reminds us that the book's visionary experiences do not proceed in a simplistic, linear sequence. Here the text revisits the theme introduced in Yahweh's instructions in 3:4-11 and symbolized in Ezekiel's seven days of silence in v 15, namely, that Ezekiel's messages will be Yahweh's own words, since Ezekiel will speak only when Yahweh has enabled him to do so. In v 27, Yahweh asserts that whatever messages Ezekiel eventually speaks will come at Yahweh's initiative: **But when I speak to you, I will open your mouth.**

With the prophet rendered silent and engaged in the initial symbolic action representing trauma, siege, and exile, Ezekiel's commissioning vision of Yahweh's presence ends by reiterating that Ezekiel is to discharge his calling faithfully regardless of the people's response (see 2:5-7; 3:16-21). As if to provide a "final verbal punctuation mark" (Block 1997, 78) on the book's opening vision, v 27 reasserts the book's most characteristic description of the people of Judah: **they are a rebellious house** (*bêt měî*).

FROM THE TEXT

Interpreters throughout the history of Christianity have often characterized the commissioning vision of chs 1—3 as being full of obscurity and difficulty. Yet, as one recent commentator remarks, the book's opening vision is theology in the form of artistic representation (Odell 2005, 32). The divine encounter that we witness at the outset of this book is, at many points, not a narrative, discursive report but a visual, sensory experience that captures our imaginations and engages a number of our senses. More importantly, this vision has particular power to speak to those who find themselves living in exile and struggling to deal with the traumatic experiences of displacement and subjugation.

For Ezekiel and his sixth-century audience, the theological significance of this vision and its power to speak to those suffering the trauma of exile rests, in the first place, on its portrayal of *God's sovereignty over human life and, indeed, the whole cosmos*. The vision of supernatural creatures and a heavenly throne is a visual demonstration of God's authority and power. As noted in the introduction to this commentary, for the priestly theology out of which Ezekiel operates, God's holiness is chiefly defined as sovereignty. In the particular context of Ezekiel's commissioning, the vision and words of chs 1—3 reaffirm God's sovereignty to those in exile and show them how they ought to envision their God. In the face of Babylonia's seeming dominance over the people's lives and world, the "first word" of the book of Ezekiel is a proclamation and demonstration that their God remains enthroned above the cosmos, with creatures of every kind subsumed under his authority.

Such a portrayal of God is a subversive image to any human persons, governments, or forces that claim dominion and power over the lives and bodies of God's people. For exiles in Ezekiel's time, the portrayals of chs 1—3 asserted an image of God as king in the face of a Babylonian emperor who demanded unquestionable loyalty. For contemporary readers, the vision and words of chs 1—3 undercut all forces that demand our loyalty or even tacitly enfold us into their mind-sets—forces of economic systems, political ideologies, and individual or corporate claims to power. Some modern readers may rightly find difficulty with Ezekiel's use of kingly/monarchical imagery for God, due to its masculine and hierarchical characteristics. However, in any context of exile and defeat, or even accommodation and assimilation, this image of God's sovereignty serves as a powerful means to "relativize" all competing claims to dominion and reorient the lives of those whose vision has been clouded by such false sovereigns (Odell 2005, 37).

A second way that the vision in chs 1—3 responds to the context of exile and trauma is through its assertion of *God's presence with the people in the midst of exile*. Immediately after an opening that describes the location of Ezekiel and his audience in a foreign, unclean land, far removed from the center of God's holiness in the temple of their homeland (see 1:1-3), the book's opening vision portrays God's presence (*kābôd*, "glory") appearing to Ezekiel in the midst of that foreign land. Though the book ultimately lifts up the ideal of a restored land and temple in which God's presence can dwell in the midst of a cleansed community (see chs 40—48), God comes to the place of the people's exile in order to begin the divine work that will ultimately lead to their full restoration. Thus, Ezekiel's commissioning vision in chs 1—3 begins the process of offering a new interpretation of the destruction and exile suffered at the hands of the Babylonians, a process that will continue throughout the book's visions, acts, and oracles. The first three chapters introduce the interpretive framework through which the exiles are to understand their past, present, and future. Rather than allowing the people to think that their plight is the result of historical contingencies or divine failure and/or cruelty, the book sets out to provide an explanation that incorporates the people's trauma into the narrative plot line of their life as God's people, as well as God's overarching plan to restore his people and land. These portrayals begin from the declaration that God's presence remains active with the people in the midst of their circumstances, whether good or bad.

As with other call experiences presented in Scripture (e.g., Exod 3; Jer 1), Ezekiel's inaugural vision in chs 1—3 offers some significant portrayals of the *nature and task of those called to be God's commissioned servants* (see sidebar "Ezekiel and the Call Experience" above). Although Ezekiel has a solitary encounter with God, the prominent use of other biblical and extrabiblical traditions, genres, and motifs in this vision demonstrates that Ezekiel came to perceive and articulate his call only in the context of his tradition and the experience of his community. Against that backdrop, Ezekiel's commissioning to be God's messenger is, in fact, only a new adaptation of his previous vocation. With his exile to Babylonia in 597 B.C., Ezekiel lost the ability to fulfill his original calling to serve as a priest at the temple in Jerusalem and minister to his people in the context of their relationship with God. The divine appearance to Ezekiel in chs 1—3, however, maintains his identity as a priest, yet offers a creative adaptation of the ways in which Ezekiel can fulfill his service to God and people (Sweeney 2005, 137). As it is presented in Ezekiel, there is a dynamic nature to God's commissioning, which may take on new forms in response to new situations in the life of the people of God and may become clear only in the context of tradition and community experience.

Even more central to Ezekiel's commissioning vision, however, is an emphasis on the weightiness of God's call. God's words to the prophet in chs 2—3 especially make it clear that a call to serve as God's messenger demands total obedience on the part of the one called. Ezekiel hears God repeatedly tell him what he must do and say, communicating both explicitly and implicitly that living out God's call demands an obedience that stands in marked contrast to the attitude of the prophet's own people: "But you, son of man, listen to what I say to you. Do not rebel like that rebellious house" (2:8). Even so, God's words in passages like 3:16-21 (see also 2:5; 3:11) make it clear that Ezekiel's obedient discharge of his call does not depend upon whether the people respond positively to his message. His life depends upon his obedient fulfillment of the call (e.g., 3:18-19), yet such obedience is not measured by the level of success he achieves but by his faithfulness to the task. If Ezekiel fails to proclaim God's message, and the people continue to rebel against God, refusing to see their experiences and lives within God's unfolding plot line, then Ezekiel will be held accountable (3:20-21). But if the people remain rebellious despite Ezekiel's faithful proclamation of God's word to them, he "will have saved" himself (3:21).

For contemporary Christians, God's words to Ezekiel may provide a new way to envision the charge to share one's faith. In the spirit of Ezekiel, perhaps the ultimate responsibility of Christians is to bear faithful witness to the love and grace of Jesus Christ, without always aiming to achieve simple, measurable conversions in people's lives. As the book of Ezekiel testifies, the "conversion" of persons to new ways of understanding and living is often a process that unfolds in dynamic ways, over periods of time, and through diverse experiences. At its heart, however, is frequently one who speaks God's words in faithful obedience.

II. ACTS AND ORACLES OF JUDGMENT (EZEKIEL 4—7)

BEHIND THE TEXT

Chapters 4—7 contain the symbolic acts (4:1—5:4) and interpretive oracles (5:5—7:27) that accompany the opening vision of chs 1—3, in which Yahweh's *kābôd* appeared to Ezekiel in exile in Babylonia. The focus steadily broadens, as the acts and oracles move sequentially to address the city of Jerusalem (4:1—5:4; 5:5-17), the mountains of Israel (6:1-14), and finally the whole land of Israel (7:1-27). Together, the visions, acts, and oracles in chs 1—7 form another part of Ezekiel's theological interpretation of the decline, fall, and restoration of Judah, which links those events inextricably with the presence, absence, and return of a holy God among the people (Blenkinsopp 1990, 6). Chapters 4—7 may be outlined as follows:

    A. Five Symbolic Acts (4:1—5:4)
    B. Explanatory Oracles (5:5—7:27)
        1. On Jerusalem (5:5-17)
        2. On the Mountains of Israel (6:1-14)
        3. On the Land of Israel (7:1-27)

The historical situation reflected by the acts and oracles is the primary background element for understanding these chapters. Although the section does not contain an explicit date, the chronological movement of the book locates these chapters in the years between the first capture of Jerusalem in 597 B.C. and the final destruction of Jerusalem that would take place in 586 B.C. Many scholars identify parts of chs 4—7 as later additions, but the acts and oracles as a whole interpret the city's initial capture and deportation, as well as the ultimate destruction to come, as divine judgment. Thus, these chapters provide some of the content of the accusations against Israel that Yahweh commissioned Ezekiel to make in the opening vision of chs 1—3 (Odell 2005, 56). Moreover, they continue Ezekiel's effort to provide a new understanding of the people's past, present, and future by interpreting the trauma they have experienced and will continue to experience as part of a larger divine plan based on Yahweh's holiness. The acts and oracles are directed on the surface to those Judeans who are still in Jerusalem after the initial events of 597 B.C. (see 5:5, 8). Even when the text describes exile/deportation (see 4:13), for example, it focuses on the exile that is to come in 586 B.C. for those still in Jerusalem.

Even so, the immediate, primary audience of Ezekiel's words and actions are his fellow exiles in Babylonia. While recounting Yahweh's instructions and oracles, Ezekiel remains among the Babylonian deportees. His attempt to persuade his hearers that the events of their past are instances of divine judgment and that such judgment is not yet complete is, in fact, a message aimed at those already in exile after 597. Apparently, Ezekiel's fellow exiles still needed to be convinced that what they had experienced was the doing of Yahweh and that Yahweh's sovereign plan included a further, more complete judgment to come (Darr 2001, 1141). Hence, Ezekiel offers symbolic actions and divine oracles that narrate past and future trauma into an unfolding, divine plot line that goes beyond what his fellow exiles can presently conceive. In so doing, he calls his audience to disassociate its loyalty and identity from the old Jerusalem upon which Yahweh's ultimate judgment has been pronounced.

A second background aspect of these chapters concerns the nature and function of the symbolic acts in 4:1—5:4. The use of such "sign-acts" or "enacted prophecies" (McKeating 1995, 19) is a characteristic feature of Ezekiel (see the sidebar "Ezekiel's Symbolic Actions" in the Introduction). Yet, the actions in 4:1—5:4 also fall into a long tradition of other prophets who use various acts and gestures to convey their messages (e.g., 1 Kgs 11:30-31; Isa 20:1-6; Jer 27:1-7; Hos 3:1-5), although Ezekiel uses a great deal more of them than other prophets (see Odell 2005, 55). Interpreters have, at times, understood these often unusual behaviors, as resulting from psychological disorders or as functioning in a semi-magical way, in which the performance of the action ensures and begins to bring about the depicted event (so Hals 1989, 33). A better view, however, is to see these actions as part of the prophets' efforts to persuade their audiences. Such acts are not magic but something more akin to street theater: acts of nonverbal rhetoric, usually followed by an explanatory oracle, designed to persuade in specific contexts (see Friebel 1999; Block 1997, 166).

Ezekiel's symbolic actions possess some unique elements when compared with the sign-acts of other prophets. Symbolic actions in prophetic books normally include instructions to execute the act, a report of the execution, and a description of the audience that witnesses the act. Here, however, one finds only Yahweh's instructions to Ezekiel (cf. 24:15-24). In light of this feature, some commentators suggest that the symbolic actions in chs 4—5 are an extension of Ezekiel's prophetic call in chs 1—3, which he undergoes privately in his house (see 3:24) as preparation for public ministry (Odell 2005, 53-56). Yet 4:3 indicates that Ezekiel's actions are to be a "sign" to Israel, and one of the acts (4:12) is explicitly to be performed in the sight of the people (Darr 2001, 1141). Hence, we should probably understand the lack of any description other than Yahweh's instruction as part of the book's tendency to keep the focus on the divine initiative and action.

Ezekiel's unusual actions, set in the years following the first exile in 597 B.C. and anticipating the coming destruction of Jerusalem in 586 B.C., offer another representation of the trauma that the people of Judah have experienced and will continue to experience. These actions portray various elements of the brutality of city-siege warfare in the ancient world (see In the Text below). In the same way as the prophet's forced eating of the scroll filled with words of lamentation and mourning in 2:8—3:3 symbolized his ingesting the people's trauma, Ezekiel, through the strange actions pictured here, displays his personal involvement in what is happening to his people. He suffers the trauma of the people's destruction and exile in his own body before he begins to relate oracles and visions of the judgment and its causes.

A third background aspect comes into play with the accompanying explanatory oracles in 5:5—7:27. Here, agricultural imagery of mountains, trees, crops, and lands becomes dominant. This passage marks the first instance of a certain type of nature imagery that appears in a number of passages throughout the book and that Ezekiel shares with several other prophets—the imagery of the devastation and rejuvenation of nature (including trees, crops, vineyards, etc.) as a part of divine judgment and restoration.

This agricultural imagery has a rich background in both the literature of the OT and the social and political realities of the ancient Near East. First, the judgments in chs 4—7 have parallels to the covenant curses in Lev 26.

This passage, appearing in the context of the priestly material associated with the covenant between Yahweh and Israel at Sinai, depicts the punishments that pertain if Israel violates its relationship with Yahweh. For example, Ezek 4:16 and 5:16 match the language of Lev 26:26 by asserting that Yahweh will bring a famine on the land by breaking the "staff of bread" (NRSV) in Jerusalem. Similarly, Ezek 5:17 corresponds to Lev 26:22, 25, as Yahweh proclaims that he will send wild animals and pestilence that will devastate the land. By using such imagery, Ezekiel, the priest, brings Israel's actions and Yahweh's reactions depicted in chs 4—7 into the context of covenant relations (Odell 2005, 71). The experiences that Israel has suffered and will suffer are not the result of failed foreign policy or Babylonian supremacy; rather, they stem from the people's violation of their covenant and represent divine responses from within the bounds of that covenant.

Ezekiel's imagery of the destruction of nature also connects to practices of warfare known throughout the ancient Near East. Extrabiblical sources indicate that the intentional destruction of trees, vineyards, crops, and other agricultural support systems was a frequent tactic of siege warfare (see Hasel 2005). While scholars continue to debate the exact purpose and sequence of this devastation of agriculture, the traumatic nature of such events is clear from texts that link the devastation of elements of nature with the simultaneous destruction of houses and deportation of peoples.

Warfare and the Devastation of Nature

The imagery of the devastation of trees, crops, vineyards, and other elements of nature that appears in the judgment oracles of Ezekiel and other prophets reflects the practices of warfare in the ancient Near East. Assyrian texts in particular depict the destruction of agriculture and land as a part of siege warfare against enemy cities. The Assyrian king Shalmaneser III (858-824 B.C.) describes his actions against a Babylonian king: "I shut him in his city, I carried off the grain of his fields, I cut down his orchards, I turned aside (*lit.*, dammed) his river" (ARAB 1:230, §622). Likewise, a later Assyrian king, Sargon II (721-705 B.C.), offers a description of the defeat of an enemy king with even more detail: "His great trees, the adornment of his palace, I cut down . . . Their abundant crops . . . I tore up by the root and did not leave an ear to remember the destruction" (ARAB 1:88, §161).

There are no explicit Babylonian references to the devastation of trees, crops, and lands among the surviving textual sources, yet it is clear that the Babylonians in Ezekiel's time destroyed cities in a similar fashion to their predecessors. Ezekiel and his audience likely experienced the devastation of nature in an even more intensified way, however, as several recent studies have observed that the Babylonians adopted what one might call a "devastated-earth policy" (see Kelle 2007, 57-75). Unlike the Assyrians, who made a regular practice of restoring cities and lands devastated by war, archaeological evidence indicates the Babylonians did not rebuild the physical and economic structures of their conquered territories. In the events surrounding the two captures of Jerusalem witnessed by Ezekiel and his audience, Babylonian armies left the lands around Jerusalem in a devastated and impoverished state.

The resonances of Ezekiel's devastation of nature imagery with the realities of ancient warfare suggest that the use of such language is another part of the prophet's effort to reinterpret the trauma experienced by his audience. To many in Ezekiel's audience, the destruction of trees, crops, vineyards, etc., was a sign of Babylonian might. Yet, Ezekiel presents this very same type of destruction as part of Yahweh's acts of judgment against Israel in accordance with the demands of the covenant (see Lev 26). In so doing, he, like other prophets, brings the traumatic experiences endured by his people under the sovereignty of Israel's God, thereby taking the power away from foreign enemies and giving it to Yahweh. Ezekiel, in fact, virtually ignores the Babylonians' role in such devastation altogether, implying that these destructive occurrences were solely Yahweh's doings from the beginning.

Overall, the symbolic acts and interpretive oracles in chs 4—7 highlight several aspects of Ezekiel's narrative theological world. While conveying Yahweh's message about the fate of Jerusalem, Ezekiel communicates that Yahweh has a sovereign plan and that Jerusalem's past capture and coming destruction are part of that larger divine work. He also begins to offer an explanation for Israel's judgment that is grounded in the demands of Yahweh's holiness. Yahweh must act because the people have defiled his temple and land (see 5:11-12).

IN THE TEXT

A. Five Symbolic Acts (4:1—5:4)

The series of symbolic actions in 4:1—5:4 forms the opening part of the section of acts and oracles that follows Ezekiel's first vision of Yahweh's presence in chs 1—3. The opening vision ended with a transitional section in 3:24-27, in which Yahweh gave instructions for the performance of a first symbolic act that represented the trauma of capture and confinement experienced by Ezekiel and his fellow exiles. In 4:1—5:4, Yahweh continues his instructions for the prophet to perform symbolic acts, but the focus of attention turns to those Judeans who remain in Jerusalem under King Zedekiah after the Babylonian capture that led Ezekiel and his group into exile in 597 B.C.

The symbolic actions described in 4:1—5:4 apparently mark the beginning of the prophet's public ministry among the exiles (see 4:3 but cf. Odell 2005, 53-56). Yet, as noted above, the text reports only the instructions for these actions as a private encounter between Yahweh and Ezekiel in which Ezekiel predominantly listens passively to the divine word (but cf. 4:14). Even the oracles of judgment that follow (5:5—7:27) take the form of direct, first person speech by Yahweh to Ezekiel, rather than a proclamation by Ezekiel to an audience.

Throughout the section, however, one finds subtle indications that Ezekiel is relating Yahweh's words to an audience. Statements such as "He then said to me" (4:16), "This is what the Sovereign LORD says" (5:5), and "The word of the LORD came to me" (6:1; 7:1) place all of the divine words to Ezekiel within the framework of a report by Ezekiel to his audience. Hence, chs 4—7 introduce two levels of discourse that remain operative throughout the entire book. On one level, Yahweh speaks directly to Ezekiel about the past, present, and future of his people. On another level, brief, occasional references addressed to the book's hearers/readers (e.g., 6:1; 7:1; 8:1) frame all of the visions, acts, and oracles as reports that Ezekiel declares to his audience and, therefore, to us as readers of the book's final form. In the case of chs 4—7, the words that Yahweh speaks directly concern the fate of those living in Jerusalem after 597 B.C. Yet, Ezekiel relates these words to the exiles living in his community in Babylonia, who must learn a new way to understand the plot line of their past, present, and future and reshape their identity in response to Yahweh's holiness.

Each of the major symbolic actions in 4:1—5:4 begins in Hebrew with a clear indication of Yahweh's address to Ezekiel (4:1, 4, 9; 5:1 ESV): "and you, O son of man" (*wəʾatâ ben ʾādām*) or simply "and you" (*wəʾatâ*). Overall, however, the organization of the series is unclear, with seemingly nine different acts being described (see Block 1997, 167). The actions also seem to jump between different phases of Jerusalem's destruction (cf. 4:1-3, 7-11, 12-13, 16-17). These complexities suggest to many interpreters that this section includes several editorial additions, especially in the passages that refer to exile. Even so, one can generally identify four major symbolic actions that Ezekiel is instructed to perform: portraying the siege of a model city (4:1-3); lying sequentially on his left and right sides (4:4-8); preparing rations for siege and deportation (4:9-17); and shaving his head to symbolize destruction (5:1-4).

These symbolic actions portray the typical stages involved in the siege of a city, as known from the practices of warfare in the ancient Near East. In such warfare, the attacking army isolates a city by constructing ramparts and siege walls around the city's outer wall in order to prohibit movement into or out of the city. Other siege machinery, including battering rams and earthen ramps, provides the means for breaking through the city's defenses and moving troops into position against the city's walls. The primary goal of such siege warfare was not necessarily to take the city by force, but to create such dire conditions of starvation and deprivation that the city's population would surrender and submit to subjugation, deportation, or destruction.

Siege Warfare in the Ancient Near East

The symbolic actions performed by Ezekiel in 4:1—5:4 provide visual representations of the stages and effects of city-siege warfare known throughout the history of the ancient Near East. The Assyrian Empire in particular perfected this practice and preserved a number of descriptions of city sieges. In one description of the siege of the Judean city Lachish during the time of Hezekiah (701 B.C.), the Assyrian king states, "As for Hezekiah the Judean, I besieged forty-six of his fortified walled cities ... Using packed-down ramps and applying battering rams, infantry attacked by mines, breeches, and siege machines, I conquered them" (COS 2.119B:303)

These are exactly the kinds of traumatic events that had likely been experienced by some of Ezekiel's fellow exiles and that would soon be experienced by the Judeans remaining in Jerusalem. Ezekiel gives this past and future trauma a new meaning as a part of the larger work of Yahweh's holiness. Yahweh, not the Babylonians, is the enemy who is at the gate of Jerusalem, and the siege and destruction, which will soon come to fruition, represents Yahweh's judgment on the unfaithfulness of the house of Israel.

■ **1-3** In a manner reminiscent of a child playing with toys, the first symbolic act (4:1-3) contains Yahweh's instructions for Ezekiel to **draw the city of Jerusalem** (v 1) upon a brick and simulate the siege of the city, complete with model siege wall, ramps, and battering rams. The reference here is probably to a mud brick (rather than a **clay** writing **tablet**; cf. NIV) that could be drawn upon while the clay was wet and left to harden in the sun. Archaeologists have recovered a number of bricks from throughout the ancient Near East with plans and maps of cities drawn upon them (see Odell 2005, 58-59).

Ezekiel's act contains the added dimensions in which Yahweh instructs him to **take an iron pan** and set it as an **iron wall** between himself and the city and then to **turn your face toward** the model city (v 3). Similar imagery appears in Lam 3:44, which grieves the destruction of Jerusalem by lamenting that Yahweh has established an impassable barrier to separate himself from his people. For Ezekiel, who operates from the context of priestly theology, this barrier is not created by the people's sin but is placed there by Yahweh to separate the divine presence from the people's uncleanness. The Hebrew phrase

set your face against **(turn your face)** designates a symbolic gesture of hostility and appears elsewhere as an action performed by Yahweh expressing his opposition and leading to defeat by enemies (e.g., Lev 26:17; Odell 2005, 59).

■ **4-8** The second symbolic act in vv 4-8 forms an aside from the stages of a siege, leading many commentators to identify the passage as a later editorial addition (e.g., Greenberg 1983, 126). Yahweh instructs Ezekiel to lie on his left side **for 390 days** and his right side for **40 days,** each of which is to symbolize the ʿăwōn (vv 4, 5, 6; **sin;** "punishment" [NRSV]) of Israel and/or Judah. Any interpretation of these verses must deal with several key questions.

First, what do the terms **Israel** and **Judah** represent in this text? Verses 4-8 seem to use **Israel** and **Judah** as designations for separate kingdoms in the north and south. If so, this would be the first instance of such usage in Ezekiel. Typically, Ezekiel uses the term **Israel** as a designation for the ideal concept of a unified north and south (e.g., 37:11), often using **Israel** and **Judah** interchangeably to refer to a single kingdom centered in Jerusalem (see 2:3; Block 1997, 176; Darr 2001, 1143). The northern kingdom had been destroyed by the Assyrians over a century before the time of Ezekiel's ministry. Even when Ezekiel addresses the history of the northern kingdom (see chs 16 and 23), usually to shed light on the behavior and fate of Judah, he designates the north by referring to its capital city Samaria or some other name like Ephraim or Joseph (e.g., 16:46; 23:4; 37:16, 19).

Second, what does the Hebrew term ʿăwōn symbolize in this passage? The text explains that Ezekiel lies on his sides in order to represent this ʿăwōn. Although the NIV translates each occurrence of this term in the section with the word **sin,** the NRSV renders it "punishment." The Hebrew term can carry both meanings. It is unclear whether Ezekiel's actions symbolize the sin/iniquity that Israel and/or Judah have committed or the punishment they have endured and will continue to endure.

Third, what do the numbers of days/years (**390** and **40**) represent? Some interpreters assume that **390 days**/years refers to the history of the northern kingdom, and **40 days**/years to that of the southern kingdom. But considering Ezekiel's typical inclusive use of the term "Israel," a number of recent commentators conclude that the days/years refer to two different phases in the life of Israel as a whole. Moreover, if there are different phases, they may use different meanings of ʿăwōn as "sin" and "punishment" in turn.

In one possible view, then, three hundred ninety years from the time of Ezekiel would go back to around 980 B.C. and the beginnings of the monarchy in Israel. Perhaps Ezekiel's first act of lying on his left side represents the **sin** (ʿăwōn) that Israel has incurred throughout its entire life as a kingdom. The **40 days**/years may then represent the next phase of Israel's life to come, in which it must bear the "punishment" (*ʿāwōn*) for its sin in the form of exile (Odell 2005, 63). The length of forty years in connection with the coming exile resonates with the story of the Israelite spies in Num 14:34, in which the Israelites were sentenced to wander in the wilderness one year for every day the spies were in the land of Canaan, with forty years being a symbolic number for the length of a generation. Through this imagery, vv 5-9 perhaps portray the coming punishment of exile as a second wilderness period, after which Israel may experience another entry into the promised land (Greenberg 1983, 118; Block 1997, 179).

While this view assumes that Ezekiel's own time is the starting point for calculating backward three hundred ninety years, and that the forty years refer to a period after Ezekiel's time, the text does not clearly indicate either of these conclusions. Perhaps the text takes as its point of departure the sweeping religious reform carried out by King Josiah of Judah in the 620s B.C. (2 Kgs 22—23; so Sweeney 2005, 138). The OT presents this reform, though apparently unsuccessful in the long run, as an attempt to reverse the sinful practices that had characterized Judah for the preceding centuries of its existence. Moving backward three hundred ninety years still places one around 1000 B.C., near the beginning of the monarchy as presented by the OT. But moving forward forty years from the 620s places one in the 580s, around the time of the destruction of Jerusalem and end of the kingdom of Judah. In this view, the word *ʿāwōn* should be understood as **sin** in each of its occurrences here (so NIV). Ezekiel's **390 days** symbolize the years that Israel lived in sin before Yahweh's attempt to bring about reform under Josiah, while the **40 days/years** symbolize Israel's failure to heed such reforms and their continuation in sin up to the end of their existence as a kingdom in Ezekiel's day. Even so, the numbers may contain a message of hope. The sum of Israel's years of sin, both before and after Josiah's attempted reform, four hundred thirty years (three hundred ninety plus forty), is equivalent to the number of years that Exod 12:40-42 says Israel dwelt in the land of Egypt before the exodus (Darr 2001, 1147). Perhaps the sum total of Israel's years of sin implies that there is hope of a second exodus that will deliver them from the bondage of their sin and its consequences, just as the first exodus delivered them after four hundred thirty years in slavery to the Egyptians.

Whatever interpretation one chooses, the imagery in this second symbolic act is another example of the priestly identity of Ezekiel and the impact of the traumatic events of exile upon it. The imagery of bearing the sin of the people (v 4) corresponds to the priest's function of taking the people's sin upon himself through eating the sin offering or transferring the sin to a representative goat to be sent away (Lev 10:17; 16:20-22). Yet, because of his situation in exile, away from the temple in an unclean land, Ezekiel's actions are no longer able to fulfill their traditional purpose of carrying away the people's sin and thereby saving them from experiencing divine punishment (Odell 2005, 63-64).

■ **9-17** The third symbolic action in Ezek 4:9-17 returns to the stages of a siege and its effects. Yahweh instructs Ezekiel to eat an unusual diet while lying on his side. The mixture of grains and beans that Ezekiel is to use to make **bread** (v 9) symbolizes the scarcity that exists during a siege, as shortages do not allow bread to be made of grain alone. Additionally, the quantities that Ezekiel is to eat each day (**twenty shekels of food** and **a sixth of a hin of water** [vv 10-11]) total only about eight ounces of bread and two-thirds of a quart of water. Such actions reflect the shortages and starvation well-known from descriptions of sieges in ancient Near Eastern texts.

Verses 12-17 jump ahead to the end result of the siege. Yahweh gives the startling directive that Ezekiel bake the bread over a fire **using human excrement for fuel** (v 12). According to the text, this is a symbol that those in Jerusalem will soon be forced to eat their food in the unclean, foreign lands of exile. Because these verses suddenly shift from the experience of a siege to the aftermath of exile, some interpreters consider them a later addition (e.g., Greenberg 1983, 118-19). Even so, in a rare moment of self-assertion in the book, Ezekiel objects to Yahweh's command on the basis of his priestly consciousness. To eat food prepared in such a way would violate ritual purity and ceremonial holiness. As a priest, Ezekiel was to eat food that was consecrated for sacrifices in the temple (see Lev 7; 10—11; Num 18), and Deut 23:12-14 commands that human excrement be relegated to a location outside the camp. Ezekiel's objection uses the primary priestly term for ritual uncleanness (*mĕṭummāʾâ;* **defiled**) and maintains that he has consistently avoided three different kinds of unclean meat (see Exod 22:31; Lev 7:18; 11:44; 17:15; 19:7).

In response, Yahweh relents from the command for human dung but insists that Ezekiel bake his bread over **cow manure** instead (v 15). While the use of animal dung for fuel was known in the ancient world in times of scarcity, cooking with it still rendered the food to be eaten by Ezekiel unclean according to the priestly purity system. In the same way, the people of Jerusalem will soon find themselves eating unclean food because they will be eating it in unclean, foreign lands (see Josh 22:19; Amos 7:17).

■ **5:1-4** The final symbolic act in 5:1-4 continues the focus on the culmination of the siege. The prophet's action here has two parts: to use a **sword** to **shave his head and . . . beard** (v 1) and to **divide . . . the hair** into three sections to symbolize different judgments that will come upon the people (vv 2-4). The act of shaving the head functioned as a sign of mourning in the ancient world, something akin to ritual self-humiliation (Blenkinsopp 1990, 38). Here again Yahweh instructs Ezekiel to perform an action that clashes with his identity as a priest. Priestly texts in the OT associate such shaving with forbidden ritual acts and thus prohibit priests from doing it (Lev 19:27; 21:5).

In the present context of siege and destruction, the act carries an added meaning. Military conquerors in the ancient world sometimes shaved the heads or beards of captives and exiles as a means of humiliation (see 2 Sam 10:1-5), an act that some of Ezekiel's own audience may have endured when Jerusalem was captured in 597. The prophet's symbolic shaving not only symbolizes the destruction to come upon Jerusalem but also gives expression to the traumatic experiences that the people perhaps have endured and will continue to endure.

The destruction envisioned here is strikingly total: Ezekiel's three clumps of hair, each symbolizing a segment of the people of Jerusalem, all suffer judgment. The first two clumps represent those who will experience death at the fall of the city. The last clump of hair, which Ezekiel scatters to the wind, represents those who will go into exile. In contrast to what we see in some of the other prophetic books, Ezekiel does not envision this final group as a righteous remnant that is divinely rescued from destruction (cf. Isa 10:20-23). Instead, these people experience exile as punishment, and Yahweh promises to unleash the sword after them for complete destruction (Ezek 5:2). Out of this third group, however, Yahweh instructs Ezekiel to take just **a few strands of hair** and place them within his cloak (v 3). Only these few of the exiles will become those who are "tucked away" by Yahweh to provide a new future plot line for the house of Israel. Yet Yahweh instructs Ezekiel to cast even some of the hairs hidden in the robe into the fire for destruction, symbolizing that even some of the ones who survive the longest will not be immune to the destruction that has come upon the others.

In this culminating act, Ezekiel subtly blends his immediate audience of fellow Babylonian exiles together with the rebellious ones awaiting divine judgment in Jerusalem and thereby reveals a significant dimension of his theology. While Ezekiel clearly sees the exiles as the ones through whom Yahweh's new future for Israel will come, he offers only a very modest hope, here taking the form of a mere remnant of a remnant of survivors (see the priestly covenant language in Lev 26). Hence, Ezekiel's symbolic acts become a message of warning to both those still in Jerusalem *and* his fellow exiles in Babylonia: a place in the future plot line of Israel on the other side of trauma and destruction is not guaranteed; it depends entirely upon Yahweh's holiness and the people's response to it.

B. Explanatory Oracles (5:5—7:27)

1. On Jerusalem (5:5-17)

The messenger formula (**This is what the Sovereign LORD says**) at the beginning of v 5 marks a shift from Yahweh's instructions to Ezekiel concerning symbolic actions to a direct divine oracle against Jerusalem (5:5-17). The oracle provides the reasons for, further descriptions of, and the intended outcome of the judgment that Ezekiel has just symbolically portrayed. It focuses especially on the character of Jerusalem and the effect of the people's behavior on Yahweh's sanctuary (Odell 2005, 68). The passage begins with an introductory comment (vv 5-6) that offers an overall characterization of Jerusalem's wrongdoing. Following this, the passage alternates between descriptions of the people's sinful actions and Yahweh's judgment acts (vv 7-12), with each new section being marked by the Hebrew term *lākēn* (**therefore**; omitted by the NIV at the midpoint of v 11). The speech concludes with a description of the intended outcomes of Yahweh's actions (vv 13-17).

■ **5-7** The description of the people's actions in vv 5-6 begins with a succinct statement (two words in Hebrew) that functions as a hinge, connecting both to what precedes and follows: **This is Jerusalem**. In relationship to the preceding chapter, the phrase clarifies that the symbolic acts portray the city of Jerusalem. In relationship to the oracle that follows, the phrase provides a transition that effectively says "now this is what Jerusalem is like." Verses 5-6 then reintroduce Ezekiel's primary description of the house of Israel known from the opening commissioning (see 2:3): **she has rebelled** (*mārâ*; v 6). As discussed earlier, this term is political in nature and carries a double nuance in Ezekiel's historical context. Drawing on the imagery of ancient political treaties, which establish the expected relationship of a vassal to an overlord, the description casts Jerusalem as a rebel that has rebelled against Yahweh, its sovereign overlord. Simultaneously, against the backdrop of the years between 597 and 586 B.C., the label of "rebel" may allude to King Zedekiah's participation in rebellious alliances against Babylonia, which Ezekiel sees as outside Yahweh's will (see Behind the Text for chs 1—3). Ezekiel offers a theo-political interpretation of the events of Israel's history, which understands all the rebellious actions of Jerusalem, even political actions related to Babylonia, as being rebellion against Yahweh.

Ezekiel's Theo-politics

Why do Ezekiel and other prophets interpret Judah's political rebellions against kingdoms like Babylonia as acts of religious unfaithfulness/disobedience to Yahweh? Political treaty-making in the ancient world involved a religious component. Particularly in the Assyrian period, treaties enacted between kingdoms evidence the practice of swearing the treaty in the names of the gods of both kingdoms (see Tsevat 1959). Other extrabiblical texts suggest that such swearing at times involved a religious ceremony in which the gods of the treaty kingdoms were worshipped with gifts (see Kelle 2005, 262-64). Following these ancient views, which thoroughly intertwine religion and politics, prophets like Ezekiel could proclaim that the Judean kings' violations of treaties, which they had entered into at Yahweh's prompting and pledged in Yahweh's name, constituted the sin of rebellion against Yahweh.

Perhaps the most striking aspect of the overall description appears in v 6, where Yahweh declares that Jerusalem's rebelliousness exceeds even that of the pagan nations surrounding it. This comparison continues in v 7, which switches to address the personified city of Jerusalem directly (**you**) and begins the first specific description of the people's actions. Yahweh describes Jerusalem with the Hebrew term *hāmôn* (**unruly**; "turbulent" [NRSV]). The word has the root meaning of "boisterous, noisy" but often occurs in political contexts to designate a type of arrogant rebelliousness. Ezekiel uses the term sixteen times in his oracles against Egypt (chs 29—32). His use here continues the characterization of Israel as a vassal in revolt against its sovereign, Yahweh.

The second half of v 7 indicates the way in which Jerusalem is **more unruly** than the surrounding nations. The NIV has correctly translated the Hebrew to indicate that Jerusalem has not just rebelled against Yahweh's laws, but the people **have not even conformed to the standards of the nations** (cf. NRSV, "but have acted according to the ordinances of the nations"). While this could refer to a failure to abide by basic, shared ethical standards, it is more likely a reference to the Judean leadership's consistent involvement in rebellious schemes. They are of such a rebellious character that they refuse to abide by even the demands of treaties into which they have entered with other nations.

■ **8-12** The word **therefore** (*lākēn*) at the start of vv 8-9 marks the shift from Jerusalem's sinful acts to Yahweh's coming judgment. Yahweh speaks directly to Jerusalem in a discourse filled with heavy first person emphasis (lit., **Behold I, even I, am against you** [v 8]) and raw emotion. The primary imagery is that of Yahweh as a divine warrior (cf. Exod 15:3; Pss 106:10-11; 135:10-12), but here Yahweh is the enemy of his own people (see Ezek 5:8). Much of the language is political and military, bearing similarities to curses and punishments found in ancient Near Eastern vassal treaties. Especially noteworthy is how the description of Yahweh's actions continues in v 10: Yahweh states that he will cause them to endure the horror of cannibalism between parents and children, which often accompanies the starvation resulting from the siege of a city (see 4:9-17; 2 Kgs 6:24-31; Isa 9:19-21; 49:26; Jer 19:9), as well as subsequent deportation.

Ezekiel 5:9-10 also returns to the categories of Ezekiel's priestly theology in order to relate the cause of Yahweh's violent acts of judgment. The text labels all of Jerusalem's actions, including acts of political rebellion, with the priestly term *tôʿăbōtāyik*, *your* [fem. sg., i.e., Jerusalem's] **abominations** (NIV adds the dimension of idol worship to the term, **detestable idols**). From Ezekiel's perspective, the rebelliousness and unruliness of Jerusalem constitute acts of defilement that render the people and their land polluted/impure (see 5:11; Lev 18:26).

Picking up on this priestly perspective, the first part of Ezek 5:11 offers a further description of the people's actions. The verse begins with the heaviest first person emphasis of the passage, combining an oath formula in which Yahweh swears by himself (**as I live**) with the emphatic expression **surely** (Heb., *ʾim lōʾ*). The oath formula occurs regularly in Ezekiel to emphasize divine pronouncements (e.g., 17:16, 19; 20:33; 33:27; 34:8). Here, Yahweh's speech drops all explicit references to political rebellions and misdeeds and now describes the people's actions solely with the categories of priestly defilement. The verse again labels the people's behavior toward Yahweh and others as **abominations** (**detestable practices**; see also v 9). Moreover, it employs the language of ritual impurity that is typical of priestly works like Leviticus (**defiled**; Heb., *ṭāmēʾ*; see Lev 18:26-27). In so doing, the oracle communicates that Jerusalem's true wrongdoing is not its political and social actions, but the fact that these actions are **abominations** that carry a polluting quality and have defiled Yahweh's sanctuary (the NIV unnecessarily implies that the people's actions here consist of idol worship [**vile images**]; but cf. NRSV, "detestable things"). A later passage in 7:22 describes foreigners as profaning Yahweh's holy place, but here it is the actions of Yahweh's own people that have defiled his dwelling. In keeping with the primary concern of the book of Ezekiel, the text's focus is on Yahweh's presence in the midst of the people, especially as it is connected to the status of Yahweh's temple and the city of Jerusalem that houses the temple (Galambush 1992, 127).

In the middle of v 11, the transitional word **therefore** (*lākēn*; omitted by the NIV) marks the switch back to Yahweh's judgment on the people's actions. The text returns to the imagery of siege, destruction, and exile known from the final symbolic action in 5:1-4 (see also Lam 2:17-22). Unlike the symbols in Ezek 5:1-4, however, this description of judgment has an emphatic and personal tone (**I myself**), which makes Yahweh the agent of destruction against his own people. The final phrase of the verse (**I will not ... spare you**) resembles the holy war language of Deuteronomy and Joshua in which Israel was told to "have no pity [mercy]" in exterminating the Canaanites (Deut 7:16 KJV). Here, however, it is Yahweh who will show no mercy to his covenant people.

■ **13-17** The final section of Yahweh's oracle against Jerusalem (vv 13-17) turns to the intended outcome of the divine judgment. It continues the presentation of Yahweh as a divine warrior who is moving against his own people. Most importantly, however, v 13 asserts that one intended outcome governs all of Yahweh's violent actions: **they will know** [*yādāʾ*] **that I the LORD have spoken in my zeal.** This is the first occurrence of the so-called recognition formula in Ezekiel (Zimmerli 1979, 38-39; Hals 1989, 31). The formula reflects the legal sphere of convincing or demonstrating. The Hebrew verb translated "to know" may also be read in this context as "to acknowledge/recognize." The formula emphasizes that Yahweh's actions have the goal of revealing Yahweh's name and identity and leading his rebellious people finally to acknowledge their true God. In the context of Ezekiel and his audience, where Yahweh's name and reputation have been impugned by his people and called into question by the exile, the divine actions have the goal of persuading the people to recognize once more who Yahweh is and what that means for the past, present, and future. Yet in a way that is perhaps disturbing for contemporary readers, Ezekiel seems convinced that the people will finally acknowledge Yahweh only when he has **spent** his **wrath upon them** (v 13). In other words, the operative conviction here is that Yahweh's acting in terrifying power and militaristic violence is the most effective way to get the people to acknowledge his sovereignty (see From the Text).

Yahweh as a Divine Warrior in the OT

Depictions of Yahweh as a warrior are a subset of warfare imagery in the OT. Such imagery finds its roots in some of the earliest poetry connected with the exodus from Egypt, which envisions Yahweh as a warrior on Israel's behalf (e.g., Exod 15:3; see also Pss 106:10-11; 135:10-12). Especially in the psalms, this imagery takes several forms: (1) Yahweh fighting alone, sometimes by miracle without any physical means and other times by using weapons (Pss 7:12-13; 17:13-14; 35:1-3); (2) Yahweh using elements of nature as weapons (Pss 18:12-19; 68:8-10; 83:13-18); (3) Yahweh leading a divine army of heavenly beings to fight Israel's battles (Ps 34:7; cf. 2 Kgs 6:8-23); (4) Yahweh serving explicitly or implicitly as the commander of Israel's army (Pss 18:34; 44:9; 60:10; 124:2-3). Ezekiel, as well as other passages, reverses this imagery and portrays Yahweh as a divine warrior who fights against Israel as an enemy (Pss 38:1-8; 60; 80; 89; Job 9:17-18; 16:12-14; Lam 2:5, 17).

As a whole, the divine diatribe on Jerusalem in Ezek 5:5-17 offers the book's first extensive reflection on the guilt of the people who have suffered and will suffer destruction and exile. If we read Ezekiel against the backdrop of this trauma, a certain irony is at work. Typically, dealing with trauma involves helping victims realize they are not to blame for the violence they have suffered, thus opening a new way of living that is free of guilt and shame (Herman 1997, 68). Ironically, however, the divine speeches in Ezekiel heap guilt upon Israel, stressing the people's liability in Jerusalem's destruction (see Garber 2004, 226). In Ezekiel's view, the people are simultaneously victims and perpetrators.

At one level, we may explain Ezekiel's perspective through the phenomenon of "survivor guilt" known from trauma studies. Survivors of tragedy often experience feelings of guilt because they survived and others did not (see Garber 2007), leading them to place indictments against themselves. At another level, however, passages like 5:5-17 function as a word of challenge to the people, pushing them to reinterpret their past and present in light of the alternative perspective of Yahweh's holiness. The book often implies that Ezekiel's audience of exiles does not feel guilt or responsibility (e.g., 11:3). Speeches like that in 5:5-17 counter this lack of acknowledgment by urging the people to recognize their culpability in the traumas they have suffered and thereby open the possibility of a new existence through future restoration (Garber 2007, 10).

2. On the Mountains of Israel (6:1-14)

5:13—
6:10

Both chs 6 and 7 begin with the so-called divine word formula (**the word of the LORD came to me** [6:1; 7:1]) and Yahweh's typical reference to Ezekiel as **son of man**. With these matching openings, Ezekiel's voice interrupts the sequence of Yahweh's speeches to address his hearers/readers directly, signaling again that he relates the divine speeches in the service of his larger theological and rhetorical purposes. The divine speeches in chs 6—7, addressed to Israel's mountains and land, respectively, broaden the preceding section's focus on the city of Jerusalem to describe the presence and effects of sinful actions upon the whole land. They also include, particularly in the case of ch 6, imagery that reflects the covenant curses in the priestly text of Lev 26 (see Block 1997, 218).

Ezekiel 6 consists of a divine oracle in two parts (vv 1-10 and vv 11-14). Each begins with the command for Ezekiel to perform a physical gesture (**set your face** [6:1]; **strike your hands . . . stamp your feet . . . cry out** [6:11]) and ends with the divine recognition formula (**they will know that I am the LORD** [vv 10, 14]). Thus, as in 5:5-17, Yahweh declares that he will enact violent judgments against Israel with the aim that the people, especially the surviving exiles (v 8), will finally acknowledge his sovereignty.

■ **1-10** Near the outset of the oracle, v 4 connects Israel's mountains with idol worship. This verse contains Ezekiel's first use of a pejorative designation for idols that will recur throughout the book: *gillûlîm* (see vv 5, 6, 9, 13). The term occurs thirty-nine times in Ezekiel, and only nine times elsewhere. This is not a typical word for idols, but a crude term that Ezekiel adopts. It derives from a Hebrew root that gives the noun the meaning of "dung pellets." Ezekiel creates a foul name (lit., "dung gods") to refer insultingly to the **idols** Israel was worshipping. From Yahweh's perspective, the entities that the people view as gods are nothing more than piles of excrement.

■ **11-14** The most notable feature of this oracle, however, is its overall address to "the mountains of Israel." This specific phrase occurs seventeen times in Ezekiel but nowhere else in the OT (6:2, 3; 19:9; 33:28; 34:13, 14*a*, 14*b*; 35:12; 36:1*a*, 1*b*, 4, 8; 37:22; 38:8; 39:2, 4, 17). The image of mountain/mountains, which occurs for the first time here, functions as a key metaphor throughout the book of Ezekiel and serves as a part of the prophet's rhetorical argument about his audience's identity and loyalty (see Casson 2004). References to either a singular mountain or plural mountains occur fifty times in twenty-two chapters. The rhetorical function of this metaphor becomes clear from the way the prophet sets up a contrast between plural mountains and a singular mountain, ultimately concluding with the plural mountains being displaced by the triumph of one mountain. Ezekiel consistently uses plural mountains (like those in ch 6) as a negative image that represents the people's past and present sin (e.g., 7:7, 16; 19:9; 20:28). But he characteristically employs the image of a singular mountain as a positive metaphor of Yahweh's presence and sovereignty (e.g., 11:23; 20:40; 34:26). These singular and plural mountains run beside each other as foils throughout the book, with the plural mountains often being associated with improper worship on the "high places" (6:3). The movement of these images reaches a climax when the hand of the Lord takes Ezekiel to a "very high mountain" at the start of the final vision of Yahweh's glory in 40:2, and Yahweh's glory/presence finally inhabits the "most holy" mountain in 43:12 (Casson 2004). By defining these images as positive (singular) and negative (plural), Ezekiel uses mountains as a metaphor to set up a foil between the exiles' past/present and future, calling them to disassociate with the old Jerusalem and its mountains and align themselves with an alternative future as a part of Yahweh's restored Jerusalem with its single, holy mountain (Renz 1999).

Mountains as Metaphors in Ezekiel

Studies of the nature and function of metaphor have demonstrated that metaphorical images, such as the "mountains of Israel" in ch 6, are not merely decorative devices but provide a means of reasoning and persuasion. Scholars have observed that Ezekiel employs plural mountains as a negative image and a singular mountain as a positive image, with the image of a single, holy mountain ultimately displacing the other images by the end of the book (see Casson 2004):

Plural mountains (negative image): 6:1-14; 7:7, 16; 18:6, 11, 15; 19:9; 20:28; 22:9; 31:12; 32:5-6; 33:28; 34:6; 35:8, 12; 36:1-12; 37:22; 38:8, 20-21; 39:2, 4, 17.

Singular mountain (positive image): 11:23; 17:22-23; 20:40; 28:14-16; 34:26; 40:2; 43:4-12.

3. On the Land of Israel (7:1-27)

■ **1-9** After beginning with the same introductory formula as ch 6, Yahweh's speech in ch 7 explicitly addresses **the land of Israel** (7:2; Heb., *ʾadĕmat yiśrāʾēl*). The first section of the speech (vv 1-9) begins with an abrupt and decisive divine declaration that announces the arrival and finality of Yahweh's judgment: **The end!** (v 2). Following this opening, the first section consists of a two-part pronouncement of destruction in vv 2-4 and 5-9 (Greenberg 1983, 157-58). Numerous translation difficulties plague the Hebrew of ch 7, and the divine speech repeats a number of themes from the oracle against Jerusalem in 5:5-17. Most notably, the text returns to priestly language and describes the offenses of the land and its inhabitants as *tôʿēbôt* (**detestable practices;** "abominations" [NRSV], vv 3, 4, 8, 9), the technical priestly term for actions that are ritually defiling and pollute Yahweh's sanctuary (Lev 18:26).

The "Day of Yahweh"

The reference in Ezek 7:7, which proclaims "the day is near," alludes to the broader notion of a "Day of Yahweh" (or "the day") found throughout the OT prophetic literature (e.g., Isa 2:6-13; 13; 34; Amos 5:18-20; 8:2-3, 9-10; Zeph 1:7-8). The motif first appears in Amos and seems to have been a prominent concept within at least some sectors of Israelite and Judean society. Popular belief apparently conceived of the "Day of Yahweh" as a future period of time when Yahweh would act in power to defeat Israel's enemies and provide the Israelites with victory and prosperity (see Amos 5:18). The prophets often invert this notion, proclaiming that the "Day of Yahweh" will, in fact, be a day when Yahweh acts in judgment against his own people as a result of their sins.

The most characteristic feature of ch 7 is the use of the unusual Hebrew phrase *ʾadĕmat yiśrāʾēl* (**land of Israel**). No other book in the OT uses this Hebrew phrase, but it occurs seventeen times in Ezekiel (see 7:2; 11:17; 12:19, 22; 13:9; 18:2; 20:38, 42; 21:2, 3; 25:3, 6; 33:24; 37:12; 38:18, 19). The unique element is the particular Hebrew word *ʾādāmâ*. While not typically a designation for the whole earth in the OT (cf. *ʾereṣ*), it can denote a political territory. More often, however, it refers to the physical ground itself, that is, the soil (e.g., Gen 2:5-6; Exod 3:5; Lev 20:25; Deut 28:4). The term's field of reference suggests that Ezekiel also uses this term to refer to the actual, physical land that belongs to Israel as the focus of Yahweh's judgment. Because **land** (*'ădāmâ*) is a grammatically feminine noun in Hebrew, the speech also contains a number of second person feminine pronouns that address Yahweh's words directly to the land/ground itself (e.g., **the end is now upon you** [fem. sg.]). Thus, the opening section of ch 7 contains Yahweh's proclamation of physical devastation to come directly upon the actual ground/land/soil of Israel. The **land** in these contexts retains its character as a metaphor for its inhabitants, but more directly represents the physical site of Yahweh's destructive activity not unlike the mountains in ch 6.

Ezekiel may be relying on the idea within priestly thought that the land can become polluted or ritually defiled because of the sinful actions of its inhabitants (Lev 18:25-28; 26:32-35; Num 35:33; see also Jer 12:10-13; Ezek 36:16-19). When used by Ezekiel in his context of exile, such imagery provides an alternative interpretation of the physical destruction of Israel's land/soil that has been and will be carried out by the Babylonians: this destruction has actually been Yahweh's doing and not that of the Babylonians. At the same time, the divine speech offers an implicit critique of those who remained in the land of Judah after the first capture and deportation in 597 B.C. (Odell 2005, 89). These survivors may have imagined themselves as the chosen ones who had inherited a promised land purged of sinful leadership (see 11:15). On the contrary, Ezekiel identifies them as sinners living in a polluted land and locates Israel's future hope with those already in exile.

■ **10-27** The second section of Yahweh's speech (7:10-27) describes defeat in battle (vv 10-25) and the disintegration of Judean society and its leadership (vv 26-27). The description features the central priestly image of the defilement of Yahweh's sanctuary (vv 21-22). The defilement is described in language that has sexual overtones and invokes the imagery of the rape of women by conquerors in war: **they will desecrate my treasured place** [sanctuary]; **robbers will enter** [Heb., *bô'*, ***penetrate***] **it and desecrate it** (v 22).

Overall, then, Yahweh's oracle against the land participates in the same rhetorical purpose as the speeches against Jerusalem and the mountains, namely, to reinterpret the trauma that has been and will be experienced by Ezekiel and his fellow Judeans. Throughout ch 7 the reoccurrence of the recognition formula (**Then you will know that I am the L**ORD [vv 4, 9, 27]) makes the daring assertion that the destruction described in these speeches is not the result of the power of the Babylonians nor the defeat of Israel's God. It is the sovereign activity of Yahweh, undertaken as a response to the people's pollution of his holiness and, as later parts of the book will make clear, forms only the first part of a larger plan that will include the future restoration of a purified people and land.

FROM THE TEXT

The symbolic acts and interpretive oracles in chs 4—7 mark the beginning of Ezekiel's construction of a new narrative plot line that can deal with the trauma experienced by his people and offer a new understanding of their past, present, and future with God. *An affirmation of God's sovereignty over the world and judgment upon sin stands at the heart of this passage.* Ezekiel attempts to convince his audience of the pervasive nature of their sin and the certainty of God's judgment. Coming after the first capture of Jerusalem by the Babylonians in 597 and before the final destruction of the city in 586, both Ezekiel's fellow exiles in Babylonia, as well as those who remained in Jerusalem, may have thought that they had already experienced the totality of God's judgment or that some kind of hope still lay with the government of King Zedekiah in Jerusalem and its constant political maneuverings (see commentary on 1:1-3). Yet Ezekiel urges his hearers to understand what they have experienced in the first capture and deportation as only the initial step in God's plan to respond to Israel's sin and reestablish divine sovereignty among the covenant people. He calls his fellow exiles to break from their attachment to the old Jerusalem and find a new identity in submission to the work that God is doing among them for the future.

Even so, these chapters, if we read them honestly, confront us with one of the most difficult and violent portrayals of God in the Bible. The God portrayed here is unforgiving, violent, wrathful, and vengeful. Rather than a process in which God convinces people to acknowledge his sovereignty and then pardons them and relents from judgment, here God deals only in sovereignty, pronouncing that the people's fate is sealed and destruction cannot be averted because it is part of an established divine plan (Darr 2001, 1170). Any future restoration lies only on the other side of judgment, but even this restoration is virtually restricted to those who went into exile with Ezekiel in 597 B.C. It is difficult for readers of Scripture to square this portrait with more characteristic OT depictions of God as a "compassionate and gracious God, slow to anger, abounding in love and faithfulness, maintaining love to thousands, and forgiving wickedness, rebellion and sin" (Exod 34:6-7). Equally difficult is the fact that physical violence is the primary way in which God accomplishes his purposes in these chapters (see Ezek 7:9). According to this text, the people will finally recognize God's sovereignty through violence that they experience.

While a reading of these texts within a Wesleyan theological perspective does not overcome all of the difficulties raised by such depictions, readers should view the violence described by Ezekiel within the book's overall theology. For Ezekiel, the violence experienced by the people is God's judgment of sin, and not some arbitrary and unbridled actions on God's part. God's wrath, then, is not an inherent part of God's nature but is connected with sin and judgment and, ultimately, with divine sovereignty. As an extension of this idea, Ezekiel makes a claim of ultimate sovereignty for God, implying that the actions of political leaders and their armies, like the Babylonians, as well as catastrophic tragedies endured by a people, should be seen as events caused by God and possessing a divine purpose. We rightly become nervous when religious leaders in our world make similar assertions, attributing a divine cause or purpose to tragedies like natural disasters and acts of military violence. Although such claims are frequent in the OT prophets, the ancient context of those prophets, as well as the nature of OT prophecy itself, should steer contemporary believers away from proclaiming such certain-sounding assessments. Still, Ezekiel sees an intimate connection between the people's sin and God's sovereign actions.

A particular point of concern with the violent image and actions of God in chs 4—7 is the harsh treatment meted out upon the natural world. In a day when Christians have much cause to be concerned for the welfare of the environment, the oracles in chs 6—7 assert that God will destroy Israel's mountains and land/ground. Ezekiel's imagery here reflects the motif of the devastation and rejuvenation of nature that appears throughout the OT prophetic books. Prophetic proclamations of judgment for sin often include statements in which God threatens to render the land desolate, lay waste to crops, and devastate trees and vines (e.g., Jer 7:20, 34; Hos 2:12; Zeph 1:2-3). Conversely, proclamations of restoration often include divine promises to replant trees, cause crops to grow, and multiply resources like grain and oil.

The Devastation and Rejuvenation of Nature in Ezekiel

Ezekiel employs the common prophetic motif that describes nature's devastation as part of God's judgment (e.g., Isa 5:10; 6:11; Jer 4:23-28; Amos 4:7-9) and rejuvenation as part of God's restoration (e.g., Isa 30:23-24; Jer 31:2-6; Amos 9:13-15). The devastation and rejuvenation of nature in Ezekiel appear in various texts with different emphases:

   a. Emphasis on recognition of Yahweh's name: 6:1-14; 12:17-20; 15:7; 21:1-5, 7-8 [MT]; 33:28-29; 38:20
   b. Emphasis on land as polluted/sinful: 7:4; 9:9; 14:12-20
   c. Oracles against the nations containing devastation of nature language: 25:12; 26:4; 29:5, 9, 10-12; 30:7-8, 10-12; 32:7-8, 13-15; 35:1-15
   d. Rejuvenation of nature texts: 34:25-31; 36:1-38; 47:1-12

Ezekiel's use of this nature motif that begins to appear in chs 6—7 has distinctive and troubling emphases (see Galambush 2004; Habel 2004). First, whereas other prophetic texts envision elements of the natural world as suffering because of human misdeeds and foreign armies, with only some attention to direct divine destruction, Ezekiel's depiction of nature in chs 6—7 places nearly all the emphasis upon God's personal, direct, and severe devastation of the natural world. Ezekiel's use of the unique phrase "the land of Israel" (see 7:2) emphasizes that God's destruction falls specifically on the physical land/ground/soil upon which Israel dwells, as well as the trees and plants rooted therein.

Second, outside of Ezekiel, one characteristic of the nature motif seems constant: although the sinful actions of human beings have a direct effect on the natural world, the land itself remains an *innocent* victim. The preaching of Jeremiah, for example, envisions the land as God's special possession, sharing a close, symbiotic relationship with the deity and able to cause God to lament its mistreatment (e.g., Jer 12:10; 23:9-12; Habel 2004, 75-76, 84). However, commentators have increasingly noticed that Ezekiel portrays the land itself as polluted, defiled, and even guilty of committing sinful actions (see Galambush 2004). He gives the land a moral status, being guilty of its own sins and therefore suffering divine punishment through famine, death of animals, and so on (e.g., Ezek 7:2-3; see also 9:9; 14:12-20; 22:24). This imagery is similar to priestly texts like Lev 18:25-28; 26:32-35; and Num 35:33 (see also Isa 24:5-6; Jer 12:10-13), which depict the land as having been defiled by its inhabitants, but Ezekiel portrays the land itself as acting sinfully, deserving by its own actions the destruction meted out upon it.

So, how are we, as contemporary Christian readers, to deal with the generally violent images of God and the specifically harsh divine treatment of nature pictured in texts such as Ezek 4—7? Perhaps a place to start is to read passages like these alongside other texts of Scripture that emphasize God's long-suffering, mercy, and forgiveness, holding the different portraits in tension with one another. Here we are reminded that the canon of Scripture does not speak with a single, unified voice but contains diverse voices that testify to different aspects of God's character and actions. We might hold together, for example, Jeremiah's emphases on God's compassion (e.g., Jer 31:3-6) with Ezekiel's emphases on God's sovereignty, even as we might read Exod 34:6-7*a* ("the compassionate and gracious God, slow to anger . . .") in conjunction with the following phrase in Exod 34:7*b* ("he does not leave the guilty unpunished").

In a surprising twist, even Ezek 4—7 contains a hint in this direction. In the midst of a passage that portrays God as a cosmic sovereign who acts out of a concern for his own holiness, one divine expression of a different reality seemingly slips through the harsh language: "I have been grieved" (6:9). Using the passive form of a term that connotes being wounded or broken (*šābar*), the text expresses a divine pathos and emotion that is more at home in the preaching of Jeremiah than Ezekiel. Yet this one comment, nearly drowned out by the thundering of God's judgments in the rest of chs 4—7, subtly reminds Ezekiel's readers that a tension of power and vulnerability, sovereignty and suffering stands at the heart of the character of God.

Perhaps another way to deal with the specific violence against nature in these chapters is to locate such imagery within the context of Ezekiel's argument and the thought-world of the ancient Near East. As we have observed, Ezekiel portrays Israel's relationship with God in the terms of ancient Near Eastern political treaties between a suzerain and vassal (see 2:1-7). These ancient Near Eastern treaties stipulate that if the vassal rebels against the suzerain, that vassal not only loses the suzerain's protection but becomes the target of military reprisals designed to put down the revolt. In line with this imagery, since Ezekiel has already declared that Israel is a "rebellious house" (e.g., 2:5, 8), that is, a house in revolt against God as its Suzerain/Lord, these chapters depict God's judgment in the expected violent and militaristic manner of a suzerain attempting to put down a revolt (Block 1997, 163). Seen in this way, Ezekiel's depiction of God's militaristic violence should be understood only as a metaphorical expression that emerges from the prophet's use of ancient political treaties as an analogy for the relationship between God and God's people.

Alongside this metaphorical context, Ezekiel's identity as a priest and his attempt to deal with the community's experience of trauma may provide another way to understand both God's violent actions and the specific portrayal of the natural world (especially the land) and its devastation. The way that Ezekiel presents the prophetic motif of the devastation of nature brings it into line with the two primary categories of priestly thought (holiness/sovereignty and purity/impurity). First, Ezekiel's assertion that God devastates the land so that people will "know/acknowledge" his name and identity brings the nature motif into line with the priestly category of God's holiness/sovereignty. In priestly thought, the holiness of God means not only that God must dwell in a ceremonially clean environment but also that God possesses a name, reputation, and authority that sets him apart (see Introduction B). In Ezekiel's cultural context, however, the fact that God's people had been sent into exile impugned his holiness by apparently demonstrating his weakness and even defeat by the patron gods of the enemy (see 36:20; 39:27-28). In response, Ezekiel ironically asserts that the traumatic destruction was, in fact, done by God and not by the Babylonians for the express purpose of demonstrating his power (see 36:22-32, 33-36, 37-38).

Second, the more unusual assertion by Ezekiel that the land itself is polluted, defiled, and even guilty of committing sinful actions and therefore suffers divine punishment likewise brings the prophetic nature motif into line with perhaps the most distinctive category of priestly thought, namely, ritual purity and its connection to God's presence in the community. In priestly theology's view, special care must be taken to guard against the defilement of what is clean and to cleanse that which has become unclean (see Lev 1—12). These convictions are important because of priestly theology's belief that God's presence dwells in the temple in the midst of the community. Hence, the people's sins are not simply transgressions against God; they are agents of pollution that create an increasing level of defilement and may cause God to withdraw his presence from the community (see Lev 16; Milgrom 1991). Later passages in the book (e.g., chs 8—11) articulate the judgment experienced by Judah precisely in these terms of God's withdrawal of his presence from the community due to the defilement caused by the people's sins. Yet, they also see God's overall goal as the cleansing of the land and people so that the divine presence may once again dwell in their midst (see 36:25-36; 48:35*b*). By describing the land itself as polluted and sinful, Ezekiel incorporates even the physical destruction of nature experienced at the hands of the enemy into priestly understandings. The land suffers not because of the triumph of the Babylonians but because it is ritually defiled. Hence, the prophet renders the destruction part of the larger sovereign plan to withdraw the divine presence, cleanse the people and land, and then return the divine presence to a purified community.

In the end, then, Ezekiel's portrayals of God's violent character and actions form another part of a powerful act of narrative imagination that takes the story of Judah's past, a story of destruction and exile that seemingly refuses to be integrated into the people's collective life in an understandable way, and reinterprets it in light of the long-standing priestly conceptions of God's holiness and the people's impurity. Ezekiel narrates a different plot line into Judah's story, which calls the people to understand their past and present in a different light. This same language also permits Ezekiel's audience to consider that the new narrative plot line introduced by Ezekiel may extend into the future and yield the possibility of a changed existence.

There is little doubt that the treatment of the earth in Ezekiel's rhetoric can be potentially dangerous, for it may foster images of domination and lead to the justification of harmful practices. This is especially true if one forgets the context of trauma out of which Ezekiel's language comes and takes these words as representing God's unmediated attitudes toward the earth. But bearing in mind this context, Ezekiel's emplotment of the devastation and rejuvenation of nature opens the possibility of a new plot line for the people's future that goes beyond what they can presently imagine. Ezekiel beckons his hearers (and readers!) into a narrative that can endure destruction and envision restoration by affirming a divine holiness that did not fail in the past and will not fail in the future.

III. SECOND VISION OF GOD'S PRESENCE: GOD LEAVES THE TEMPLE (EZEKIEL 8—11)

BEHIND THE TEXT

Up to this point in the book, readers of Ezekiel have encountered a variety of references to the defilement of Yahweh's sanctuary and the divine judgment that is to come as a result. Throughout the first seven chapters, however, Ezekiel's words and actions have not yet provided specific images and elements of that defilement. The vision of the Jerusalem temple in chs 8—11 transports both the prophet and the reader to the scene where the defilement takes place and now allows them to see directly the nature of the people's actions and the divine response.

Chapters 8—11 contain the second vision of Yahweh's presence or glory/presence (*kābôd*), which features Yahweh's departure from the defiled temple in Jerusalem. As we have noted in the overall structure of the book, this is the second of three major visions that depict the movement of the divine glory/presence (chs 1—3; 8—11; 40—48). In the same way that the opening vision of Yahweh's *kābôd* (chs 1—3) was followed by a series of symbolic acts and explanatory oracles (chs 4—7), this second vision stands before an extended section of symbolic acts and pronouncements of judgment in chs 12—24. In the narrative progression of the book, the opening vision depicts Yahweh's presence/glory appearing to Ezekiel among the exiles in Babylonia and commissioning him to act as a messenger. The second vision in chs 8—11 pictures the divine glory back in Jerusalem but only in order to portray the final move of Yahweh's presence out of the defiled temple to dwell among the exiles in Babylonia. For Ezekiel and his audience, this vision describes what is going on in Jerusalem while they are in Babylonia, but more importantly it offers a theological explanation of their deportation into exile and the coming destruction of Jerusalem by the Babylonians. The people's sinful actions have driven Yahweh's holy presence out of Jerusalem, and Yahweh has abandoned the city to destruction. Even so, these things are parts of the larger movement of a divine plot line in which Yahweh is purifying the city and people in preparation for his return and their restoration.

The opening verses of ch 8 provide the setting for the vision. They locate the prophet in his house in Babylonia, with the elders of the exiles sitting before him. Similarly, the conclusion of the vision (11:24-25) indicates that Ezekiel related what he had seen to his fellow exiles, presumably the elders mentioned at the beginning of ch 8. As we have noted, this context of private consultation is characteristic of much of Ezekiel's activity among the exiles. In this case, the setting serves as a reminder that, while the persons and circumstances mentioned in Ezekiel's vision relate on the surface to the Judean community in Jerusalem after the initial events of 597 B.C., the real audience of the prophet's vision report is the group of Babylonian deportees among whom he lives. In this capacity, the vision in chs 8—11 forms another part of Ezekiel's effort to reshape the exiles' understanding of the traumatic experiences of their time in light of Yahweh's plan for judgment and restoration.

The first words of ch 8 also associate this vision with a particular historical context. As in the case of chs 1—3 and 4—7, the chronological movement of the book locates chs 8—11 in the years between the Babylonians' first capture of Jerusalem in 597 B.C. and final destruction of the city in 586 B.C. More specifically, 8:1 once again uses the date of King Jehoiachin's exile as a point of departure and sets the prophet's vision "in the sixth year, in the sixth month on the fifth day," that is, September 18, 592 B.C., or about one year after Ezekiel's initial commissioning vision (see 1:1-2). The significance of this date relates to happenings in the larger political world of the ancient Near East around this time. Zedekiah of Judah, the king who was on the throne in Jerusalem, had been put into power by the Babylonians after the exile of Jehoiachin in 597 (2 Kgs 24—25). As discussed previously, he quickly became involved in plans for a potential rebellion against Babylonia, perhaps even hosting a conference in Jerusalem with officials from surrounding kingdoms (Jer 27:1-3; see Behind the Text for chs 1—3). This revolt never materialized, and Nebuchadnezzar brought Zedekiah to Babylon in 594-593, likely as a means of insuring his loyalty (see Jer 51:59).

Just a year or so later, the dynamics of the situation around Judah changed. In 592 B.C., while the Babylonians' efforts were concentrated elsewhere, Pharaoh Psammetichus II, who had come to the Egyptian throne three years earlier, won a decisive victory against Ethiopia that established his power in the region. Shortly thereafter, Egyptian records indicate that he embarked on a victory tour of Syria-Palestine, demonstrating his newfound power and status. For Zedekiah and other regional rulers under Babylonian dominance, this resurgence of Egypt fanned the flames of rebellion against Babylonia. For the next few years after 592 B.C., Judah and other similar kingdoms looked increasingly to Egypt as the inspiration and means for rebellion against the Babylonians. Eventually, Zedekiah would withhold Judah's required tribute to Babylonia and enter into open rebellion (ca. 590 B.C.), with biblical and extrabiblical texts indicating that Judah appealed to Egypt for horses and troops and sent royal officials to Egypt for direct negotiations. This rebellion would, of course, lead to the final destruction of Jerusalem in 586 B.C. Already in 592, however, the draw of Egypt was powerful for those who believed Yahweh's will was to rebel against the Babylonians and find success with the aid of the Egyptians.

The date reference in 8:1 sets the prophet's second vision of Yahweh's presence/glory against this background. The link with this historical context raises two issues. First, the prophet's report clearly emphasizes that he was transported to Jerusalem only "in visions," while he remained physically present in exile. Yet, the level of detail with which Ezekiel describes the actions and persons in Jerusalem raises questions concerning the literalness of his report. Should we understand these descriptions as reports of actual events that occurred in Jerusalem at this time? Did the prophet have some source by which he knew of the things he reports? Though it is possible to attribute Ezekiel's vision to direct divine revelation of contemporary events, it is clearly not a vision of things actually happening at the moment, at least not in its entirety, since the extensive killing of Judeans depicted in ch 9 would not occur until the Babylonians took the city several years later. One may approach this question by treating the happenings described in chs 8—11, such as the death of certain individuals (see 11:13), as actual events about which Ezekiel had knowledge either through direct revelation or through some other source. The prophet then gives a theological interpretation of these events as Yahweh's judgment. Another approach to this question would be to treat these events as paradigmatic examples of the kinds of actions the prophet imagines to be going on in Jerusalem. In this case, the prophet envisions the forms of divine judgment that will take place upon those actions in the near future.

The second issue raised by the text's historical setting concerns the theopolitical aspect of Ezekiel's prophecy that appears throughout the book. The prophet's depictions of the polluted temple, violent punishments of the people, and withdrawal of Yahweh's presence attribute a theological meaning to the political and social affairs going on in Judah. He links these affairs to the center of the people's life with Yahweh in the temple, effectively condemning the present configuration of Judah's life, as well as their path toward dependency upon Egypt and rebellion against Babylonia, as ritual abominations that pollute the dwelling of Yahweh's presence among them and will result unavoidably in the destruction of the city as divine judgment. In other words, by concentrating on activities related to worship in the temple, rather than political maneuverings in the royal palace, the vision in chs 8—11 indicates that the real problem with the people's actions is not a specific policy or treaty, but that their actions constitute a defilement of Yahweh's sanctuary and a threat to Yahweh's holiness. Such a depiction is part of the prophet's ongoing attempt to provide his audience with a new understanding of their past, present, and future by interpreting the ultimate destruction of Jerusalem to come as divine judgment sent to deal with a polluted sanctuary in which Yahweh's holy presence can no longer dwell.

Ezekiel's vision of judgment against the people remaining in Jerusalem consists of two vision couplets in between an introduction and conclusion:

   A. Introduction: Visionary Movement to Jerusalem (8:1-4)
   B. First Vision Couplet (8:5—9:11)
      1. Four Scenes of Abomination in the Temple (8:5-18)
      2. The Executioners in Jerusalem (9:1-11)
   C. Second Vision Couplet (10:1—11:23)
      1. Yahweh's Glory Begins to Depart the Temple (10:1-22)
      2. Interruption 1: Judgment on Wicked Officials (11:1-13)
      3. Interruption 2: Promise of Restoration for the Exiles (11:14-21)
      4. Yahweh's Glory Departs the City (11:22-23)
   D. Conclusion: Visionary Return to the Exiles (11:24-25)

As the above outline shows, the vision as a whole is framed by references to Ezekiel's setting amid the exiles in 8:1 and return to that setting in 11:24-25. Between the two parts of this inclusio, the first vision couplet (8:5—9:11) focuses on the abominations in the temple and the summoning of the executioners to bring judgment on the city, while the second couplet (10:1—11:23) features the movement of the divine glory/presence out of the temple and city. At one level, then, the sequence of the vision follows the movement of Yahweh's glory, as it meets Ezekiel when he arrives in Jerusalem (8:4), then proceeds in stages out of the temple and eventually out of the city (11:23-24). As we will see, however, the exact sequence of the divine glory's movement is confusing at various points. Moreover, the second couplet of the vision in 10:1—11:23 presents special problems for interpreters, as the straightforward plot line of Yahweh's *kābôd* beginning its movement (10:1-22) and then ultimately leaving the city (11:22-23) is interrupted by two sections (11:1-13, 14-21) that are not well integrated into their present context and seemingly out of sequence after the preceding scenes.

These observations of unevenness lead many interpreters to identify parts of chs 8—11 as later additions (but cf. Greenberg 1983, 192). The nonlinear, confusing sequence of chs 8—11 is perhaps best explained, however, by one of the key background features of the passage as a whole, namely, its genre as a vision. As discussed previously, a major feature of Ezekiel's ministry presented in the book is the experience of visions in which Ezekiel himself participates and offers a report, often providing detailed descriptions of the vision's elements and their corresponding effects on his person. Prophetic visions frequently do not proceed in a linear and logical fashion, but present various episodes that double back on each other, even sometimes in contradictory ways (compare, for example, the confusing repetition of Ezekiel's vision of Yahweh's glory moving from the cherubim to the threshold in both 9:3 and 10:4). The understanding of Ezekiel's visions as attempts to articulate and explain traumatic events further clarifies the disjointed nature of these chapters, as traumatic experiences are often "missed" by conscious memory, and a victim must rely on images and symbols to express events a piece at a time. Such expression, however, frequently requires multiple attempts with a number of nonuniform images to give voice to experiences that remain somewhat elusive (Garber 2004, 221; Geller 2000, 261-62).

The final and probably most significant background issue for Ezekiel's vision in chs 8—11 is its focus upon the Jerusalem temple. Priestly theology and temple imagery, especially the connection among concepts such as ritual purity, holiness, pollution/defilement, and the divine presence, play the defining role in how the vision communicates the people's sinfulness and Yahweh's response in judgment. The priestly importance of distinguishing among unclean, clean, and holy (see Lev 1—12) largely derives from the conviction that Yahweh's presence dwells in the temple in the midst of the community. For priestly theology, then, the people's sins are not simply transgressions against Yahweh but agents of pollution that create an increasing level of defilement or uncleanness on the temple and endanger the dwelling of Yahweh's presence in the midst of the community (see Lev 12). Given that Yahweh is holy, and that holiness must be kept separate from uncleanness, continued acts of sin will defile the temple and cause Yahweh to withdraw his presence, thus leading to the destruction of the city.

This situation is precisely what appears in Ezekiel's description of the Jerusalemites' actions and the city's status in chs 8—11. Clearly, the text is concerned with sins that are cultic/ritual in nature (see 8:5-17). Yet, perhaps the most apparent indicator of this operative priestly conception is the text's use of the distinctively priestly term *tôʿēbôt* ("detestable things" [NIV]; "abominations" [NRSV]) to designate various acts by the people. This term from the OT's priestly discourse gives their actions a ritual interpretation and indicates that they pollute the temple where Yahweh's presence must dwell in holiness (see Lev 18:26).

With the depictions given in this vision, the reader receives a fuller picture of Ezekiel's interpretation of the traumatic events that his people have experienced and will continue to experience: Judah's destruction and exile is the result of the withdrawal of Yahweh's presence from their midst, which, in turn, results from the people's sinful actions that have defiled the holiness of his sanctuary. This interpretation of events draws upon the widespread ancient Near Eastern understanding that a temple could only be destroyed if its patron god had abandoned it, either by choice or after being vanquished by a more powerful deity (see Greenberg 1983, 200-201). Ezekiel emphasizes the people's culpability in Yahweh's withdrawal that will lead to the destruction of Jerusalem, as his vision intertwines the movement of the glory/presence out of the city with descriptions of the people's sinful actions.

Ancient Near Eastern Temples and the Divine Presence

Ezekiel's depiction of Yahweh's glory/presence departing from the Jerusalem temple that has been defiled by the people's actions relates to several ancient Near Eastern texts from other cultures that describe a deity's withdrawal from a temple because of the improper conduct of the god's followers. As in Ezekiel, this withdrawal results in the destruction of the temple and/or city. The Lamentation over the Destruction of Sumer and Ur, a lengthy Sumerian composition lamenting the destruction of the ancient city of Ur, names various gods leaving the city: "Nanna, who loved his city, departed from the city; Sin who loved Ur (no longer) dwelt in his house; Ningal . . . [put on] a garment, departed [from her house]" (*ANET* 617). Similarly, a later Persian inscription from King Cyrus (557-529 B.C.) describes a god leaving his temple out of anger over the conduct of his worshippers: "Upon their complaints the lord of the gods became terribly angry and [he departed from] their region, (also) the (other) gods living among them left their mansions" (*ANET* 315).

IN THE TEXT

A. Introduction: Visionary Movement to Jerusalem (8:1-4)

■ **1-4** Following the date reference of **the sixth year, in the sixth month on the fifth day** of the month (September 18, 592 B.C.; see Behind the Text), Ezekiel begins his first person vision report by providing the setting: he was in his house with **the elders of Judah** sitting before him (v 1). Although many of Ezekiel's oracles and sign-acts seem to be given before a wider audience or contain no specification of any audience (e.g., chs 4—7; 33), this small-group consultation with the leaders of the exiles occurs at various places throughout the book (8:1; 14:1; 20:1). In a manner evocative of the Elisha traditions (e.g., 2 Kgs 5), the leaders of the Judean exiles in Babylonia come to the prophet, presumably to inquire about some question or issue. Ezekiel's introductory comment, however, omits the crucial piece of information concerning the content of the leaders' inquiry. As the vision unfolds across chs 8—11, this gap remains open. Ultimately, as we will see, the vision as a whole suggests that the elders had inquired after an interpretation of their status as exiles, especially in relation to the circumstances in both Jerusalem and Babylonia after 597 B.C. How should they understand themselves and the people who remained in Jerusalem theologically in light of the identity of the people of Yahweh and the work Yahweh is doing in history? Seen in this way, Ezekiel's vision is part of his effort to help the exiles understand themselves and their present situation theologically in light of the larger plan of Yahweh and the unfolding of Yahweh's holiness in human life.

After establishing the setting, the last part of v 1 signals the beginning of the divine vision, as Ezekiel states, **the hand of the Sovereign LORD came upon me.** As we have seen elsewhere (1:3), this expression indicates a type of divine possession that initiates a visionary experience. Here, and throughout the introductory verses that follow (e.g., **in visions of God he took me** [v 3]), the text's language reminds the reader that the scenes and events described in chs 8—11 are only visionary. Immediately upon this possession, Ezekiel describes the appearance of a figure who will be his guide on the vision of the temple (v 2). Although the Hebrew text of v 2 reads *a figure that looked like fire*, most translations see that reading as a confusion of two similar Hebrew words ("fire" and "man") and follow the Greek rendering **a figure like that of a man**, thus picturing a figure with a shining radiance who is consumed in flames below the waist. The figure resembles nearly exactly the humanlike figure who appeared above the throne in 1:26-28 to represent the glory/presence (*kābôd*) of Yahweh in exile. From the outset, then, the reader recognizes that Ezekiel's vision places him before the same divine presence that had commissioned him to service in the opening of the book.

As in the case of ch 1, the Hebrew of Ezekiel's description of the divine figure is indirect and opaque, referring literally to **the likeness** [*dĕmût*] **of the appearance of** [*kĕmarʾēh*] **a human being** (see 1:5, 10, 13, 14, 16, 22, 24, 26, 27, 28). True to the nature of such visionary experiences, Ezekiel does not express things in their actual essence but only in relationship to analogous concepts and entities ("like," "as"). While it is possible that this language represents a reticence to disclose fully things that are seen as too holy, we have noted that such indirect descriptions may also relate to traumatic experiences that are often missed, or partially comprehended, and thus are difficult to articulate fully or directly. The most important element of the divine figure in ch 8, however, is the action he undertakes in vv 3-4. In Ezekiel's vision, the fiery figure stretches out **what looked like** (lit., *the form of*) a hand and lifts Ezekiel off the ground by his hair. The **Spirit** (*rûaḥ*) once again combines with the divine hand as the agent of visionary transportation (see 3:14, 22-24), and the prophet's vision suddenly places him in the temple complex in Jerusalem.

The location in which Ezekiel's visionary transport comes to rest provides the transition to the first major part of the vision in vv 5-18. The spirit transports Ezekiel to what the Hebrew text describes as **the entrance of the gateway to the inner court that faces north** (v 3). The precise location is difficult to discern, but Ezekiel apparently finds himself standing in a gate at the northernmost end of the temple complex's outer courtyard (i.e., the southernmost end of the inner courtyard), through which one proceeds north into the inner courtyard (see Odell 2005, 104; Darr 2001, 1175). Perhaps we should think of the gates described here and in the following verses, which are the sites of a significant amount of material and action, along the lines of the gates depicted in the vision of the ideal temple in chs 40—42: large rooms (ca. 40 by 80 feet) that provide passage between sections of the temple area (see commentary on chs 40—42; Odell 2005, 105).

In general, the visionary portrayal of the temple that begins in v 3 fits with what can be gathered from other biblical descriptions of the Jerusalem temple before the exile (e.g., 1 Kgs 6—8; see "Excursus: The Jerusalem Temple" below). The temple in Jerusalem reflected the pattern of most ancient Near Eastern temples, consisting of three main sections that moved from an outer area, to an inner room, and finally to the most holy place. The sense of holiness increased as one drew closer to the innermost area, the holiest place in which the deity's presence was thought to dwell. What creates difficulties for the interpretation of the temple scene that dominates the rest of ch 8 is that Ezekiel envisions a complicated series of specific courtyards, gates, and rooms that finds no parallel in other sources of knowledge about the preexilic temple in Jerusalem and of which no archaeological remains have survived (see also chs 40—42). In fact, our knowledge of the specifics of the preexilic temple is very limited. Various biblical texts give differing indications of such things as the existence of courtyards (cf. 1 Kgs 6—8; 2 Kgs 21:5; 23:12), and the temple likely went through numerous renovations and additions throughout the period of its existence.

Excursus: The Jerusalem Temple

The detailed references to the layout of the temple in both chs 8—11 and 40—48 introduce the issue of the history of the temple in ancient Jerusalem. The history of the temple (at least according to the biblical accounts) stretches from its origins in the tenth century B.C. (attributed to Solomon) to the Roman capture of Jerusalem in A.D. 70. Yet throughout this time, the temple did not have a continuous existence. Hence, scholars now identify the first temple (destroyed in 586 B.C.), the second temple (rebuilt in 515 B.C.), and Herod's temple (a completely refashioned temple built sometime during Herod's reign between 37 and 4 B.C.). Even in between these major phases, however, the Jerusalem temple underwent numerous modifications and additions, most of which are not fully described in any textual sources. Moreover, no physical evidence of any phase of the temple building has survived in the archaeological record to date (e.g., the famous Western Wall is the remaining portion of a supporting wall built for Herod's temple). Most of our conceptions about the Jerusalem temple come from biblical descriptions, which do not all coincide, as well as inferences drawn from evidence of other temples throughout the ancient Near East.

In general, temples in the ancient world were not places for public worship, although the exterior spaces and courtyards could host such events. Rather, ancient Near Eastern temples were thought of as dwelling places for the patron god or gods. Note, for example, how Ezekiel's description of the Jerusalem temple in ch 8 describes it as Yahweh's "house" (see 8:14, 16). The major biblical description in 1 Kgs 6—8 (paralleled in 2 Chr 2—4) indicates that the temple building itself was a rectangle, approximately 165 feet long and 84 and a half feet wide. It consisted of three sections: (1) an outer foyer or porch, likely not closed off and functioning as a public court that marked the transition into the interior space; (2) the main room, separated by large double wooden doors and constituting the largest room in which most of the priestly and cultic activity took place; and (3) the most holy place (holy of holies), taking the form of a perfect cube and housing the ark of the covenant as the symbol of Yahweh's presence. Various outdoor spaces, perhaps including Ezekiel's "courtyards," surrounded the temple building, but these areas are only alluded to in the OT, so knowledge of them remains limited. Most importantly, the temple operated with a sense of "graded holiness," in which the areas become more holy and restricted as one moves toward the holy of holies from the outside. The public could enter the porch area, but the main room was restricted to priests, and the most holy place was entered once per year by the high priest alone.

Despite the description in 1 Kgs 6—8, detailed knowledge about the Jerusalem temple remains very limited. Hence, Ezekiel's elaborate references to courtyards, gates, and other structures are difficult to interpret. His descriptions come from a period very late in the first temple's existence, just before its destruction in 586 B.C., and the temple of his day may have differed significantly from the description in 1 Kings. Additionally, Ezekiel's descriptions of the temple in both chs 8—11 and 40—48 occur in visionary contexts, and the latter envisions an ideal temple and promotes certain conceptions of arrangement and architecture.

8:1-4

Whatever the details of the temple architecture, Ezekiel's vision report focuses on what he saw in this gateway from the outer to the inner court (vv 3-4). The prophet sees two representations, which, at this point in the chapter, receive no further explanation. He sees something described literally in Hebrew as ***the image of jealousy that provokes to jealousy*** (*sēmel haqinĕʾâ hamaqĕneh*). The wording here (*sēmel*) indicates some sort of sculptured image but gives the structure no specific content (contra the NIV's **idol**). Nonetheless, the statue is a representation of some kind of sinfulness located in the very place of Yahweh's holiness (see discussion of v 5 below). Simultaneously, Ezekiel reports that he also finds himself before the **glory**/presence (*kābôd*) of Yahweh, the very one that he **had seen in the plain** during his commissioning vision in chs 1—3. Over the course of chs 8—11, the prophet's observation of the movement of Yahweh's *kābôd* occupies the central place in the vision narrative, as he watches it move in phases out of the temple and city. Here, before Ezekiel begins his visionary journey into the main room of the temple, the text places the divine **glory** alongside the ***image of jealousy,*** presenting two contrasting images that characterize the problematic situation of the people's current life. One image represents the people's rebellious posture and actions, and the other signifies the very presence of Yahweh that should rest comfortably in their midst, but is, in fact, being displaced from its own dwelling by the people's doings.

B. First Vision Couplet (8:5—9:11)

1. Four Scenes of Abomination in the Temple (8:5-18)

Following the introductory description, Ezekiel reports his visionary tour of the Jerusalem temple, with Yahweh serving as a type of personal tour guide. The remainder of ch 8 consists of four scenes of "abominations" (NRSV; *tôʿēbôt*; **detestable things**) that the prophet witnesses in the temple. The scenes have a tightly integrated structure, as each one moves progressively inward from the gateway into the inner court. If one includes the transition in vv 3-4 with the first scene in vv 5-6, each of the four scenes begins with Ezekiel stating that Yahweh **brought me** and **said to me** (vv 5, 7-8, 14-15, 16-17). Additionally, each scene except the last ends with Yahweh's pronouncement that Ezekiel will see **things that are even more detestable** (vv 6, 13, 15).

In these structuring formulas, Yahweh consistently refers to the prophet with the book's characteristic designation **son of man** or "mortal" (NRSV), thus again stressing Ezekiel's mortality in comparison to divine sovereignty. The text's language also employs specifically priestly categories to describe the people's sinful actions by labeling the deeds that Ezekiel witnesses in these four scenes with the technical Hebrew term *tôʿēbôt*. In this way, the prophet's vision in ch 8 gives a particularly priestly explanation of why Yahweh's glory is abandoning the temple. Unlike the characterizations in prophets such as Amos and Hosea, Yahweh's actions are motivated here not primarily by ethical concerns but by infractions of proper cultic behavior and the preservation of Yahweh's holiness. In keeping with the priestly understanding of the relationship between purity, holiness, and the divine presence in the midst of the people, Yahweh's words in v 6 summarize the vision's perspective: the people's actions constitute **detestable things** that ritually defile the holy dwelling and thus **will drive me far from my sanctuary**.

■ **5-6** The first scene of abominations occurs in vv 5-6, when Yahweh instructs Ezekiel to observe what is in the **entrance of the gate** to which he was transported in the vision, and the prophet focuses on *the image of jealousy*. Still at this point, while the image clearly represents something negative, the text provides no description of the image or what it symbolizes (contra the NIV's **idol**). The typical understanding of this image identifies it as an idol to another god, which the people in Jerusalem have set up in rebellion and which provokes the jealous anger of Yahweh (e.g., Greenberg 1983, 168-69; Darr 2001, 1175). Second Kings 21:7, for instance, mentions a statue (Heb., *pesel*) of the goddess Asherah that King Manasseh of Judah had set up in the temple about a century earlier, and 2 Chr 33:7, 15 calls this statue a *sēmel* ("image"). If one adopts this interpretation, each of the following scenes witnessed by Ezekiel (8:7-18) represents practices of idolatrous worship of other gods by the Jerusalemite people in Yahweh's own sanctuary (see Greenberg 1983, 169; Hals 1989, 50). In this view, the primary sin of the people that brings divine judgment is forsaking Yahweh to serve other gods.

The text's nondescript language for this image, however, permits another view. There is no indication in Ezekiel that the statue depicts the goddess Asherah or a foreign deity. Moreover, as some recent commentators have observed, the Hebrew term usually translated **jealousy** (*haqiněʾāh*) may be rendered as "zeal," indicating only that this statue was a depiction of an act of religious zeal, perhaps a monument symbolizing human devotion, and not necessarily to a god other than Yahweh (Odell 2005, 106). It stands at the entrance to the gate of the temple like a picture of a person at prayer may hang at the entrance of a modern-day church sanctuary. If it is true that there is nothing overtly idolatrous about this image, the text at this point leaves open the question of why such an image is one of the people's **utterly detestable things** that defile the temple (v 6; see discussion of vv 17-18 below).

Perhaps more importantly, reconsidering the nature of this image in vv 5-6 potentially changes our understanding of the scenes that follow in vv 7-18. Rather than a collection of idolatrous elements and practices, the actions Ezekiel witnesses may represent what the Jerusalemites took to be legitimate and honest attempts to seek Yahweh. What Ezekiel condemns in the following verses may be unorthodox forms of worship that were made necessary by the capture of Jerusalem and subsequent deportation of religious leaders in 597 B.C. Left without the established priestly leadership, the community tried to make their own way with worship to carry on life before Yahweh, not realizing that from Yahweh's point of view they were merely awaiting the full divine judgment to come upon the city. As one recent treatment has argued, the scenes Ezekiel witnesses fit the pattern of a ceremony of lament to Yahweh that the people undertake elsewhere in times of crisis (see Joel 2; Odell 2005, 104-16). Having experienced the traumatic events of 597 B.C., the people remaining in Jerusalem under Zedekiah perhaps implore Yahweh to remain with them and bless them as his chosen community. Ironically, however, Yahweh reveals to Ezekiel that the people's very efforts to seek Yahweh are so tainted as to constitute defiling "abominations" that drive Yahweh away and ensure the city's destruction. Something about the character of the community's life invalidates their worship, even their worship to Yahweh (see discussion of vv 17-18 below).

■ **7-13** After telling Ezekiel that he will see "even more detestable things" (*tôʿēbôt*; v 6), Yahweh brings the prophet into the actual entryway of the inner court in vv 7-13, revealing the second scene of abomination in the temple. The text's imagery is strange, as Ezekiel observes **a hole in the wall,** follows Yahweh's command to dig through it, and discovers a hidden chamber behind the wall (vv 7-8). The description accords with the typical architecture of temple buildings, in which side rooms surrounded the main halls (see temple excursus above). Even so, the text presents a visionary experience, and the location of this scene in a hidden chamber is symbolic, emphasizing the theme of being hidden from Yahweh's sight (see v 12; Darr 2001, 1176).

In this hidden location, the abominations that Ezekiel witnesses are twofold. First, he sees artistic depictions of animals and other creatures lining the walls of the room (v 10). Such iconographic drawings were common in ancient Near Eastern temples. Yet, the language here (**detestable animals**) suggests creatures that were considered ritually unclean by priestly standards. Ezekiel also states that the wall art included depictions of the people's **idols** (*gillûlîm*; v 10). This statement again (see 6:4 above) utilizes the term that Ezekiel characteristically adopts as a pejorative designation for idols throughout the book, a crude term that carries the meaning of "dung pellets" and denounces the people's idols as literally "dung gods." Nonetheless, the text itself gives no indication that these iconographic images are necessarily non-Yahwistic. We should perhaps think of them as artistic representations of beings in Yahweh's service or intermediaries between Yahweh and the people (see Odell 2005, 109). However, given their use by a sinful people, perhaps in improper ways, Ezekiel labels them **idols**.

8:7-13

Alongside these iconographic images, Ezekiel secondly observes **seventy elders** of the Jerusalemite community led by an individual named **Jaazaniah** performing a ceremony with censers and incense (vv 11-12). The text provides no further identification for **Jaazaniah,** who was perhaps a recognizable figure to Ezekiel's audience. The elders' use of ceremonial elements such as incense is in keeping with ordinary temple rituals. Yet, this group of Jerusalem elders contrasts with the elders of the exiles mentioned in v 1. While the exiles in Babylonia seek divine instruction from Yahweh's prophet, the Jerusalem leaders conduct their own religious ceremony in a secret chamber of the temple. This portrayal reinforces the book's perspective that the community remaining in Jerusalem after 597 B.C. is the old Israel that stands under judgment, while the Babylonian exiles represent Israel's future with Yahweh.

Despite this contrast, as well as Ezekiel's repetition of the label **idols** (v 10), the language and actions of the Jerusalem elders do not necessarily imply the worship of another god besides Yahweh. Rather, Yahweh draws Ezekiel's attention to the sentiment expressed by the elders: **The** Lord **does not see us; the** Lord **has forsaken the land** (v 12). One can take this language as an expression of arrogance and rebellion, as the people assert their ability to hide from Yahweh and their freedom to worship other gods (see Greenberg 1983, 170). Yet, the language here may also represent a genuine cry of lament to Yahweh, similar to what one finds in various lament psalms (e.g., Pss 22:1-2; 88:14). Having experienced the Babylonian capture of their city, many in the Jerusalem community likely concluded that Yahweh had already abandoned them and was no longer responsive to their prayers. Moreover, with the removal of the Zadokite priests into exile, the Jerusalem elders found themselves without properly ordained priestly leadership and left to fend for themselves in their efforts to seek and maintain Yahweh's presence among them. Nonetheless, these actions, too, stand condemned in Ezekiel's vision as "abominations" that pollute the dwelling place of Yahweh's presence. Ironically, then, the Jerusalem elders fear that Yahweh has already withdrawn from them, yet the vision in chs 8—11 indicates that the very actions the people undertake to try to maintain the divine presence in their community are adding to the defilement that drives Yahweh away.

■ **14-15** The third scene of abominations in the temple (vv 14-15) likewise permits more than one specific interpretation. After Yahweh once again declares that Ezekiel will see things that are **even more detestable** (v 13), the prophet finds himself inside another part of the **north gate** of the temple. There he observes a group of women performing some type of mourning ritual. Most translations render Ezekiel's description as **mourning for Tammuz,** thus suggesting that the women are carrying out a ritual associated with the worship of the Sumerian god Tammuz or Dumuzi, a dying and rising god of vegetation and fertility in Babylonian religion (see Darr 2001, 1176). If this is the case, it is clear why the vision presents the women's action as an "abomination" that pollutes Yahweh's dwelling. The Hebrew of v 14, however, does not contain the preposition **for** and is better translated *weeping the Tammuz.* This translation suggests that Ezekiel refers to the title of a traditional lament song or genre ("the Tammuz"), rather than a ritual to a foreign god. Given the name, this song or genre may have been adapted from rituals originally associated with the Babylonian dying and rising deity but has now come to have a different content and function for people using it to pray to Yahweh (see Odell 2005, 110). In much the same way that originally secular musical tunes have been adapted for Christian worship throughout history, for Judean worshippers in sixth-century Jerusalem, "the Tammuz," although retaining a name traditionally associated with a foreign god, may have become a genre or song of mourning that could be offered to Yahweh in times of distress and lament. From Ezekiel's perspective, of course, no difference exists between the idolatrous act of worshipping foreign gods and the vain expressions of mourning by those whose lives have consistently profaned Yahweh's holiness in their midst.

■ **16-17** After once again telling Ezekiel that he will see things "even more detestable" (v 15), Yahweh brings the prophet to the scene of the last abomination (vv 16-18). The very location of this scene indicates its function as the climax of the sequence. Having moved around various parts of the north gate and entry area, Ezekiel now enters the inner court or main room of the temple. More specifically, the abomination that he observes takes place between the porch and the altar in the main room (i.e., the incense altar). In this sacred space, Ezekiel reports seeing twenty-five unidentified men bowing down toward the sun in the east. On the surface, the depiction again seems to indicate apostasy and idolatry, namely, the solar worship of the sun as a deity. The OT contains various prohibitions of sun worship, as well as some indications that sun worship existed in Judah before the exile (e.g., Deut 4:19; 17:2-5; 2 Kgs 23:11). Yet biblical and extrabiblical data indicate the existence of a longstanding tradition in ancient Israel in which language and imagery associated with the sun were used to describe Yahweh (e.g., see the similarities between Ps 104 and the Egyptian "Hymn to Aten," or sun deity). Additionally, many commentators recognize that the scene here is similar to the national lament to Yahweh undertaken by the people of Jerusalem in Joel 2:15-17 (Darr 2001, 1117; Odell 2005, 111). As in the scene that Ezekiel sees, Joel describes a group gathered in the temple's inner court between the porch and the altar, with priests imploring Yahweh to spare his people and city (Joel 2:17). Once more, then, the prophet's vision may depict a Yahwistic ritual in which the people of Jerusalem beseech Yahweh, their sun-like source of light and life, to spare the people and city. The reason for the text's condemnation may appear in a subtlety of language. In contrast to the scene in Joel, Ezekiel refers to this ritual as being led only by certain **men** (v 16) rather than "priests" (Joel 2:17). Thus, even in the people's Yahwistic ceremonies, they now act with improper, unsanctified leadership, which renders illegitimate their attempts to seek Yahweh in a sinful community.

In the midst of this final scene of abomination, Yahweh's voice in v 17 interrupts Ezekiel's observations to provide perhaps the most definitive explanation of the whole series of temple scenes throughout ch 8. Up to this point, the focus has been on cultic and ritual acts taking place within the temple. Now Yahweh adds a new dimension. The divine voice asks rhetorically whether the people's participation in the cultic abominations depicted throughout ch 8 has been so **trivial** in their eyes that they have felt free to compound it with other, even more problematic actions that also **provoke me to anger**. The logic of the texts suggests that the actions mentioned in v 17 are even more offensive to Yahweh than the cultic abominations described previously. Yahweh asserts first that the people **fill the land with violence** (*ḥāmās*). The Hebrew term here (*ḥāmās*) is a general word connoting many kinds of harmful actions, but it especially carries the meaning of violent crimes against human persons at the individual and societal levels, sometimes with a military connotation. The word appears, for example, as the main description of humanity's evil deeds that lead Yahweh to send the flood in Gen 6:11.

Verse 17 also includes the description of another anger-provoking action that is more specific: **putting the branch to their nose.** The background and meaning of this act remain debated. It may, for instance, be an obscene gesture indicating rejection of Yahweh or some kind of ritual to a foreign god. Given the preceding reference to **violence,** however, the gesture may constitute a political symbol used as part of a ceremony for forging a treaty. Such treaty-making ceremonies with corresponding ritual acts are known from ancient Near Eastern sources. As discussed above (see Behind the Text), in the historical context of 592 B.C. Judah found itself caught in an Egyptian resurgence that saw Pharaoh Psammetichus II tour triumphantly through Syria-Palestine. Sometime shortly thereafter, King Zedekiah entered into rebellion against Babylonia. Perhaps the divine vision here offers a theo-political condemnation of a Judean alliance being made with Egypt, which the prophet saw as another example of the people's rebellion against Yahweh.

The descriptions of these social, ethical, and political misdeeds in v 17 may provide the key to understanding the overall imagery and condemnations throughout the whole of ch 8. The above commentary has suggested that the elements and practices described in the vision report, beginning with the "image of jealousy" in vv 3 and 5 (NRSV), may not constitute the worship of other gods but may be genuine, even if unorthodox, elements of Yahweh worship in Jerusalem after the initial deportation in 597 B.C. This interpretation raises two larger considerations for the chapter as a whole. First, the scenes may represent the kind of response to trauma in which a religious community attempts to refashion its practices in light of events that have drastically altered their circumstances and outlook. The Jerusalem elders and other worshippers (vv 11-12, 16) moved outside of the standard rules of acceptable practices for worship in the temple, at least from Ezekiel's Zadokite perspective. Yet, they attempted to seek Yahweh in a changed situation by these modified actions. A similar circumstance appears in 2 Chr 30, for instance, which describes the unorthodox observance of the Passover ritual during the reign of Hezekiah due to the conglomeration of historical circumstances that had unfolded in Judah over the preceding years. In the midst of this observance, Hezekiah prayed that Yahweh would pardon those who were seeking him with their hearts, "even though not in accordance with the sanctuary's rules of cleanness"

(2 Chr 30:19 NRSV). In that instance, the people received grace for their actions due to the earnestness of their seeking.

In Ezekiel's vision, however, no such grace is granted, at least to the community remaining in Jerusalem (cf. 11:16-21 concerning the exiles). If the people's practices do not constitute idolatry or apostasy, the second larger consideration for ch 8 concerns why Ezekiel's vision condemns these practices as abominations that pollute Yahweh's sanctuary and drive out his presence. At one level, the practices depicted here are out of keeping with and inadequate by the standards of strict Zadokite temple practices, which the book will outline in detail in chs 40—48 (see Sweeney 2005, 141-42). Yet, the social, ethical, and political language of v 17 suggests that the issue is one of hypocrisy. Yahweh's final description of the people's deeds indicates that though they carry on worshipping and beseeching Yahweh through various cultic practices, perhaps in altered ways due to the new situation post-597 B.C., they simultaneously engage in violence against others and rebellion against Yahweh in the social, ethical, and political dimensions of their life. These actions not only invalidate whatever worship they may bring but also turn the very acts by which the people seek Yahweh into impure deeds that pollute the sanctuary and drive Yahweh to withdraw from their midst.

■ 18 Having established the nature and seriousness of the people's polluting actions, Yahweh concludes the first part of the visionary couplet in 8:5—9:11 by declaring his resolve to bring the decisive judgment upon the people: **I will deal with them in anger** (v 18). There will be no compassion or relenting; Yahweh will act to protect his own holiness. Through such language, Ezekiel once again renarrates the trauma that is to come upon Jerusalem at the hands of the Babylonians. The city's coming destruction is part of a divine plan to remove the polluted sanctuary and create a new people among whom Yahweh can dwell in holiness. Yet the language at the end of ch 8 is extreme, providing a segue to the widespread slaughter depicted in ch 9. Yahweh rejects the very laments and appeals that the people have offered throughout ch 8, declaring that he will not listen to the cries of his people even if they **shout in my ears** (lit., **they cry in my hearing with a loud voice**).

2. The Executioners in Jerusalem (9:1-11)

Ezekiel's vision of Jerusalem continues in ch 9, which forms the second part of the first visionary couplet in 8:5—9:11. Following from the divine declaration to bring judgment upon the people without pity at the end of ch 8 (8:18), the vision in ch 9 portrays the actual judgment of Jerusalem, particularly in the form of the slaughter of its people. The images and actions described in the text are horrifying in their violence (even to Ezekiel; see 9:8), especially the direct and personal role that Yahweh plays in the killing of men, women, and children (see From the Text). Even so, the depiction here remains at the visionary level only, as the actual destruction of Jerusalem by the Babylonians would come six years later (586 B.C.).

■ **1-2** The opening line of ch 9 makes it clear that the vision Ezekiel witnesses in the following verses is a continuation of the temple vision in ch 8. The language of 9:1 repeats the Hebrew wording of the final verse of ch 8. As the Hebrew reads literally, Yahweh had previously declared that he will not hear the people's prayers even if **they cry in my hearing with a loud voice** (8:18), and Ezekiel opens the second part of the vision in ch 9 by reporting that Yahweh himself **cried out in my hearing with a loud voice** (v 1). Yahweh's cry summons six humanlike figures, which the text describes with the Hebrew term *pĕquddôt* (**guards**; "executioners" [NRSV]) and one linen-clad scribe, who carries a case for writing used in ancient scribal practice. Although Yahweh instructs the six humanlike figures to bring weapons (v 1), the Hebrew term describing them leaves the reader initially in suspense concerning their character and function. The term simply designates any appointed visitor and can connote both one who comes to punish, as well as one who comes as a simple functionary (see Greenberg 1983, 175). As the vision unfolds beyond vv 1-2, however, it becomes clear that these figures represent the divine execution squad summoned to carry out Yahweh's slaughter of the city's inhabitants. The imagery used with the executioners and scribe throughout the rest of the chapter resembles that of the angel of death in the stories of the exodus and Passover (Exod 12), as well as artistic depictions of such divine warriors known throughout the ancient Near East (see Odell 2005, 112-13).

Scribes in the Ancient World

The description of a linen-clad figure carrying a writing kit in 9:2 reflects the typical equipment and function of a scribe in the ancient Near East. Scribes were members of professional guilds that functioned within the bureaucracy of various civilizations, generally fulfilling tasks of writing and record keeping. They often trained in schools run by the temple or royal palace. Since the number of literate people in ancient societies was probably small, scribes served to record events, note transactions in the temple, and compose official correspondence. One of the best-known biblical examples is Baruch, who served as a scribe for the prophet Jeremiah (e.g., Jer 36). Visual depictions of scribes from the ancient Near East often picture them holding hinged wooden tablets or various types of scrolls.

■ **3a** Once the executioners have assembled beside the altar, the text prolongs the reader's suspense by not moving directly to a description of their instructions or action. In the first part of v 3, Ezekiel momentarily turns his attention away from these figures to Yahweh's **glory**/presence (*kābôd*), which met him initially at the entry gate at the beginning of his visionary journey (8:4). Ezekiel witnesses the **glory** leave its place **above the cherubim** in the holy of holies and move to the outer **threshold** of the temple building. This description introduces a key element that will figure prominently in the rest of the vision in chs 9—11, namely, the movement of Yahweh's presence out of polluted Jerusalem, thus leading to the city's destruction in judgment. The glory's shift in v 3 from the holy of holies, where Israelite tradition envisions Yahweh to be enthroned above the **cherubim** (see Exod 25:18-22; 37:7-9), to the doorway of the temple is the first part of the larger movement that will progress in stages across the following chapters.

The movement of Yahweh's glory/presence in Ezekiel's vision is one of the most complicated parts of chs 8—11. The reference in 9:3, for instance, seems to relate the initial move out of the temple, but 8:4 already described the glory as present with Ezekiel at the outside gate into the inner court. Perhaps one of the references in 8:4 or 9:3 is a later redactional insertion. Additionally, the glory's movement introduced in v 3 does not figure again in the vision until 10:1-4. Even from that point, the progression of the movement is difficult to follow coherently, with some instances of repetition and nonlinearity (see "The Movement of Yahweh's Glory/Presence" sidebar). Overall, however, one can trace a generally sequential movement of Yahweh's presence out of the holy of holies to the temple threshold (9:3; cf. 10:4), to a cherubim throne on the south side of the temple (10:1-3, 18), to the east gate of the temple (10:19), and finally to the Mount of Olives east of Jerusalem (11:22-23). We should perhaps attribute the sometimes confusing sequence depicted in Ezekiel's vision report to various phases of editing over time, or to the fact that visions by nature tend to be episodic and nonlinear. Either way, the vision's intertwining of the glory's steady departure with descriptions of judgment and destruction being carried out against Jerusalem establishes an inextricable link between these two events. As we see with the book's overall structure featuring three visions of Yahweh's glory (chs 1—3, 8—11, 40—48), the temple vision in chs 8—11 identifies Jerusalem's existence and destruction as directly tied to the presence or absence of a holy God among the people. This link is the interpretation of Judah's past and future trauma that Ezekiel wants to give to his community: Judah's destruction and exile is not the result of Babylonian military might but the withdrawal of Yahweh's presence from their midst, which, in turn, results from the people's sinful actions that have defiled the holiness of his sanctuary.

The Movement of Yahweh's Glory/Presence

The commentary on 9:3 has noted that the movement of Yahweh's glory/presence (*kābôd*) in Ezekiel's vision in chs 8—11 is difficult to follow and may be the product of several phases of editing. Overall, however, the references to the movement of the glory/presence across chs 9—11 are as follows:

9:3	glory moves from the holy of holies to threshold of temple
10:1-3	a mobile throne appears above the cherubim on the south side of the temple
10:4	repetition of the glory's movement from the holy of holies to the threshold of the temple (cf. 9:3) (redactional addition?)
10:18	glory moves from the threshold to the throne above the cherubim on south side of the temple
10:19	glory (riding on cherubim throne) moves to the entryway of the east gate of the temple
11:22-23	glory (riding on cherubim throne) moves out of the temple to the Mount of Olives east of Jerusalem

■ **3b-4** Following the interjection concerning the movement of the divine glory, the second part of v 3 returns to Ezekiel's report, as he describes Yahweh's instructions to the figures standing beside the altar. Yahweh's first instructions go to the scribe dressed in linen, telling him to move through the city and **put a mark [*tāv*] on the foreheads of those who grieve and lament over all the detestable things** (*tôʿēbôt*) (v 4). The scene resembles the blood placed on the doorways of the Hebrews' houses in Egypt to spare them from Yahweh's executing angel (Exod 12). In a sense, Yahweh here reenacts the terrible night when the angel of death took the life of all the firstborn in Egypt, yet this time the divine execution falls upon Yahweh's own people. The Hebrew word translated **mark** here is simply the last letter of the Hebrew alphabet (lit., ***put the letter tāv on the forehead***), which is written in the shape of an "X" in ancient cursive Hebrew script. This action breaks with the book's characteristic outlook, which maintains that there is no hope for those remaining in Jerusalem between 597 and 586 B.C., now seemingly raising the possibility that some in Jerusalem are troubled by the polluting actions depicted in the temple vision in ch 8 and are able to be saved along with the exiles in Babylonia (see 5:1-4).

The "Mark" on the Forehead (Ezek 9:4)

The enigmatic mark on the forehead of the faithful in Jerusalem (9:4) has had a rich interpretive history. Unlike the mark on the right hand or forehead in Rev 13:16, which has a negative association with the "beast," the mark in Ezekiel's vision is a positive designation of the righteous. Since the name for the mark is actually the last letter of the Hebrew alphabet (*tāv*), some ancient Jewish rabbis suggested that it signified the recipient had fulfilled the Torah from beginning to end, from A to Z, so to speak. Some early Christian interpreters saw the shape of this Hebrew letter, which was written as an X in the early Hebrew script, as related to the Greek symbol of the letter *chi* that came to represent "Christ" and thus as a mark in the shape of Christ's cross (see Greenberg 1983, 177; Block 1997, 310-14).

■ **5-7** Yahweh's instructions to the armed execution squad follow immediately upon his words to the scribe. Ezekiel reports that the executioners are to follow behind the scribe and mercilessly slaughter any person who does not have the "mark." The language of the instructions repeats precisely Yahweh's declaration at the end of the temple vision in 8:18: the executioners are to act **without . . . pity or compassion** (v 5). In keeping with his earlier statement, Yahweh dispatches the armed killers to carry out a virtually indiscriminate slaughter of men, women, and even children who do not possess the scribe's mark (v 6). Moreover, Yahweh's instructions reflect the priestly concerns that have dominated the vision thus far. Implicitly acknowledging the defiled state of the temple, Yahweh commands the executioners to **begin at my sanctuary** (v 6). After the initial slaughter of **the elders who were in front of the temple**, perhaps the twenty-five men bowing toward the sun in 8:16 (but cf. 11:1-4), Yahweh not only sends the executioners to kill throughout the city but also commands them to complete the defilement of the sanctuary that the people have begun by bringing the corpses into the temple courts (v 7). Within the priestly purity regulations, contact with dead bodies rendered people and places unclean (see Num 19). Thus, through this command Yahweh himself orders the defilement of his own sanctuary. The divine instruction even takes such defilement to its extreme, not simply calling the executioners to bring corpses into the sanctuary precincts, but to **fill the courts with the slain** (v 7).

■ **8-11** As the executioners proceed through the city, Ezekiel finds himself standing alone in the middle of a scene of mass slaughter. In v 8, the horrifying nature of the scene moves the prophet to both a physical and verbal response, as he falls prostrate and cries out, **Ah, Sovereign Lord! Are you going to destroy the entire remnant of Israel?** This exclamation represents one of the few times in the book where the prophet deviates from simply speaking Yahweh's script and raises his own voice in an act of objection or attempted intercession that is more typical of the prophetic role (see 4:14; 11:13; Amos 7:1-5). The language employs the book's characteristic divine title (**Sovereign Lord**) used to emphasize Yahweh's separateness and power over against Ezekiel's merely mortal status ("son of man"). But the question has a desperate tone, as Ezekiel's exclamation implies that, despite the initial impression given by Yahweh's instructions to the scribe, no one has been marked to escape destruction and everyone in the city is being slaughtered. The language of this question reveals that the book of Ezekiel does not use the term **remnant** (šĕʾērît) with the same theological connotations as it appears in some other prophets (e.g., Isa 37:32; 46:3). This book does not possess a "remnant theology" in which Yahweh selects a righteous or faithful group to preserve in the midst of the people's sin and judgment. Ezekiel largely reserves the language of **remnant** and "remaining" for the Jerusalemites who survived the initial capture of the city in 597 B.C., and these people are nearly rejected entirely in favor of the Babylonian exiles (see 5:10; 11:13).

Ezekiel will provide an answer to his own question later in the unfolding vision (see 11:13). At this point, however, Yahweh's words to Ezekiel in 9:9-10 do not offer an answer to the prophet's question. Rather, the divine words emphasize again the severity and extent of the people's sin and defilement (note the reference here to both **Israel and Judah;** see commentary on chs 2 and 4), echoing much of the language from earlier portions of the vision concerning violence through **bloodshed,** social **injustice,** and a sense that Yahweh has **forsaken the land.** Yahweh then again declares that he will act without **pity** or ***compassion*** (see 8:18; 9:5). Both the implication of Ezekiel's desperate question and the hard resolve of Yahweh's repeated declaration give an ominous tone to the ending of this part of Ezekiel's vision. Verse 11 reports that the scribe sent to mark those to be spared returned to Yahweh, declaring, **I have done as you commanded.** And the reader is left to wonder whether he searched in vain for anyone to mark.

C. Second Vision Couplet (10:1—11:23)

After depicting the abominations that have defiled the temple and the brutal judgment on the people, Ezekiel's vision proceeds in chs 10—11 to a portrayal of Jerusalem's destruction and the climax of Yahweh's glory/presence finally leaving the city. This narrative movement is interrupted, however, by two contrasting episodes addressing the judgment to come on Jerusalem's wicked officials (11:1-13) and the restoration to come for the Babylonian exiles (11:14-21).

I. Yahweh's Glory Begins to Depart the Temple (10:1-22)

In the first part of the visionary couplet that spans chs 10—11, the divine glory makes its initial move from the holy of holies to the threshold of the temple and then to the east gate of the temple (cf. 9:3). The structure of the chapter is difficult to follow, seemingly jumping from scene to scene without a logical progression and, at times, going back over scenes and actions a second time (see Hals 1989, 60-61). Such disjointed structure may be the result of editorial activity, but could also be attributed once again to the nature of visionary material and its link to the expression of traumatic memory, the character of which often produces an episodic series of images without a necessarily straightforward sequence. Although ch 10 builds to the climax of the glory's movement out of the temple, the bulk of the narrative focuses on the detailed description of the creatures and apparatus that provide the transportation for the divine presence. In this way, the scene has the appearance of being a diversion from the overall progression of chs 8—11, but given the connection of these elements to temple and ritual, they would have been a source of great interest to someone from a priestly background.

Throughout ch 10, Ezekiel describes the reappearance of several elements that he had witnessed in his first encounter with the divine glory beside the Kebar River in ch 1 (an elevated throne, jewel imagery, living creatures with four faces, burning coals, and wheels with eyes). Yet there are also significant differences between the two visions that should not be harmonized. For instance, the descriptive language in ch 10 is generally more direct and less analogical (**as;** "something like" [NRSV]) than that of ch 1, a feature that may be the result of later editing, or, some interpreters suggest, of Ezekiel seeing these things within the familiar context of the temple where they make more sense than they did in the foreign setting of exile (see Odell 2005, 119). Most noticeably, however, there is a more explicit identification of and role for the **cherubim,** which were not mentioned by this name in ch 1's vision and first appeared as the resting place of Yahweh's glory inside the holy of holies in 9:3. The statues from the holy of holies now seem to come to life as a wheeled flying chariot for the divine glory. This portrayal is a direct expansion of the generic "living creatures" from ch 1, linking that previous image with explicitly temple elements from the most holy place of the sanctuary.

Cherub/Cherubim in the OT

The terms "cherub" and "cherubim" (pl.) occur more than ninety times in the OT, sometimes describing statues or drawings of inanimate objects and sometimes, as in ch 10, constituting living creatures. Representations of such creatures are known from throughout the ancient Near East and bear no resemblance to Western art's conception of cherubs as round-faced infants. The cherubim known from the ancient world appear in a wide variety of forms but are always fierce-looking composite creatures, combining human and animal forms, who fly with wings and often have multiple faces and legs. In the OT, they are always winged and associated with sacred places or temples. Three-dimensional cherubim appear, for instance, in descriptions of the biblical tabernacle and temple, and two golden cherubim with outstretched wings cover the ark of the covenant in the holy of holies, providing the throne for Yahweh's invisible glory/presence (Exod 25:18-22; 37:7-9; 2 Kgs 19:15; see Meyers 1992).

■ **1-2** At the opening of the chapter, Ezekiel uses indirect language to describe **the likeness of a throne of sapphire** (v 1; lit., ***something like the appearance of the likeness of a throne***) standing above the **cherubim**. This description immediately draws the reader back to the initial vision of ch 1, as Ezekiel now finds himself once again standing before Yahweh's glory/presence and its accompanying throne-chariot. At the same time, v 2 refers to **the man clothed in linen** who had been present with the divine executioners in ch 9, thus linking the scene to come with the preceding scene of the slaughter of the people. Yahweh now instructs the scribe to retrieve **burning coals** from among the wheel structure under the cherub-throne and **scatter them over the city**. Whereas the previous scene depicted the judgment on the people of Jerusalem through the killing activity of the divine executioners, the imagery here symbolizes the destruction of the city itself in a massive conflagration. Some commentators have noted the priestly dimension of this depiction, as the touching of burning coals resembles the kind of cleansing act described in texts such as Isa 6:6-7 (Greenberg 1983, 181; Sweeney 2005). Yet the imagery more directly evokes the tradition of divine judgment through the use of fire from heaven (e.g., Gen 19:24; Pss 11:6; 140:10; see Odell 2005, 117).

■ **3-17** Most of the remainder of the chapter (vv 3-17) is a detailed description of the **cherubim** and the ways in which they move. First, however, vv 3-4 repeat the movement of the divine glory from the holy of holies to the threshold on the south side of the temple building (cf. 9:3). The text then describes how a cherub extends a humanlike hand to give fire to the scribe who has entered among the wheels (vv 6-8). At this point, when the reader is prepared for the man wearing linen to proceed into the city and set it on fire and for Yahweh's glory to complete its movement out of the city, vv 9-17 interrupt the narrative movement. They take the reader into an interlude that devotes extended attention to the details of the appearance of the cherubim, evoking the description of the creatures and throne in the initial vision of ch 1: wheels with eyes (10:9-13; cf. 1:15-18), four faces on each cherub (10:14; cf. 1:10), and the method of movement (10:11, 16-17; cf. 1:17-21). While one can identify differences with the description in ch 1 (e.g., one of the faces of the cherubim in ch 10 is that of the cherub itself rather than an ox; cf. 1:10; 10:14), the key point to which this interlude builds in v 15 explicitly identifies these **cherubim** with the **living creatures** from ch 1. In other words, this latter vision offers an interpretive explanation of the unidentified creatures that appeared with Yahweh's presence in Babylonia: they were none other than the temple cherubim from the holy of holies.

■ **18-22** Following this interlude, the scene in ch 10 returns to the main story line of the overall temple vision in vv 18-19. Ezekiel reports that he watched as the glory of Yahweh moved from **the threshold of the temple** building and took its place **above the cherubim.** The entire chariot-throne then went into motion, as the cherubim **spread their wings and rose from the ground** (v 19). In this majestic scene, the divine glory moved one step further outward from its dwelling place in the sanctuary, now stopping **at the entrance to the east gate of the** LORD's **house** (v 19). With the divine glory/presence poised to abandon the city altogether, vv 20-22 offer one final description of the cherubim, which again identifies them with the living creatures from Ezekiel's commissioning vision.

2. Interruption 1: Judgment on Wicked Officials (11:1-13)

■ **1-7** By the end of ch 10, Ezekiel's vision has portrayed the annihilation of the sinful people of Jerusalem (ch 9), the destruction of the city itself by fire (10:1-8), and the movement of the divine presence to the gate of the temple, poised to exit the city (10:18-19). In the logic of the vision, all that remains is for Yahweh to exit entirely from the now destroyed city. With the beginning of ch 11, however, the text interrupts the basic story line of chs 8—11 with the first of two deviations. The first interruption (vv 1-13) declares divine judgment on the wicked officials in Jerusalem. The second interruption (vv 14-21) announces the divine promise of restoration for the exiles in Babylonia. Not surprisingly, the placement and content of these passages lead some commentators to suggest that they are later additions to the original vision report (e.g., Hals 1989, 69). The opening verses of ch 11, for example, appear to be the introduction to a new vision. The **Spirit** once again serves as the agent of transportation for Ezekiel (see 8:3), as he is taken in the vision to the new location of Yahweh's glory at the east gate of the temple (11:1), and the text turns its focus to the group of people in that place. This strains the logical sequence of chs 8—11, however, since the vision has already portrayed the city's total annihilation in chs 9—10. Even so, the text's visionary character reminds us not to expect a simple, linear development, and the passage can be read as a type of close-up view of some of the activities going on within Jerusalem during the broader judgment scene that was depicted in the two preceding chapters.

The opening verses of the chapter (vv 1-2) make clear why Yahweh's glory stopped at the east gate of the temple on its way out of the city (see 10:19). Something is going on there that provides a significant revelation for Ezekiel's and his audience's understanding of Judah's situation in the present and future. The prophet sees **twenty-five men,** a reference perhaps meant to evoke the group mentioned in 8:16-18, and especially takes note of **Jaazaniah** and **Pelatiah,** who are described as the **leaders** or ***officials*** of the Jerusalem community. As with the mention of **Jaazaniah** in 8:11, nothing more is known of these individuals, although the text's failure to provide any further identification suggests that they were well-known to Ezekiel's audience. The key factors in this opening scene, however, are what Yahweh says about these men (v 2), and what the men themselves are saying (v 3). Yahweh tells Ezekiel that **these are the men who are plotting evil and giving wicked advice** in Jerusalem (v 2). While this verse could be read as a description of the entire group of twenty-five, it more likely refers to the actions of Jaazaniah and Pelatiah in their capacity as governmental officials. Their **wicked advice** was perhaps political policy counsel that these leaders provided to King Zedekiah, advice likely urging the forging of alliances with Egypt and rebellion against Babylonia (see Behind the Text). The description has resonances with Isaiah's oracle against two Jerusalem officials, Shebna and Eliakim, condemning them for leading Judah into a rebellion against Assyria without Yahweh's approval (Isa 22:15-25).

In Ezek 11:3, Yahweh tells Ezekiel what these leaders have been saying about themselves and the Jerusalem community. The saying here is ambiguous, yet it is clearly meant to be the leaders' interpretation of the status of those remaining in Jerusalem after 597 B.C. The first part of the saying should be read as a declarative statement (contra NIV): ***The time for building houses is not near*** (v 3). The second part of the leaders' statement is evidently meant to provide the reason for the first: **This city is a cooking pot, and we are the meat.** The meaning of this description is open to various interpretations, most of which center on the meaning of the metaphor of the **cooking pot** and **meat** (see Darr 2001, 1186; Odell 2005, 120). On the surface, the people's description of their situation seems to be a negative one: this is no time to divert resources to rebuilding destroyed houses or building new ones, since we are in jeopardy like meat being boiled in a pot. The context of such cooking imagery in the OT, however, suggests that the metaphor, and therefore the Jerusalemites' assessment of themselves and their situation, are positive, even arrogant (Greenberg 1983, 187; Odell 2005, 120). The boiling of meat in a pot is sacrificial imagery in other parts of the OT, in which the meat in the pot represents the choicest cuts, the holy offerings (see 2 Chr 35:13). Later, Yahweh will instruct Ezekiel to use this same metaphor to describe those left in Jerusalem as the "choice pieces" of meat in a pot that are ironically destroyed like all the rest (24:4). Read in this way, the Jerusalemites tout their self-perceived status as the choicest, even holiest parts of the people of Judah that remain in the sacred vessel of Jerusalem. In their view, those taken into exile in 597 B.C.

constitute the less worthy parts that have been discarded in favor of the best. The first part of the leaders' statement, then, becomes an assertion that they do not need to build houses, since they now have the right as the chosen group to take over the deserted properties of those who have gone into exile.

The people's self-assessment in v 3 takes on an added significance when read within the context of the entire vision in chs 8—11. As noted above, the opening of ch 8 implied that the vision came in response to some inquiry made to Ezekiel by the elders of the exile. The text thus far suggests that the inquiry concerned their present and future status as exiles. In 11:3, we hear the perspective of those who had remained in Jerusalem on just that point: they are Yahweh's choice portion and the exiles are those who have been rejected and discarded. The remainder of the first half of ch 11, however, consists of Yahweh's judgment upon the Jerusalemite leaders and their claims. After commanding Ezekiel to **prophesy against them** (v 4), Yahweh reinterprets the metaphor of the meat and pot to speak judgment against the Jerusalemites (vv 5-7). The accusation here (**you have killed many people in this city** [v 6]) echoes the emphasis on the people's political and social "violence" set out in 8:17. Ironically, Yahweh asserts that the corpses of those slain by the officials are the choice cuts of **meat** in the sacred **pot** of Jerusalem, while the leaders themselves will be driven out (11:7).

■ **8-12** Ezekiel then relates Yahweh's climactic pronouncement of judgment on the Jerusalemites in vv 8-12. The language and imagery here echo the description of the slaughter depicted in ch 9, as Yahweh declares that he will bring the **sword** against the city and the people **will fall by the sword** (v 8, 10). Moreover, the judgment speech states Yahweh's intention to drive those remaining in Jerusalem into exile, giving them **over to foreigners** for **punishment** (v 9). As part of this judgment oracle, Yahweh again rejects the leaders' sacrificial pot metaphor for their own self-understanding (**this city will not be a pot for you** [v 11]). Perhaps most significantly, however, twice in vv 8-12 the text uses the recognition formula to express Yahweh's ultimate goal in the destruction and exile that is to come upon the people of Jerusalem: **you will know that I am the LORD** (vv 10, 12). As discussed previously, this formula indicates that the goal of such divine actions is to bring the people to an acknowledgment of Yahweh's sovereignty and holiness, leading them to follow Yahweh's will in religious, social, and political life, rather than to pursue courses of action **conformed to the standards of the nations around you** (v 12; for the interpretive possibilities of this phrase, see discussion of 5:7). From this text's perspective, Yahweh's coming actions against Jerusalem, especially divine acts of violence and destruction, are the key to bringing the people to recognize Yahweh's lordship and power (see 6:7, 10, 14; 7:4, 9; see From the Text).

■ **13** The first interruption section in 11:1-13 concludes with Ezekiel's report of the aftermath of Yahweh's speech to him (v 13). When Yahweh's first person pronouncement ends (v 12), Ezekiel speaks again in v 13 and reports the astonishing detail that in the vision he was experiencing, Pelatiah (see 11:1) **died** as the prophet was proclaiming Yahweh's oracle of judgment. Given the chapter's visionary character, it is unclear whether readers are to take this as a literal statement that one of the officials in Jerusalem dropped dead as Ezekiel was experiencing this vision (i.e., in 592 B.C.) or as a description of a specific death that will occur when the judgment of Yahweh unfolds in the coming years or simply as a symbol of the deathliness of Yahweh's coming judgment (see Greenberg 1983, 189). The language of the verse (**as I was prophesying**) places this death within the vision of things to come rather than as a separate event that took place while the vision was occurring. In any case, Pelatiah's death functions as a symbol of the power of the divine word spoken through the prophet (Hals 1989, 67).

Ezekiel's response to this death is once again both physical and verbal (see 9:8). In line with his characteristic response throughout the book's visions, the prophet is overwhelmed and falls prostrate (see 1:28; 3:23; 9:8). From that position, Ezekiel's cry to Yahweh uses the book's characteristic title for emphasizing divine power and otherness (**Ah, Sovereign LORD**) and returns to the language of the question he posed earlier as the divine executioners were going throughout the city (see 9:8). While some translations render v 13 as a question (**Will you completely destroy the remnant of Israel?** NRSV: "Will you make a full end of the remnant of Israel?"), the Hebrew lacks the traditional indicator of a question and should perhaps be read as an exclamation of despair: *you are making a complete end of the remnant of Israel!* Read in this way, Ezekiel here thinks he has discovered the answer to the similar question he had posed to Yahweh in the middle of the executions in ch 9. From the prophet's perspective, it seems that Yahweh's words and actions symbolized in chs 8—11 add up to a total annihilation of the house of Judah, leaving no chosen people and no sanctuary for the divine presence among them.

3. Interruption 2: Promise of Restoration for the Exiles (11:14-21)

■ **14-15** Seemingly in response to the despairing conclusion that Ezekiel has drawn in v 13, Yahweh's speech in vv 14-21 forms a second interruption of the movement of the glory/presence out of Jerusalem. As if to correct Ezekiel's understanding, Yahweh addresses the present and future status of Ezekiel's community that has gone into exile in Babylonia. Using the standard prophetic word formula (**The word of the LORD came to me**) to mark a new oracle, v

14 begins a hopeful promise of future restoration for those already in exile, a promise that interrupts the vision's consistent focus on the sin and judgment of the Jerusalemites and teases the book's readers with a taste of restoration language that will be developed more fully later in the book. In his address to Ezekiel, Yahweh uses familial language (**your brothers; your blood relatives**) to indicate to the prophet that those destined to receive restoration are the exiles with him in Babylonia (v 15). Some ancient Greek and Syriac manuscript traditions, in fact, render v 15 as an explicit reference to *your own kin, your fellow exiles* (see NRSV). This identification takes the reader back to the mention of some inquiry made by the elders of the exiles (8:1), to which Ezekiel's vision in chs 8—11 serves as a response. Perhaps providing insight into the nature of the elders' inquiry, Yahweh's words in 11:14-21 offer an explanation of the present and future status of the exiles.

The rhetoric of the divine speech in vv 14-15 implies that from Yahweh's perspective there are two groups that need to be distinguished in the theological understanding of the prophet and his audience: Ezekiel's **brothers** (fellow exiles) and **the people of Jerusalem** who remain in the city after 597 B.C. In keeping with the rhetoric of the book as a whole, the speech suggests that in Yahweh's eyes the exiles are **the whole house of Israel** (v 15), discounting those remaining in Jerusalem as a type of old Israel that has no part in the future reserved for the new Israel represented by Ezekiel's Babylonian community. In contrast to this divine perspective, however, Yahweh relates the words that those remaining in Jerusalem are saying about themselves and the exiles: **They** [i.e., the exiles] **are far away from the LORD; this land was given to us as our possession** (v 15). Said differently, the Jerusalemites interpret the deportation of Ezekiel's group as evidence that the exiles represent the sinners within Judah and their deportation should be understood as divine judgment that cleared them away from the faithful community remaining in Jerusalem.

■ **16-21** In vv 16-21, the divine address rejects the Jerusalemites' assessment of the character and status of the exiles, and declares that the latter are the ones who will experience restoration and among whom the divine presence will dwell. The language and imagery of this section are similar to a divine message to Jeremiah that is set in the same period between the first and second captures of Jerusalem (Jer 24). In that oracle, Yahweh metaphorically describes those who remain in Jerusalem under King Zedekiah as the "bad figs" that must be thrown away, while those sent into exile with King Jehoiachin are the "good figs," to whom Yahweh will give "a heart to know . . . that I am the LORD" so that they will "return to me with all their heart" (Jer 24:4, 7-8; see especially Ezek 11:19-20).

Scapegoat Imagery in Ezekiel 11

Ezekiel's depiction of the judgment and restoration of the Judean people in ch 11 makes a clear distinction between the group remaining in Jerusalem after 597 B.C., who will suffer destruction as a result of their sins, and those taken into exile in Babylonia, who will experience divine restoration. Some commentators suggest that imagery connected with the priestly ritual of the two goats on the Day of Atonement (the so-called scapegoat ritual) may underlie the prophet's depictions (Lev 16; see Sweeney 2005, 142). In this ritual, two goats served as sin offerings for the people, one of which was sacrificed, while the other was sent into the wilderness to carry away the community's sins. Ezekiel depicts the city of Jerusalem and those remaining in it after 597 B.C. as being slaughtered, even using the metaphor of sacrificial meat in a pot to describe this group (11:5-12). By contrast, another group is sent away into exile. Perhaps the prophet uses the lens of the two goats ritual to assert his conviction that atonement for sin will come through the slaughter of one group and the carrying away of the other into exile. Through this perspective, Ezekiel offers his fellow exiles a theological understanding of their status as exiles in the larger perspective of Yahweh's redemptive activity.

11:16-21

To communicate the divine perspective, Yahweh's first person speech (**I sent them** [v 16]) asserts that he, rather than the power of the Babylonians, sent Ezekiel and his group into exile, yet only as part of a larger plan for the restoration of the divine presence within a purified community. Moreover, although Yahweh sent this group into exile, the speech makes clear his identification of them as the new Israel for the future in two ways. First, Yahweh declares that even while they have been in exile he has been a **sanctuary** (*miqĕdāš*) for them in their midst (v 16). It is unclear whether the Hebrew here should be read to indicate that Yahweh has been their sanctuary **for a little while** (NIV and NRSV), or that he has been a ***little/diminished sanctuary*** for them in their current situation. Either way, the priestly categories of Ezekiel's theology, especially the notion that the sanctuary represents the dwelling place for the divine glory/presence in the midst of the people, make this assertion remarkable. Contrary to the Jerusalemites' assertion that the exiles have been removed **far away from the** LORD (v 15), the divine word states that Yahweh's dwelling place has been among them even while in exile, although not visible in a physical structure. More surprisingly, while the holy temple in Jerusalem, the definitive location of Yahweh's presence, is portrayed in this vision as defiled and destroyed, Yahweh discloses that he has temporarily dwelt among the exiles in the foreign **countries where they have gone,** lands that are unclean according to the priestly regulations for ritual purity and holiness (see also the appearance of Yahweh's glory in Babylonia in ch 1).

The second way that the divine oracle makes clear the identification of the exiles as the new Israel begins in v 17, where Yahweh's speech shifts to direct second person plural address to the exiles themselves and makes a promise of restoration: **I will gather you [pl.] from the nations . . . I will give you [pl.] back the land of Israel.** To flesh out this promise, Yahweh's words in vv 18-21 switch back to addressing Ezekiel and further describe the fate of the exilic community. The language in these verses is not simply that of restoration (**they will return** [v 18]) but also that of transformation. It resembles the language and imagery that will appear in the climactic promise of the people's transformation in ch 36, but with some differences.

The promise of restoration and transformation in v 18 employs the priestly language of ***abominations*** (*tôʿēbôt;* **detestable idols**) to assert that when the exiles are restored to the land, they will purify it by removing the elements that have rendered it unfit for Yahweh's holy presence. The verse's language is striking for Ezekiel. Although the following verses describe acts of transformation that Yahweh will perform for and upon the people, they are preceded here by an uncharacteristic portrayal of human agency as the means by which cleansing and change take place. As discussed previously, Ezekiel's theology of divine holiness and sovereignty typically restricts such acts solely to Yahweh's initiative and action, with humans as passive recipients of the change (cf. 36:25). The language of 11:18 thus raises the complex issue of divine and human agency in Ezekiel's vision of the people's transformation, which we will discuss in detail with ch 36. For now, we may note that while Ezekiel has characteristically little place for human agency, there are places in the book that suggest a different perspective on how people's hearts are changed before the divine. Here, the text seems to envision an important role played by human agency in cooperating with the divine action for the transformation of moral character. This human agency will become most explicit in ch 18, where Yahweh instructs the people: "Get yourselves a new heart and a new spirit!" (v 31 NRSV). By the climactic statement in ch 36, however, such moral transformation is solely Yahweh's doing, including the removal of idols and other defiling elements from the community (see 36:25). Perhaps these texts indicate a development in Ezekiel's reflections on moral agency, but at this point, Yahweh's oracle seems to envision a cooperative effort between divine and human action.

Whatever the role of human agency, 11:19-21 makes clear that the primary transformative actions in the exiles' future will be performed by Yahweh. The remaining elements of the divine promise illustrate this through the image of the transformation of the **heart.** In v 19, Yahweh declares that he will give the people **an undivided heart** (lit., ***one heart,*** although some ancient manuscripts read "new heart" as in 18:31 and 36:26) and **a new spirit.** Further, Yahweh promises to change the people's **heart of stone** into a **heart of flesh.** In the context and usage of the OT, the **heart** refers not to the seat of emotions but to the locus of a person's will, motivations, and actions (see O'Rourke 2001). Hence, the transformation to **an undivided heart** signifies the possession of a singular will or intention toward obedience, as opposed to a set of divided loyalties that pull one in various moral directions. The image resonates with John Wesley's conception of a "simplicity of intention" to the love of God and neighbor, a "purity of affection" that comes to the believer through the sanctifying grace of God (e.g., in Wesley's *Plain Account of Christian Perfection;* see Wesley 1971, 10). Similarly, the notion of transformation from **a heart of stone** to **a heart of flesh** symbolizes a move away from a hardened obstinacy and self-determination to a malleable will, which divine instruction can shape toward obedient action.

The promise of restoration and transformation culminates in covenant language. Verse 20 declares that Yahweh's redemptive actions will result in the people's abandonment of the rebelliousness that Ezekiel sees as having characterized their life with God (see commentary on 2:1-7) in favor of faithful obedience to the divine **decrees** and **laws.** This change will mark a return to the initial and proper relationship between Yahweh and the people, which the words of Yahweh describe with the OT's classic formulation of Israel's constitution as Yahweh's chosen community: **They will be my people, and I will be their God** (see, e.g., Exod 19:5-6). The final statement of Yahweh's response (Ezek 11:21) to Ezekiel's question or exclamation from v 13 then sets the future promised to the exiles in contrast to that of the Jerusalemites, whose **hearts** remain unchanged and whose *abominations* (**detestable idols**) will result in their ultimate destruction.

4. Yahweh's Glory Departs the City (11:22-23)

■ **22-23** Following the two interruptions devoted to the Jerusalemites and exiles respectively (11:1-13, 14-21), the main narrative plot line of the withdrawal of Yahweh's glory/presence from the temple and city reaches its conclusion in vv 22-23. Ezekiel reports that the cherubim-throne lifted off the ground (v 22), carried the divine glory/presence out of the city, and **stopped above the mountain east of it** (v 23). Geographically, the description charts the glory's path out of Jerusalem, across the Kidron Valley, coming to rest on the Mount of Olives to the east. Even here, at the culmination of the divine withdrawal, the text's rhythm communicates hesitancy, as Yahweh's glory does not simply fly off toward Babylonia but stops at the first way point just outside the city. Perhaps the description implies that something is stirred within Yahweh's character, producing a reluctance, even if only momentary, to leave the holy city. Within ancient Jewish tradition, for instance, some interpreters took this pause as a symbol of Yahweh's desire to hold out some final hope for the repentance of Jerusalem (see Greenberg 1983, 191). Or, perhaps, as in the Christian tradition of Jesus' lament over Jerusalem (Matt 23:37-39; Luke 13:34-35), the divine presence takes a final moment to weep over the defilement and destruction of Jerusalem that has been so vividly portrayed in the preceding vision.

D. Conclusion: Visionary Return to the Exiles (11:24-25)

■ **24-25** The entire report of chs 8—11 ends with a reminder that the actions and words depicted in these chapters have been only a visionary representation of the present and future condition of Judah and its people. Ezekiel's visionary experience ends as it began: he is transported by the **Spirit** back to the exiles in Babylonia (v 24; see 8:1-3). Presumably finding himself once again before the elders of the exile who had come to inquire of him, Ezekiel reports, **I told the exiles everything the LORD had shown me** (v 25). From this visionary portrayal of Jerusalem's defilement, the withdrawal of Yahweh's presence from the temple, and the promised restoration of the exiles, Ezekiel offers his fellow deportees a new understanding of the trauma they had experienced and a new view of their own status before Yahweh in the present and future.

FROM THE TEXT

The vision of God's glory leaving the temple in chs 8—11 forms another part of Ezekiel's construction of a new narrative plot line that can deal with the trauma experienced by his people and offer a new understanding of their past, present, and future with God. *An affirmation of the demands of God's holiness, the seriousness of God's judgment, and the hopefulness of God's intentions stands at the heart of the passage.* The vision in chs 8—11 offers a way for those in exile to interpret theologically the deportation that they have experienced and the final destruction of Jerusalem that will come a few years later: these events should be understood as part of a larger divine plan to purify the community and restore God's presence among them. This interpretive move attempts to deal with the trauma that Ezekiel and his people are experiencing by taking the seemingly unconnected traumatic events of destruction and forced displacement and integrating them into a coherent story line that makes them comprehensible in a larger framework of holiness, judgment, and restoration. The prophet's rhetoric effectively emplots the traumatic experiences of war, especially the destruction of Jerusalem and the death of its inhabitants, into the priestly understanding of God's activity in the world. In this light,

Ezekiel's primary theological claim is that the holiness of God must not be compromised, and God will act in both judgment and redemption in order to restore that holiness.

In affirming God's holiness, judgment, and hopeful intentions in the face of trauma, Ezekiel's vision report urges readers to see behind the veil of historical-political realities and see God's presence. For Ezekiel, the capture of Jerusalem and the deportation of his fellow exiles was not the result of Babylonian military cunning or supremacy, nor Judean weakness or misfortune; it was, rather, the result of the people's long history of unfaithful actions that polluted the holiness within which God's presence must dwell, driven God away from their community, and rendered their life unsustainable as God's people. Ezekiel's historical-theological constructions here, however, go in a somewhat different direction from those found in most of the OT prophetic books. Many prophetic texts attribute actions of historical agents to divine causation, thus bringing the collective memories of enemy actions into the purview of Israel's God (e.g., Isa 10:5-19). By emphasizing God's control of foreign armies, the prophets in some measure take the power away from the enemy conquerors and give it to Israel's God. But Ezekiel's rhetoric goes further than his fellow prophets and pushes a different rationality for Judah's traumatic events. His emphasis on God's direct role in Jerusalem's destruction and exile (see chs 9—10) does not merely reinterpret the Babylonians as instruments in the plan of Israel's God. In contrast to the apparent reality, namely, that Judah's misfortunes have been accomplished by the Babylonian war machine, Ezekiel allows the Babylonians no explicit involvement in the events, insisting that this was entirely God's doing from the beginning. Note, for example, that Ezekiel's vision of Jerusalem's coming destruction does not mention the Babylonians but pictures the true agents of these events as divinely appointed assistants working under God's direction (ch 9). Ezekiel's language expresses a concrete conviction that God was the only one involved in Judah's defeat and trauma from the very beginning.

As discussed previously (see From the Text for chs 4—7), such attempts to identify theological meaning behind specific traumatic experiences can provide suffering persons and communities with a coherency and understanding that moves them toward wholeness. But these kinds of interpretive moves should give contemporary interpreters pause. Ezekiel's interpretations certainly affirm divine sovereignty over the most chaotic aspects of human existence, yet given a broader understanding of our present interpretive context and the nature of ancient Israelite prophecy, contemporary readers should likely resist the temptation to attribute direct divine causation to specific tragedies like acts of military violence. Nonetheless, today's readers of Ezekiel can operate in the spirit of the prophet's attempt to situate historical, political, and social events within a conviction that God is active alongside of and within the events of human life and history. Without suggesting direct divine causation, Ezekiel's theological descendants can affirm that all of life unfolds in God's presence and then seek ways in which God may be at work, often through the means of God's own people, in the midst of particular circumstances, conforming them to a larger divine purpose and story line. Moreover, the text invites readers to link the character of a community's life, even in destruction and restoration, not with social and political forces but with God's presence or absence in their midst.

The presentations of judgment and restoration in the second vision of God's glory also point to an "already-not yet" tension within which God's people exist. Despite the definitiveness of Ezekiel's presentations of Jerusalem's destruction (chs 9—10) and the exiles' restoration (11:14-21), both of these realities remain in the future from the perspective of the time in which this vision is set (see 8:1-3). The text's rhetoric reveals the classic tension known well from discussions of eschatology in both Jewish and Christian tradition. From the outlook of the book of Ezekiel, God's judgment on the sin of his people has begun with the first capture of Jerusalem in 597 B.C. and will be finally accomplished in the city's destruction by the Babylonians at a time in the near future. Likewise, the salvation and restoration of the Judean exiles has already begun, as God's glory/presence dwells among them as a temporary "sanctuary" in exile (see 11:16), and will be finally accomplished with their purification and return to the land in years to come (11:14-21). For now, however, the people of God must live in the tension between the start of the accomplishment of God's purposes, which even now has broken in among them, and the delayed full realization of those purposes, which await God's action at some unknown future time but remain certain in their coming.

Such a tension has resonated with the Christian church throughout history, as it exists in the time between the beginning of God's decisive action in Jesus Christ and the fulfillment of God's redemptive purposes at the end of the age. Ezekiel's visionary rhetoric, certain though it is of the reality of judgment and redemption to come, pushes its readers to direct their efforts not to calculations and scenarios of the coming events but to the present life of the community as it lives before God in the time of delay. Just as Ezekiel envisions for the Jerusalemites after 597 B.C. (see ch 8), the call upon God's people is to consider how the knowledge that God's kingdom has already broken in among them redefines their understanding of the world and their life within it. God's people live in a world in which God's presence is active, drawing creation toward the fulfillment of the divine redemptive purposes. Such a knowledge should lead the community of faith not to end-time speculation or easy dismissal of their world, but to the consideration of how they are to live faithfully in the presence of God's holiness and participate in God's ongoing redemptive purposes.

For contemporary readers, perhaps the most poignant consideration raised by chs 8—11 concerns worship, morality, and ethics in the midst of difficult circumstances. *Ezekiel especially condemns hypocrisy on the part of the community, in which God's people fail to link worship and ethics in a holistic vision of life and society before God.* While examining the temple vision in ch 8, for example, we noted that God's address leads the reader through the various cultic abominations in temple practice, only to conclude that these ritual sins are surpassed by the "violence" perpetrated by the people throughout the land (8:17). The vision describes a people who seek God at the temple, perhaps through both traditional and unorthodox means, all the while refusing to follow God's will in the realms of social justice, personal compassion, and political policy. This dimension of Ezekiel's critique of Judean life resonates with other prophetic voices (e.g., Isa 1:10-17; Amos 5:1-7) and provides a particularly sharp word to the contemporary Christian church, often living its life of worship too compliantly within the social structures and political ideologies of modern nation-states. Ezekiel's conviction is that belief and worship are inextricably linked with personal and communal ethics, such that the failure to live according to God's purposes in all aspects of life invalidates even seemingly sincere attempts to seek God. Moreover, the imaginative pictures of destruction in chs 9—10 communicate that such hypocrisy ultimately leads to an inability to remain in God's presence, and thus an inability to sustain life in the face of ruin. To worship God, one must follow God's ways in all areas of life.

This commentary's more sympathetic interpretation of the Jerusalemites' actions in the temple, however, takes the question of worship, morality, and ethics in times of crisis to another level. If the interpretation given here is correct, Ezekiel does not picture the people remaining in Jerusalem after 597 B.C. as turning to other gods in idolatry but as continuing to mourn before and seek Israel's God in the midst of their situation (see commentary on ch 8). In so doing, however, they engage in activities that break with proper practices (at least as defined by Ezekiel's priestly perspective) and ironically further offend God. The description of the people's mind-set in ch 8 suggests that a sense of being abandoned by God leads them to try new means of relating to God that violate the established standards. As we have seen, the sentiments attributed to the people in Ezekiel's vision echo those of the psalmists who lament over their sense of God's abandonment, as well as the words of later exiles in need of prophetic messages of hope: "Why do you say, O Jacob, and speak, O Israel, 'My way is hidden from the LORD, and my right is disregarded by my God'?" (Isa 40:27 NRSV). Ezekiel's descriptions suggest that the sense of abandonment that comes from trauma hinders the people's theological insight into the meaning of the events they have experienced and how they ought to respond, leading them desperately to devise attempts to beseech and appease God. Such a connection between a sense of abandonment and the involvement in religious practices that fall short of God's ideal may provide a warning to contemporary communities that suffer trauma: *persons and communities that have experienced the kinds of traumatic events known by the Jerusalemites often live with a sense that God has abandoned them, a sense that leaves them vulnerable to acts of unfaithfulness and desperation.* Ezekiel suggests that there are times when persons and communities should curb desperate attempts to seek connection with God and begin to allow God's restoration to take place by recognizing the sinfulness that characterizes their lives and by looking to God's holiness as the only path to redemption.

Finally, alongside the theological dimensions discussed above, readers of the vision in chs 8—11 must take note that these chapters once again confront us with difficult and violent portrayals of God. We have examined this issue already in the context of chs 4—7 (see From the Text). Here again the God portrayed in Ezekiel's vision is violent, wrathful, and vengeful, not trying to convince people to acknowledge their sin and receive pardon but pronouncing that their fate is sealed and judgment cannot be averted. Any restoration is restricted to those who went into exile with Ezekiel in 597 B.C. The divine discourse of chs 8—11, for instance, as in chs 4—7, features the "recognition formula" ("you will know that I am the LORD" [11:10, 12]; see previously 6:7, 10, 14; 7:4, 9), an assertion that apparently establishes physical violence as the primary evidence by which the people will acknowledge that God is at work in the world.

The previous discussion of chs 4—7 highlighted in particular the portrayals of God's violent acts against nature and the interpretive issues raised by those portrayals. The Jerusalem vision in chs 8—11 adds a new aspect to the issue of divine violence. In these chapters, God's violence is more *personal* on two levels. First, the violent acts depicted here are directed specifically against the physical bodies of human persons. Divinely appointed agents will "mark" the bodies of individuals and use their cutting weapons to "slaughter" those unmarked (9:4, 6). God will wield God's own sword against the bodies of sinners (11:8), and the slaughter will include not only responsible adults but also young men, young women, and children (9:6). Second, and perhaps more troubling, the vision in chs 8—11 seemingly links such violence more intimately to God's own character. The text asserts that God's anger (God's anger is his wrath, from the book's perspective, on his covenant people who have trivialized/profaned his holiness) has been provoked and God will act without any sense of mercy or pity (8:17-18; 9:5, 10). As the preeminent American OT theologian Walter Brueggemann has noted, all biblical interpreters "must acknowledge the violence that is present in the Old Testament that is seemingly without much irony assigned to YHWH," whether that be violence done by God or by humans at the behest of God (Brueggemann 2008, 135, 137).

For readers from the Wesleyan theological tradition, such depictions of divine violence do not lead to the conclusion that violence is an inherent part of God's nature. God's holy love stands at the center of God's nature, and the theological context of the book of Ezekiel associates the depicted violence with God's judgment on sin within a covenant context. Still, the issue of how contemporary Christian readers should deal with these portrayals of God is pressing due to the danger that interpreters can use such language to legitimate violence, both in present historical circumstances or simply in violent end-times scenarios that revolve around the warlike destruction of God's "enemies." Hence, the suggestions made in our earlier discussion of chs 4—7 remain important possibilities: holding these portrayals in tension with other biblical texts that emphasize divine mercy and forgiveness and reading the images as metaphors drawn from Ezekiel's use of ancient Near Eastern political treaties. Yet we may also consider again the significance of the context of trauma out of which Ezekiel's portrayals come. These depictions of violence form another part of a powerful act of imagination that takes the story of Judah's past, a story of killing, destruction, and exile that seemingly refuses to be integrated into the people's collective life in an understandable way, and reinterprets it in light of the long-standing priestly conceptions of God's holiness and the people's impurity. For the sixth-century priest-prophet himself, the troubling portrayals may reflect the trauma and violence that Ezekiel and his fellow Judeans have experienced in their own bodies.

IV. ACTS AND ORACLES OF JUDGMENT (EZEKIEL 12—24)

Overview

The vision of the status and fate of the Jerusalem temple recounted by Ezekiel in chs 8—11 is the second major vision of Yahweh's glory/presence (*kābôd*) in the book (see chs 1—3; 40—48). In the collection of material that follows in chs 12—24, the book moves from the report of the temple vision to the description of various symbolic acts, rhetorical addresses, and metaphorical discourses that constitute Ezekiel's work among his fellow exiles over the final years leading up to the Babylonian destruction of Jerusalem in 586 B.C. As in the case of the vision in chs 8—11, Ezekiel's words throughout this section have a dual focus, at once depicting the sin and judgment of those who remained with King Zedekiah in Jerusalem between 597 and 586 B.C., and addressing his audience of Babylonian exiles who still need to understand the unfolding events, their own status before Yahweh, and their role in the movement from judgment to restoration being driven by divine holiness.

As noted concerning the overall structure of Ezekiel, each of the book's three visions of the divine glory connects to a series of acts and oracles. Just as chs 1—7 move from a vision of Yahweh's glory in chs 1—3 to symbolic acts and explanatory oracles in chs 4—7, the vision of Yahweh's glory leaving the temple in chs 8—11 gives way to a collection of acts and oracles in chs 12—24. These chapters contain a wide variety of genres that explore several theological dimensions of the people's past, present, and future with Yahweh. The genres include symbolic acts, prophetic oracles, metaphorical and allegorical discourses, and imagistic portrayals. Both the genres and topics, however, group fairly well into coherent subsections within chs 12—24, perhaps due to the work of later editors or collectors. The discussion that follows will explore the groupings of genres and topics in turn, offering comments concerning Behind the Text, In the Text, and From the Text for each subsection. On the whole, the material in chs 12—24 exhibits a parallel structure that begins and ends with symbolic acts and features a centerpiece in which Ezekiel offers a reinterpretation of the entire sweep of Israel's history as a history of sin and rebellion:

A. Part 1: Acts and Oracles of Siege, Exile, and Intercession (12:1—14:23)
   1. Symbolic Acts of Siege and Exile (12:1-28)
   2. Explanatory Oracle: Lack of True Prophets (13:1-23)
   3. Explanatory Oracle: Lack of True Intercession (14:1-23)
B. Part 2: Metaphorical Discourses (15:1—17:24)
   1. The Useless Vine (15:1-8)
   2. The Faithless Bride (16:1-63)
   3. The Two Eagles and the Vine (17:1-24)
C. Part 3: Oracles of Judgment and Lament (18:1—19:14)
   1. Retribution and Judgment (18:1-32)
   2. Lament over Jerusalem (19:1-14)
D. Part 4: Israel's History of Sin/Rebellion (20:1-49)
   1. Introduction (20:1-4)
   2. Historical Rehearsal (20:5-29)
   3. Application to the Exiles' Present and Future (20:30-44)
   4. Oracle of Destruction Against the Negev (20:45-49)
E. Part 5: Metaphorical Discourses and Symbolic Acts (21:1—24:25)
   1. The Sword of God (21:1-32)
   2. Jerusalem, the Bloody City (22:1-31)
   3. The Two Wives of God (23:1-49)
   4. The Boiling Pot (24:1-14)
   5. Symbolic Act: Ezekiel's Muteness (Beginning of Siege) (24:15-27)

Taken as a whole, Ezekiel's message across these chapters makes the case that the people's past and present existence has been and is consistently characterized by rebellion against Yahweh. This condition of Yahweh's people applies equally to those remaining in Jerusalem, as well as those already in exile with the prophet. More importantly, however, the defilement of divine holiness produced by this rebellion has now led Yahweh to act in judgment in order to purify his sanctuary and people. The exiles, Ezekiel proclaims, have the possibility of receiving the transformation and restoration that flows out of the activity of Yahweh's holiness, but only if they recognize their own culpability in Israel's history of rebellion, the nature of Yahweh's work among them, and the need to break with the old Jerusalem that stands condemned in judgment.

Before proceeding to the subsections within chs 12—24, there is one overall background issue that is relevant for the section as a whole. Following the vision of the Jerusalem temple in chs 8—11, which is dated to 592 B.C. (see 8:1), no dates occur in the text between chs 12 and 19. The only two dated oracles within chs 12—24 occur in ch 20, which refers to 591 B.C., and ch 24, which coincides with 588 B.C., the beginning of the Babylonian siege of Jerusalem. The lack of dates creates uncertainty concerning how much time has passed since Ezekiel's temple vision, yet the material in chs 12—24 all seems to reflect the situation before the destruction of Jerusalem. Hence, the overall movement of the book's final form places these acts and oracles between 592 and 588 B.C., that is, between the rise of Egyptian power under Psammetichus II (see Behind the Text for chs 8—11) and the beginning of the Babylonian reprisal against Jerusalem's rebellion.

The years between 592 and 588 B.C. saw significant developments in the area of Syria-Palestine that no doubt shaped Ezekiel's theological proclamations. As discussed with chs 1—3, the seeds of rebellion grew almost immediately after Zedekiah had been placed on the throne in Jerusalem by the Babylonian king Nebuchadnezzar II in 597 B.C. Around 593 (see 1:1-3), Zedekiah convened a meeting of emissaries from the kingdoms of Moab, Ammon, Edom, Tyre, and Sidon, apparently to plot a rebellion against Babylonia (Jer 27). Although such a rebellion failed to materialize, the rise to power of the Egyptian pharaoh Psammetichus II, and his subsequent victory tour of Syria-Palestine around 592, fanned the flames of rebellion among those thinking that Babylonian strength had waned (see Behind the Text for chs 8—11). Probably as a result of this Egyptian resurgence, coupled with long-standing Judean religious beliefs in the inviolability of Jerusalem, Zedekiah withheld annual tribute and entered into open rebellion against Babylonia in the late 590s or early 580s. Biblical and extrabiblical texts depict Judah appealing to

Egypt for horses and troops and sending royal officials to Egypt for direct negotiations. According to the date sequence in the book, these were the events unfolding in Judah while the prophet proclaimed the messages in chs 12—24 to those who were living in exile.

Perhaps the most significant aspect of these historical developments that would shape both Jerusalem's fate and Ezekiel's preaching was a shift in Babylonian imperial policy that apparently occurred around this time. Since their rise to dominance, the Babylonians had typically dealt with a rebellious kingdom by forcibly subduing it, removing the rebellious king, but maintaining the kingdom's continuity by leaving the capital in the same location and appointing another member of the royal family as the new king. These were, for instance, the very actions Nebuchadnezzar apparently undertook at Jerusalem in 597 B.C. that brought Zedekiah to the throne formerly held by his nephew Jehoiachin (see 2 Kgs 24). Likely as a result of the combination of regional unrest and Egyptian resurgence in the late 590s, however, the Babylonians altered their earlier policy of maintaining stability. Nebuchadnezzar apparently decided henceforth to replace currently ruling families of rebellious kingdoms, relocate the kingdoms' centers of power, and rule them more directly. In the late fall of 589 B.C., Nebuchadnezzar apparently set out from Babylonia to make Jerusalem the first example of this new policy. He led his forces to central Syria and established a base of operations at Riblah. There he evidently divided his army and sent one contingent down the coast toward the border of Egypt and another toward Jerusalem where they placed the city under siege sometime in 588 B.C. (see 24:1).

The siege of Jerusalem would last for more than a year and involve a number of developments, including the expedition into Syria-Palestine by an Egyptian force under the new pharaoh, Hophra or Apries, which caused Nebuchadnezzar to lift the siege temporarily. Eventually, however, sometime in the summer of 586 B.C., the Babylonians captured and destroyed Jerusalem. We will see the historical details of this event later in our discussion of ch 33. Yet, the biblical texts particularly highlight two elements of the fall of Judah that are relevant for chs 12—24. First, Jerusalem experienced dire straits during the siege, especially severe famine among the people (see 2 Kgs 25:1-3). Second, in the final moments, Zedekiah and a military escort attempted to flee south toward the Transjordan but were captured and brought to Nebuchadnezzar at Riblah. Probably in keeping with the stipulated punishments of his vassal treaty, Zedekiah's sons were killed in front of him, his eyes were put out, and he was sent to Babylonia blind and in chains (see 2 Kgs 25:7). These kinds of horrific realities associated with siege and destruction find a prominent place in Ezekiel's symbolic acts and oracles given to his audience of exiles in the tumultuous years between 592 and 588 B.C.

A. Part 1: Acts and Oracles of Siege, Exile, and Intercession (12:1—14:23)

BEHIND THE TEXT

Chapters 12—14 form the first subsection within the larger unit of symbolic acts and oracles (chs 12—24) that follows the second vision of Yahweh's glory/presence. Chapter 12 is the focal point, as it relates Ezekiel's interaction surrounding two symbolic acts that give explicit pictures of the siege and exile that are to come upon Jerusalem and its people. Expanding from these depictions, chs 13 and 14 contain two explanatory oracles that elaborate on current social and theological conditions among both the exiles and Jerusalemites, especially the lack of true mediators or means of intercession that could give the people understanding or rescue them from the consequences of their sin:

A. Part 1: Acts and Oracles of Siege, Exile, and Intercession (12:1—14:23)
  1. Symbolic Acts of Siege and Exile (12:1-28)
  2. Explanatory Oracle: Lack of True Prophets (13:1-23)
  3. Explanatory Oracle: Lack of True Intercession (14:1-23)

These prophetic acts and oracles are set against the background of the historical events surveyed above surrounding Jerusalem's rebellion against Babylonia from 592 to 588 B.C. Although the prophet's proclamations describe words and actions related to the people remaining in Jerusalem under King Zedekiah, the audience of Ezekiel's messages is the exilic community with him in Babylonia. His primary concern is to provide them with the proper theological understanding of the events that have occurred and will continue to occur in Jerusalem and to exhort them to break with their former identity bound up with the old Jerusalem and look to a new identity on the other side of Yahweh's coming judgment.

The first significant background aspect of chs 12—14 relates to the prophetic genre of the symbolic action report, which figures prominently in ch 12. We have previously examined the nature and function of such "sign-acts" or "enacted prophecies" (McKeating 1995, 19) in connection with Ezekiel's actions depicted in chs 4—5. As noted in that context, the use of these symbolic acts is a characteristic feature of Ezekiel (with about a dozen identifiable acts in the book), and should be understood as a type of street theater or performance rhetoric in the service of audience persuasion (see Friebel 1999). Most importantly for chs 12—14, the previous discussion noted that while symbolic action reports in prophetic books normally give the divine instructions to execute the act, an account of the execution, and a description of the audience that witnesses the act, the texts of Ezekiel typically provide only Yahweh's instructions for the act (cf. 24:15-24), a feature in keeping with the book's tendency to maintain the focus on the divine initiative and action. Ezekiel's symbolic acts in ch 12, however, are unusual in this regard. At least for the chapter's main symbolic act (12:1-16), the text provides not only Yahweh's instructions but also a report of Ezekiel's execution of the act and the audience's puzzled response. In so doing, the prophet is able to communicate explicitly the divine intentions behind the symbols.

A second background element for chs 12—14 involves the extended focus on prophets and the prophetic office in ch 13 in particular. This first explanatory oracle highlights the activity of other prophets both among the exiles in Babylonia and back in Jerusalem. In so doing, it attests to a widespread phenomenon of prophecy known throughout the ancient Near East and to the contentious nature of the relationships among various prophets and the messages they proclaimed. These references raise important definitional questions such as, "What was a prophet in the ancient world?" and "What was the nature of prophecy in ancient Judean society?" Biblical figures such as Amos, Hosea, Micah, and Isaiah stood within a broad phenomenon of prophecy known throughout the ancient Near East, and texts from a variety of cultures attest the activity of prophets from as early as the eighteenth century B.C. While prophets in ancient Israel and elsewhere exhibit great diversity in their roles and actions, the majority of available evidence indicates that far from being simply, or even primarily, predictors of the future, particularly the distant future, prophets in cultures throughout the ancient Near East were divine spokespersons who spoke an authoritative message from a deity concerning social, religious, and political issues of their day. They often functioned within societal institutions like the temple or royal government. Prophets in ancient Israel in particular were something akin to rhetorical orators, who spoke carefully crafted speeches or engaged in symbolic actions in order to provide a word from Yahweh, often introduced with the so-called messenger formula ("Thus says the LORD" [NRSV]). These words aimed to persuade an audience of what the prophet believed was the proper interpretation of contemporary events or the true call of Yahweh upon the community's belief and practice (see Kelle 2005).

Ezekiel's words in ch 13 are especially interesting because they indicate the presence of female prophets within Judean society (see 13:17-23). Although the vast majority of prophets that appear in biblical texts are men, a variety of biblical and extrabiblical evidence indicates that many prophets in the ancient world were women. This is especially true for some cultures outside Israel, such the city of Mari in Mesopotamia, for which the surviving texts indicate a preponderance of female prophets. The OT identifies only five specific women as prophets (Miriam, Exod 15:20; Deborah, Judg 4:4; Huldah, 2 Kgs 22:14 and 2 Chr 34:22; Noadiah, Neh 6:14; woman associated with Isaiah, Isa 8:3). Yet textual references and evidence drawn from archaeology and sociology strongly suggest that female prophets were as well-established in Israel as elsewhere, and the women mentioned in ch 13 were a vibrant part of an established phenomenon of female prophecy in the ancient Near East (see Gafney 2008).

As we will see in the discussion of ch 13 below, Ezekiel condemns the male and female prophets equally (and without regard for gender) for the messages they proclaim and the intentions they possess. Yet none of these prophets are charged with being in the service of other gods. Hence, Ezekiel's accusations against these prophets highlight the perennial difficulty of discerning between true and false prophetic messages. Given prophecy's nature as proclamation and interpretation based on the prophet's theological assessment of historical circumstances, it is common to have differing, even contradictory, proclamations concerning the meaning or expected outcome of significant events, such as Zedekiah's decision to pursue liberation from Babylonia or Jerusalem's capture and the people's deportation. The issue of adjudicating between true and false prophetic messages, especially when all prophets involved are claiming to speak for Yahweh, is one that is recognized by many OT texts (see Deut 13:1-5; 1 Kgs 22), but without clear resolution (see From the Text).

A final background aspect of chs 12—14 emerges from the conviction among many commentators that several parts of these chapters have undergone later editing or were added in the years after Jerusalem's destruction. For example, the application of Ezekiel's first sign-act to the "prince" in Jerusalem (12:10-16) leads some interpreters to conclude that it was fashioned after the actual fate suffered by Zedekiah in 586 B.C., whether by the prophet himself or another hand (e.g., Zimmerli 1979, 267).

Regardless of one's views on these matters, the discussion of the text's compositional history has especially highlighted a number of connections between the language and content in some sections of chs 12—14 and the legal terminology and cases found within Pentateuchal laws from the Priestly tradition (P), and, especially, the so-called Holiness Code in Lev 17—26 (H). The prime example of these connections appears in the hypothetical legal case presented in ch 14, which resembles the legal terminology in Lev 17 and threats of punishment that are similar to the curses for breaking the covenant in Lev 26 (see Odell 2005, 162; Zimmerli 1979, 312). We have examined the question of Ezekiel's relationship to the Priestly and Holiness traditions in the introduction to this commentary, especially the long-standing scholarly attempt to determine which traditions are earlier and which are dependent. The observable similarities in ch 14 remind us that Ezekiel's preaching shares the Priestly tradition's special emphasis on holiness associated with sacred space and sacred personnel, as well as the Holiness Code's expansion of this notion of holiness into an ideal for the whole community, which is lived out through proper social relations (see Kohn 2002). These perspectives provide some of the thought-world that underlies Ezekiel's interpretation of the people's trauma and exile.

IN THE TEXT

1. Symbolic Acts of Siege and Exile (12:1-28)

Building upon the visionary description of Jerusalem's defilement and destruction in chs 8—11, Ezekiel's words and actions in ch 12 offer further depictions of the divine judgment that is to come on Jerusalem and, most especially, the meaning of that divine action for the present and future of the Judeans already living in exile after 597 B.C. Chapter 12 contains reports of two symbolic acts performed by the prophet among his fellow exiles (vv 1-16, 17-20) and two disputes over common proverbs concerning the power and relevance of the prophetic word (vv 21-25, 26-28). The prophetic word formula (**the word of the LORD came to me**) serves as the primary structural marker of the chapter's units, occurring at the beginning of each new act or dispute (vv 1, 8, 17, 21, 26). In keeping with the book's characteristic style, virtually all of the chapter's elements are presented as personal interactions between Yahweh and Ezekiel upon which the reader is allowed to eavesdrop. The interactions describe the instructions Yahweh gives the prophet or provide Yahweh's perspective on certain matters, rather than detailing Ezekiel's interaction with his audience.

In comparison to the vision in chs 8—11, which focused on the people and circumstances of the city of Jerusalem under Zedekiah between 597 and 586 B.C., Ezekiel's words in ch 12 shift the attention to the character and mind-set of the exiles in Babylonia. Yahweh's strong words about **a rebellious people** who **do not see** or **hear** (v 2) describe the exiles themselves, reflecting the description of them in Ezekiel's divine commissioning (see 2:1-7; 3:1-11) and reminding the reader that for Ezekiel, these exiles share the culpability for Jerusalem's past and present sin. The repeated attempts to communicate and dramatize the inevitable and total nature of Jerusalem's coming destruction also suggest that the exiles continue in some measure to attach their identity to the old Jerusalem that stands under judgment, harboring false hopes for Zedekiah's plans to throw off Babylonian domination and a quick return to a spared Jerusalem. Taken as a whole, Ezekiel's words and actions urge the people to abandon their previous identification with sinful Jerusalem and understand the larger plan of Yahweh that entails the city's destruction in judgment.

■ **1-7** The opening unit of the chapter contains the first of two symbolic actions that depict the coming siege and exile of Jerusalem (vv 1-7, 8-16). Following the prophetic word formula and the now-expected designation of Ezekiel as **son of man,** v 2 provides an introduction, as Yahweh warns Ezekiel that he is living in the midst of **a rebellious people** (lit., ***house of rebellion, bêt měrî***). As discussed with Ezekiel's commissioning vision, this title occurs fourteen times in the book and represents the prophet's primary designation for the people of Judah (see 2:6, 8; 3:9, 26, 27). It recasts the entire character and history of Judah as one of rebellion and carries overtones of both sinful rebellion against Yahweh, the cosmic king of all creation (see ch 1), and political rebellion of a vassal such as Zedekiah against a treaty partner or overlord (see Odell 2005, 43). Strikingly, however, in ch 12 Yahweh uses this designation five different times (vv 2 [twice], 3, 9, 25), apparently to describe the exiles in particular, rather than the Jerusalemites or simply the Judean people historically. Yahweh's introduction in v 2 adds to this description by asserting that the exiles lack sensory perception: **they have eyes to see but do not see and ears to hear but do not hear** (v 2). This motif appears throughout the prophetic books in reference to a number of subjects (e.g., Isa 6:9; 43:8; Jer 5:21). In this context, it introduces the theme of sight, perception, and understanding that runs throughout the symbolic acts and dispute oracles in the whole of Ezek 12 (see the emphasis on vision in vv 21-28).

How should we understand this negative portrayal of the group that elsewhere plays a favorable role in the book's descriptions of Yahweh's overall intentions and actions? Clearly, Ezekiel's description here indicates once again that although he understands the exiles of 597 as the group that will constitute Judah's future, he nonetheless sees them as sharing in the guilt and responsibility for Jerusalem's past and present condition. Many commentators suggest that Ezekiel's rhetoric attributes a level of spiritual blindness or forgetfulness to those who have experienced deportation: although they have lived within the tradition of Yahweh's faithfulness throughout their history, years of rebelliousness have rendered them unable to remember Yahweh's saving acts in the past or understand Yahweh's ways in the present (see Odell 2005, 142).

Yet the text's language of being unable to perceive and understand also evokes the aftermath of trauma, wherein the traumatic experience often has the effect of blinding the sufferer to any kind of meaningful understanding of the events they have experienced. No broader perspective can find its way through the past experience that has overshadowed the victim's present and become the defining reality for their view of the foreseeable future. Although the end of Ezekiel's vision in chs 8—11 reported his explanation of the vision to his fellow exiles, the opening of ch 12 indicates that those whose lives have been so severely disrupted remain unable to understand the meaning of past and future events and in need of further explanation. The exiles—by virtue of both their own rebellion and the trauma they have suffered as a result—apparently still lack the ability to integrate their experiences into a larger meaningful narrative and correctly perceive Yahweh's intentions and actions in the world.

The actual report of the first prophetic sign-act and its accomplishment appears in vv 3-7. Yahweh's instructions to Ezekiel command two related actions. By day, Ezekiel is to prepare what the text designates as "exile's baggage" (v 3 NRSV; **pack your belongings for exile**) and symbolically leave his dwelling place as if being deported. As with the eating of the scroll in 2:9—3:3, this action represents another instance in which Ezekiel literally acts out something that Jeremiah described only rhetorically, as a word addressed to the Egyptians (cf. Jer 46:19; see Block 1997, 369). The imagery here reflects the depictions of citizens of conquered cities, even Judean cities such as Lachish, on ancient Assyrian relief sculptures, which often portray deportees heading out of a city carrying packs of belongings. Additionally, by night, Yahweh instructs Ezekiel to **dig through the wall** of his house and carry out his **belongings,** while covering his face (vv 5-6). The imagery here fits the prophet's Babylonian context, in which houses were constructed of mud brick, yet the text remains unclear as to whether Ezekiel is to dig a hole in the wall from inside or outside of his house. The former would symbolize an attempt to escape from a city under siege (so Wevers 1969, 99; Greenberg 1983, 209-10). The instruction to dig in the sight of his audience in v 4, however, suggests that Ezekiel is to dig through his wall from the outside, an act that would symbolize an attacking army's puncture of a city's defensive wall (so Block 1997, 370; Odell 2005, 137). In either case, the prophet is to proceed with his face covered, a gesture that may represent grief or shame, an attempt at disguise, inability to see, or the finality of exile (Block 1997, 375; see vv 12-13 below).

Throughout vv 3-7, the language suggests that Ezekiel took these actions repeatedly over the course of several days and nights (see, especially, v 7). He thus engages in a series of acts of street theater or performance rhetoric designed to symbolize experiences that form part of Yahweh's judgment on Judah. Later parts of ch 12 relate these acts to the coming fate of Jerusalem in 586 B.C., but they undoubtedly draw upon the traumatic experiences suffered by Ezekiel and his fellow deportees during the Babylonian siege of Jerusalem just a few years earlier. As Ezekiel reenacts their trauma before their eyes, the chapter as a whole links their experience to Yahweh's coming actions against Jerusalem. In this way, the prophet once again becomes a **sign** for his people (see 4:3). By contrast to the book's earlier designation of Ezekiel with the neutral Hebrew term *'ôt* ("sign" [4:3]), v 6 identifies him with the more ominous word *môpēt*, connoting a negative **omen** or **portent** (so also in 24:24, 27).

■ **8-16** The next section of ch 12 provides Ezekiel with the divine interpretation of the first symbolic act. The giving of the interpretation is triggered by the people's query in vv 8-9. As noted above, the report of the carrying out of Yahweh's instructions (v 7) and the description of the audience's response (vv 8-9) are typical features of the genre of symbolic action reports, but do not usually appear in the book of Ezekiel (see Hals 1989, 76). Beginning with the prophetic messenger formula (**This is what the Sovereign LORD says**; see also vv 19, 23, 28), the divine response that Ezekiel is to give his audience identifies his previous actions as symbolizing the future judgment of siege and deportation that is to come upon King Zedekiah and those who remained in Jerusalem after 597 B.C.: **This oracle concerns the prince in Jerusalem and the whole house of Israel who are there** (v 10).

The language of Yahweh's statement raises a number of interpretive possibilities. The Hebrew term translated **oracle** (*maśśā'*) may also carry the meaning of **burden.** Since Ezekiel nowhere else uses this term with the sense of **oracle,** and the passage as a whole focuses on **the prince in Jerusalem,** one should perhaps read v 10 as a condemnatory statement that identifies Jerusalem's current ruler as the primary cause of the sinful situation: ***This burden is the prince in Jerusalem*** (Greenberg 1983, 212; Block 1997, 372-74). The use of the term **prince** (*nāśî*; see also v 12) rather than "king" (*melek*) to refer to Zedekiah also gives Yahweh's statement the character of theo-political commentary. In the same way that Ezekiel's date references use the exiled King Jehoiachin, rather than the reigning Zedekiah, as their point of departure (e.g., 1:2), the prophet's words here relegate Zedekiah to a **prince** who does not have the status of being the true king. Simultaneously, the language evokes the status of a subordinate vassal to an overlord, perhaps highlighting Zedekiah's current involvement in plotting rebellion against his treaty obligations to Nebuchadnezzar, who had installed him as king in Judah (Odell 2005, 139). For those wondering whether rebellion against Babylonia is part of the divine will for Judah in response to the catastrophe of 597 B.C., Ezekiel's rhetoric makes clear that Yahweh is against Zedekiah's actions, which will ultimately lead to Jerusalem's destruction.

Along with this political dimension, the text's designation of **prince** for the most powerful ruler in Judah once again sounds the book's theme of the incomparable sovereignty of Yahweh. While Ezekiel does use the term "king" on occasion to refer to the future human ruler in the restored Jerusalem to come (37:24), he nearly always designates Judah's human authorities in both the sinful present and restored future as **prince** (e.g., 19:1; 21:12, 25; 34:23-24; 37:25; 44:3; 48:21). In the prophet's perspective, all of Judah's human rulers are penultimate authorities at most, standing under the governance of Yahweh, the cosmic king (see ch 1).

The part of Yahweh's explanation that raises the most interpretive issues appears in 12:12-14. Here, the focus of the explanation narrows to the **prince** himself. These verses recast Ezekiel's earlier symbolic actions as things that will be experienced by Jerusalem's ruler specifically, and not simply as the general experience of those in the city. Although the text does not name Zedekiah, it is clear that Ezekiel depicts the current king's plans for rebellion as futile and Yahweh's judgment as coming upon him at the hands of the Babylonians, including his being taken into exile to Babylon (v 13). Repeating the list of actions from vv 3-6, Ezekiel proclaims that the **prince** will carry his **things on his shoulder** and **leave** the city, as **a hole will be dug in the wall** (lit., ***they will dig*** [cf. NRSV]; perhaps a reference to the Babylonian breach of the city; see v 5 discussion above). Zedekiah himself, Ezekiel says, will be the one to **cover his face so that he cannot see the land** (v 12).

In keeping with the prophet's emphasis on divine sovereignty, vv 13-14 explain these coming events as entirely Yahweh's doing. The verses contain repeated first person divine statements (**I will spread; I will bring; I will scatter; I will pursue**) that identify Yahweh, rather than the Babylonians, as the real agent, even in Zedekiah's coming capture and deportation to Babylon. As we have seen already, Ezekiel's identification of the coming siege and exile of Jerusalem as acts carried out by Yahweh, with virtually no active role given to the Babylonians who historically performed these actions, rhetorically takes away the power of Israel's enemies in favor of continued affirmation of Yahweh's sovereignty. This rhetorical move also offers his audience a way to reconsider the trauma that they have experienced and will continue to experience: even the destruction of their city and fellow citizens by the invading Babylonian army does not stand outside the comprehensible categories of their story and identity but has a larger meaning within the ongoing purposes of Yahweh in the world.

The Absence of Babylon in Ezekiel's Rhetoric

The first occurrence of the name "Babylon" in the book of Ezekiel is in 12:13, coming after many of the preceding chapters have detailed actions of siege and destruction. Although Ezekiel's preaching revolves around the wars and destruction carried out by the Babylonians in Jerusalem between 597 and 586 B.C., the Babylonians are not explicitly named as killing the people (e.g., 5:1-4; 9:3-7), destroying the city (e.g., 10:1-2), devastating the land (20:45-49), or deporting the people (12:13-15), even though they were the ones who performed these actions historically. In Ezekiel's rhetoric, Yahweh alone (often described in divine first person statements) is the sole agent for the realities that Judah has experienced and will continue to experience, and this rhetorical feature may best be read in the context of the search for meaning in the trauma that Ezekiel's audience has experienced.

The specific application of Ezekiel's symbolic acts to Zedekiah has suggested to many commentators that vv 12-14 may be a later update to the text, perhaps added after the actual events surrounding Zedekiah and Jerusalem had unfolded in 586 B.C. as a type of *ex eventu* (or "after the event") prophecy (so Cooke 1937, 129; Zimmerli 1979, 267; Hals 1989, 77). Many details here are similar to the biblical accounts of what happened to Zedekiah at the end of the siege (see 2 Kgs 25:4-7; Jer 39:2-7; 52:7-11). When the Babylonians breached the city, Zedekiah and his entourage broke out of the city at night and fled east toward the Jordan River. They were captured, and Zedekiah was taken to Nebuchadnezzar's headquarters in Riblah. Probably in keeping with the stipulations of the vassal treaty he had signed, the rebellious king's sons were executed before him, his eyes were put out, and he was taken in chains to Babylon. Ezekiel's references to the **prince** sneaking out at night (12:12) and going to Babylon but being unable to see it (v 13) seem close to what apparently transpired in 586 B.C. Even so, the prophet's acts and descriptions depict common practices of the treatment of captives in the ancient Near East (see Block 1997, 366-67). In any case, Yahweh's explanation in vv 12-14 serves primarily to portray the current king of Jerusalem in a negative and cowardly light, as one who flees rather than face the consequences of his rebellion and one against whom Yahweh has already declared judgment (Odell 2005, 138).

Following this focus on the prince, vv 15-16 conclude Yahweh's interpretation of Ezekiel's first symbolic act by returning to a more general focus on the Jerusalemites who will experience the coming destruction. These verses provide another statement of the reason for the judgment to come, once again cast in the terms of priestly concerns over divine sovereignty and the pollution of Yahweh's holiness. Using the divine recognition formula (**they will** know that I am the LORD), v 15 asserts that the experience of exile will lead the rebellious Jerusalemites finally to acknowledge Yahweh's sovereignty. The divine statement in v 16, however, adds an element that has been sounded only lightly elsewhere in the book: **I will spare a few of them** (see 5:1-4). The Hebrew root used here (*yātar*) is not the typical term used to designate a "remnant," especially a "righteous remnant," which is delivered by Yahweh because of its faithfulness, but simply a group that is "left over" or "survives" (see also 14:22). As noted previously (see 9:8), the book of Ezekiel does not contain the notion of a "righteous remnant"; the sinfulness and judgment of the Jerusalemites is all-encompassing. Thus, while some may survive, they are only the leftovers, not those saved by their own merit.

These survivors will have a specific function. As they scatter among various nations, they will testify to their **detestable practices** ("abominations" [NRSV]; Heb., *tôʿēbôt*). By describing the people's actions with this priestly term, the text once again offers a theological interpretation of the people's coming fate. Destruction and exile are the result of the ways Yahweh's people have defiled his holiness and driven his presence out of their midst. Moreover, Yahweh declares that as these survivors from Jerusalem scatter, they, too, will become a type of sign, which will lead even foreign nations to acknowledge Yahweh's sovereignty.

12:8-20 ■ **17-20** Beginning with another occurrence of the prophetic word formula (see also vv 1, 8, 21, 26), v 17 introduces Yahweh's instructions for Ezekiel to carry out a second symbolic act. Verses 17-20 relate only the instructions for the act, the more typical form of these reports in Ezekiel. The prophet is to **tremble** and **shudder in fear** as he eats and drinks (v 18). As with the first symbolic act in vv 1-16, although the act itself symbolizes the fearful conditions of living under siege and experiencing widespread military destruction that are to come upon those remaining in Jerusalem (vv 19-20), the explanation and, ultimately, the message of the act is addressed to Ezekiel's fellow Babylonian exiles. There is some ambiguity concerning whether the Hebrew construction in v 19 should be rendered **say to the people of the land** (i.e., referring to the exiles; so also in NRSV), or ***say of the people of the land*** (i.e., referring to those in Jerusalem), but the context suggests the former. If so, Ezekiel here uses a technical designation known from elsewhere in the OT that reminds the reader of the identity of the deportees. The **people of the land** in some contexts carries the technical meaning of the land owner class in Judean society and reminds Ezekiel's readers that the exiles of 597 had primarily consisted of these upper levels of Jerusalem's social classes (Hals 1989, 80; Block 1997, 382; Darr 2001, 1196).

To those who had the status of relative social privilege during their life before deportation, this second sign-act once again aims to convince them of the finality of Yahweh's coming judgment on the city and society that had previously given them their identity. The force of this message is highlighted by the switch to direct second person plural address to the exiles at the close of v 20. By means of the divine judgment and destruction of Jerusalem, **you [pl.] will know that I am the** LORD. Hence, Ezekiel's second symbolic act provides another theological interpretation of the traumatic events experienced by the people, thereby leading those searching for understanding to the acknowledgment of Yahweh's sovereignty and design.

■ **21-25** Another instance of the prophetic word formula (see vv 1, 8, 17, 26) in v 21 marks the transition from the reports of symbolic acts to two "disputations" or "dispute oracles" that constitute the remainder of the chapter (vv 21-25, 26-28). As noted above, these oracles complement the symbolic acts by offering further elaboration concerning the power and relevance of the prophetic words that Ezekiel has been instructed to proclaim to his fellow exiles. The disputation genre typically includes a common saying of the people and a response by a divine or human figure that alters, challenges, or rejects the popular understanding (see Hals 1989, 81). In the first disputation (vv 21-25), Yahweh queries Ezekiel concerning a **proverb** (Heb., *māšāl*) that is circulating among the people (v 22). The label *māšāl* designates a variety of types of material in the OT, including parables, allegories, and instructional speeches, yet Ezekiel seems to use it here with the basic sense of a traditional saying that is popular within a culture or community (Darr 2001, 1197). Interpreters remain divided over whether the popular sayings in vv 22 and 27 were being promulgated by the exiles, the people remaining in Jerusalem, or both. Some suggest the proverb in vv 21-25 was popular among the Jerusalemites and the saying in vv 26-28 represents the exiles' point of view (Block 1997, 387; Darr 2001, 1198). Others conclude that both sayings constitute sentiments current among Ezekiel's fellow exiles (Odell 2005, 141). The text does not permit a firm conclusion, and the sentiments expressed would likely be at home among both groups, especially given the apparent personal and ideological connections between the groups that the prophet continually challenges with his calls for the exiles to break their attachment to their old city and identity.

Both common sayings seem to express popular disillusionment or even cynicism about the reliability of prophetic proclamations concerning Israel. Standing as they do immediately after Ezekiel's symbolic acts in vv 1-20, the people's expressions illustrate their continued blindness and deafness to the nature and meaning of Yahweh's acts in the world (see vv 1-2). The proverb in v 22 expresses the sentiment that prophetic predictions like those of Ezekiel have no force because they simply go unfulfilled, as **the days go by and every vision comes to nothing.** The saying's use of the term **vision** is especially relevant, as Ezekiel's prophetic message as a whole is dominated by major visions concerning Yahweh's glory/presence and its relationship to the past, present, and future state of the people (see chs 1—3; 8—11; 37; 40—48). In the present context, the saying's most direct referent is the Jerusalem vision reported in chs 8—11. If this proverb was circulating among the people in Jerusalem, it suggests a cynical indifference or defiant rejection of messages that expose their sinfulness and announce a coming judgment (see Zimmerli 1979, 284; Block 1997, 387-88). If the saying was circulating among Ezekiel's fellow exiles, it perhaps expresses a regretful skepticism born out of disillusionment and disappointment (see Greenberg 1983, 227). As the oracle against the false prophets in ch 13 will indicate, the exiles had heard and continued to hear numerous, sometimes competing, prophecies, many of which announced some sort of deliverance for which they should hope, yet none of which had materialized over the course of nearly a decade.

In response to the people's proverb, Yahweh instructs Ezekiel to issue a rebuttal that expresses the exact opposite sentiment: **the days are near when every vision will be fulfilled** (v 23). The delay in the fulfillment, Yahweh asserts, has not been due to the unreliability of the prophetic word but due to the timing of Yahweh's plan and work in the world. Now, however, the time of preparation is nearing an end, and Yahweh's holiness/sovereignty is about to manifest itself fully. The time is near when Yahweh will silence the propagation of all **false visions** (v 24) and bring about the fulfillment of his own words **without delay** (v 25).

■ **26-28** The second disputation concerning a popular saying also begins with the prophetic word formula and Yahweh's instructions to Ezekiel (vv 26-27). The text identifies the source of the saying with the general title **house of Israel,** and the sentiment makes sense on the lips of both the Jerusalemites and the exiles. The saying asserts that Ezekiel's prophetic visions relate only to **many years from now** in **the distant future** (v 27). On the lips of the Jerusalemites, the saying deflects the accusation of sin and the warning of judgment as something meant for another generation. On the lips of the exiles, however, the saying once again takes on a tone of disillusionment and disappointment. For this audience, the **vision** that they see as only for the future may well be that of their restoration (e.g., 11:14-21). Faced with the inability to integrate their trauma into a larger plot line, the exiles lament the possibility of actually experiencing any of the future divine restoration for themselves. Such pessimism may also have been present among the second generation of readers of the book of Ezekiel, those who knew the outcome of the prophecies of destruction on Jerusalem and now wondered about the continuing relevance of Ezekiel's promises for a later community (Odell 2005, 141-42). As in the first disputation, Yahweh's response is a succinct but forceful rebuttal that none of the prophetic words **will be delayed any longer** (v 28).

The concern over the reliability of the prophetic word that stands at the heart of the two disputations in ch 12 provides a transition to the condemnations of false prophets in ch 13. As Judah's story moves toward the siege and deportation depicted by Ezekiel's symbolic acts, the people's prophets fail to offer true words from Yahweh, and thus Judah faces the coming trauma without any meaningful intercession or counsel.

2. Explanatory Oracle: Lack of True Prophets (13:1-23)

Chapter 13 begins the first of two oracles in which Ezekiel denounces the lack of true intercession for the people of Judah during the days of their sin and rebellion. In the same way that chs 4—7 move from the prophet's symbolic actions (chs 4—5) to accompanying oracles (chs 6—7), ch 13 constitutes the first explanatory oracle that elaborates on the symbolic acts described in ch 12. Ezekiel's discourse here consists of two oracles against false prophets: 13:1-16 addressing male prophets and vv 17-23 addressing female prophets (see Behind the Text). The text is not explicit about where these prophets are located, simply designating them as **prophets of Israel** (v 2). Given the content of their messages, it is likely that they are prophets active in supporting the Jerusalem community between 597 and 586 B.C., although some commentators suggest the group of male prophets may represent those in Jerusalem, while the female prophets may be active among the exiles (Darr 2001, 1192).

12:26—
13:23

One can certainly imagine the sentiments attributed to these prophets as having been present in both communities. For Ezekiel, the falsehood of their message, especially that of the male prophets in vv 1-16, lies in the fact that they say destruction will not come upon Judah, but **peace** and security will prevail (see v 10). Juxtaposing these prophets with the mention of the "prince" in ch 12 suggests an overtly political interpretation of the prophetic conflict (see Odell 2005, 145). Ezekiel's targets here are perhaps royal prophets who were active in supporting Zedekiah's plans for rebellion against Babylonia with promises of divine approval and success (compare Jeremiah's conflict in Jer 28—29, where two such prophets are named, Hananiah and Shemaiah). Once again, Ezekiel's theo-political concerns show through, as these prophets are accused not of being non-Yahwistic but of advocating a political policy that lies outside of Yahweh's plans for the people. Even so, as we will see, the primary aspect of these prophets' behavior that brings them in for condemnation is not the simple untruthfulness of their message but their failure of responsibility and impure intentions (Hals 1989, 87). These prophets preach with the intent to give a false sense of security, rather than to provide the people with a theological understanding of Yahweh's purposes and acts in the world.

a. Condemnation of Male Prophets (13:1-16)

■ **1-3** The denunciation of the male prophets begins with Yahweh's instructions to Ezekiel in vv 1-3. The typical beginning with the prophetic word formula (**the word of the LORD came to me** [v 1]) and the messenger formula (**this is what the Sovereign LORD says** [v 3]) takes on a new force in the present oracle. In this context dominated by the question of who speaks truthfully for Yahweh, the text emphasizes that Ezekiel's words come as a direct mandate and message from Yahweh. By contrast, the divine instructions in vv 1-3 identify the central problem with the prophets that Ezekiel is to address as the fact that they do not receive a vision or message from Yahweh, but **prophesy out of their own imagination** (lit., **heart;** Heb., *lēb*) and **follow their own spirit** (vv 2-3). Readers of Ezekiel immediately notice the contrast between the character of these prophets' experiences and the way in which Yahweh's Spirit has been actively involved with, and even serving as the agent of motion for, Ezekiel throughout the course of his ministry (e.g., 2:2; 3:12; 8:3; 11:1).

The discussion of ch 11 highlighted that the Hebrew term "heart" (*lēb*) represents the seat of decision-making, reason, and will in ancient conceptions of the human person. Hence, the use of **heart** and **spirit** here suggests that these prophets formulate their messages out of their own reasoning, ability, and critical assessment of the situation, rather than out of divine direction. The use of such reasoning was a part of the task of all ancient prophets, even those such as Jeremiah and Ezekiel, as they functioned as rhetorical orators aiming to persuade their audiences in particular circumstances (see Behind the Text). But the accusation here seems to assert that these prophets have not subjected their own reasoning and ability to Yahweh's direction and sovereignty, and thus they do not see clearly the meaning of Yahweh's ways in the world. We should probably conclude that the fault of these prophets lies not with an intentional deception in their messages but with a failure to discern rightly. That is, in all likelihood, these spokespersons believed in the genuineness of their message (note that they wait expectantly for "their words to be fulfilled" [v 6]), and the accusation made against them is that they have failed to perceive Yahweh's leading and arrived at the incorrect conclusion concerning the meaning of Yahweh's work and the fate of Judah's people.

■ **4-7** The next verses outline the problematic actions carried out by the prophets as a result of the faulty character of their messages. Throughout the accusation as a whole, the text switches back and forth between third person description of the prophets and direct, second person address to the prophets themselves (second person: vv 5, 7, 8; third person: vv 3, 4, 6, 9). In so doing, it outlines how the prophets' actions have been especially harmful to the welfare of their own people. In addition to offering their false messages (vv 6-7), the prophets have, on the one hand, acted **like jackals** among their own people (v 4). The metaphor here draws upon the imagery of jackals as scavengers who move among the ruined and barren places. In the same way, these prophets, with their uninspired words of false security, have preyed upon the ruin and devastation that their people have experienced over the last decade.

On the other hand, the prophets have failed to carry out one of the most crucial tasks of the prophetic role, namely, they have not interceded on the people's behalf in order to strengthen them during these days. The text presents this accusation with the imagery of a dilapidated city wall that the prophets have failed to fortify: **you have not gone up to the breaks in the wall to repair it** (v 5). This language parallels that in Ps 106:23, where Israel's doxological tradition remembers Moses as one who "stood in the breach" to intercede for Israel and turn away Yahweh's wrath. For the tradition articulated in Deuteronomy, Moses stands as the paradigm for the prophetic role in Israel (see Deut 18:15), and such intercession through speaking words of truth forms a crucial part of the prophetic task. By contrast, these prophets fail to meet the standard of prophetic identity. As a result, Yahweh says, Israel is not prepared to stand **in the battle on the day of the LORD** (v 5). The phrase **day of the LORD** has a technical meaning throughout the prophetic books, marking the time when Yahweh's judgment will fall upon the people (see, e.g., Amos 5:18-24). Ezekiel's own preaching has consistently emphasized that Judah's judgment at the hands of the Babylonians is imminent, and yet the people's own prophets have failed to communicate Yahweh's purposes and left them unprepared to deal with the coming events.

■ **8-16** The transitional word **therefore** in v 8 marks the shift from the accusations against the male prophets to the announcement of divine judgment that is to come upon them (vv 8-16). The passage continues to alternate between third person description and second person direct address to the false prophets, often recapitulating the accusations of their wrongdoing through misleading the people by proclaiming **peace** and false security rather than divine judgment and its meaning within Yahweh's larger plan (see vv 8-10; see the similar condemnations of prophets in Jer 6:14; 8:11; 14:3-13; 23:17; 28:9).

In a construction that reflects previous expressions that Yahweh will become an enemy against his own people (e.g., 5:8; 6:14), the first stage of divine judgment is that Yahweh's **hand will be against the prophets** (v 9). This

13:4-16

outstretched hand will effect three particular punishments. Yahweh will exclude the prophets from **the council of my people, ... the records of the house of Israel,** and **the land of Israel** (v 9). The exact referents of these designations remain unclear, yet each of them seems to connote some kind of political status or position that is stripped away from the prophets (Odell 2005, 148). **The council of my people,** a designation that is unique to Ezekiel, suggests a group of close advisers, perhaps serving the king, within which the prophets functioned as counselors concerning social and political decisions (see, e.g., Isaiah's role with King Ahaz in Isa 7). While these prophets may have contributed their message of false security to the inner circle of King Zedekiah, Yahweh announces that they will be excluded from the group that will shape Israel's future when restoration occurs. The remaining two designations exclude the prophets from increasingly wider groups, moving next to the "citizenship roll" of the kingdom, and finally to residence in the land itself (Zimmerli 1979, 294). As is common in Ezekiel's rhetoric, the conclusion of v 9 reports the imagined result of this divine judgment with the recognition formula: **Then you will know that I am the Sovereign Lord.** The text remains ambiguous as to whether it is the false prophets who will come to acknowledge Yahweh's sovereignty when they experience these things, or Ezekiel's exilic audience whose recognition of Yahweh's lordship will increase when they witness these acts of judgment on those who have proclaimed a message of peace and security.

Verses 10-16 introduce the dominant image of Yahweh's description of the prophets' deeds and the judgment to come upon them, an image that returns in some fashion to the wall metaphor of vv 4-5. Yahweh likens the false prophets to shoddy builders who fail to fortify properly the protective wall built by the people. More specifically, Yahweh compares the prophets' actions to those who take the people's **flimsy wall** and simply **cover it with whitewash** (v 10). The language here envisions an unfinished wall of piled stones that has not been constructed with mortar between the stones or covered with a plaster or mud seal to protect against the weather (Odell 2005, 149). Rather than providing the kind of mortar and seal that can help the wall stand against destructive forces, these shoddy builders simply apply **whitewash,** perhaps a thin layer that merely improves appearance (Zimmerli 1979, 287), or a poorly made plaster missing key ingredients (Greenberg 1983, 237). The metaphor is transparent but operates on various levels. Perhaps the prophets should have exposed the faultiness of the people's current social, political, and religious life, or perhaps they should have interceded to try to bring about change that could spare the people from destruction. In either case, their message of false peace and security has simply covered over Judah's sin and rebellion and left the people vulnerable to divine judgment. As a result, Yahweh concludes his pronouncement with repeated first person emphasis (**I will send** [v 11]; **I will unleash** [v 13]; **I will tear down** [v 14]), declaring that his judgment will come like a storm that will destroy the shoddy wall and those who covered it with whitewash, leading once again to the demonstration of his sovereignty (vv 11-16).

b. Condemnation of Female Prophets (13:17-23)

■ **17** With the reference to the **daughters of your people who prophesy out of their own imagination** (*lēb*; v 17; cf. v 2), Yahweh directs Ezekiel to turn the focus of his accusations to female prophets and their activity among the people. As noted above, this passage (vv 17-23) is the second section that offers an accusation followed by a pronouncement of judgment (see vv 1-16). We have observed that female prophets are well attested as a historical reality from an early date in the ancient Near East in general and ancient Israel in particular (see Behind the Text). It is significant to note in this context that Ezekiel's condemnatory language for these prophets mirrors that directed at the male prophets in vv 1-16. The gender of these female prophets plays no role in the reason for their condemnation.

■ **18-19** The text provides the specific accusations and reasons for judgment against the female prophets in the form of a woe oracle. The exact actions attributed to the women remain unclear, however, as some of the key Hebrew terms are uncertain in their meaning (see Block 1997, 413-14). The description probably communicated clearly to a more familiar audience, but in general terms the prophets' inappropriate behavior involves several practices: sewing something (**magic charms;** "bands" [NRSV]) for the arms, making something (**veils**? bonnets?) for people's heads, causing the death of undeserving people, and keeping alive those who do not deserve to be spared. A long tradition in scholarship, still occasionally manifest today, has labeled these women as sorcerers and associated their actions with magic rituals, especially connected with the consultation of the spirits of the dead (note the NIV's translation **magic charms** in vv 18, 20; see also Zimmerli 1979, 296; Hals 1989, 86; Block 1997, 410; Darr 2001, 1203). Yet, as Odell (2005, 144) has recently observed, the text does not associate their actions with the kinds of sorcery that are condemned elsewhere in the OT (e.g., Deut 18:10), and their actions are generally in line with the typical prophetic practices of visions and divination.

Scholarship's impulse to identify these women as sorcerers may, in fact, have its origins in a perhaps unconscious gender bias that negatively labels women's religious leadership and practice as "other" and fails to appreciate the prevalence of legitimate women prophets in the ancient world and the OT literature. The available evidence for such prophetic activity suggests that female religious professionals in ancient Israel often served in roles associated with medical practices, especially health services related to childbirth and other sicknesses (see Bowen 1999; Gafney 2008). This evidence, along with the text's reference to actions involving who lives and dies, suggests that we should perhaps understand the women described in ch 13 as using implements such as armbands and head coverings in ceremonies related to healing practices (Odell 2005, 151).

Even though these female prophets may have functioned within the accepted practices of Yahwistic religion, Ezekiel draws upon priestly theology and labels their actions as serving to ***profane/defile*** (*ḥll*) the holy reputation of Yahweh among the people (v 19). The book's consistent connection of Yahweh's holiness and reputation to the notion of divine sovereignty suggests the possibility that the prophet condemns the women's actions because they usurp Yahweh's sovereignty over the granting of life and death and subvert Yahweh's determinative view of justice in which the righteous are allowed to live but the wicked perish (Zimmerli 1979, 299; Odell 2005, 151). In a book dominated by an uncompromising conviction in Yahweh's sovereign control of the fate of the righteous and wicked, these actions represent a challenge to divine holiness.

■ **20-23** As in the address concerning the male prophets in v 8, the transitional word **therefore** in v 20 marks the change from the accusations to the punishment to come upon the female prophets. At its most basic level, Yahweh declares that he will take away the things that the prophets use to carry out their acts and ensure that they no longer experience **false visions or practice divination** (v 23). Accordingly, even these prophets will come to acknowledge Yahweh's sovereignty (**you will know that I am the Lord** [vv 21, 23]). The declaration of punishment, however, contains an unusual assertion for Ezekiel. Yahweh says he will take these actions so as to **save my people from your hands** (vv 21, 23). As we have seen, Ezekiel's rhetoric throughout the book has consistently disavowed any such concern on Yahweh's part to rescue those remaining in Jerusalem from the coming judgment. Moreover, Yahweh's repeated designation of the victims in this passage as **my people** (vv 18, 19, 21, 23) implies an intimate connection between Yahweh and the Jerusalemites that is not in evidence in the book's general interpretation of Judah's circumstances. Perhaps this text offers a different (inconsistent?) nuance in Ezekiel's theological understanding. Yet the nature of these references may also suggest that the women prophets addressed here were active not in Jerusalem (like the male prophets in vv 1-16) but among the exiles, the ones that Yahweh has identified as the community through which Judah's future restored life with Yahweh will unfold (so Darr 2001, 1192).

3. Explanatory Oracle: Lack of True Intercession (14:1-23)

Along with the preceding condemnation of false prophets, ch 14 constitutes the second of two oracles in which Ezekiel denounces the lack of true intercession for the people of Judah during the days of their sin and coming destruction, which were starkly depicted through the symbolic acts in ch 12. One can imagine the concern for the possibility of successful intercession being palpable, even among Ezekiel's fellow exiles, who still do not yet seem to have fully broken with their old identity or completely understood the nature of Yahweh's plan for Jerusalem's present and future. Chapter 14 opens, in fact, with Ezekiel's report that **the elders of Israel** once again came to inquire of him (v 1; see also 8:1; 20:1). As in ch 8, the text does not specify the content of their inquiry, but the balance of the chapter suggests that, perhaps in light of Ezekiel's acts and oracles depicting siege and condemning false prophecy, they inquire about the possibility of intercession before Yahweh that would alter their present circumstances and Jerusalem's future fate.

Seen in this light, the first section (vv 1-11) seems to focus primarily on the possibility of divine intercession on behalf of Ezekiel's fellow exiles. It offers a divine response to the general case of whether sinful people can successfully inquire of Yahweh through a prophetic mediator. Implicitly, the text states that no intercession is possible because of the sinfulness of those seeking intercession and the ways they have defiled Yahweh's holiness. If, however, they break with their former identity, Yahweh will open the possibility of a new future. The second section (vv 12-23) maintains the impossibility of intercession but offers a slightly different perspective, focusing more upon the Jerusalemite community remaining in the land between 597 and 586 B.C. The section asserts that the people have so defiled Yahweh's land and presence that even the most righteous persons are no longer able to intercede and turn away judgment. Taken together, these two sections make the point that there can be no intercession for Jerusalem; judgment is a decisive part of Yahweh's plan, but it stands within the larger divine purposes of validating Yahweh's holiness and purifying the community for the future.

a. No Intercession for the Sinful (14:1-11)

■ **1-5** Following the report that certain **elders of Israel** (v 1) came to seek Ezekiel's counsel, the prophet uses the prophetic word formula (**the word of the LORD came to me** [v 2]) to announce a divine condemnation on idolatry and a refusal by Yahweh to be consulted. The reference to **these men** (v 3), which apparently refers back to the **elders** in v 1, suggests that Ezekiel once again includes the exiles in those who share the culpability for the sinfulness of Judah and the judgment to come upon Jerusalem (see 12:1-3). Even though they are in exile and Yahweh's future plans revolve around them, the deportees apparently remain wedded to their former identity centered in Jerusalem.

Specifically, Yahweh condemns the exilic inquirers because they have **set up idols** [*gillûlîm*] **in their hearts** (v 3). The language, which again employs Ezekiel's derogatory term for idols as "dung pellets" (see commentary on 6:1-10), may indicate an internalizing of idols in which the people have committed their devotion to these objects (Zimmerli 1979, 306-7; Block 1997, 425). Yet one may also understand this statement as a reference to cultic objects worn by worshippers or ritual practices performed even as worship of Yahweh (Odell 2005, 159-60). As the description of the activities in the temple in 8:7-13 suggests, the use of images and objects as mediators for intercession was likely a well-established part of Yahweh worship in Jerusalem before 586 B.C. In this text, however, Yahweh declares that the very objects the people have used for intercession before Yahweh ironically call into question the very possibility of such intercession. Moreover, throughout vv 1-11, the passage describes the people's sinful actions with priestly terminology such as **detestable practices** (v 6; *abominations;* Heb., *tôʿēbôt*) and "defile" (v 11; Heb., *tmʾ*), interpreting them not simply as inappropriate deeds but as polluting acts that contaminate Yahweh's holy presence among the people.

The messenger formula in v 4 (**This is what the Sovereign LORD says**) marks the beginning of the divine response to the question of the possibility of intercession before Yahweh for those guilty of idolatry. The language takes the form of a hypothetical legal case that resembles the style and terminology found in the laws of the Holiness Code in Lev 17—26. Several parts of this code, such as Lev 17, address the necessity of uncompromised devotion to Yahweh (see Hals 1989, 90-92). In this vein, v 4 presents a generic case (**when any Israelite**) concerning whether a sinful/idolatrous person can successfully receive intercession that allows him or her to inquire of Yahweh. Perhaps surprisingly, the divine statement asserts that any idolater who seeks Yahweh through a prophet will indeed receive an answer (v 5; but cf. Odell 2005, 161-63). Significantly, however, the text at this point does not indicate the nature of that divine response. Rather, Yahweh declares that his response, whatever form it is revealed to be, will serve the larger purpose to **recapture the hearts of the** sinful **people** (v 5), a phrase that resonates with the book's recurring statement that the divine actions of judgment to come upon Judah will lead the people to "know that I am the LORD" (see v 8).

■ **6-8** Before revealing the nature of the divine response, Yahweh interrupts his presentation of the legal case and instructs Ezekiel to call the people to **repent** and **turn from** their **idols** and **detestable practices** (*abominations*), which, in the priestly conception, defile Yahweh's holiness among the people (v 6). For the first time in the book, the prophet offers a direct call for repentance as an appeal for change among his audience. Although rare, the presence of such an appeal in this context hints at some measure of hope for Ezekiel's fellow exiles who will break with their former identity, as it implicitly offers a perspective that identifies the trauma of their sin and judgment as only one part of a larger divine movement toward purification and restoration (Darr 2001, 1207).

Verses 7-8 reveal the urgency of the prophetic call for repentance in v 6. Yahweh resumes the hypothetical legal case but now shows the nature of the divine response to sinful idolaters who seek intercession. Ironically, sinners who attempt to come before Yahweh without turning away from their defiling practices will receive a direct divine answer, but it will be a hostile word of judgment. The response, Yahweh asserts, will be to **set my face against** the sinner and **cut him off** from the future congregation of Yahweh's **people** (v 8). The language here reflects that of Yahweh's instructions to Ezekiel in the symbolic act concerning judgment on Jerusalem in 4:3, with the phrase "set [the] face against" representing a symbolic gesture of opposition and hostility (see Lev 26:17). The language also reflects that of the covenantal punishments in many of Leviticus's priestly and holiness laws, in which to be cut off/put out of the community is a prescribed punishment for sin that threatens the community (e.g., Lev 17:14; 18:29; 19:8). In keeping with one of the book's themes, Yahweh's direct address at the end of Ezek 14:9 ("you [pl.] will know that I am the Sovereign LORD") presents the intended effect that this judgment will have among the exiles, presumably on the ones who heeded the call to turn away from their former identity (v 6).

■ **9-11** The same goal of securing the acknowledgment of divine sovereignty attends to Yahweh's first person address in vv 9-11. In a manner that is typical for the case law material in the OT, these verses introduce a "subcase" into the larger legal issue (Hals 1989, 92). Yahweh's words reiterate the earlier judgment against the false prophets and those who seek intercession through them (13:1-16). Unlike ch 13, however, which attributes the prophets' false messages of hope to their own machinations, the text here asserts the total sovereign control of Yahweh, as he claims that he is responsible for deceiving the false prophets (14:9; see 1 Kgs 22). While such a claim creates some problems concerning Yahweh's character and integrity, we have observed that it provides a powerful reframing of the chaotic and meaning-denying experiences of trauma and exile. When read within that context, these verses affirm that Yahweh will remove these false prophets so that his future community will, in priestly terms, no longer **defile themselves** (*tm'*) with actions that pollute Yahweh's holiness, but will be drawn into a newly constituted covenant relationship between Yahweh and people (Ezek 14:11).

b. No Intercession by the Righteous (14:12-23)

The prophetic word formula in v 12 begins a new section of Yahweh's address to Ezekiel that continues the theme of the impossibility of successful intercession but from a different perspective. In this section, the focus shifts from those in exile with Ezekiel to those who remain in Jerusalem under Zedekiah. Whereas in vv 1-11 the text asserts that the sinfulness of those who seek intercession for themselves prohibits their ability to achieve it, vv 12-23 indicate that Judah's sinfulness has become so great that even the most righteous individuals are now unable to intercede effectively. To make that point, Yahweh's speech begins in vv 12-20 with another general and hypothetical case of any sinful land, and then turns in vv 21-23 to apply the scenario described directly to Jerusalem.

■ **12-20** The general test case of a sinful land that is **unfaithful** to Yahweh presents four hypothetical divine judgments that Yahweh might send upon such a land: **famine** (v 13), ravaging animals (v 15), **sword** (v 17), and **plague** (v 19). These punishments are archetypal judgments known from elsewhere in the OT, specifically in the context of divine curses that result from the violation of the covenant in the Holiness Code (see Lev 26:22-26). They have also appeared previously in Ezekiel's speeches about the judgment to come upon Jerusalem (see 4:16; 5:12, 16, 17). In the present context, each of the judgments is interwoven with references to three persons who function as archetypal righteous individuals: **Noah, Daniel and Job** (vv 14, 20). In the case of each potential judgment, Yahweh concludes that even these three righteous figures would be unable to intercede successfully for the kind of sinful and unfaithful land under consideration in the general scenario. The imagery here draws upon the OT tradition of righteous individuals interceding on behalf of other persons and groups (e.g., Abraham at Sodom in Gen 18; Moses in Exod 32—33 and Ps 106:23; Samuel in 1 Sam 7).

The figures of **Noah** and **Job,** as represented in their stories elsewhere in the OT, are non-Israelites who intercede to save a group of others (Noah saves a remnant; Job intercedes first for his children and then for his three friends). Problems attend, however, to identifying Ezekiel's reference to **Daniel** with the character known from the OT book of Daniel. The Hebrew text does not give the name "Daniel" as it is spelled in the OT book by that name, but reads "Dan'el," the name of a non-Israelite figure who appears in extrabiblical texts from Ugarit dating to the fourteenth century B.C., and whose name occurs again in Ezek 28:3. The "Dan'el" known from these texts is an archetypal wise person who successfully prays for a son and then tries to intercede on his behalf after his sudden death (see sidebar "Dan'el and the Aqhat Legend"). The story of this figure apparently circulated throughout the area in ancient times. The biblical book of Daniel presents Daniel as a contemporary of those in exile, although the vast majority of scholars see the book of Daniel as having been written significantly later in the Hellenistic period. It is unlikely that the Daniel figure presented in the biblical traditions had achieved status as a legendary wise person by the time of Ezekiel. Accordingly, virtually all recent commentators conclude that Ezekiel draws upon the Ugaritic tradition of Dan'el, a third non-Israelite figure who intercedes on behalf of another person (e.g., Zimmerli 1979, 314; Darr 2001, 1213; Odell 2005, 165; cf. Block 1997, 447-49; see the text note in NIV). Seen in this way, these three figures highlight the gravity of the sinful land's situation even more. All three figures not only are archetypal righteous individuals but are known for their ability to intercede with the divine specifically on behalf of their children. Yet, Yahweh asserts in this context that even if these three were present in the faithless land, they would only be able to save themselves.

Dan'el and the Aqhat Legend

The figure of Daniel or Dan'el mentioned in 14:14, 20 and 28:3 is probably not Daniel known from the biblical tradition but a wise king named Dan'el known from the extrabiblical tradition called the Legend of Aqhat. The text was discovered among written remains at the city of Ugarit (modern Ras Shamra) in northern Syria and dates to the fourteenth century B.C. The legend tells the story of King Dan'el, who prays for and receives a son named Aqhat. When the son is grown, a certain goddess kills him, and Dan'el attempts to intercede in order to bring him back or retrieve his remains. King Dan'el became a legendary figure of righteousness and wisdom, whose story circulated throughout ancient Syria-Palestine and may have influenced the composition of the OT books of Ezekiel and Daniel.

14:12-23

■ **21-23** The messenger formula in v 21 marks a new section in which the text applies the hypothetical case of the sinful land and its inescapable punishment (vv 12-20) directly to the current situation of **Jerusalem** in Ezekiel's time. Although some interpreters consider this final section to be a later update to Ezekiel's words, especially since it seems to move away from the picture of total destruction envisioned in vv 12-20, in its present form Yahweh's pronouncement gives a clear expression of the motive and meaning for the destruction that the people of Judah have suffered and will continue to suffer. Jerusalem will suffer the standard punishments for covenant breaking, but some **survivors** will come to join those already in exile (v 22). For Ezekiel's audience of exiles, their observation of these events, especially their firsthand encounter with the sinfulness of those former Jerusalemites who survive, will finally yield understanding of what has happened. Those in exile seeking understanding of the meaning of the past, present, and future (see 14:1) will realize not only that Yahweh did these things, but that his actions were not **without cause** (v 23). Literally, the Hebrew phrase here denotes actions that were taken "not undeservedly" or "not gratuitously." Ezekiel once again speaks to the people's need to deal with the trauma they are experiencing and witnessing, a need to find ways to render the trauma of destruction and deportation comprehensible. Yahweh's words in this text assert that the trauma has not been senseless or gratuitous. Rather, it is an outworking of the people's own unfaithfulness and stands as part of Yahweh's larger actions concerning his own sovereignty and holiness.

FROM THE TEXT

The symbolic acts and explanatory oracles in chs 12—14 move the reader progressively through various aspects of Jerusalem's future judgment and its causes and significance. Ezekiel provides explicit pictures of the siege and exile that is to come upon the people and city and offers oracles that elaborate on previous and current social and theological conditions among both the exiles and Jerusalemites that have contributed to the present circumstances.

The references to the people's blindness at the beginning of ch 12, taken within the context of trauma presumed by the book, illustrate once more that the experience of trauma can blind even believers to the ways and work of God in the world. The text explicitly links the blindness and deafness of the exiles to their rebellious nature. Even so, the traumatic experience of destruction and exile has further blinded the people to the correct perception of the exile. As trauma theory indicates, a traumatized person or community often struggles particularly with the reception of the events and experiences that have been destructive or disorienting. In a similar manner, Ezekiel sees the exiles as an initially rebellious people, but also as a community that continues to be rebellious, perhaps even more rebellious after that initial rebellion, largely because they now fail to perceive the proper theological meaning of their experiences within the context of the work of God's holiness in the world. The prophet sees the people as directly responsible for the initial rebelliousness that led to judgment, yet also seemingly acknowledges the ongoing effect of blindness (willful or not) that may be caused by traumatic experience.

In the same way, the experience of traumatic loss or suffering even for victims who are in no way responsible for that trauma can, at times, render them unable to see beyond the trauma to the nature of God's presence and work in their lives and the reality of God's ongoing vision for the world. In much the same way as Ezekiel's symbolic actions in ch 12 addressed his traumatized audience, those of us who find ourselves in the midst of trauma may need to work for ways to create space in which others can speak a word that offers a new perspective within which we might view that trauma, even as we must refuse the temptation to deny the trauma's reality. By the same token, we may open ourselves to the recognition of the role of trauma in the blindness that we so often readily identify in others, perhaps offering ourselves as one who could be in their midst and gesture toward a vision of God's ways and work. In either case, the people's inability to hear the prophetic words as relevant for their own situation at the end of ch 12 reminds us that we must often resist the temptation to dismiss words given to us as being relevant only for other persons and circumstances, a temptation that overlooks the very present ways that God may speak, even through exile or the words of a fellow sufferer.

On another level, the connection between the motif of blindness and the people's rebelliousness in chs 12 and 14 also points to how our own habits and practices may blind us to the ways of God in the world, even apart from the experience of trauma. Ezekiel reflects on the ways that the people's rebelliousness is not simply limited to religious beliefs and practices, but characterizes their ideologies and courses of actions in the political and social realms, as well. In the prophet's view, these elements contribute to the people's inability to understand God's character and actions in the world. As one recent commentator has suggested, this very perspective pushes us to ask how our habits, practices, and ideologies make us blind, often without our recognition, to God's character and ways (Odell 2005, 144). Are there political ideologies, social-economic convictions, and cultural values that have become so ingrained among the people of God that they no longer allow us to see clearly the character of God and the ways that character would manifest itself in life and society?

As one reflects on the need to perceive correctly God's ways in the world, the condemnation of the false prophets in ch 13 highlights the perennial difficulty of discerning authentic voices speaking for God in the midst of a cacophony of voices claiming to do so. As noted in the Behind the Text section, the struggle to identify true and false prophetic messages was a palpable issue in ancient Israel, especially in times of trauma, when the people attempted to understand the meaning of the present and God's role in it. In these circumstances, the people often heard competing words from prophets who all claimed to speak for the same God, just as did the prophets whom Ezekiel condemns in ch 13. The various texts of the OT that address this issue come to no clear conclusion and offer little help to contemporary readers, who often find themselves in need of the same kind of discernment. Odell has recently noted that the recognition that Ezekiel and the prophets he condemns offer different interpretations but stand within the same community of faith and speak for the same God raises the issue of how to think about the diversity of theological opinion and interpretation within contemporary believing communities (2005, 153-54). Clearly, she concludes, there is a need for a certain measure of unity, yet we should bear in mind the particular historical and rhetorical context of Ezekiel's hard-edged rejection of any diverse perspectives when considering the relevance of this issue for contemporary believing communities, especially for a climate in which certain perspectives are often marginalized or condemned in the interest of a particular version of "unity." The process of considering which theological perspectives are credible and appropriate is often more complex than the certitude expressed in Ezekiel's context, and, perhaps ironically, the dialogue among a variety of perspectives may be the most enriching for a community of faith.

Even so, the nature of Ezekiel's condemnations in ch 13 might provide a helpful specific insight into the question of discernment. As noted above, Ezekiel condemns these prophets not simply for the untruthfulness of their message, but more so for the irresponsibility and hurtful effects of their proclamations. *By asserting that these prophets' false words of hope and security make them into agents of harm for their community and bring them under divine judgment, this text highlights the accountability that attends to speaking words on behalf of God.* Ezekiel's words alert contemporary readers to the presence of those who speak in God's name, yet proclaim messages that do not reflect the character and ways of God in the world. In some cases, such "preaching" provides a message of exclusivism, violence, and authoritarianism, proclaiming condemnation from a position of power and offering a militant view of God's purposes and ways. In other cases, such messages receive their shape from political and social ideologies, such as industrialized capitalism, and conceal underlying structures of injustice and oppression beneath a thin "whitewash" of piety and civility (13:10). Much too easily, the self-assured proclamations of peace and prosperity or judgment and nationalism drown out God's prophetic calls for justice for the poor, the establishment of a nonexploitative economy, and care for the vulnerable and marginal. Ezekiel's critique in ch 13 reminds all readers of the accountability attached to words spoken on God's behalf, especially by those in positions of authority. As one commentator concludes, Ezekiel makes clear that "those who occupy positions of power will answer to God for the manner in which they exercised their authority" (Block 1997, 419).

B. Part 2: Metaphorical Discourses (15:1—17:24)

BEHIND THE TEXT

Chapters 15—17 form the second subsection within the larger unit of symbolic acts and oracles (chs 12—24) that follows the second vision of Yahweh's glory/presence (chs 8—11). These chapters constitute a well-defined collection of three metaphorical discourses. Chapters 15 and 17 revolve around the agricultural image of a vine as a representation of the people, while the lengthy centerpiece of ch 16 focuses on the city of Jerusalem in particular, using the often unsettling metaphor of a promiscuous woman to represent the capital city:

B. Part 2: Metaphorical Discourses (15:1—17:24)
    1. The Useless Vine (15:1-8)
    2. The Faithless Bride (16:1-63)
    3. The Two Eagles and the Vine (17:1-24)

Within the context of chs 12—24, the discourses in chs 15—17 continue Ezekiel's addresses to his fellow exiles during the final years leading up to the Babylonian destruction of Jerusalem in 586 B.C. They reiterate the prophet's overall message that the people's past and present existence has been characterized by rebellion against Yahweh. As with the preceding section, Ezekiel's discourses maintain a dual focus, at once describing words and actions related to the people remaining in Jerusalem under King Zedekiah and addressing the immediate audience of the exilic community in Babylonia. His primary concern is to provide the exiles with the proper theological understanding of the events that have occurred and will continue to occur in Jerusalem and to exhort them to break with their former identity bound up with the old Jerusalem and look to a new identity on the other side of Yahweh's coming judgment. Ezekiel makes use of the power of metaphor to offer a new perception of the past and future acts of Yahweh and the status of both the Jerusalemites and the exiles.

The first significant background aspect of chs 15—17 relates to the nature and function of metaphor. As we noted in the Introduction, the genre of metaphorical discourses stands alongside vision reports and symbolic actions as one of the three most prominent literary forms in Ezekiel's theological constructions. The book's heavy concentration of extended metaphorical discourses—about a dozen in various locations—is one of the distinguishing traits of the book among the OT prophets. Ezekiel's metaphors, perhaps rivaled only by Jeremiah's, are extended, complex, and often offensive in their language, with some narratives, such as that in ch 16, being nearly fifty or more verses long (see also ch 23).

The study of modern metaphor theory provides a helpful window into the nature and function of these discourses (see Moughtin-Mumby 2008; Durlesser 2006). Metaphors are not as straightforward as they may appear. They are frequently complex and indeterminate, producing a complicated range of possible meanings. In this way, metaphors serve to reshape the reader's or hearer's understanding of both the subject of the metaphorical expression and the image used to represent it. Metaphorical comparisons (e.g., Jerusalem is an unfaithful bride) depend upon common cultural understandings that are associated with both elements of the expression within a given social context. When two elements are brought together in a metaphorical expression (e.g., Jerusalem and adulterous woman), the associated cultural understandings interact to affect the audience's view of both elements and to produce a new meaning for the expression as a whole that goes beyond any literal meaning. As a result, metaphorical expressions always stand as parts of broader cultural conceptions and require knowledge of their cultural context for proper understanding (see Lakoff and Johnson 1980).

Most importantly for the interpretation of Ezekiel's metaphorical discourses is the relationship between metaphor and rhetoric. A metaphor is not simply a decorative way of expressing a literal statement but a type of linguistic "weapon" used to persuade an audience in a particular situation (Booth 1979). Metaphorical expressions persuade by reframing an audience's way of viewing reality and structuring experience, even dismantling previous understandings and constructing new perspectives (see Kelle 2005; Darr 2001, 1220; Newsom 1984). When seen in this way, Ezekiel's metaphorical discourses offer his audience new ways of perceiving the realities of their past, present, and future, traumatic realities including their own exile and the coming destruction of Jerusalem.

The second significant background aspect of this section involves the specific metaphor of the vine/vineyard employed in both chs 15 and 17. The vine is a common symbol for the people of Israel and Judah throughout the OT (as well as in some NT texts; e.g., Matt 20:1-16). It appears in a variety of contexts and with a diversity of meanings. The image gains its resonance from the importance of viticulture as a key element of the agrarian society of ancient Israel and Judah, yet the vine/vineyard appears as a metaphor with both positive and negative connotations in different texts' depictions of Yahweh's relationship with the people. Positively, vines symbolize peace and prosperity (see 1 Kgs 4:25; Mic 4:4), and Israel appears as Yahweh's special vine, planted and nurtured to fruitfulness (see Ps 80:8-11; Hos 10:1). Negatively, however, the vine can be a symbol of the people's failure to produce the kind of justice and righteousness that Yahweh expects, or an image of Yahweh's coming judgment in which the vine is uprooted from the ground (see Isa 5:1-7; Jer 2:21; Ezek 19:10-14).

The third significant background aspect of this section concerns the metaphor of a promiscuous woman/adulterous wife used to depict the city of Jerusalem in ch 16. This personification of Jerusalem is one of a set of texts in the OT prophets that employ marital and sexual metaphors to represent the relationship between Yahweh and some portion of the people, and most of these texts personify the capital cities of Samaria and Jerusalem in particular. Debate remains over whether these texts indicate the existence of a single, coherent marriage motif (the so-called prophetic marriage metaphor; see Moughtin-Mumby 2008), but they appear in significant numbers throughout the prophetic books (see Isa 1:8, 21-31; 23:1-18; 49:14-26; 50:1-3; Jer 2:2, 16-28*a*; 5:7-11; 49:3-6; Ezek 23:1-49; Hos 2; Amos 5:2; Mic 1:6-9; Nah 3:1-7). In these texts, Israelite and non-Israelite cities appear as wives, brides, mothers, and prostitutes. At the heart of these depictions is an ancient cultural understanding of marriage as a relationship between two unequal partners that may involve love and intimacy but also a high degree of exclusivity and jealousy akin to property ownership. Additionally, as ch 16 demonstrates, the language of these metaphorical depictions is often extreme, lewd, and offensive in its portrayals of female bodies, experiences, and sexuality. These kinds of marital and sexual metaphors have been misused over the years in ways that have been harmful to the lives of women and the relations between women and men. As one might expect, they have generated a substantial amount of analysis, particularly from perspectives concerned with gender studies (see Galambush 1992; Abma 1999; Baumann 2003; Yee 2003; Kelle 2005; Moughtin-Mumby 2008). The In the Text section below will examine the rhetorical function of the female metaphorization of Jerusalem in ch 16 in its literary and historical context, and the From the Text discussion that follows will consider the metaphor's possibilities and problems for contemporary readers.

The background of the female city metaphor, however, provides a necessary starting place for interpretation (see Kelle 2008). Much of the research on these depictions has focused on trying to uncover the possible mythological backgrounds (e.g., goddesses associated with capital cities; ancient Near Eastern city lament texts) that stand behind the OT's practice of personifying cities as females. While the origins of the imagery remain unclear, the available biblical and extrabiblical writings make it clear that there was a long-standing and widespread metaphorical tradition, evidenced throughout the ancient Near East, in which cities were personified as various types of female figures.

A close analysis of the female city texts in the OT prophets reveals some defining characteristics. First, prophetic personifications of cities as female appear exclusively in contexts that envision the destruction of the cities, even if that destruction takes the form of a threatened action or already existing condition (e.g., Isa 47:1-3; 54:1; 62:4; Jer 49:23-27; Mic 1:6-7). Additionally, when these texts describe the destruction of the personified city, they frequently employ the metaphorical language of physical and sexual violence against a woman (e.g., Isa 47:1-5; 52:1-2; Jer 13:22-27; Ezek 16; 23; Nah 3:1-7). Note, for instance, the imagery of the stripping and dismemberment of the "woman" Jerusalem in Ezek 16:39-41. In fact, the language of physical and sexual violence against women, which many readers rightly note as a point of concern in the prophetic books, appears only in these contexts that depict the destruction of a city that is personified as a woman (see the possible exceptions in Jer 3:1-13 and Hos 2; but cf. Kelle 2008, 99). Together, these characteristics suggest the important conclusion that the language of physical and sexual violence against women in prophetic texts such as chs 16 and 23 does not have established societal practices or accepted treatment of actual women in view but is conventional metaphorical language used in the ancient world to represent the destruction of cities. Even so, recognizing the ancient metaphorical conventions that stand behind these gendered texts does not remove the dangerous potential for the misuse of such language, nor the ways in which it reflects hierarchical worldviews in which women were thought of as subordinate and vulnerable to dominant males (see From the Text).

Perhaps the most important observation about the city personification texts in the prophets is that the female figure in such OT passages almost always personifies a *capital* city, especially, Samaria and Jerusalem. When combined with the other characteristics mentioned above, this particular focus on capital cities suggests that the cities themselves are symbols that represent the ruling houses and political elite who governed from these locales. Thus, the complete prophetic metaphor uses capital cities to represent the political rulers and then employs female figures to represent the capital cities. The prophetic metaphorization of cities as females, then, has the rhetorical effect of casting the political rulers, who were predominantly male, as vulnerable or faithless females, effectively feminizing the most powerful males in the society (see Yee 2003; Kelle 2005).

In the cultural context of ancient Judah, with its attachment of honor and shame connotations to the proper sexual behavior of women in particular, this metaphorical feminizing of the male ruling elite casts them in a negative light. The discourse symbolically depicts the male rulers as those who engage in behavior that was considered culturally to be repulsive, shameful, and worthy of punishment. By using such metaphorical portrayals, Ezekiel plays on the cultural mores of the day, which would have led people to want to disassociate from a woman who is unfaithful or promiscuous. He creates something of a populist discourse that advocates political, theological, and rhetorical distance between the general population and the political rulers. Hence, chs 16 and 23 not only present Jerusalem and its current leaders under Zedekiah in a new light, exposing them as unfaithful to Yahweh in every dimension, but also continue one of Ezekiel's central appeals, namely, that the people, especially his fellow exiles, should distance themselves from the old Jerusalem and the ways associated with it.

A final background aspect of chs 15—17 is the possibility that some parts of these chapters have undergone later editing or were added to the material in the years after Jerusalem's destruction. For example, some interpreters conclude that the hopeful sections in ch 16 (vv 53-63), which abruptly depart from the lengthier judgment sections, or the prose interpretive section in ch 17 (vv 11-21), which interrupts the chapter's poetic materials (vv 3-10, 22-24), may be later additions to the text (e.g., Zimmerli 1979, 334). Such suggestions remain speculative, however, and the discourses accomplish a significant rhetorical effect in their present form.

IN THE TEXT

I. The Useless Vine (15:1-8)

The speech in ch 15 begins a series of three metaphorical discourses (chs 15—17) that continue this portion of the book's focus on the people and circumstances in Jerusalem under King Zedekiah after 597 B.C., albeit with the ostensible aim of addressing the audience of Ezekiel's fellow exiles and offering an interpretation of the traumatic events of the recent past and immediate future. Each of the metaphorical discourses begins with the now familiar prophetic word formula ("The word of the LORD came to me") and Yahweh's designation of Ezekiel as "son of man" (15:1-2; 16:1-2; 17:1-2). Chapter 15 divides into the presentation of the metaphor (vv 2-5) and its interpretation (vv 6-8).

■ **1-5** Yahweh's speech reported by Ezekiel centers on the image of a **vine** (v 1). As noted above, the vine metaphor is at home in the viticulture of ancient Judah's agrarian society and appears with both positive and negative connotations in different OT texts' depictions of Yahweh's relationship with the people. In this instance, the prophet's metaphor uses the particular image of the **wood of a vine** (ʿēṣ hagepen) and its comparison to any other kind of **branch** (ʿēṣ hazĕmôrâ; lit., ***pruned wood***), that might be cut off from a tree. Rather than focusing on the grapevine as a whole or the fruit that it produces, which is more typical of the vine/vineyard metaphors in the OT (e.g., Isa 5:1-7), the image here is that of a vine branch that has been cut away from the vine itself.

The text develops the vine metaphor through a series of rhetorical questions in Ezek 15:2-5. The questions center on the issue of the wood's usefulness, and all of them are designed to elicit a negative response from the audience. From the opening sarcastic question in which Yahweh asks Ezekiel to say how the wood of the pruned vine branch is **better than** that of other kinds of wood (v 2), the rhetorical questions go on to make the point that the vine branch's wood is worthless for making **anything useful** (v 3). Verse 4 perhaps suggests that such wood is useful only to be burned for fuel. Even this usefulness remains uncertain, however, as the text may imply that the vine branch's wood only burns on the ends rather than throughout the whole and thus is not even useful for fuel (cf. Greenberg 1983, 268; Odell 2005, 175). In any case, the overall verdict is clear: unlike a vine branch that remains attached to its vine and produces appropriate fruit, a pruned vine branch yields only wood that is useful for burning, and perhaps not even for that.

■**6-8** The transitional word **therefore** (*lākēn*) marks the shift from the description of the metaphor in vv 1-5 to the divine interpretation in vv 6-8. Given the frequent use of this term in prophetic literature to introduce the judgment that follows an indictment, the reader already anticipates that the divine explanation will offer a negative interpretation of the vine image as a symbol of judgment. Yahweh's description, however, directs this judgment specifically against those remaining in Jerusalem under Zedekiah.

Verse 6 offers a first person divine declaration in which Yahweh states that just as he has **given** (*nětattîw*) the wood of the vine branch to be burned in the fire, so he will **give** (*nātattî*; treat) those who are in Jerusalem to destruction in fire. The allusion to the coming destruction and conflagration of the city in the remaining verses collects some language and themes known from earlier in the book: (1) **set my face** as a gesture of hostility (15:7; see 4:3; 7:22; 14:8); (2) destruction by **fire** (15:7; see 5:2, 4; 10:2); and (3) making **the land desolate** as a result of the people's sin (15:8; see 14:13, 15-16). Through this description, the metaphor of the vine functions to recast those still in Jerusalem as useless, unable to serve a meaningful purpose in Yahweh's larger plan of restoration, and now good only for judgment (15:8). When this divine pronouncement is read in the context of the whole metaphorical discourse, an implicit reason for the vine's/Jerusalemites' worthlessness emerges. The wood of the vine branch is useless because it has been severed from the plant that gives it life; it can no longer fulfill its proper role of drawing nourishment from the plant and bearing usable fruit. Likewise, the people's unfaithfulness has cut them off from their life-giving relationship with Yahweh, rendering them unable to yield the kind of obedience that can lead to the accomplishment of Yahweh's purposes (Odell 2005, 174).

Even so, the appearance of the second person recognition formula (**you will know that I am the** LORD) in v 7 reveals that this metaphorical discourse is actually a proof saying designed to communicate to those living in exile with Ezekiel (Darr 2001, 1216). Ironically, the destruction of the good-for-nothing-but-the-fire Jerusalemites turns out to have one meaningful function. Through this metaphor, Ezekiel offers his audience yet another way to interpret the traumatic events surrounding Jerusalem's destruction that renders them understandable as part of Yahweh's sovereign actions. Such an effort to deal with trauma by attributing destruction to divine causation rightly calls for caution in the contemporary appropriation of this text. Yet, in Ezekiel's context the metaphorical discourse recasts the old Jerusalem as that which has been severed from Yahweh and lost its potential to be a part of the larger divine work.

2. The Faithless Bride (16:1-63)

The extensive metaphorical discourse in ch 16, which constitutes the longest chapter in the book, stands at the center of the series of three metaphorical discourses in chs 15—17. Like chs 15 and 17, the opening prophetic word formula and designation **son of man** for Ezekiel (16:1-2) frame it as a divine address to the prophet. Unlike ch 15, however, this discourse is not presented just as a teaching to Ezekiel. Throughout the discourse, for example, the divine words speak directly to the city of Jerusalem (note the second person ["you," "your"] address throughout; e.g., vv 3-4). In these ways, the metaphor portrays the capital city as a promiscuous and adulterous woman, whose unfaithfulness is punished in violent and graphic ways.

15:6—
16:63

The chapter's extended metaphor of Jerusalem as a faithless bride presents the reader with a high number of interpretive difficulties (so also the female personification of Samaria and Jerusalem in ch 23). The imagery as a whole draws upon a wide range of ancient practices and traditions, including the care of infants, adoption and marriage customs, political treaty-making, legal and judicial processes, and religious activities. Perhaps most pressingly, however, the reader encounters here a deeply troubling metaphorical portrayal, set on the lips of Yahweh himself, which features graphic portrayals of women and the blatant, physical abuse of a woman's body by a husband who is seen as justified in his actions (see Galambush 1992). As suggested in the Behind the Text discussion, at least as an initial move, interpreters should attempt to locate this disturbing, even offensive imagery within the context of the ancient traditions and experiences that underlie it, asking why Ezekiel may have spoken as he did, examining the ancient metaphorical traditions represented in the text, and seeking the experiences of war-related trauma that such imagery may express. Yet, one must also attend to the ongoing, potentially damaging implications that such an ancient discourse may have and the challenges raised for contemporary readers by this discourse's portrayals of women and sexual violence (see From the Text).

The chapter as a whole takes the form of a controversy oracle, using the imagery of a court case being brought against the personified Jerusalem (see Mic 6:1-8). It divides into several main sections that reveal the movement of Yahweh's accusations and judgments against the city:

vv 1-3a   Introduction
vv 3b-34   Accusations Against Jerusalem
vv 35-43   Yahweh's Judgment Against Jerusalem
vv 44-52   Renewed Accusations Against Jerusalem
vv 53-58   Oracle of Restoration
vv 59-63   Covenant Renewal with Jerusalem

The Behind the Text discussion observed that the chapter's imagery draws most directly from the wider ancient Near Eastern tradition of personifying capital cities as females, and using these personified females as negative symbols for the male, ruling elite. In Ezekiel's case, the adulterous woman (Jerusalem) in ch 16 represents King Zedekiah and those who share power with him in Judah between 597 and 586 B.C. The discourse uses the same marital and sexual imagery that appears in other OT texts (e.g., Hos 2; Jer 2—3) but develops the female personification more fully, as ch 16 recasts Jerusalem's entire history as the tragic story of an unwanted child, rescued, adopted, married, and ultimately gone bad (Darr 2001, 1225). The message here is not new in the book, but the metaphor provides another way for Ezekiel to communicate his view of the past history and present condition of the people's relationship with Yahweh, highlighting sins of both a religious and political nature.

a. Introduction (16:1-3a)

■ **1-3a** The discourse opens with Yahweh's command for Ezekiel to **confront Jerusalem with her detestable practices** (v 2), making immediately clear that the referent of the female figure described in the following verses is the capital city itself. The imperative here (*hôdaʿ*; "make known" [NRSV]), occurs in judicial contexts and carries a legal sense of presenting a charge against the accused (Greenberg 1983, 273). Yahweh's opening command also features the priestly label **detestable practices** (*tôʿēbôt*; lit., ***abominations***) as the overall designation for all of the sins attributed to Jerusalem in the discourse that follows. The Hebrew term appears eleven times in the chapter. In keeping with the priestly perspective we have seen throughout the book, Ezekiel gives a ritual, cultic interpretation to all of Jerusalem's wrongful actions—religious and political (cf. vv 16-22, 23-29)—which casts them as acts that defile Yahweh's holiness and pollute the temple where the divine presence must dwell, thus leading to the judgment and destruction that result from Yahweh's withdrawal from the community.

b. Accusations Against Jerusalem (16:3b-34)

■ **3b-5** The extended accusations in vv 3b-34 leveled against the female Jerusalem (and the ruling elite that the personified city represents) begin with a description of her birth in poor circumstances. Yahweh describes Jerusalem as having begun her life as a disadvantaged, unwanted, and vulnerable infant. In the first place, Yahweh reminds Jerusalem of what was from a later Judean point of view her questionable ancestry in the land of Canaan, with an **Amorite** father and a **Hittite** mother (v 3). This description was surely meant as an insult to the political and priestly leaders of Jerusalem who were often concerned with proper ethnic purity and descent, but it also reflects the historical tradition of Jerusalem as a city (Tuell 2009, 87). The OT presents Jerusalem as originally a Jebusite city brought into Israel through the actions of David (2 Sam 5:1-10; 1 Chr 11:1-9). The Amorites and Hittites both designate historical peoples, but perhaps more importantly, both terms appear in the OT's conventional listings of the foreign peoples who inhabited the promised land and were to be driven out before the Israelites (e.g., Gen 15:19-21; Exod 3:8; Deut 1:7-8). Jerusalem from the beginning, Yahweh asserts, possessed this foreignness and deserved rejection.

The divine discourse goes on to portray Jerusalem as an infant that was unwanted and abandoned to die. Verses 4-5 depict Jerusalem as having received none of the typical ancient practices of caring for a newborn; rather, she was **thrown out into the open field**. Such exposure and starvation was a common practice of infanticide in the ancient world, a means of eliminating infants, especially females, who were unwanted or for whom the parents could not provide. While the description in v 5 may indicate emotional enmity (**you were despised**), the phrase may also reflect a legal act of the formal renouncement of parenting rights (***you were disowned***), clearing the way for someone else to claim an unwanted child, if a willing rescuer could be found (Odell 2005, 189).

■ **6** In contrast to the fate that the infant Jerusalem should have suffered, Yahweh's words in v 6 remind Jerusalem of a sudden and gracious turn of events that altered her destiny. The imagery of these verses depicts Yahweh as a traveler who happens upon the exposed infant girl. He finds her abandoned, having not even been washed of the birth blood. In the priestly conception, the necessity of contact with blood, which was itself a ritually unclean event (Lev

12:4; 17:10-14), rendered childbirth a defiling activity that required rituals of purification (Lev 12:1-8). Jerusalem, however, received no acts of purification of any kind. She began her life as one who was unwanted and in a hopelessly unclean/defiled state. As a sudden reversal of Jerusalem's condition, Yahweh's declaration to the infant in v 6 (**Live!**) may again reflect the formal procedures for legal adoption in the ancient world. The imagery is similar to that found in the Old Babylonian Code of Hammurabi, which stipulates the permanence of an adoption that takes place while the child is still in its amniotic fluid (Darr 2001, 1226).

■ **7-14** With this adoption, Yahweh's narration of the past in v 7 quickly summarizes the girl's development through puberty and into full womanhood. At this point, however, Jerusalem once again finds herself in a vulnerable situation. The text's description of her as having fully formed breasts but being **naked and bare** indicates that she has reached the age of sexual maturity but has no male guardian to provide for her. Just as in the moment of Jerusalem's life-threatening vulnerability as a discarded infant, Yahweh once again **passed by** the now young woman and took note of her vulnerability (v 8). The imagery is almost as if Yahweh had adopted the infant and then left her alone through adolescence, only to return at the next moment of greatest danger. In the previous circumstance, Yahweh acted to claim the unwanted; now, Yahweh recounts how he took the woman Jerusalem to be his wife. Although the notion of marrying an adopted daughter may seem strange to contemporary readers, the language in v 8 (**I spread the corner of my garment over you;** or, *spread my cloak/wing over you*) appears elsewhere as a formal expression of the intent to initiate a marriage relationship and provide for the needs of the woman (see Ruth 3:9). Yahweh's subsequent words make this intent explicit: **I gave you my solemn oath and entered into a covenant with you . . . and you became mine** (Ezek 16:8).

Verses 9-14 relate a series of dramatic transformations that followed Yahweh's initial act of marriage, transformations through which Jerusalem moves from a bride to a queen (note especially vv 12-13). The actions reverse the desperate and vulnerable situations that have attended Jerusalem's existence up to this point. In Yahweh's first action, for example, he **washed the blood** from the young woman (v 9). Scholars differ over what blood is envisioned here (birth blood, see v 6; menstrual blood, signaling puberty; blood after first intercourse, representing consummation of the marriage; see Darr 2001, 1228), but the reference indicates that Jerusalem's condition was still marked by the uncleanness she had known in birth (Odell 2005, 190). With Yahweh's intervention, however, Jerusalem's circumstances change once again. Verses 10-14 follow with a description of Yahweh providing the needs of his wife in clothing, adornments, and food that befit royalty, completing her transformation to **queen** (v 13). As Galambush (1992, 95) observes, the terms used in these verses for Jerusalem's clothing are used elsewhere in the OT only in descriptions of the tabernacle and temple. Hence, the text's rhetoric once again makes clear that the metaphorical woman in ch 16 is the capital city Jerusalem and links the discourse back to the book's primary concern with Yahweh's holiness and Jerusalem's (especially the temple's) defilement.

Yahweh's description of the bride's transformation reaches its climax with v 14, which provides the end result of the divine actions: female Jerusalem's **fame spread among the nations**. The wording here, which literally describes Jerusalem's *name* becoming well-known among the nations, resembles the book's common references to Yahweh's name (reputation) that has been defamed among the nations by Israel's actions (e.g., 36:16-38). Yet Yahweh's words in v 14, with their repeated first person references (lit., ***my splendor; I had set on you***) and prophetic utterance formula (**declares the Sovereign Lord**), assert that Jerusalem's beauty and fame result only from Yahweh's graciousness bestowed upon her.

■ **15** The opening words of v 15 create a jarring contrast with Yahweh's first person statements in v 14 and mark the transition to the accusations against Jerusalem. An adversative *vav* in Hebrew, followed by repeated second person pronouns (**But you . . . your beauty . . . your fame . . . your favors**), quickly shift from the picture of good gifts bestowed by Yahweh to declare that Jerusalem claimed these gifts as her own and **trusted** in them for her security. The language in this verse provides the general introductory statement for the rest of Yahweh's accusations against Jerusalem in vv 16-34 by introducing the metaphor **committed fornication** (Heb., *zānāh*; **become a prostitute**) to identify the general indictment against the bride/queen Jerusalem. Metaphorically speaking, Jerusalem's actions about to be described were a way of taking the gifts of beauty and splendor that Yahweh had given and offering them indiscriminately to **anyone who passed by.**

Various forms of the Hebrew term *zānâ* ("fornicate") occur more than fifteen times in this chapter, and this sexual metaphor of promiscuity and adultery occurs regularly in prophetic texts that personify cities as females (e.g., Isa 23:15; Jer 2:20; 3:1-3; 5:7; Nah 3:4; out of 134 occurrences of the root in the OT, ninety occur in the Latter Prophets and forty-two are in Ezek 16 and 23). As the NIV implies, the root's basic meaning involves a literal sexual relationship outside of a formal union, perhaps most narrowly an act of prostitution (i.e., sex for hire) but also designating a wide variety of sexual transgressions (Kelle 2005, 100). However, the prophetic texts that personify cities as females, especially those that depict Samaria and Jerusalem as Yahweh's wives, do not typically use the term to refer to actual sexual activity but as a metaphor for a variety of deeds that the prophets see as acts of unfaithfulness to Yahweh. Although the most common action that the prophets label with the metaphor of fornication is the worship of other gods, prophetic city personification texts employ the imagery to characterize misconduct that is political and commercial, as well (e.g., Jer 3:1-3; Ezek 3:3, 5, 7-8; Nah 3:4). In the context of Yahweh's speech to Jerusalem in Ezek 16, the declaration that Jerusalem committed fornication functions as the general characterization of the specific deeds listed in the following verses, all of which are presented as Jerusalem's inappropriate and ungrateful responses to Yahweh's benevolent acts bestowed in vv 6-14.

■ **16-22** The first of Jerusalem's wrong responses to Yahweh's benevolence—and the first action described as *fornication* (v 16; Heb., *zānâ*; prostitution)—is apostasy through idol worship (vv 16-22). The egregious nature of Jerusalem's actions appears, however, not simply in the fact that they made idols. Yahweh's indictment depicts female Jerusalem as using the precise gifts that she received from Yahweh in vv 10-14 (**garments, fine jewelry, embroidered clothes, food** [vv 16-19]) to construct **high places** (v 16), make **male idols** (v 17), and present offerings before them (vv 18-19). Although the language here is overtly sexual (**you made for yourself male idols and engaged in prostitution with them** [v 17]), given the metaphorical conventions at work in this discourse, readers should refrain from interpreting these verses as literal descriptions of actions being done in Jerusalem (Darr 2001, 1229). The once well-established theory that sexual rites or cultic prostitution was a part of the practices of some religions in ancient Syria-Palestine is not supported by the most recent assessments of the available evidence (see Kelle 2005, 122-68; see sidebar "Theories of Cultic Prostitution"). Rather, the text's repeated use of first person verbs and pronouns (**my gold and silver** [v 17]; **my oil and incense** [v 18]; **food I provided** [v 19]) keeps the indictment in the realm of a metaphorical marriage and emphasizes that Jerusalem was unfaithful with the very gifts and resources that resulted from her special relationship with Yahweh (see Hos 2:5-9).

Theories of Cultic Prostitution

In previous decades, a high number of scholars contended that various religions in ancient Syria-Palestine, most notably the worship of the god Baal that receives occasional mention in the prophetic books, included fertility rituals in which sexual activities took place in sanctuary contexts. One of the most popular theories was that temples had cult prostitutes with whom worshippers would engage in sexual activity in order to secure fertility for animals and crops from gods and goddesses. Based on this hypothesis, scholars often associated the sexual imagery in prophetic texts like Hos 2 and Ezek 16 and 23 with these fertility rites. In recent years, however, numerous studies have reevaluated all of the biblical and extrabiblical evidence, and interpreters increasingly doubt the existence of such ritual prostitution and its influence on prophetic texts (see Kelle 2005, 122-32).

Verses 20-21 present perhaps the most dramatic betrayal of Jerusalem's relationship with Yahweh, as they accuse Jerusalem, here envisioned as a mother as well as a wife, as engaging in child sacrifice to her idols. Ezekiel may refer here to an actual practice, sometimes acknowledged to have taken place in Judah despite condemnations elsewhere in the OT (see 2 Kgs 16:3; 21:6; cf. Exod 34:20; Deut 12:29-32), or the reference may remain metaphorical, alluding to Judah's sons and daughters being handed over to death as a result of misguided alliances and rebellions. In any case, once again Yahweh's repeated first person language asserts that these were **my children** (Ezek 16:21), who were born **to me** (v 20). Verse 22 then provides a summary statement for the first category of Jerusalem's metaphorical fornication that describes her actions as **detestable practices** (*tô'ēbôt*; lit., ***abominations***), the technical Hebrew term that once again gives a priestly interpretation that casts Jerusalem's actions as defiling the place where Yahweh's presence dwells. The summary statement also introduces a theme that will reappear throughout the rest of Yahweh's address. Jerusalem has failed to **remember**—to keep before her as a present and defining reality—the situation of hopelessness and death she knew at the beginning. This lack of remembering that her life is a gift, sustained not by her own resources but by Yahweh's benevolence, provides the text's base explanation for why Jerusalem has failed to respond appropriately (see vv 43, 60-63).

■ **23-29** The divine oracle formula (**declares the Sovereign LORD** [v 23]) marks the beginning of another general description of Jerusalem's misconduct in vv 23-25, which again refers to the building of **a lofty shrine** (v 24) and uses the metaphor of **promiscuity** (*zānâ*; v 25). Verse 26 then introduces a second category of Jerusalem's inappropriate responses to Yahweh's gifts that constitute this fornication. Now, the tenor of the metaphor of fornication changes from religious apostasy with idols to political relations with other kingdoms (Darr 2001, 1231). The text describes the city's various political alliances and entanglements as acts of unfaithfulness in which Jerusalem betrayed Yahweh in order to trust in other entities. In succession, the rhetoric describes Jerusalem's inappropriate relations with the Egyptians, Assyrians, and Babylonians. Even when Yahweh acted in judgment, allowing enemies such as the Philistines to take away Judean territory (v 27), Jerusalem was undeterred.

The relations envisioned could refer to a variety of scenarios throughout Judah's history in which the kingdom participated in shifting alliances and rebellions with these major powers (see discussion of Judean history in the Introduction). Yet, the metaphorical rhetoric recasts these kingdoms as Jerusalem's adulterous lovers. The use of adulterous lovers as a trope for foreign allies and inappropriate political relationships is well-established in the OT prophets and extrabiblical texts (e.g., Jer 22:20, 22; Ezek 23:5, 9; see Kelle 2005, 111-22). In this instance, the Hebrew in some of Yahweh's accusatory statements is sexually lewd and explicit, obscured by virtually all modern English translations, perhaps with good reason (e.g., v 25: **offering your body** [lit., *you spread your legs*]; v 26: **Egyptians, your lustful neighbors** [lit., *with large flesh;* here, a euphemism for *penises*]). The rhetorical aim of such discourse is to change the audience's perspective from seeing these alliances as a necessary function of political practicality to understanding them as acts of betrayal against Yahweh. Yet, as Odell observes, when placed within this chapter's overall metaphor of the abandoned female child, and when considered from the perspective of traumatic experience, the picture of Jerusalem continuously jumping from suitor to suitor resembles the classic symptom of a neglected child who is unable to form any lasting attachments (2005, 190).

■ **30-34** Yahweh's accusations against Jerusalem reach a climax in vv 30-34. In a type of summary of the religious and political *fornication* described in the preceding verses, Yahweh declares that Jerusalem's **heart** (*lēb*) is **sick/weak** (*'amāl*). As discussed previously, the **heart** serves in the OT as the seat of the will/decision-making faculty (note the NIV's **weak-willed** [v 30]). Within Ezekiel, this declaration connects to the emphasis on the corrupt state of the people's heart/will and the need for its renewal/transformation, an emphasis that has already appeared (11:19) and will play a prominent role in the book's restoration visions (18:31; 36:26-27). Yahweh then extends this description of the personified Jerusalem's condition by declaring that in her fornication she even went beyond the typical behavior of a prostitute (16:33-34). Rather than the normal exchange in which a client seeks out a prostitute and pays her for her services, Yahweh asserts that Jerusalem's disloyalty was so great that she abandoned her fee and pursued her clients (i.e., foreign allies), offering them money to come to her.

c. Yahweh's Judgment Against Jerusalem (16:35-43)

■ **35-36** The transitional word **therefore** at the head of v 35 (again in v 37), along with two versions of the prophetic messenger formula and another designation of Jerusalem as **prostitute** (*zônâ*), mark the change from accusations to punishment. Yahweh's opening statement in vv 35-36 brings together references to the female Jerusalem's religious and political misdeeds described as fornication in the preceding section. The second person address indicates that the sentence is rendered by Yahweh, who stands as both the injured party and judge.

■ **37-41** The description of punishment against the personified Jerusalem in the following verses is one of the most problematic sections of Ezekiel for contemporary (and probably ancient) readers, prescribing vicious acts of physical and sexual violence against the female body at Yahweh's direction. The passage blends portrayals of Jerusalem as a woman who commits adultery (vv 37-38, 39*b*, 40, 41*b*) and a city that suffers destruction (vv 39*a*, 41*a*), reinforcing that the historical subject here is a city and not a woman, but also reminding us of the slippage that is present in any metaphorical construction. Overall, the discourse, which remains only at the level of a prediction, provides a metaphorical depiction of the fate that Ezekiel sees as coming for Jerusalem at the hands of the Babylonians and their allies.

In an ironic twist, Yahweh appoints Jerusalem's **lovers** to carry out the violent actions of judgment (v 37). The metaphor describes the coming judgment in several stages. First, Yahweh declares that he will **strip** Jerusalem (lit., *I will uncover your nakedness*) in front of her lovers (v 37). Within the female personification of Jerusalem, this act may be a prelude to the physical and sexual assault described in the following verses, or a symbolic gesture indicating, as it does in some ancient Near East divorce documents, the husband's withdrawal of material support and inheritance from a former wife (see Kelle 2005, 59-79). The nakedness may also indicate a return to the woman's initial state of exposure and abandonment (vv 4-7; Darr 2001, 1234). Perhaps more significantly for Ezekiel's aims, however, in the OT prophetic texts, especially those that personify cities as females, to "uncover the nakedness" of a woman often functions as a metaphor for the destruction of a city (e.g., Jer 13:22-27; Hos 2:3; Nah 3:5-6; see Kelle 2005, 90-92). Along these lines, v 38 likens Jerusalem's coming punishment with that prescribed for **women who commit adultery,** referring not to some ritual of stripping but to the death penalty (Lev 20:10; Deut 22:22; contra Block 1997, 501-2; see Tuell 2009, 90).

The next stage of judgment continues to intertwine descriptions of violence against a woman and the destruction of a city. The text states that Jerusalem's lovers will tear down the city's **mounds** (v 39), **lofty shrines** (v 39), and **houses** (v 41). In short, Yahweh declares, Jerusalem's lovers with whom she sought security will destroy the city. Verses 40-41 describe this destruction metaphorically in a way that depicts even more violence against the woman's body. In a scene reminiscent of a gang attack, Yahweh threatens Jerusalem with a **mob** that will **stone** her and **hack** her **to pieces with . . . swords,** completing the ultimate destruction of the city (note the burning of houses in v 41).

■ **42-43** The truly terrifying and most disturbing part of the rhetoric, however, appears in v 42, where the extreme violence and murder of the metaphorical woman is depicted as a type of divine catharsis in which Yahweh is able to "satisfy" (NRSV; **subside**) the rage he has felt and thereafter **be calm** (Darr 2001, 1235). The troubling nature of this portrayal of Yahweh becomes clear when we think of the common patterns of modern domestic abuse, in which a jealous husband's rage turns to physical violence, after which he speaks tenderly to the abused woman. Ezekiel's own experience of physical and emotional trauma, which lies at the heart of the book's rhetoric as a whole, may provide an explanation of—though perhaps not an inoculation against—this portrayal, as the prophet's characterizations of Yahweh may reflect the imprint of violence upon the prophet's own psyche. Even so, Yahweh's conclusion to the indictment (v 43) once again (see v 22) attributes Jerusalem's misbehavior to a failure to **remember** her desperate beginnings—a lack not of passive recollection but of present application of the past's meaning. The conclusion also once again identifies her actions from the priestly perspective as defiling ***abominations*** (**detestable practices**) that threaten Yahweh's presence among the people.

d. Renewed Accusations Against Jerusalem (16:44-52)

■ **44-52** Just as Yahweh's accusations and judgment of Jerusalem seem to reach their conclusion, the Hebrew particle **Look/Behold!** (*hinnēh;* omitted by NIV) at the start of v 44 suddenly introduces a further indictment. The rhetoric of Yahweh's speech in this section continues the female personification of the city—recapitulating earlier references to her bad stock of foreign parents (v 45)—but adds a new condemnation of Jerusalem through a comparison with Samaria and Sodom, personified as Jerusalem's sinful "sisters" (vv 46-52). There is no clear OT tradition for the representation of Sodom (see Gen 19) as a sister to Samaria and Jerusalem, although the city appears as a negative example in some prophetic texts (e.g., Isa 1:9-10). The section may be a later addition to the text, but the rhetorical point of the comparison is clear: Jerusalem's wrongdoings have surpassed those of Samaria and Sodom, even making these notoriously evil—and now destroyed—cities appear righteous by comparison (see Ezek 16.47, 48, 51, 52). By relating this divine discourse, Ezekiel seeks to reshape his audience's understanding of Jerusalem, further leading them to break with any remaining attachment to it.

The Sins of Sodom

The city of Sodom is notorious within the biblical literature as an example of sin that results in divine destruction. The primary story appears in Gen 19, but the city appears in several prophetic texts as an example of wickedness and judgment (see Isa 1:9-10; 3:8-9; 13:19; Jer 23:14; 49:18; Amos 4:11). Some readers and interpreters read the story of Gen 19 and identify Sodom's sin as sexual in nature, particularly involving homosexuality, likely because of the scene concerning Lot's guests, daughters, and the men of the city. However, the prophetic texts in the OT, as in Ezek 16:49-50, consistently identify Sodom's wrongdoing as social and economic injustices coming from a sense of pride and a failure to extend hospitality to strangers (help to **the poor and needy** in the land [v 49]).

e. Oracle of Restoration (16:53-58)

■ **53** Yahweh's words in v 53, extending the references to Samaria and Sodom from the preceding section, make an abrupt and surprising reversal from judgment to restoration (note the NIV's **However** [v 53]). Without any transitional statement, Yahweh declares that he will bring restoration to Samaria and Sodom, as well as the smaller towns (**daughters**) associated with them. Yet, the text does not dwell on these cities' restoration. The word order of the verse creates suspense, as it moves first through Samaria and Sodom. Is it possible that Jerusalem, whose destruction seemed so dramatic and final in vv 35-43, may also experience restoration after judgment? Indeed, at the end of the verse, Yahweh adds a statement to Jerusalem, **and your fortunes along with them** (v 53*b*).

■ **54-58** The verses that follow, however, add another surprise concerning Jerusalem. Verse 54 provides an unexpected rationale for Jerusalem's restoration. Yahweh asserts that he will restore Jerusalem **so that** the people will be **ashamed** (Heb., *kālam*), language that returns at the close of the chapter (vv 61, 63). The eventual restoration of Jerusalem will somehow result in a sense of shame rather than simple joy for the people, which will even serve as a consolation to Samaria and Sodom, who have experienced similar destruction (v 54). Scholars differ on how to understand this language, proposing connections to formal (psalm-like) complaints the people previously made against Yahweh's inaction (Darr 2001, 1236-40), or priestly purification rites for the temple (Odell 2005, 196-97). It is best, however, to interpret this sentiment in the context of Ezekiel's address to his exilic audience who have experienced and will continue to experience the envisioned destruction. The text seems to imply that Yahweh will deliver the people so that in the moment of deliverance they will realize their past ingratitude and present undeserving status. The sense of shame about the past in response to a newly changed situation may play a positive role for those attempting to make sense out of trauma, as it may lead to a new assessment of the past and a sense of ownership over it (Lapsley 2000b). In the case of Ezekiel, who continues to urge his fellow exiles to accept their culpability in the sins of the past and to disassociate from the old Jerusalem, experiencing shame at the time of restoration may lead to a clearer understanding of what happened and an acceptance of their responsibility for it (Odell 2005, 199).

f. Covenant Renewal with Jerusalem (16:59-63)

■ **59-60** The final section of Yahweh's address to the personified Jerusalem returns to the certainty of the judgment that is to come (**I will deal with you as you deserve** [v 59]), even while continuing the emphasis on a future restoration. The section now recasts both the past sin and promised restoration in new terms: the making, breaking, and restoring of a **covenant** (*bĕrît*) between Yahweh and Jerusalem (vv 59-60). Although a covenant between Yahweh and the people is a prevalent image with a variety of meanings throughout the OT, this text uses the term to characterize the initial relationship that Yahweh established with the abandoned infant Jerusalem at the start of the chapter (**covenant I made with you in . . . your youth** [v 60]). The new promise then—that Yahweh will one day **establish an everlasting covenant** with Jerusalem—represents not the making of a new covenant but a renewal and extension of the ancient relationship (so also the "new covenant" in Jer 31:31-34). Here again we find Ezekiel's theological conviction that any future hope for the people emerges from Yahweh's own initiative and as a result of his concern to reestablish divine sovereignty and holiness (see v 62).

■ **61-63** Yahweh's final promise of covenantal restoration is also cast in the language of remembering that has appeared throughout the discourse. In contrast to Jerusalem's repeated failure to remember her desperate beginnings and Yahweh's benevolence (vv 22, 43), Yahweh now declares that he will "remember the covenant" he formed with the abandoned infant at the beginning (v 60). Furthermore, Yahweh's remembering will cause Jerusalem to **remember**—to make present in a fully realized way—her rebellious practices and inappropriate responses to Yahweh's grace (v 61). Among other benefits of these promised transformations, including Jerusalem's elevation over her **sisters** (v 61) and the people coming to **know that I am the** LORD (v 62), the discourse concludes by affirming that Yahweh's final and ultimate word to Jerusalem will be forgiveness (v 63). As the NIV reflects, the term here (*kippēr*) often carries the meaning of "to atone," functioning in priestly contexts to refer to the ritual cleansing activities done on behalf of the people and sanctuary (Lev 4—6; 16). In this final statement, Yahweh promises that he will act as a priest for the people, accomplishing the cleansing and holiness that Ezekiel so often asserts is missing (Tuell 2009, 96).

Nonetheless, the chapter does not have a simplistically happy ending. Even after the description of restoration, Jerusalem is once again left in ***shame*** (*kālam*; **humiliation** [v 63]), rendered speechless in light of their past actions.

One can imagine this rhetoric as another attempt by Ezekiel to give his audience a different view of and response to their past and present circumstances, further urging them to disassociate from the old identity that had shaped their former realities.

I often ask my biblical studies students what contemporary Christian readers should say about a passage like ch 16. How should we understand and explain a text that seems so far from our usual conceptions of a loving God? The From the Text section below will more fully consider this chapter's challenges for contemporary readers, but at this point it is helpful to provide some comments on the text's overall imagery from the perspective of Ezekiel's traumatic experiences and ancient context.

The chapter's depictions of physical and sexual violence likely reflect Ezekiel's own experience of trauma in the wake of the capture of Jerusalem and deportation to Babylonia in 597 B.C., experiences that had been suffered by earlier generations of Judeans and that were still to be suffered at the climactic destruction of Jerusalem in 586 B.C. While the graphic images of physical and sexual violence in ch 16 are metaphorical portrayals related to the city of Jerusalem, the imagery may have been shaped by real-life war experiences suffered by women and men among Ezekiel and his fellow exiles (see Tuell 2009, 91-92). In the ancient world, capture and defeat in battle often involved the stripping, brutalizing, rape, and murder of male and female captives. Several biblical texts, as well as extrabiblical inscriptions and pictorial reliefs, attest to this violent treatment of war prisoners, especially stripping, rape, and other forms of sexual humiliation (Isa 3:16—4:1; 20:4; Jer 13:18-22; Amos 7:17). Tragically, recent evidence of such abuse and humiliation of prisoners by the U.S. military in early twenty-first-century conflicts testifies to the ongoing reality of these practices. Ezekiel and his fellow deportees likely experienced or, at least, witnessed such abusive treatment, and the depictions of physical and sexual violence in ch 16 may arise out of these experiences. The chapter's imagery may especially reflect the psychological humiliation of the male elite class, who, in the ancient cultural understanding that saw maleness as representing power, had lost their masculinity and been forced symbolically into the role of a victimized woman (see Kamionkowski 2003).

In the metaphorical discourse that portrays Jerusalem as an adulterous wife who suffers humiliation and violence, Ezekiel makes the war-related experiences endured by his audience a part of reconceptualizing Jerusalem's story. Within its rhetorical-historical context, the gendered and violent imagery of ch 16 functions to renarrate the trauma of capture and exile, providing some meaning to these events by interpreting them within the larger plot line of Yahweh's covenant and Judah's sin. The discourse takes physical, social, and psychological experiences that do not fit the normal categories of understanding and recasts them into some of ancient Judah's common theological and cultural conceptions of holiness, judgment, gender, and marriage. These conceptions provide a new way to explain what happened and why. More specifically, as discussed in the Behind the Text section, the prophetic personifications of capital cities as women function rhetorically to cast the political rulers—those represented most directly by the symbol of the capital cities—as faithless wives that act disgracefully and deserve punishment according to the ancient cultural norms. Although Ezekiel's discourse does not move beyond the gender conceptions of his culture or the lingering effects of his own trauma, it advocates a new self-understanding for his audience and continues his appeal that the people, especially his fellow exiles, should distance themselves from the old Jerusalem, its character, and its leaders.

3. The Two Eagles and the Vine (17:1-24)

The metaphorical discourse in ch 17 constitutes the last in the series of three discourses. Like chs 15 and 16, the discourse opens with the prophetic word formula and designation **son of man** for Ezekiel (vv 1-2), which frame it as a divine address to the prophet. Unlike chs 15 and 16, however, after the main metaphorical narrative (vv 3-10), vv 11-21 provide a detailed interpretation of the images and their meaning. This is followed by a vision about the future in vv 22-24 (although the chapter may include some later additions [see Odell 2005, 205]). The chapter as a whole gives a theological interpretation of the maneuverings of Judean royal politics, which asserts that Yahweh is the controlling force at the center of all history and characterizes Zedekiah's movement toward rebellion against Babylonia as unfaithfulness to Yahweh.

■ **1-2** Yahweh's introductory word to Ezekiel in v 2 identifies the content of the message as an **allegory** (*ḥîdâ*) and **parable** (*māšāl*). These Hebrew terms, which have a range of meanings (e.g., "riddle," "allegory" [NRSV]), share the basic sense of a saying that requires interpretation. What follows is a type of fable, something akin to a modern political cartoon, which stands in the tradition of other biblical fables (e.g., Judg 9:8-15; 2 Kgs 14:8-10).

■ **3-10** The parable uses images from nature (animals, trees, vines) to represent the kings of Judah, Babylonia, and Egypt and offers a symbolic political commentary on the Babylonian capture of Jehoiachin in 597 B.C., Nebuchadnezzar's appointment of Zedekiah on the Judean throne, and, subsequently, Zedekiah's apparent reliance on Egypt and anti-Babylonian forces following Pharaoh Psammetichus II's successes in the region after 592 B.C. (see Behind the Text for chs 12—24). Verses 3-6 represent this series of events by describing how a **great eagle** (Nebuchadnezzar [v 3]) carried away the top part of a cedar tree in Lebanon (Jehoiachin) and then planted a **seed** from the land (Zedekiah [v 5]), which grew into a **vine** (v 6). Verses 7-8 describe how a second **great eagle** (Psammetichus II) drew the attention of the vine, which began to seek its nourishment from the second eagle.

The text's power lies in its metaphors, all of which appear in various contexts throughout the OT (see Darr 2001, 1245). Eagles (used for Nebuchadnezzar and Psammetichus) are often symbols of military power and royalty (Deut 28:49; Jer 48:40; 49:22). While trees often symbolize kings and kingdoms (Judg 9:7-15; 2 Kgs 14:8-10; Ezek 31:1-9), cedars from Lebanon were regarded as especially tall and strong, and OT texts often use them to represent strength and power (Song 5:15; Isa 10:34). The use of the vine as a symbol for Zedekiah's kingdom not only contrasts with the cedar that represents Jehoiachin but is especially resonant in light of the prophet's portrayal of the Jerusalemites as a useless vine in ch 15 (cf. Ps 80). The parable's metaphors subtly reveal Ezekiel's view of Zedekiah as a worthless vine, who contrasts most unfavorably with Jehoiachin. Verses 9-10 conclude the parable with Yahweh posing a series of open-ended questions that rhetorically lead the hearer/reader to a conviction of the dismal fate of Zedekiah's vine-kingdom, perhaps again seeking to change the exilic audience's understanding of Jerusalem and its rulers at the time.

■ **11-21** The transition from Yahweh's description of the parable (vv 3-10) to its interpretation (vv 11-21) is marked by the same prophetic word formula (**the word of the LORD came to me** [v 11]) that began the discourses in 15:1, 16:1, and 17:1. The text also returns to Ezekiel's primary description of the people, as Yahweh commands him to give the interpretation to the **rebellious house** (v 12; *bêt měrî*; see commentary on 2:1-7). The political overtones of this designation are apt in this context. Without using any personal names, 17:11-15 unpacks the preceding parable by describing Nebuchadnezzar's placement of Zedekiah on the Jerusalem throne, with an oath of allegiance to rule as a loyal vassal, as well as Zedekiah's collusion with Egypt to rebel against Babylonian authority. Verse 16 contrasts Zedekiah's unreliable oath with a divine oath formula (**As surely as I live**) in which Yahweh answers the open-ended questions from vv 9-10 and asserts that Zedekiah will suffer Nebuchadnezzar's wrath and die in Babylonia.

The most interesting part of this political commentary comes in vv 19-20, where Ezekiel gives Zedekiah's actions and fate a theological interpretation, thoroughly intertwining Yahweh with the political realities of the day. Already the text has characterized Zedekiah's vassal oath to Nebuchadnezzar as a *běrît* (vv 13-15; **treaty**; "covenant" [NRSV]). While this term can simply designate political agreements, it often carries theological overtones in the

OT. Verse 19 brings this theological dimension to the fore, as another oath from Yahweh declares that the vassal treaty with Nebuchadnezzar broken by Zedekiah was, in fact, **my oath** (*'ālātî*) and **my covenant** (*bĕrîtî*). In Ezekiel's perspective, rebellion against Babylonia constitutes rebellion against Yahweh because Zedekiah's covenant with Nebuchadnezzar was actually Yahweh's covenant. This conception likely derives from the ancient practice, evidenced especially in the Neo-Assyrian period, in which the parties enacting a treaty swore the pact in the names of their gods (see Tsevat 1959; Kelle 2005, 262). The deities functioned as guarantors of the treaty, and disloyalty to the treaty was disloyalty to the god in whose name it had been sworn. In the context of ch 17, Yahweh's description of Zedekiah's rebellion against Babylonia as an act of religious unfaithfulness provides Ezekiel's audience of exiles with a new interpretation of the traumatic events that have unfolded in Judah and resulted in the present and coming circumstances. Here is Ezekiel's depiction of Yahweh as the lord of history, which simultaneously recasts Jerusalem as a disloyal vassal to Yahweh, further urging the exiles to break away from their old identity with the city.

The first person assertions in v 20 go on to claim direct divine agency for Zedekiah's fate (**I will bring him to Babylon**) and reiterate that Zedekiah's real treason is against Yahweh (**he was unfaithful to me**). Verse 21 concludes the explanation section with the now-familiar divine recognition formula, with second person pronouns shifting the focus back to Ezekiel's immediate audience and declaring that Yahweh's actions against Jerusalem will lead the exiles to ***acknowledge*** (*yāda'*) that he is the power behind the past and future events.

■ **22-24** Yahweh's discourse continues in vv 22-24, which constitute an addendum that looks beyond the judgment to come. This passage also begins with the messenger formula (see vv 1-3, 11, 19) and returns to the tree imagery of the parable in vv 3-10. In a close parallel to Nebuchadnezzar's actions depicted at the beginning of the chapter, Yahweh declares that he will take a **shoot from the . . . top of a cedar and plant it** so that it grows into **a splendid cedar** in which all birds can find rest. This passage constitutes one of several in Ezekiel—appearing with increasing number in later chapters—that envision a future restoration for Judah centered on a human ruler and a renewed Davidic dynasty in Jerusalem (see 34:23-24; 37:15-28; 46:1-18). Given the imagery's similarity to that in 17:3-4, the text likely provides another example of Ezekiel's conviction that Judah's future lies with the exiled Jehoiachin (recall the book's dating scheme based on Jehoiachin's reign) rather than Zedekiah, whom the chapter depicts as a vine left to die (v 9).

Even so, the future vision reflects the prophet's overall theological perspective that calls for a dramatic break with the old Jerusalem. Verses 22-23, for example, use the imagery of a cosmic mountain of Yahweh to represent the dwelling place of the restored kingdom, an image often linked to descriptions of the old capital of Jerusalem as "Zion" in the so-called Zion Psalms (e.g., Pss 46; 48). Ezekiel's restoration passages, however, do not describe Jerusalem as "Zion"—a term that never appears in the book. For Ezekiel, Yahweh's restoration is a new act, not to be identified with the old Jerusalem around whom the former Zion traditions were built. Furthermore, vv 23-24 assert that the purpose of this restored kingdom is not parochial or imperialistic, but to demonstrate Yahweh's sovereignty to all kingdoms of the world. In Ezekiel's time, this kind of vision, as well as those in similar passages (often labeled "messianic" texts because of their references to a future, ideal king), related most directly to historical figures such as Jehoiachin. Over the following centuries, however, as the ideal persons and circumstances failed to emerge in history, such passages gave rise to a number of traditions that reinterpreted their language toward various conceptions of a future "messiah" who would fulfill the larger divine purposes.

FROM THE TEXT (CHS 15—17)

The metaphorical condemnation of the Jerusalemites as a useless vine in ch 15 brings to the fore an interpretive issue that has appeared elsewhere in the book: the notion that God may utterly reject a people (see Odell 2005, 176). At various places in the book, the people remaining in Jerusalem after 597 B.C. are subject to wholesale divine rejection, as the prophet's rhetoric casts them as having reached a point when they are no longer useful for anything other than destruction. This kind of totalizing rhetoric has sometimes found a place in contemporary political, social, and religious discourse, as entire ethnic, cultural, and faith communities are labeled as dangerous and targeted for exclusion or elimination. Surely, readers from the Wesleyan tradition will want to temper such rhetoric—no doubt originally shaped by the traumatic experiences of Ezekiel and his fellow exiles—with convictions about the efficacy of God's prevenient grace and loving nature, which suggest that no people or person is outside the realm of God's redemptive activity and God may, perhaps, be at work for good in places that seem otherwise to us. Ezekiel, too, contains some moments where another perspective breaks through and speaks of God's continued involvement with the Jerusalemites, even into the future on the other side of judgment (e.g., 5:1-4; 6:8-10; 12:16).

Ezekiel's assertion in ch 17 that God's holiness/sovereignty is the ultimate power behind even the political realities of his day, brings to the fore another interpretive issue that has appeared elsewhere in the book: the conviction that historical events have a theological explanation in terms of God's direction and control. *As we have discussed previously (see From the Text for chs 4—7 and 8—11), such attempts to identify theological meaning behind specific historical and political happenings can provide suffering persons and communities with a coherency and understanding that moves them toward wholeness but should give contemporary interpreters pause.* As Darr (2001, 1253) explains, "In a world where holocausts occur, Ezekiel's correlation of historical events with Yahweh's administration of justice can be lethal." Perhaps the depictions in chs 15—17 can again remind us to begin any consideration of God's sovereignty and historical events by recognizing that all such rhetoric in Ezekiel is an extreme way of countering his audience's possible conclusion that the trauma they had experienced signified God's weakness or defeat.

Perhaps there are no harsher words to deal with in Ezekiel, however, than those in the metaphorical portrayal of Jerusalem as the faithless bride in ch 16. The portrayals of women, gender, sex, and violence are unquestionably problematic, disturbing, and even offensive, especially for those who consider Ezekiel to be part of the church's sacred Scripture. *While the commentary discussion has offered some window into the background and rhetorical dynamics of this chapter, its challenge to contemporary readers demands ongoing attention.* Such attention should also be paid to the similar metaphor of Jerusalem and Samaria as promiscuous women in ch 23, and the comments made here apply to that discourse, as well. As we have already observed, the origins of the gendered metaphor in ch 16 lie in Ezekiel's attempt to deal with the trauma experienced both psychologically and physically by his fellow exiles, but the prophet's cultural situation leads him to make use of ancient conceptions of marriage and domestic life and graphic portrayals of physical violence to the female body.

No fully satisfactory answer exists to the question of how contemporary readers should handle a passage like ch 16. Perhaps the most important step in any consideration is to recognize and emphasize that the text is problematic and articulate why this is so. Toward this end, ch 16 has generated a wide variety of scholarship within the field known as "feminist biblical interpretation"—a very diverse field of study that engages a variety of issues related to biblical portrayals of women and gender and the treatment of these issues within past and present biblical scholarship from a wide range of viewpoints (see Galambush 1992). These studies help identify clearly the problematic aspects of the chapter's sexual and violent metaphors. Most fundamentally, the portrayal of Jerusalem as a faithless bride who is punished by her divine husband is intertwined with a patriarchal worldview in which men are the dominant players and the norm of society. Chapter 16 portrays female experience and sexuality as the object of male control, denying the female character any voice or agency and suggesting that physical violence is an appropriate means of maintaining male control and bringing reconciliation.

Such depictions also depend upon cultural conceptions of honor and shame in ancient patriarchal societies (Odell 2005, 198-99). In these conceptions, the culturally defined misbehavior of a woman who was associated with a man brought shame to the man in the society's eyes, and the husband could vindicate his honor by punishing the woman. Chapter 16 applies precisely these conceptions to God. While the chapter's depictions are indeed only metaphors, it is not adequate to dismiss them as *merely* metaphors. The study of metaphor theory has demonstrated that metaphors are not simply decorative devices but have cognitive effects that shape how people think, act, and conceptualize reality. And these metaphors in particular are dangerous to both men and women, as they have the potential to produce a surplus of unintended effects and meanings. As Darr summarizes, "Imagery, especially biblical imagery, that details the degradation and public humiliation of women . . . and then suggests that such violence is a means toward *healing* a broken relationship can have perilous, even lethal repercussions. The files of police officers and social workers are filled with cases of women battered and murdered by males . . . who regard them as personal possessions" (Darr 2001, 1241).

Beyond the initial recognition of the problematic elements, contemporary Christian readers in particular need to consider some appropriate strategies for engaging the metaphorical discourses of texts like ch 16. First, at the canonical level alone, the diversity of divine portrayals in the OT as a whole may provide a helpful way forward. The OT contains some markedly different portrayals of God that perhaps provide a counterbalance to passages such as ch 16. To cite just one example, the book of Hosea contains a similar passage that portrays God acting in jealousy and violence against his metaphorical "wife" (Hos 2:1-23), but only a few chapters later offers an extended discourse that portrays God as a loving and long-suffering parent to Israel, who is portrayed as a rebellious child (Hos 11:1-11).

Second, while not attempting to explain away the problems, readers should surely begin by emphasizing the historical and cultural context from which these depictions come. The conceptions of men, women, and marriage evident in ch 16 reflect those of an ancient culture no longer shared by modern readers. This historical context provides some necessary distance from the text's rhetoric. Christian readers might approach the text's assumptions and portrayals in much the same way that most of them would understand Paul's admonition for women to cover their heads in church (1 Cor 11:2-16)—a text with important meanings to convey but embedded within particular ancient cultural ideas.

Third, contemporary readers should likewise emphasize that the depictions in ch 16 are only metaphors, even as they avoid the temptation to dismiss them as merely metaphorical. The subject actually being portrayed by the woman is the city of Jerusalem, the inappropriate actions envisioned are idolatry and political alliances (not literal sexual activity), and the punishments described are actually elements of city destruction. These subjects of the metaphors provide a fourth strategy in which readers can emphasize the function of the discourse in its rhetorical context. As discussed above, ch 16, like the other prophetic texts that personify capital cities as females, uses the female city to represent the male ruling elite and thereby portray them as worthy of shame and judgment (see Behind the Text). In an ancient patriarchal culture that equated strength with masculinity, the metaphor effectively feminizes the male rulers as promiscuous women. This rhetorical effect means that contrary to the ways this text has been used by men to justify conceptions of and violence against women, the ancient Judean male hearers/readers of the text would have seen themselves as the female Jerusalem, especially if the depictions reflect the physical abuse and humiliation suffered by Judean captives and deportees.

In and among the various problems and their potential solutions, however, the discourse in ch 16 offers a significant theological message that is especially resonant with readers from the Wesleyan tradition. At the heart of this discourse is a call for the people to have an undivided loyalty to God. The text's descriptions of Jerusalem's turn to idols and reliance upon political allies represent divided loyalties that keep the people from a fully devoted relationship with God and ultimately result in the deathliness in which the people now find themselves. In this language, readers from the Wesleyan tradition may hear a message that is similar to John Wesley's articulation of Christian perfection and entire sanctification in the Christian life (see also commentary on ch 36). At its most basic level, Wesley's formulation of entire sanctification involves an inward surrender and outward obedience that result in all of one's life being characterized by a single motive to love God—a pure love that evicts sin and governs the heart and life (Greathouse and Dunning 1982, 88). For Wesley, entire sanctification is not a state into which one simply passes but a moment-by-moment disposition of living that represents the process of being freed from improper self-love and renewed into the image of God in Christ. As ch 16 indicates, sin becomes identified as the directing of one's devotion or love to an object other than God, producing a divided loyalty or mixed love. By contrast, entire sanctification is the replacement of the believer's lingering measure of self-centeredness and misplaced love with a pure, wholehearted love for God (and thus others through God). The implicit call in ch 16 for the people to put away the loyalties/devotions that have characterized their life finds an echo in Wesley's vision that God's ultimate grace to the believer is the gift of a "single eye" and "pure heart" (Wesley 1971, 32).

C. Part 3: Oracles of Judgment and Lament (18:1—19:14)

BEHIND THE TEXT (CHS 18—20)

Chapters 18—20 form the third subsection within the larger unit of symbolic acts and oracles (chs 12—24) that follows the second vision of Yahweh's glory/presence (chs 8—11). These chapters constitute a series of three oracles that explore the question of the responsibility for Judah's exile, proclaim Yahweh's judgment that is rooted in the people's long history of rebellion, and cast some glances toward restoration beyond judgment. Within the context of chs 12—24, the oracles continue Ezekiel's addresses to his fellow exiles during the final years leading up to the Babylonian destruction of Jerusalem in 586 B.C., maintaining a dual focus, at once describing words and actions related to the people remaining in Jerusalem under King Zedekiah and addressing the immediate audience of the exilic community in Babylonia. The chapters proceed through two oracles featuring legal forms and fable imagery, respectively, to a lengthy historical rehearsal of Israel's past:

   C. Part 3: Oracles of Judgment and Lament (18:1—19:14)
      1. Retribution and Judgment (18:1-32)
      2. Lament over Jerusalem (19:1-14)
   D. Part 4: Israel's History of Sin/Rebellion (20:1-49)

The first significant background aspect of chs 18—20 emerges from the date formula in 20:1, which locates Ezekiel's rehearsal of Judah's history in "the seventh year, in the fifth month on the tenth day" (August 14, 591 B.C.). This is the first date that has appeared in the book since the temple vision in 8:1, dated a year earlier (September 18, 592 B.C.). As discussed in the Behind the Text section for chs 8—11, the time around 592-591 B.C. saw the rise of Egyptian power under Psammetichus II, who achieved major military success and conducted a victory tour into Syria-Palestine. This apparent resurgence of Egypt as a power that could challenge Babylonia further nurtured seeds of rebellion that had been planted almost immediately after Zedekiah had taken the throne in Jerusalem (see the regional council in Jer 27). Sometime shortly after 591, these seeds would sprout, as Zedekiah withheld annual tribute and entered into open rebellion against Babylonia. The date in 20:1 places Ezekiel's presentation of Judah's history of rebellion in the time of Psammetichus's victories, when Zedekiah and those in Jerusalem moved further toward open revolt—an act that Ezekiel sees as yet another rebellion against Yahweh in a long history of rebelliousness.

The second significant background aspect of chs 18—20 concerns the legal nature of the material that appears in ch 18. In the midst of a disputation in which Ezekiel argues for a new understanding of responsibility and retribution, the text employs three scenarios (vv 5-9, 10-13, 14-18) that take the form of case law known from the ancient world's legal traditions (so also 14:4-11). Unlike so-called apodictic laws, which issue an unqualified prohibition ("you shall not murder" [Exod 20:13]), case laws issue an "if . . . then" statement, which presents a range of scenarios and subscenarios, as well as their corresponding verdicts (e.g., "When someone steals an ox or a sheep, and slaughters it or sells it, the thief shall pay five oxen for an ox, and four sheep for a sheep" [Exod 22:1 NRSV]). The vast majority of law codes from the ancient Near Eastern world take this form, with perhaps the most extensive example being the Babylonian Code of Hammurabi (ca. 1800 B.C.; see sidebar "Case Law and the Code of Hammurabi"). This type of case law also appears predominantly throughout the OT legal corpus and deals with a wide variety of ethical, ritual, property, and family issues (e.g., Exod 21:8—22:14; Deut 22:1-30). The case law in ch 18 reflects the typical pattern: a governing case is set out, followed by a series of subcases that extend the general principle of the governing case. Ezekiel's specific usage represents priestly case law in particular, which invests the hypothetical scenarios and verdicts with priestly and ritual concerns such as defilement with idols and blood impurity (e.g., 18:6; Odell 2005, 224).

Case Law and the Code of Hammurabi

> The Babylonian law code of King Hammurabi (ca. 1792-1750 B.C.) is one of the best preserved legal collections from the ancient world. The majority of its formulations take the form of case laws—scenarios that present verdicts in an "if . . . then" style: "If a member of the artisan class took a son as a foster child and has taught him his handicraft, he may never be reclaimed" (ANET 175-76); "If a seignior hired an ox or an ass and a lion has killed it in the open, (the loss) shall be its owner's" (ANET 176). A significant amount of the same content also appears in OT laws, and Ezekiel's disputation over responsibility in ch 18 uses the case law format to express his priestly ideals.

The third significant background aspect of chs 18—20 relates to the genre of historical rehearsal in ch 20. This type of text recounts the broad sweep of the people's history, offering a particular interpretation of the past. Ezekiel uses his historical rehearsal to recast Judah's past as a history of continuous rebellion from the very beginning, but the genre appears elsewhere in the OT with a variety of styles, lengths, and purposes (e.g., Jer 2; Hos 11; Amos 2:9-16). The liturgical materials in the Psalms, which served to sustain the people's memory and identity through worship, provide instructive examples of historical rehearsals in Pss 105 and 106. While Ezekiel's rehearsal takes the form of a narrative discourse, these psalms are poetic, liturgical compositions that constitute a praise litany and communal confession of sin. Even so, they resemble ch 20 in content and function. Psalm 105 retells the story of Israel from the time of Abraham to the people's entrance into the land of Canaan, but this telling casts Israel's past entirely as a story of Yahweh's constant goodness, making no mention of any failure or ingratitude on Israel's part. Psalm 106, viewed by scholars as a continuation of the preceding psalm, offers another retelling of Israel's story, beginning from the time of the Hebrews in Egypt and proceeding down to the Babylonian exile. In this telling, Israel's entire history has been a story of covenant failure, in which the people have been repeatedly saved only by Moses and other intercessors.

The fact that these psalms, which portray Israel's story from two different perspectives, stand side by side illuminates the nature and function of historical rehearsals like that in ch 20. Such rehearsals do not aim to provide a historical account of the past; rather, they provide an interpretation that recasts the people's history from a particular perspective and for a specific rhetorical purpose. Ezekiel's discourse in ch 20 likewise recounts the entire history of the people as a history of disobedience to illustrate the thoroughgoing nature of their rebellion against Yahweh.

A final background aspect of chs 18—20 is the possibility that some parts of these chapters have undergone later editing or were added to the material in the years after Jerusalem's destruction. For example, some interpreters conclude that the fable-like discourse in ch 19 gives indication of having passed through two stages of development, with the vine imagery in vv 10-14 perhaps representing a postexilic addition (so Zimmerli 1979, 397; but cf. Block 1997, 591). Others identify the judgment (vv 5-31) and restoration (vv 32-44) sections in ch 20 as preexilic and postexilic compositions, respectively (so Zimmerli 1979, 414; but cf. Greenberg 1983, 376-88). These theories remain speculative, however, and the discourses accomplish a significant rhetorical effect in their present form.

IN THE TEXT

1. Retribution and Judgment (18:1-32)

■ 1 The discourse in ch 18, which begins the series of three oracles that explore the question of the responsibility for Judah's exile, opens with the now-familiar prophetic word formula (see also 15:1; 16:1; 17:1; 20:2, 45; 21:1), characteristically presenting the entire passage—even the people's reported speech (see 18:2, 19, 25)—as Yahweh's direct discourse to Ezekiel, given from the divine point of view. The use of second person plural pronouns in the Hebrew of v 2, however, quickly transforms Yahweh's address to Ezekiel into a direct challenge to the prophet's audience. What follows is a divine dispute oracle with legal and priestly elements, which challenges the people's use of a popular saying to describe the realities of their situation (see Block 1997, 554-55). Unlike the immediately preceding chapters, which have focused on the people and circumstances in Jerusalem under King Zedekiah after 597 B.C., the discourse in ch 18 is both addressed to and concerned with the exiles themselves, responding to a deeply felt need and aiming to change their theological self-understanding.

■ **2-4** Yahweh's words in v 2 refer to a popular saying (**proverb;** *māšāl*) being used by the exiles that constitutes the primary point of contention in the oracle. As in the description of the eagle fable in 17:2 (see also 12:22, 27; 16:44), the Hebrew term designates a saying that requires interpretation; yet, in this context it has the sense of a common expression that has become popular in a certain cultural setting. Although the Hebrew preposition (*'al*) in the final phrase of v 2 can have an adversarial nuance ("against"), the description of this saying as **about the land of Israel** suggests that the exiles were using this proverb as a general characterization of the reality that had shaped Israel's story as a whole and their experiences in particular. The proverb, which is also quoted in Jer 31:27-30, expresses the notion of generational punishment in which later generations suffer as a result of the sins of their ancestors: **The fathers eat sour grapes, and the children's teeth are set on edge** (v 2). The imagery draws upon the common experience of a bitter taste left in one's mouth after eating fruit that has gone **sour** (or, is **unripe;** see Odell 2005, 222). After a divine oath formula in v 3 (**As surely as I live**), Yahweh forcefully refutes this proverb, particularly with two assertions (v 4): *all lives are mine* and *only the person that sins shall die* (the NIV's use of **soul** misses the meaning of the Hebrew construction here).

From this opening, modern commentators have typically understood the exiles' use of the proverb in v 2 as an attempt to maintain their own innocence, protesting that they are not guilty of the sinfulness Ezekiel has charged by appealing to a belief in corporate responsibility in which later generations may suffer for their ancestors' sins. The exiles, it is often argued, use the notion of corporate responsibility to protest that they find themselves in exile only because of the sins of an earlier generation. In this view, their protest is similar to the lament expressed in Lam 5:7, which also comes out of a context of destruction and exile for Jerusalem: "Our fathers sinned and are no more, and we bear their punishment" (e.g., see Darr 2001, 1254). This notion of corporate responsibility finds expression in some pentateuchal texts such as Exod 34:6-7, which explicitly affirm generational punishment: "Yet he does not leave the guilty unpunished; he punishes the children and their children for the sin of the fathers to the third and fourth generation" (v 7; see also Exod 20:5-6; Deut 5:9-10).

Many commentators have thus understood Ezek 18 to be Ezekiel's refutation of such corporate responsibility and an assertion of a new doctrine of individual accountability, dismissing the belief that anyone can suffer for another's sins. Interpreters have often lauded this supposedly innovative doctrine of personal responsibility as one of the most important contributions made by Ezekiel to the developing OT theological tradition (see Block 1997, 556-61; Joyce 1989; Matties 1990). According to this interpretation, the prophet insists that sinfulness and punishment are individual matters; hence the present experience of judgment can only be the responsibility of the ones being punished. Contrary to the texts noted above that assert generational punishment, the rejection of such corporate judgment also appears in the Pentateuch and elsewhere: "Fathers shall not be put to death for their children, nor children put to death for their fathers; each is to die for his own sin" (Deut 24:16; see also 2 Kgs 14:6; 2 Chr 25:4).

Although the interpretation of ch 18 as an endorsement of personal accountability resonates with modern conceptions of individualism that have been prevalent in Western society, recent assessments have proposed new understandings (see Mol 2009; Tuell 2009, 107-9; Odell 2005, 220). The text's use of plural language, especially in the closing section (vv 27-32), as well as the roles of the father, son, and grandson (vv 5-18) as representatives of whole generations, suggest that the chapter remains focused on collective responsibility and does not relegate matters of sin and judgment to the personal realm (see Mol 2009; Joyce 1989). Moreover, the rhetorical context of the trauma experienced by Ezekiel and his fellow deportees points to a different understanding of what the proverb in v 2 expressed and how Ezekiel responded to it. Rather than a protest of innocence, one may hear in the exiles' use of this proverb the defeated expression of a deterministic and fatalistic sentiment. Through the words of this common saying, the exiles acknowledge their own sinfulness and their deserved judgment but give voice to the feeling that they were destined to sin because of the bad moral character and actions of those who went before them. They express the fatalistic and despairing notion that the cycle of sin and judgment cannot be broken; their moral behavior was determined beforehand by the lifestyle of their ancestors. They became sinners because that is how they were raised. It follows, then, from the exiles' perspective that even now they have no ability to break the cycle and change the fate that has been determined by their past. In seeking to understand the trauma they have experienced, the exiles see themselves as "victims of an immutable law of the universe: the fate of one generation is inexorably determined by the actions of the previous" (Block 1997, 561).

Yahweh's opening declarations in v 4 establish ch 18 as a refutation of this deterministic and fatalistic conception. In contrast to the notion of an unbreakable scheme of forces to which a people's character and destiny are bound, Yahweh asserts that ***all lives are mine*** (v 4), rendered anew with possibility and responsibility in each successive generation (**the father as well as the son** [v 4]). As noted above, OT passages exhibit differing viewpoints on the reality of generational consequences to which the proverb alludes (cf. Exod 20:5-6; 34:6-7; Deut 5:9-10; 24:16; 2 Kgs 14:6), and human experience testifies to the powerful, often injurious effects of parents upon the lives of children. Even so, Ezekiel's rhetoric challenges the deterministic way in which the exiles have applied the proverb's meaning to their particular case. The remainder of the chapter develops Yahweh's opening declarations to mean that the exiles bear the responsibility for their own sinfulness and the judgment they have experienced; their moral character was not determined solely by their ancestors. Simultaneously, however, since the life of the present generation is not solely determined by the past, the exiles have the ability to change their fate and determine their future by their present actions, if they will break with their past identity (the old Jerusalem) in order to receive a new future brought about by Yahweh's holiness.

■ **5-18** Following the opening statements, Ezekiel offers a three-part hypothetical case study (vv 5-18) to explicate Yahweh's assertion that each generation has the possibility of (and responsibility for) forging its own moral destiny. The case study describes three generations of a single family, beginning with a righteous father (vv 5-9), who is followed by a wicked son (vv 10-13) and then a righteous grandson (vv 14-18). Rather than a simplistic statement that affirms the personal moral accountability of individuals, Ezekiel's depiction illustrates the conviction that successive generations are not locked into a moral destiny—good or bad—by the actions of their predecessors—good or bad. When read in the context of the exiles' fatalism and despair, Ezekiel's words counter the sense of a loss of control over life often experienced by trauma sufferers. The deeds and experiences of the preceding generation do not bind the next generation to a certain way of living or guarantee the results of judgment and salvation that attended to choices of the past.

The lists of righteous and wicked deeds attributed to the father (vv 5-9), son (vv 10-13), and grandson (vv 14-18) reflect the form and content of OT priestly laws, especially the Holiness Code in Lev 17—26 with its emphasis on ritual purity and defilement (see Lev 18—19). The descriptions for each family member contain many of the same actions but do not match each other precisely in the deeds or their order. The similarities perhaps indicate that Ezekiel drew from a familiar list of righteous and unrighteous behaviors, and some interpreters suggest that the actions reflect demands for entrance to the temple (e.g., Pss 15; 24) or requirements for justice placed upon kings (e.g., Ezek 34:1-10; see Block 1997, 566-69). More evidently, in a manner similar to the often underappreciated nature of the OT priestly legislation (see Lev 19), the actions described for each family member blend priestly/ritual deeds with those of social justice and ethics, rejecting any dichotomy between purity and morality. This blending, however, results in lists that contain some deeds that continue to resonate with contemporary readers (e.g., feeding **the hungry** and clothing **the naked** [vv 7, 16]) and others that seem culturally bound and foreign (e.g., lending at interest [vv 8, 17]; having intercourse **with a woman during her** menstrual **period** [v 6]; Tuell 2009, 109).

The specific priestly concerns and terminology in the lists establish the defiling nature of some of the actions as **detestable things** (*tôʿēbôt*; lit., ***abominations*** [v 13]) that threaten Yahweh's presence among the people. Additionally, the references to **idols** in vv 6, 12, and 15 use Ezekiel's pejorative term *gillûlîm*, dung pellets, and the phrase, **eat at the mountain shrines** (vv 6, 11, 15), unique to Ezekiel, likely connects with both the Holiness Code's prohibition against killing and eating animals in places other than the Jerusalem temple and Ezekiel's associations of mountains with idol worship (e.g., 6:13; Tuell 2009, 110). The sinful act to **lie with a woman during her period** (v 6), seen as only a minor defilement in some priestly texts (Lev 15:19-24), appears in the Holiness Code as one of the "abominations" (*tôʿēbôt*) that endanger Yahweh's holy presence (Lev 18:19, 24-25). When these ritual concerns are mixed with moral abominations in which one **does not oppress anyone** (vv 7, 12, 16) and **does not commit robbery** (vv 7, 12, 16), both of which refer not to simple mistreatment or thievery but to the particular denial of land rights and economic resources to the poor by the rich, it becomes clear that Ezekiel's conception of righteousness involves right relationship before Yahweh and right actions toward neighbor. Ezekiel's point is that each generation can follow this path of righteousness, regardless of who has gone before them.

■ **19a** After illustrating the message that the exiles have not been helplessly doomed to repeat the moral failures of their ancestors, Yahweh cites another statement that the exiles are allegedly saying about their situation (v 19*a*). The exiles, apparently assuming the accuracy of the initial proverb of generational determinism (v 2), ask, in effect, how it could possibly be otherwise.

Although the NIV renders the people's question in v 19 in terms of a child that must unavoidably **share the guilt** of the parents, a better translation suggests the sense that a child must "suffer for the iniquity" of the parents, regardless of its own guilt (so NRSV). We may perhaps read this question as an expression of deep resignation, as the exiles despair with some sarcasm, "Why shouldn't it be this way? That's just how the moral order works! It only makes sense that your parents' actions can lock you into a certain destiny and force you to live under their consequences." The people's sentiment again reflects the statements about generational punishment in the Ten Commandments (Exod 20:5; Deut 5:9) and also expresses the common experience that children indeed often suffer for the misdeeds of their parents and cycles of injurious behavior often seem unbreakable. We may recognize here, however, the exiles' continued attempt to forge a coherent framework to explain the trauma of exile in a way different from Ezekiel's narrative of Yahweh's holiness. The exiles place their trauma within a deterministic scheme as a function of the unavoidably mechanical way they say life operates.

■ **19b-24** Yahweh's response does not allow the people's resignation to stand. What follows in vv 19b-24, cast once again in terms of the generations of a family rather than simple individuals, is the clearest articulation of the chapter's argument that each generation has the possibility and responsibility to choose their own moral path, even if they cannot avoid all the consequences of their ancestors' choices. The righteous will receive the benefits of their righteousness and the wicked will bear the consequences of their wickedness—no matter who has gone before them (vv 19b-20). The past does not determine the future. Verses 21-22 go even further, however. The rejection of any deterministic fatalism means that even those people who have made their own choice for wickedness have not unalterably sealed their destiny. If the wicked one **turns away from all the sins** (v 21), a new moral destiny of life takes effect.

Readers may find this affirmation surprising in light of the book's consistent emphasis on the people's thorough defilement and inability to do anything to avoid the judgment that is to come. Perhaps the prophet's words here relate only to the group of Babylonian exiles with whom Ezekiel locates Judah's future made possible by Yahweh's holiness. The statement in v 23, however, seems broader. Most references to restoration in Ezekiel locate that hope solely in Yahweh's self-concern to demonstrate his holiness/sovereignty and redeem his reputation in the eyes of the nations (see 11:17-20). Yet, Yahweh's assertion in 18:23, which finally provides the reason for the open possibilities that the chapter has maintained, locates the willingness to allow each new generation the chance for hope within the essence of Yahweh's character: **Do I take any pleasure in the death of the wicked?** Alongside Yahweh's concern for holiness, Ezekiel asserts that Yahweh is fundamentally committed to life, and this character leaves open the ending of every generation's story.

■ **25** The next section begins by citing a third statement that the exiles are allegedly saying about their situation, this one more accusatory: **The way of the Lord is not just** (v 25). It is unclear whether this statement is an objection to Yahweh's assertion in vv 21-24—objecting that Yahweh's willingness to set aside the past makes him unreliable—or, a further expression of the exiles' despair that they were locked into a life of sin. While the primary Hebrew root (*tkn*) in the exiles' statement can carry the meaning of "inscrutable/unpredictable" (see Odell 2005, 227), the sense of "unfair/unjust" links the statement to the people's interpretation of the original proverb (v 2) and again expresses the exiles' sense that they were unfairly doomed to sinfulness and punishment by their lineage in a rebellious people.

■ **26-29** In vv 26-29, Yahweh rejects the people's statement by recapitulating the claims made in the preceding verses, again asserting that each generation's fate is determined only by their present actions. Moreover, Yahweh's response turns the tables on the exiles, contending that their ways have been unfair (v 29). This unfairness lies in the divine conviction that the exiles' original proverb is not true. They had a fair opportunity to follow a righteous path, and when they did not, they used a belief in fatalistic determinism as an excuse. The closing reference to the **house of Israel** in v 29 (also vv 30, 31) returns to Ezekiel's broad reference for Yahweh's people throughout their history (see 2:3), linking the exiles back into the larger story of Israel that will constitute the focus of ch 20.

■ **30-32** The transitional word, **Therefore** (*lākēn;* v 30) marks the shift to a pronouncement of judgment in vv 30-32, giving the concluding part of Yahweh's speech the typical style of a judgment saying. Yahweh declares that he will carry out judgment, but it will not be dictated by an inherited moral condition; rather, it will be for **each one according to his ways** (v 30). Even after holding out this hope, Yahweh's reference to the **house of Israel** in v 30 confirms that the exiles indeed share in the guilt that has resulted and will result in Jerusalem's present and future exile and destruction. Suddenly, however, double imperatives from the same Hebrew root (**repent; turn away;** Heb., *šûb*) in the middle of v 30 shift the final section from a judgment saying to a call to repentance. The final verses emphatically call the people to act on the real possibility to change, breaking with their former identity, and thus avoid judgment. The most surprising language of this invitation appears in v 31, where Yahweh commands the exiles to **get a new heart and a new spirit.** Although the NIV is ambiguous concerning from where this **heart** and **spirit** come, the Hebrew text points to the people's own initiative and action: ***get for***

yourselves (*lākem*). This heart and spirit imagery has appeared in 11:19 and will reappear in the book's extensive vision of transformation in 36:26-27, yet these passages stress that the **new heart** and **spirit** can only be received as a gift from Yahweh, due to the people's thoroughgoing rebellion and defilement. Moreover, although earlier chapters have included some calls to repentance, the invitation here is difficult to understand in light of the fact that judgment has already fallen upon the exiles and Ezekiel consistently affirms the inevitability of the decisive judgment still to come on Jerusalem (see chs 9; 16). Although Ezekiel maintains the exiles' culpability, he unexpectedly suggests that the people are capable of changing and attaining a righteousness that avoids full judgment.

The divine invitation at the close of ch 18 thus complicates Ezekiel's apparent understanding of the human moral self. As Bowen observes, "The fundamental assumptions about human nature in this chapter stand in tension with assumptions elsewhere in the book" (2010, 100). Does Ezekiel see human beings as possessing a "neutral moral selfhood" in which they are incapable of change or a "virtuous moral selfhood" in which they have the capacity to act rightly (see Lapsley 2000a)? We will address this issue more fully in the commentary on ch 36, but the divine command at the close of ch 18 reveals a tension maintained throughout the book. Although Ezekiel characteristically adopts the pessimistic view that humans are incapable of acting for the good, the book as a whole affirms the moral self as both something attained through human action and received as a divine gift. Later in the book (ch 36), Ezekiel seems to conclude that humans are incapable of moral goodness, yet he augments this view so that a divine act of the spirit enables a moral self that is then capable of virtue. In a manner similar to Wesley's prevenient grace, the book maintains the tension of initiative and gift—a human capacity to change through repentance, as Yahweh's Spirit reveals human need and empowers human response.

2. Lament over Jerusalem (19:1-14)

■ 1 Chapter 19, as the second in the series of three oracles that explore the question of the responsibility for Judah's exile, offers a fable-like condemnation of Judah's royal house, drawing on animal and agricultural imagery. Yahweh's opening command to Ezekiel makes clear the discourse's subject and character: **Take up a lament concerning the princes of Israel** (v 1). The reference to **princes** (*niśi'ê*) uses Ezekiel's preferred term for monarchical rulers (cf. *melek*; see 12:10), perhaps employed to stress their penultimate status under Yahweh's sovereignty. Here, the term also connotes the entire dynastic line of Judean kings and their sons/successors. Over the following verses, Ezekiel offers an allegorical portrayal of recent Judean rulers and the downfall of the royal house. Verse 1 labels this portrayal as a **lament** (*qînâ*; see also v 14*b*), a term that designates the genre of a funeral song, characterized by an uneven ("limping") 3:2 meter in Hebrew syllables and best represented in the book of Lamentations but also common in Ezekiel and other prophetic literature (e.g., Amos 5:1; Jer 7:29; Ezek 2:10; 19:1, 14; 26:17; 27:2, 32; 28:12; 32:2, 16; see Block 1997, 592).

■ **2-9** The first section of the discourse (vv 2-9) is a lament centered on the image of Jerusalem and its dynasty as a **lioness** and **her cubs.** The reference to the princes' **mother,** for which no subject is identified, continues the female personification of Jerusalem from ch 16, although here the city is given a double metaphorization, first as **mother** and then as **lioness.** The language again aims to change the audience's view of the capital city that Ezekiel sees as defiled and worthy of destruction. The precise identities of the kings (**cubs**) in the following verses remain uncertain. The first cub (vv 1-4), who was taken to Egypt, must be Jehoahaz II (ca. 609 B.C.; 2 Kgs 23:31-35), Jehoiakim's immediate predecessor. The second cub (vv 5-9), who was brought before the Babylonian king, could represent Jehoiakim, Jehoiachin, or Zedekiah (or perhaps all of them), although Jehoiachin seems likely (leaving the "stem" that suffers destruction in vv 11-14 to represent Zedekiah) (cf. Sweeney 2005, 147; Block 1997, 605).

■ **10-14** The second section (vv 10-14) continues the lament by shifting to the agricultural image of Jerusalem (**your mother**) as **a vine** (v 10) and its kings as **branches** (v 11). The language returns to Ezekiel's earlier vine imagery, where it was a symbol for Jerusalem (ch 15) and Zedekiah's reign (ch 17). For Ezekiel, the future of Jerusalem and its ruler(s) is bleak: the vine is transplanted into the wilderness and the branches are consumed by fire (19:13-14).

Together these animal and agricultural images cast the capital city and its rulers as guilty of violence, bloodshed, and injustice, all constituting acts of rebellion against Yahweh. Lions in the ancient Near East served as royal symbols, often appearing on royal seals and described as adorning Solomon's throne in 1 Kgs 10:19 (Odell 2005, 236). Yet, OT texts also use lions as an image for violent enemies, armies, and kingdoms (Pss 7:2; 10:9; Isa 5:29; Hos 5:14; Nah 2:11-12; see Block 1997, 599). More significantly, the combination of lion and vine imagery like that seen in ch 19 appears elsewhere in Jacob's blessing of Judah and his descendants in Gen 49:9-12. This connection gives Ezekiel's condemnation a broader focus, not limited to the particular Judean kings of the early sixth century B.C. but ultimately casting the entire dynasty of Judah as unrighteous and worthy of judgment.

D. Part 4: Israel's History of Sin/Rebellion (20:1-49)

I. Introduction (20:1-4)

As if to build upon the links between the imagery in ch 19 and Jacob's blessing of Judah and his descendants in Gen 49, Ezek 20 offers an extensive retelling of Israel's story from slavery in Egypt to the time of the exile. This historical rehearsal (see discussion of genre in Behind the Text)—the third oracle in a series of explorations of the responsibility for Judah's exile—is a full-scale reenvisioning of Judah's past that recasts their story as a history of continuous rebellion from the very beginning. Across chs 18—20, the prophet's shifting focus from the exiles, to the Judean kings, and now to the whole people of Israel throughout their history resists charging any one party as solely responsible for the exile but illustrates Ezekiel's view that Judah as a whole, including those exiled with the prophet in 597 B.C., share in the culpability for what has and will come upon Jerusalem.

■ **1-4** The introduction (vv 1-4) sets the scene for Ezekiel's historical rehearsal with familiar elements. The date formula in v 1 (August 14, 591 B.C.) places the oracle one year after the temple vision in chs 8—11, during the rise of Egyptian power under Psammetichus II, one of the influences that drew Judah toward open rebellion against the Babylonians in the following years (see Behind the Text). The immediate context given in the oracle is another visit to Ezekiel by a group of the **elders of Israel** who seek some kind of word from Yahweh through consultation with the prophet (see 8:1; 14:1). As in ch 14, Yahweh initially rejects the elders' inquiry (20:3) with a prophetic messenger formula (**This is what the Sovereign LORD says**) and divine oath (**As surely as I live**). In v 4, however, Yahweh concedes to respond, yet not to whatever unstated question the elders may have had in mind. Rather, he instructs Ezekiel to **confront** (lit., ***explain/make known***) the exiles **with the detestable practices** (*tôʿēbōt*; ***abominations***) of their ancestors. The use of the designation **detestable practices** here gives a priestly interpretation to all of the sinful acts described in the historical rehearsal that follows (see also 16:2). From Ezekiel's perspective, the rebellious deeds throughout the people's history constitute defiling acts that pollute Yahweh's holiness and endanger his presence among them. Yahweh's question to Ezekiel in v 4 (**Will you judge them?**) is an implicit call for both the prophet and his fellow exiles to break with their attachment to their past identity and the ways of their ancestors and consent to Yahweh's perspective on their history as one of rebellion that deserves judgment.

2. Historical Rehearsal (20:5-29)

After the introductory scene, another prophetic messenger formula marks the beginning of Yahweh's first person rehearsal of Israel's story (v 5). The rehearsal consists of two sections: (1) the historical rehearsal of Israel's rebellions (vv 5-29) and (2) an application of the past to the exiles' present and future (vv 30-44).

■ **5-29** Yahweh's rehearsal of Israel's past moves through the periods of Egyptian slavery and the exodus (vv 5-10), first (vv 11-17) and second (vv 18-26) wilderness generations, and life in the land of Canaan (vv 27-29). Each section follows the same pattern, giving the people's past a predictable and cyclical character: Yahweh reveals himself, the people rebel, Yahweh becomes angry to the point of destruction, and Yahweh ultimately decides to spare the people. The descriptions of the different eras repeat much of the same wording, especially describing the people's sin in each period with language that represents rebellion (Heb., *mārâ*) against a political overlord (**they rebelled against me;** vv 8, 13, 21—note the reassertion of Yahweh's kingship in v 33).

Ezekiel's characteristic priestly language recurs throughout the descriptions, as well, bringing the people's rebellions into the priestly conceptions that structure the book and casting them as defiling acts that impugn Yahweh's holiness (e.g., **defile** [*tāmʾē*; vv 7, 18, 26]; **idols** [*gillûlîm*; vv 7, 18]). For example, the text gives special emphasis to the **Sabbaths,** a term that occurs six times in the chapter, and the ways they were repeatedly profaned by the wilderness generation (vv 11-24). The historical origins of the Sabbath remain debated, but the notion of Sabbath as a sign of Yahweh's covenant that sets Israel apart as his people is a distinctly priestly idea (Exod 31:13-17), and the Holiness Code in particular emphasizes the connection between Sabbath observance and holiness (Lev 19:3, 30; 23:3; 26:2; see Tuell 2009, 129). Additionally, in keeping with Ezekiel's overall emphasis on Yahweh's sovereignty and initiative as the sole cause of the people's judgment and future restoration, the rehearsal presents each of Yahweh's gracious acts of relenting toward Israel as motivated not by Yahweh's compassion for Israel (cf. Hos 11:8-9) but by Yahweh's concern for his own holiness/reputation that has been defamed by the people's misdeeds: **For the sake of my name . . . being profaned in the eyes of the nations** (vv 9, 14, 22).

"Statutes That Were Not Good" (Ezek 20:25-26)

In the midst of recounting the rebellious deeds of the second wilderness generation (20:18-26), Yahweh asserts that in response to their sinfulness he **gave them over to statutes that were not good and . . . let them become defiled through their gifts—the sacrifice of every firstborn** (vv

25-26). Because these verses seem to imply that Yahweh actually commanded the people to practice child sacrifice (in order to increase their defilement for judgment), Yahweh's statement has become an interpretive crux. The challenge is even more difficult given that the Pentateuch does not mention any laws given to the second wilderness generation, and Ezekiel's claim seems to contradict Jeremiah's assertion that Yahweh never commanded child sacrifice (Jer 7:31-32). Moreover, elsewhere Ezekiel condemns child sacrifice, at least as offered to idols (16:7-21; 23:37-39). Laws in Exodus (Exod 13:13; 34:20) imply that the Israelites should satisfy Yahweh's demand that the firstborn be offered to him (Exod 22:29-30) by substituting a sheep, but texts in the historical books indicate that the Judean kings Ahaz and Manasseh practiced child sacrifice following the customs of other nations, at least under certain circumstances of distress (see 2 Kgs 16:3; 21:6; 23:10).

Early Christian interpreters used Ezek 20:25-26 as a disparaging polemic against the Jewish law. While some modern interpretations suggest that Ezekiel is condemning laws found in other Israelite law codes such as Deuteronomy (Hahn and Bergsma 2004) or implying that the ancestors misinterpreted Yahweh's demands (Odell 2005, 253), the most common interpretation concludes that the statement is similar to Paul's rhetoric in Rom 1:24-25, claiming that since Israel's heart was already so corrupt, Yahweh simply gave the people over to their evil desires (see Tuell 2009, 129-31). Perhaps, however, interpreters should give more weight to the chapter's nature as a rhetorical presentation and take Ezekiel's comment in a less literal way. The genre of ch 20 indicates that it is not intended to be an account of literal historical happenings but a rhetorical depiction designed to present Israel's past as having a particularly defiled and defiling character.

Taken as a whole, the most distinctive aspect of Ezekiel's rehearsal of Israel's history appears when ch 20 is compared with other prophetic books. The perspective on Israel's history in Jeremiah and Hosea in particular (see Jer 2; Hos 2; 11) envisions the people as having begun in faithfulness and obedience, with the exodus and wilderness time as a type of honeymoon for Yahweh and Israel, only after which Israel became unfaithful. By contrast, Ezekiel describes the people as already rebellious and unfaithful to Yahweh even while in Egypt (so also 23:1-3). This notion has some connections with Deut 29:16-17, which allude to the people remembering idols they had seen in Egypt, and more directly with Ps 106, which refers to the ancestors rebelling while in Egypt, yet no known tradition precisely resembles Ezekiel's presentation. Here again, we see Ezekiel's propensity not simply to refer to previous traditions but to reconfigure them in creative ways. For Ezekiel, the people's rebelliousness that extends to the very beginning of their history is an indicator of their thoroughgoing defilement and an explanation of the trauma that has come upon them.

3. Application to the Exiles' Present and Future (20:30-44)

■ **30-32** With the transitional **therefore** and a new messenger formula, Yahweh in v 30 breaks from the historical rehearsal and commands Ezekiel to address his fellow exiles with a challenge. Direct second person plural address (**you**) presents the exiles with the question of whether they will continue to **defile** themselves like their ancestors did. Verses 30-32 reiterate the ancestors' misdeeds, especially priestly/ritual purity violations such as child sacrifice and defilement with idols. As at the beginning of Ezekiel's encounter with the elders of the exiles (vv 1-3), Yahweh asserts that he will not be consulted by the people if they do not break with their old, impure identity.

■ **33-39** A divine oath formula in v 33 (**As surely as I live**) marks a sudden change from a challenge to the exiles to an unqualified divine determination to act. In the following verses, Yahweh asserts that he will, in fact, reestablish his lordship over the people and restore them from the places where they have been scattered. However, this envisioned restoration is an unusual, even unhappy, one, as the text describes a forcible act in which Yahweh presses his kingship upon the people and subjects them to his lordship, seemingly against their will: **I will rule over you with a mighty hand . . . and with outpoured wrath** (v 33). Yahweh's words have the feel of someone clenching their teeth in exasperation and determining to act unilaterally. The speech uses motifs that cast the future restoration as a second exodus from Egypt (vv 35-36; see Hos 2:14-23), but these are overshadowed by royal imagery of Yahweh as a conquering monarch who asserts authority, places his subjects on trial, and purges those who are rebellious (Ezek 20:36-38; see also ch 34). Yahweh's reference to making the people **pass under my rod** (20:37)—an expression found elsewhere only in Lev 27:32 as a means to set apart the tithe animals from the flock and herd—implies a selective numbering of those to be included in the new community and connects with depictions of Yahweh as king elsewhere in the book, especially in the shepherd/king imagery of ch 34. In keeping with Ezekiel's understanding of Yahweh's holiness that has been profaned among the nations, the divine address in 20:39 concludes that Yahweh will act to restore Israel, even if the people do not heed the calls to break with their old identity of rebellion and impurity, because Yahweh will no longer allow his name/reputation to be defamed. Those who choose not to live under Yahweh's kingship will simply be outside of the covenant community; thus, their actions will no longer defame Yahweh's reputation (Bowen 2010, 119).

Yahweh's heavy-handed actions reflect Ezekiel's notion of an all-encompassing divine sovereignty/holiness that provides the only possibility for a change in the people's situation, since the people do not possess the required heart and spirit that would allow them to live in holiness before Yahweh (see 11:19-20; 16:30; 18:31). As we will see in ch 36, Ezekiel ultimately comes to envision this unilateral divine action as having a transforming effect on the people, so that they are, in fact, changed, receiving a new heart and spirit that enable them to live in the presence of a holy God (see 36:22-30).

■ **40-44** The conclusion of Yahweh's address (vv 40-44) describes further what the restoration will entail. The regathered **house of Israel** will serve Yahweh with proper offerings. Verses 41-42 present the culmination of Yahweh's actions in characteristically Ezekielian terms: Yahweh's holiness will be made manifest in Israel for all the nations to see, and the exiles will finally **know/ acknowledge** (*yādaʿ*) Yahweh as sovereign.

The climax of ch 20 demonstrates again that the historical rehearsal provided here is not designed as an objective recording but as a rhetorical recasting of Israel's entire story from the priestly perspectives of Yahweh's holiness and the people's impurity. The point is to show the thoroughgoing nature of the people's sinfulness—from their very beginning and through every generation—yet, ironically, this makes Yahweh's decision to restore them in the end a truly gracious act. In the context of the trauma of deportation experienced by Ezekiel and his fellow exiles, the historical rehearsal incorporates the entirety of Israel's experiences—past rebellion, present destruction, and future restoration—into the larger plot line of Yahweh's aim to restore his holiness, cleanse the people and land, and reestablish his presence in a purified community. In Ezekiel's account, even the trauma of exile had been divinely determined in advance as early as the wilderness period (vv 23-24; see Deut 31:16-21) and was not a meaningless or incoherent event. As Darr (2001, 1291) concludes, "For Ezekiel, *everything* hangs on securing Yahweh's sovereignty and control over history," precisely because this assertion gives some meaning to the trauma that threatens to shatter Israel's existence.

The creation of a new memory for the people that is accomplished by Ezekiel's recasting of their history also addresses the issue of memory among trauma victims in particular (Bowen 2010, 122). Victims often struggle to remember and articulate the trauma they have experienced, or repress it altogether, and, as a result, they continually reexperience the trauma through intrusive emotions, images, and reactions (see Allen 1995, 122). Articulations such as Ezekiel's offer trauma victims a way to recover the memories of the experience and avoid continuously reexperiencing the trauma through indirect means.

4. Oracle of Destruction Against the Negev (20:45-49)

■ **45-49** The final verses of ch 20 in English translations stand apart from the preceding section in form and content. In the Hebrew text, vv 45-49 appear as the first five verses of ch 21, and the oracle belongs with the series of metaphorical judgment images against Jerusalem in chs 21—23. Like the following chapters, 20:45-49 uses an image—the burning of a forest—to symbolize Yahweh's destruction of Jerusalem. The Hebrew geographical term used in v 47 (*Negeb*) designates the drier area south of Jerusalem (**southern forest**; "forest of the Negeb" [NRSV]) but may serve here as a part that represents the whole of Judah or as a nickname for Jerusalem (cf. Odell 2005, 264; Block 1997, 663). In this image, readers encounter again the troubling portrayals of the divine devastation of the natural world discussed earlier with chs 4—7, yet the forest also serves as a symbol of the human inhabitants of the land (see "the mountains of Israel" in 6:1-3).

FROM THE TEXT (CHS 18—20)

Ezekiel's response to the exiles' proverb in ch 18 presents an unexpected vision of hope that combats a sense of defeatism and determinism—a strong rebuttal of the notion that some kind of generational curse unalterably defines the lives of some people. The preceding commentary has suggested that the exiles acknowledge their own sinfulness, yet they express the despairing sentiment that the destructive course of their life was unavoidably determined in advance by the actions and circumstances of those who went before them, effectively lamenting, "We ended up in sin because we had no chance against the powerful, formative conditions of our past."

In the exiles' painful sentiment, we can sense the despair of those in our world who know all too well that people often suffer for the sins of others, especially as destructive behaviors of family members shape the lives of the next generation, seemingly locking them into a harmful and dysfunctional cycle they are powerless to break. Beyond familial relations, we know the realities of how innocent persons suffer—sometimes randomly—because of the violent and unjust actions of persons they do not know, even as systemic societal sins such as racism, sexism, and economic injustice press their effects upon each new generation. Trauma studies offer an important window into these dimensions through the investigation of the possible effects of secondary and indirect trauma upon subsequent generations (see Smith-Christopher 1999, 139-43; Bowen 2010, 106). Certainly at one level ch 18 resists any conception by which persons might place all blame for their actions or circumstances on other people, but more significantly, the divine response to the exiles asserts that whatever forces and events have impacted a person or generation, it is possible to make a new present and future with God. Because all lives—individually and collectively—belong first and foremost to God (18:4), powerful cycles and destructive effects, though real, can be overcome, giving way to a new "turn," with a "new heart" and a "new spirit" (18:30-31).

The possibility of new beginnings with God also extends into the realm of human relationships and communities. God's gift of a new present and future invites persons and communities today to envision new beginnings for relationships and situations with negative histories. The future of these realities need not be determined by their past. As Odell suggests, the possibilities of new beginnings extend to the social, ethnic, and political "hot spots" of the world's conflicts, as well as the hurtful dynamics of damaged interpersonal relationships. These possibilities call us to recognize the "liberating power of forgiveness," an act that refuses to let "past hurts to dominate our hopes and dreams" or "the heart to become hardened by old patterns" (Odell 2005, 230).

Ezekiel's incorporation of both ritual/cultic concerns and economic/social practices in the case studies of ch 18 provides a vision of the holy life that integrates purity and justice. The OT's priestly material, especially the Holiness Code (Lev 17—26), regularly intertwines God's calls for purity/set-apartness through proper ritual and sacrifice with demands for social justice through provision for the poor and vulnerable (see Lev 19). By listing what constitutes righteous and wicked behavior in these terms, Ezekiel articulates the purity and justice trajectories as equal parts of the vision of holiness, noting the demands for the ritually pure to secure the economic and physical well-being of the poor by giving food to the hungry and clothes to the naked. Churches in the historic holiness traditions have often struggled to maintain the integration of purity and justice, at times emphasizing demands for cultural separateness to the neglect of the practices of social and economic justice. Ezekiel's holistic vision may provide a corrective, defining holiness as a call not only to purity but also to the physical, social, and material well-being of the other. Christian readers will sense a connection between Ezekiel's words and Jesus' parable of the final judgment (Matt 25:1-46), in which those who receive eternal life are those who fed the hungry, clothed the naked, and visited the sick (Tuell 2009, 112).

Ezekiel's historical rehearsal in ch 20, especially when combined with similar rehearsals such as Ps 105, invites people of faith to look back over the story of their lives and see a history of God's faithfulness to them. This perspective, which, as for Ezekiel, may only be recognizable in hindsight, allows one to see through eyes of faith God's gracious activity in his or her life, even without whitewashing those times of sin and failure. This kind of retrospective highlights, as does Ezekiel's rehearsal, God's repeated mercy and relenting—the divine "yet" with which God regularly turns away from often deserved judgment or abandonment. Rehearsals such as ch 20 lead contemporary believers to pray for a continuation of this divine mercy, asking God not to give up, but to hold the often unfaithful people in steadfast love and compassion.

At the same time, the practice of rehearsing our lives as stories of God's faithfulness elicits repentance, as our unfaithfulness becomes apparent by comparison. No such repentance prayer is offered by the exiles in ch 20, but a national prayer of repentance set on the lips of Daniel (Dan 9:4-19)—a prayer also placed in the context of exile—represents the kind of response to Ezekiel's rehearsal that one might imagine. Daniel's prayer looks back over Israel's history and contrasts God's faithfulness with the people's disloyalty, using language and categories at home in Ezekiel's discourse. He speaks of the people's shame (9:7), the temple's desolated state (9:17), and God's name that has been disgraced among the nations (9:16, 18). Yet Daniel goes on to articulate the repentance that might be generated by Ezekiel's historical rehearsal, a hopeful prayer grounded solely in God's initiative and holiness:

> We do not make requests of you because we are righteous, but because of your great mercy. O Lord, listen! O Lord, forgive! O Lord, hear and act! For your sake, O my God, do not delay, because your city and your people bear your Name. (Dan 9:18b-19)

E. Part 5: Metaphorical Discourses and Symbolic Acts (21:1—24:27)

BEHIND THE TEXT

Chapters 21—24 form the fourth subsection within the larger unit of symbolic acts and oracles (chs 12—24) that follows the second vision of Yahweh's glory/presence (chs 8—11). Following the series of oracles in chs 18—20 that explored the question of the responsibility for Judah's exile, chs 21—24 provide specific condemnations of Jerusalem and its leaders, further detailing their misdeeds and describing divine judgment. The chapters contain a variety of types of material, including judgment oracles, metaphorical narratives, allegories, and symbolic action reports, yet they revolve around the central images of Yahweh's sword (21:1-32), a blood-soaked city (22:1-31), faithless wives (23:1-49), and a boiling pot (24:1-14).

E. Part 5: Metaphorical Discourses and Symbolic Acts (21:1—24:27)
  1. The Sword of God (21:1-32)
  2. Jerusalem, the Bloody City (22:1-31)
  3. The Two Wives of God (23:1-49)
  4. The Boiling Pot (24:1-14)

5. Symbolic Act: Ezekiel's Muteness (Beginning of Siege) (24:15-27)

The most notable feature of chs 21—24 is the presentation of the various materials as direct personal communication from Yahweh to Ezekiel. Each chapter begins with the prophetic word formula ("The word of the LORD came to me" [21:1; 22:1; 23:1; 24:1]), and, with the exception of ch 23, pairs this expression with the prophetic messenger formula ("Thus says the LORD/Lord GOD" [21:3; 22:3; 24:3 NRSV]). Moreover, nearly every subunit within the chapters is marked by one or both of these formulas (21:1, 3, 8, 18, 24, 26, 28; 22:1, 3, 17, 19, 22, 23, 28, 31; 23:1, 22, 28, 32, 34, 35, 46; 24:1, 3, 6, 9, 15, 20, 21). The density of these repeated formulas places an even heavier emphasis than elsewhere in the book on the divine origin of the judgment images in the chapters. The speeches in chs 21—24 also contain several genres and elements that we have explored in previous Behind the Text sections. Chapters 21, 22, and 24 feature metaphorical discourses (see Behind the Text for chs 15—17), and ch 23 relies on the prophetic tradition of personifying cities (especially Samaria and Jerusalem) as females, in general, and Yahweh's wives, in particular (see Behind the Text for chs 15—17). Symbolic actions appear throughout the chapters (21:6-7, 14, 18-23; 24:15-27; see Behind the Text for chs 4—7), and, as with most passages in chs 12—24, scholars propose various texts as later additions that presuppose Jerusalem's fall (e.g., 21:28-32; 22:23-31; e.g., Zimmerli 1979, 467; Hals 1989, 161).

Perhaps most significantly, 24:1 contains the next date formula in the book ("ninth year, in the tenth month on the tenth day"; January 15, 588 B.C.), the first since 20:1, which was set two years earlier. The surrounding verses (24:1-2) reveal the date's significance. Ezekiel's metaphorical discourse (24:3-14) and symbolic action (24:15-27) are set on the day that Nebuchadnezzar's Babylonian forces began their siege of Jerusalem. As discussed previously (see Behind the Text for chs 12—24), Zedekiah's moves toward rebellion against Babylonia had increased after 592 B.C., especially under Egyptian influence, until he entered into open rebellion likely in the late 590s or early 580s. In response to Judah and perhaps others, the Babylonians appear to have subsequently adopted a new policy toward rebellious kingdoms that entailed removing the ruling family from power and relocating the kingdom's capital. Sometime in the fall of 589 B.C., Nebuchadnezzar set out from Babylonia to make Jerusalem the first example of this new policy. He led his forces to central Syria and established a base of operations at Riblah. There, he apparently divided his forces (see 21:18-20) and sent one contingent southward to place Jerusalem under siege. The Babylonian siege of Jerusalem would last for more than a year and involve a number of developments such as an ineffectual Egyptian intervention, eventually ending when the Babylonians breached Jerusalem's walls in the summer of 586 B.C. (see Behind the Text for chs 33—37).

With the commencement of the Babylonian siege, trauma again moves to the fore of Ezekiel's experience, tone, and message. For the final siege of Jerusalem, the biblical texts depict dire conditions, especially severe famine in the city (2 Kgs 25:1-3). These descriptions fit well with the attested realities of ancient siege warfare, known primarily from the Assyrian Empire, the immediate predecessors of the Babylonians (evidence for Babylonian tactics is much more limited). Assyrian texts and pictorial reliefs depict the standard siege practices of surrounding a city to cut off supplies, constructing siege ramps of earth and stone (the archaeological remains of one such ramp, nearly two hundred feet long, still appear at the site of the ancient city of Lachish), and moving large battering rams into place against the walls. City sieges often involved practices of brutality and psychological warfare aimed at the barricaded inhabitants, including the displaying of severed heads and the impaling of captured warriors or citizens on tall stakes around the outskirts of the city. For those in a city under siege, starvation, fear, and desperation characterized daily existence, as the threat of enemy swords, bloodshed, and capture loomed just outside the walls. These realities, likely experienced on a prolonged basis by the Jerusalemites beginning in 588 B.C., clearly fit with the definition of traumatic events as physical, psychological, social, and economic experiences of terror, death, helplessness, oppression, warfare, and more, experiences that resist integration into the narrative of the individual's or community's life (Geller 2000, 261).

For Ezekiel, these realities signaled the beginning of the final destruction of Jerusalem that he has repeatedly identified for his fellow exiles as the full manifestation of Yahweh's judgment. Rather than gleeful satisfaction, however, the prophet's tone and words in chs 21—24 reflect the trauma associated with the horrific experiences of siege warfare. As trauma study has revealed, the effects of trauma can be experienced even indirectly or secondarily by associated groups not directly involved in the immediate events (Smith-Christopher 1999, 139-43; Herman 1997). Yet Ezekiel and those who had been deported after the Babylonians' first capture of Jerusalem in 597 B.C. had also experienced such war realities firsthand. The metaphorical discourses and symbolic acts in chs 21—24, with their vivid depictions of swords, armies, slaughter, bloodshed, and even sexual violence, are among the book's most explicit representations of the experiences of warfare and represent the culmination of Ezekiel's judgment preaching. As Bowen states, "For a moment, the veil over the trauma is lifted and readers are given a glimpse of the terror they must have faced" (2010, 123). Combined with the high number of prophetic word and messenger formulas, these images give chs 21—24 an intensity that resembles a wartime communiqué, written under the duress of battlefield conditions.

IN THE TEXT

I. The Sword of God (21:1-32)

■ 1-7 After the prophetic word formula and the characteristic designation of Ezekiel as **son of man,** Yahweh begins his discourse to Ezekiel with the recurrence of a command that designates hostility or opposition (**set your face against** [v 2]; see also 4:3; 6:1). The opening verses direct Yahweh's judgments specifically to **Jerusalem,** the political center for Zedekiah and those remaining with him in Judah, but also expand the address to include the people's *sanctuaries* (Heb., pl.; cf. **sanctuary**) and the whole **land of Israel.** The beginning of Yahweh's discourse adds another metaphorical image of the coming judgment to the fire in the Negev that appeared in 20:45-49. Verse 3 introduces the image of Yahweh's **sword** that he has unsheathed and will now wield against Judah. The use of the **sword** as a weapon has appeared throughout the book (e.g., 5:1-2; 6:3, 8, 11-12; 11:8, 10; 12:14, 16; 14:17, 21; 16:40; 17:21), but here the text introduces a series of oracles within ch 21 that together chart the "military 'career' of a sword unsheathed by Yahweh [vv 1-7], sharpened and polished for battle [vv 8-17], handed over to the king of Babylonia [vv 18-29], and finally destroyed by the fiery breath of God [vv 30-32]" (Darr 2001, 1292).

The opening declaration of judgment in vv 1-7, however, contains the surprising assertion that Yahweh will cause his destruction to fall on **both the righteous and the wicked** (vv 3-4), an assertion that contrasts with Ezekiel's theological argument in ch 18 and elsewhere (see 9:4-6; 14:12-20) that only the wicked will die for their sins. These contrasts, which should not simply be dismissed, remind us that Ezekiel was not attempting to construct a systematic theology of the divine-human relationship. Rather, the sentiment expressed in 21:3-4 is perhaps better understood as a reflection of the realities of warfare experienced by Ezekiel and his people where innocent people die and collateral damage is seemingly unavoidable. For Ezekiel, as so often for contemporary people of faith, the traumatic experiences of war seem to problematize any neatly packaged theologies of judgment and responsibility. In response to this opening declaration of judgment, Yahweh instructs Ezekiel to carry out the first of the chapter's symbolic acts (vv 6-7): to **groan** in mourning before his fellow exiles and identify the action as a response to the total divine destruction that is to come (see also v 12).

■ 8-17 Another pairing of the prophetic word and messenger formulas (vv 8-9) shifts from Yahweh's opening declaration of judgment to a poetic reflection on the divine sword, itself (vv 9b-17). Textual difficulties make any interpretation of the passage provisional, as portions of vv 10 and 13 are incomprehensible in Hebrew and nearly every verse is unclear at various points. The oracle as a whole pictures the divine sword as sharpened, polished, and drawn for battle, and the conclusion in vv 14-17 depicts the sword in action, describing the siege of a city with soldiers surrounding its gates. Yahweh's first person reflection on his sword also includes instructions for Ezekiel to carry out two symbolic actions—one again representing mourning over the slaughter and destruction (**Cry out and wail** [v 12]) and the other symbolizing the furious slashes of the sword in action (**strike your hands together** [v 14]—mirrored by Yahweh in v 17; see also 6:11).

At the heart of this reflection on the sword is Yahweh's depiction of the people as a rebellious child. The notoriously difficult Hebrew in vv 10 and 13, which the NIV renders as a specific condemnation against Jerusalem's royal house (**scepter of my son Judah** [v 10]; **scepter of Judah** [v 13]), is more adequately translated without the addition of the word "Judah," which does not appear in the Hebrew: "you have despised the rod [šēveṭ] and all discipline" (v 10 NRSV); "you despise the rod" (šēveṭ; v 13 NRSV). The imagery invokes the parent-child metaphor for Yahweh and Israel/Judah used elsewhere in the prophetic books (e.g., Isa 1:2-6; Hos 11:1-9). The prophetic metaphor of childhood and discipline draws upon the legal procedure for dealing with a repeatedly rebellious child in Deut 21:18-21, which prescribes a two-step process. First, the rebellious child is subjected to an initial act of discipline by the parents, often represented by the "rod" in prophetic texts, and then given a chance to reform, so as to avoid further punishments. If, however, the child scorns the initial discipline and continues to rebel, the law prescribes a second, final punishment that constitutes the death penalty (by stoning in Deut 21:21). While contemporary readers must surely reject the kind of physical punishment that this ancient law envisions, prophetic texts such as Ezek 21 use the metaphor to depict Yahweh's people as a rebellious child who has already suffered the initial blow of punishment (perhaps, for Ezekiel, Jerusalem's first capture and deportation in 597 B.C.) and yet seems determined to continue to rebel. Hence, in the context of Ezekiel's oracle, the people's continual rebellion means Yahweh now turns to the death penalty represented by the divine sword, as the rod that disciplines gives way to a steel rod (i.e., a sword) that kills (Bowen 2010, 126).

■ **18-23** The prophetic word formula at the start of v 18 marks the second half of the chapter, which begins with instructions for Ezekiel to perform another symbolic action (vv 18-20) and proceeds through an explanation of the act (vv 21-23) and a two-part judgment oracle (vv 24-27, 28-32) (Odell 2005, 268).

Yahweh instructs Ezekiel to make a **signpost** at a fork in the road (v 19) for Nebuchadnezzar and the Babylonian army, indicating the roads toward **Rabbah,** the capital of Ammon, and **Jerusalem,** at the heart of Judah (v 20). The oracle extends the image of Yahweh's sword from the first half of the chapter, but with Yahweh now placing the **sword** into the hands of the Babylonian king to wield against Jerusalem (v 19). The depiction here likely reflects the traumatic realities underway in the years leading up to the Babylonian siege of Jerusalem, as commentators generally associate this oracle with Nebuchadnezzar's campaign to the west in 589/588 B.C. and his establishment of a base of operations at Riblah in northern Syria from which he apparently divided his forces westward toward the border of Egypt and eastward toward Jerusalem (see Behind the Text). Though Nebuchadnezzar uses divination to seek direction from his own gods, Ezekiel's oracle implies that Yahweh directs Nebuchadnezzar's steps (and sword!) to the path that leads to Jerusalem (vv 21-23).

■ **24-27** The transitional word **therefore** and the prophetic messenger formula in v 24 begin a judgment oracle that connects Ezekiel's symbolic action about the Babylonian king to the sins and punishment of Judah's king (vv 24-27). The oracle is general at first (v 24), addressing the people with plural pronouns in Hebrew (e.g., **you people**) and highlighting actions that, in the context of ch 21, carry the connotations of political **rebellion** wherein Judah has violated its treaties/oaths to Babylonia—a **guilt** that has now come to light before Nebuchadnezzar (Odell 2005, 270). The appearance of a second person singular pronoun in Hebrew at the start of v 25 (**you;** omitted by NIV), however, abruptly shifts to a specific condemnation addressed directly to King Zedekiah in Jerusalem. As elsewhere in Ezekiel's rhetoric, the oracle designates Judah's monarch merely as a **prince** (see 19:1; 45:7-9)—and a **wicked** one, at that! Not only does this designation assert a penultimate status for Zedekiah compared to Yahweh (and perhaps also to Nebuchadnezzar, his overlord, or Jehoiachin, the exiled Judean king), vv 26-27 specifically envision his removal from the throne (**remove the crown**) and Jerusalem's ultimate destruction (**A ruin! A ruin!**).

■ **28-32** The chapter closes with a two-part judgment oracle that is "extraordinarily difficult" to read both textually and exegetically (see Greenberg 1997, 435-38). The oracle combines elements from earlier sections and returns to the image of the sword drawn for battle, yet it remains nearly impossible to sort out who is doing what, to whom, and under what circumstances (cf. Odell 2005, 273-74; Bowen 2010, 131). On the surface, vv 28-29 constitute an oracle against Ammon, one of the kingdoms located east of the Jordan River and Dead Sea that will later (25:1-7) be the first kingdom condemned in Ezekiel's oracles against the nations (chs 25—32) for their joy at Jerusalem's destruction. Verses 30-32 of ch 21, however, seem to shift to an oracle addressed to the sword itself, with Yahweh ordering the sword to cease from its destruction and even passing judgment on the sword. If the sword here represents Nebuchadnezzar (see v 19; but cf. Odell 2005, 274-75), the oracle may proclaim that Yahweh will eventually judge Nebuchadnezzar for his arrogance and violence after he has completed his role as Yahweh's instrument of punishment for Judah (so also the Assyrian king in Isa 10). Yet, such a condemnation would be unusual in Ezekiel, as the book contains no other explicit judgment against Babylonia (but perhaps see chs 38—39), likely due to Ezekiel's conviction that rebellion against Babylonia constituted one of Judah's primary acts of unfaithfulness against Yahweh.

2. Jerusalem, the Bloody City (22:1-31)

Yahweh's address to Ezekiel in ch 22 adds another metaphorical image for Jerusalem, its sin, and its judgment that builds upon the image of the divine sword in ch 21. The chapter divides into three oracles marked off by the prophetic word formula (vv 1-16, 17-22, 23-31) and reads like a type of greatest hits collection, repeating several elements that have appeared elsewhere in Ezekiel's messages (especially ch 18) and drawing heavily upon Israel's legal tradition: idols (22:4), social injustice (vv 7, 29; Exod 22:21-22; Lev 19:33-34), taking interest (Ezek 22:12; Exod 23:8; Lev 25:36-37), profaned Sabbaths (Ezek 22:8, 26; Exod 20:8-11; Lev 19:30), eating upon mountains (Ezek 22:9), defiling sexual activity (vv 10-11; Lev 18:7-20; 20:11-21), and prophets who smear whitewash (Ezek 22:28; 13:8-15).

■ **1-5** The discourse employs these elements in the service of an overall metaphor describing Jerusalem as a **city of bloodshed** (v 2; or *bloody city*) and alternating between words from Yahweh to Ezekiel and to the city. Ezekiel may have borrowed this title (**city of bloodshed**) from Nah 3:1, where it is used for Nineveh, the capital of the Assyrian Empire. The image and the descriptions that follow have multiple nuances, presenting Jerusalem both as a violent shedder of blood and as impure because of blood contamination (as in contact with a menstruating woman, Ezek 22:10). The depictions combine to give the impression of Jerusalem as a thoroughly *blood-soaked city*. As at the beginning of the historical rehearsal in 20:4, Yahweh asks Ezekiel if he will **judge** the city (v 2), rhetorically signaling the need for the exiles to break with any attachment to Jerusalem and their old identity. Yahweh also commands Ezekiel to make known Jerusalem's **detestable practices** (*abominations; tôʿēbôt*), using the now familiar priestly term to cast all of the sins that follow as defiling actions that pollute Yahweh's sanctuary and push his holy presence away from the people (v 2).

■ **6-16** The first section detailing how those in Jerusalem have **shed blood** (vv 6-16) especially singles out the city's political rulers, again labeled only as **princes** (see 21:25; 22:25). The list of misdeeds is similar to that of the wicked son in 18:10-12, reflecting several of the priestly laws for Sabbath and sexual purity (22:8-11; Lev 18:6-20), and highlighting unjust social practices toward the **alien, fatherless,** and **widow** (Ezek 22:7). Together, these misdeeds give a chilling picture of a society in which no one explicitly commits murder but people use unjust, even legally sanctioned, economic and power systems to do violence against the vulnerable in society (Greenberg 1983, 154; Odell 2005, 282). The special attention given to wives, daughters, and sisters in vv 11-12 presents an even more troubling, and still familiar, picture of a society in which women are particularly vulnerable to being preyed upon even by those in their own families. Yahweh's culminating pronouncement against Jerusalem in vv 15-16 employs the typical priestly language we have come to expect in Ezekiel. Yahweh declares his intention to exile the Jerusalemites as a means of removing their **uncleanness** (the cultic impurity term, tm'), dealing with his or their defilement in the eyes of the nations (cf. NIV and NRSV on v 16) and causing the people finally to **know/*acknowledge*** (*yāda'*) Yahweh. Here again we see Ezekiel's primary theological effort to explain the exile and destruction in the priestly terms of dealing with the people's impurity and establishing Yahweh's holiness.

Immigrants, Orphans, and Widows

Many prophetic oracles (e.g., 22:7-12) deal particularly with the just treatment of immigrants, orphans, and widows—three groups that represent members of society who are often vulnerable and disenfranchised within both ancient and modern economic and political systems. Laws dealing with the treatment of such vulnerable persons appear throughout the OT's legal texts (e.g., Exod 22:21; 23:9, 12; Lev 19:9-10; Deut 14:29; 16:11, 14; 24:14-21; 26:12-13; see Darr 2001, 1309). The command to provide for these persons is a command to seek out and give to those who will never be in a position to reciprocate the kindness.

■ **17-22** Verses 17-22 introduce a new image of Jerusalem's coming destruction drawn from ancient metal-working practices and similar to that in Isa 1:21-26. The imagery reflects the process of extracting metals such as silver, tin, and iron from lead ore and the impure byproduct (**dross**) left over from the extraction (Darr 2001, 1312). Unlike Isaiah, in which the people become pure by having the impure residue melted away, Ezekiel portrays the people as **dross** and impure metals, left only to be destroyed like metals in a smelter.

■ **23-31** In vv 23-31, the judgment against Jerusalem reaches its climax, as Yahweh commands Ezekiel to relay an extensive condemnation of the major groups of political, religious, and socioeconomic leaders. Similar lists of judgments against leaders appear in various prophetic texts (e.g., Jer 5:31; Mic 3:11), and Ezekiel's oracle may be most directly dependent upon the earlier seventh-century oracle in Zeph 3:3-4. The NIV follows the Septuagint for v 25 (Heb., **prophets**) and so places the **princes** at the head of the list, as in v 6, returning to ch 19's imagery of vicious animals to describe the violence of the royal house. Verse 26 condemns Jerusalem's **priests** for their failure to teach Yahweh's **law** (*tôrâ*) concerning ritual and cultic purity/holiness, and v 27 again employs animal imagery to condemn the bloodshed done by other groups of **officials** (*śar*). The judgment on the **prophets** in v 28 repeats the imagery of ch 13, casting them as smearing **whitewash** over a cracked wall by preaching falsely (see also v 30). Verse 29 then extends the divine condemnations beyond political and religious leaders to **the people of the land.** Although the exact identity of this group remains unclear, the label, which appears in numerous OT texts, often designates a particular class of well-off landowners with significant political and social influence.

The condemnation against the priests in v 26 is a fitting climax to the sins of Jerusalem, as it brings together all the major categories and concerns of Israel's holiness/purity system (see Lev 10:10) and represents a microcosm of the priestly framework within which Ezekiel interprets the trauma of Judah's exile and destruction. The people have failed to maintain the distinction **between the holy and the common . . . the unclean and the clean,** and, as a result, Yahweh's holiness has become **profaned among them.** Instead of maintaining these boundaries and preserving a holiness in which Yahweh could dwell with the people, Jerusalem's defiling actions have forced Yahweh to withdraw and produced the need to cleanse the land from their impurities.

3. The Two Wives of God (23:1-49)

Chapter 23 introduces a new image in the series of metaphors in chs 21—24 by recapitulating the portrayal of Jerusalem as Yahweh's unfaithful wife from ch 16, this time portraying both the capital cities of Samaria and Jerusalem as adulterous wives married to the same divine spouse. Here again, the reader encounters the troubling marital/sexual metaphor, which features graphic portrayals of women and the violent, physical abuse of a woman's body by a husband who is seen as meting out justifiable punishment (see Galambush 1992). The Behind the Text discussion for ch 16 identified the ways such portrayals draw upon ancient Near Eastern and OT traditions of personifying cities as females to achieve certain rhetorical aims, and the From the Text section for ch 16 highlighted the problems these metaphors present for contemporary readers. The reader should consult those discussions again for ch

23, although another iteration of such sexual and violent imagery only makes these discourses more difficult to endure.

While chs 16 and 23 reflect the same type of metaphorical discourse, they have notable differences (see Block 1997, 729-30). In addition to the inclusion of Samaria, ch 23 is closer to ch 20 in accusing the people of unfaithfulness already during their time in Egypt rather than only in the land of Canaan (cf. 16:1-5; 20:5-8). The misdeeds depicted by the sexual imagery in ch 23 also focus more on political alliances and international relations, rather than cultic sins. Perhaps most notably, the language and descriptions in ch 23 are even more violent and graphic than those in ch 16. Ezekiel's portrayal, for instance, resembles both ch 16 and Jeremiah's depiction of "faithless Israel" and "unfaithful Judah" as Yahweh's adulterous wives in Jer 3:6-11, but multiplies explicit details of the women's sexuality, murder, and dismemberment, now depicting, rather than simply threatening, the attack on the women/cities.

■ **1-4** The opening prophetic word formula (v 1) establishes ch 23 as another divine address to Ezekiel. The remainder of the discourse alternates between divine speech to the prophet that describes the women in third person (especially Samaria, vv 5-10) and direct speech to female Jerusalem, in particular (vv 22-35, 40-41, 49). Verses 2-4 present the basic metaphor of two sisters, already engaged in sexual misbehavior in Egypt. Verse 3 introduces the Hebrew root *znh* ("to fornicate"; **became prostitutes**) as the primary, overall metaphor for all of the actions that follow. As discussed with ch 16, the term need not indicate professional prostitution, but serves in various contexts as a metaphor for religious, political, and economic misdeeds that the prophets see as wanton and illicit, representing acts of unfaithfulness to Yahweh. The opening also assigns names to the sisters: **Oholah** for the older Samaria and **Oholibah** for the younger Jerusalem. Both names derive from the Hebrew word for "tent," with **Oholah** ("her [own] tent") perhaps referring to the northern kingdom's independent sanctuary or sanctuaries, and **Oholibah** ("my tent [is] in her") referring to Yahweh's sanctuary in Jerusalem (Eichrodt 1970, 322). The precise meaning of these names remains unclear, yet v 4 establishes their identities as **Samaria** and **Jerusalem,** respectively.

Already in the opening of the discourse, however, there is an ambiguity in the text's portrayal of the sisters in Egypt. On one hand, the text describes them as engaging in fornication, yet the detailed language of their sexual activity presents the women as passive recipients upon whom others force themselves: **their breasts were fondled and their virgin bosoms caressed** (v 3; see also v 8). Readers examining the text with gender concerns in mind can see here a slippage in the metaphor that betrays the text's patriarchal perspective, seemingly blaming these young girls for misbehavior and masking the reality that they were actually victims (see van Dijk-Hemmes 1995). From another perspective, Odell proposes that the text uses this ambiguity to suggest that the women initiated relations with their lovers for what they thought would be their own benefit, but eventually lost control of these illicit relationships, which became destructive to them: "Dalliance turns into rape, trade into plunder" (Odell 2005, 298). Perhaps the passive language in v 3, however, connects more directly with the portrayal of Jerusalem as an abandoned infant at the outset of ch 16. The passive language in v 3 initially presents the young sisters as sympathetic and vulnerable figures, subject to molestation and sexual exploitation while in Egypt. The Hebrew pual (passive) verb form (*mōʿăkû*; **they were squeezed**) is perhaps best understood not as indicating toleration (**they let their breasts be squeezed**) but compulsion (**they had to let their breasts be squeezed**) (contra Block 1997, 732). Just as in ch 16, v 4 then depicts Yahweh's intervention that rescues the sisters from this helpless situation (lit., **they became mine**), as Yahweh marries them and establishes a family (cf. 16:8-14). Yet, just as in the previous metaphor in ch 16, the sisters quickly turned away from this relationship into fornication with other lovers (23:5; cf. 16:15).

■ **5-10** The first section of accusations (23:5-10) retells the history of the northern kingdom as the life story of the elder sister, **Oholah** (Samaria). This section begins what is a chapter-long, thoroughgoing, and one-sided portrayal of the two sisters as out-of-control sex addicts, driven by lust and insatiable desire for any males that seem attractive and powerful. Yahweh narrates Oholah's story to Ezekiel, employing **prostitution** (*znh*, v 5) first and foremost as a political metaphor and condemning the woman Samaria for pursuing alliances with the Assyrians, which are seen as a way of being unfaithful to Yahweh. The text describes Assyria's political and military leaders as Oholah's **lovers** (v 5), who are stately, attractive, and powerful (v 6). The use of **lovers** as a metaphor for political allies reflects the common language of ancient Near Eastern political treaties in which vassal peoples are commanded to "love" their overlords through obedience and loyalty (see Kelle 2005, 112-22). Verse 7 not only adds a religious dimension to these political relationships (**idols**) but also employs the priestly language of defilement (*tāmēʾ*) to place Samaria's actions within Ezekiel's category of ritual impurity that threatens Yahweh's presence among the people.

Each of the accusation sections for Samaria and Jerusalem are followed by a section of consequences introduced by the transitional word, **therefore** (*lākēn;* vv 9, 22). Verses 9-10 conclude the depiction of Oholah with Yahweh's first person recounting of the ironic judgment that fell upon the city. At Yahweh's direction, the very lovers after whom Oholah had sought came against her and **stripped her naked** (v 10). The sexually violent language here is a common metaphor for city destruction in prophetic texts that personify cities as females (see Hos 2:2-3), and the text appears to be a clear reference to the Assyrian capture of Samaria in the late 720s B.C. (2 Kgs 17:1-6).

■ **11-21** Yahweh's first person narration continues in vv 11-21 with the accusations against **Oholibah** (Jerusalem). The indictment continues the overall metaphor of the city as a faithless bride, as well as the use of *fornication* (*znh*) as a metaphor for unacceptable political alliances. Yahweh charges that **Oholibah** did not learn from the fate of her older sister but became even more corrupt in her **lust** and **prostitution** (*znh*; v 11) by pursuing alliances not only with the **Assyrians** but also with the **Chaldeans/Babylonians** and *Egyptians*. The specific accusations divide into three sections based on these different lovers: vv 11-13 (Assyrians), vv 14-18 (Chaldeans), vv 19-21 (Egyptians). Two themes are evident throughout Yahweh's accusations. First, there are several apparent connections with Judean history, especially events during the reign of Zedekiah leading up to the Babylonian siege of Jerusalem in 588 B.C. The sequence of Jerusalem's turning from Babylonian to Egyptian lovers, for instance, reflects Zedekiah's placement into power by the Babylonians in 597 B.C. and his subsequent rebellious involvement with Egypt during the resurgence of Pharaoh Psammetichus II around 590 B.C. For Ezekiel, however, this shift simply represents a return to the illicit relationships that characterized the woman Jerusalem in Egypt (see vv 2-3).

Second, Ezekiel's priestly interpretation of Judah's past sets the terms once again, as the discourse repeatedly casts Oholibah's political dalliances as ritually *defiling* acts (*tm'*) that polluted Yahweh's dwelling among the people (vv 13, 17). By drawing on the sexual purity taboos of priestly laws, Ezekiel describes the personified Jerusalem's political dealings with some of the most sexually explicit, lewd, and even pornographic metaphors found in the chapter, often obscured by English translations. The text portrays Oholibah as filled with lust over the physical attractiveness of the foreigners (v 12), even moved to solicitation by the mere sight of **figures of** the **Chaldeans** portrayed in wall carvings (vv 14-16). Verse 17 euphemistically depicts a bedroom scene in which the Babylonians **entered** and **defiled her,** and v 20 gives a graphic depiction in which Oholibah is attracted to the Egyptians because of the large size of their **genitals.** Clearly, these portrayals serve to cast the southern kingdom's political maneuverings as shameful activities by someone who knows that the deeds are harmful but is unable to stop. Part of this depiction portrays Oholibah as having gone to bed with one set of lovers and then immediately **turned away from them in disgust** (v 17). At one level, this kind of jumping from lover to lover reflects the instability of Jerusalem's political actions over the last years of its existence. At another level, however, such actions again resonate with the realities of trauma, reflecting especially the lingering effects often faced in adulthood by one who was uncared for as a child—namely, the inability to form healthy, lasting relationships (see the portrayal of the sisters in Egypt).

Chaldeans and Babylonians

Ezekiel's discourse in 23:14-17 uses the term "Chaldeans" to refer to the Babylonians whose empire dominated the ancient Near East from the late seventh to mid-sixth centuries B.C. The Chaldeans were actually a specific ethnic group of Arameans from the area of the Persian Gulf south of Babylonia. Not native Babylonians, they came to power in Babylonia around 625 B.C. and led the resurgence that came to be designated as the Neo-Babylonian Empire (ca. 625-539 B.C.). Ezekiel's terminology may reflect his knowledge of the nonnative origin of the rulers in Babylonia.

■ **22-35** Yahweh's sudden switch to direct, second person address to Oholibah in v 21 constitutes a hinge between the preceding indictment (vv 11-21) and the following pronouncement of judgment (vv 22-35). Beginning with the transitional **Therefore** (*lākēn*; v 22), Yahweh pronounces the sentence of destruction and exile on Jerusalem, once again revealing Ezekiel's theological explanation for the trauma that he and his fellow exiles have experienced and will continue to experience vis-à-vis their religious and political capital. The description of destruction remains within the discourse's marital metaphor and provides an ironic judgment in which the same **lovers (Babylonians, Chaldeans, Pekod, Shoa, Koa, Assyrians)** that Jerusalem had pursued will turn against her (vv 22-23). Rather than giving a precise historical account of sixth-century B.C. events, the depiction seems to draw together Jerusalem's various encounters with hostile forces like the Assyrians and Babylonians into a comprehensive picture of assault (unless the Assyrians are envisioned as having been incorporated in the forces of the Babylonians). Most emphatically, however, the opening prophetic messenger formula and repeated divine first person statements (**I will stir up . . . I will bring them** [v 22]) emphasize that Yahweh is the agent behind all of the political and military events being described. In the face of traumatic events open to various interpretations, Ezekiel again asserts Yahweh's sovereignty/holiness as the sole force behind Judah's experiences.

23:11-35

Verses 22-29 portray Jerusalem's divine judgment with the imagery of a well-outfitted ancient army, conducting a military invasion, siege, and capture of a city. Yet because the text's rhetoric keeps this portrayal within the metaphor of Jerusalem as the wife of Yahweh, these military actions are described as personal, violent, and sexual acts against a woman's body: **cut off your *nose* [noses] and your ears** (v 25); **strip you of your clothes** (v 26); **leave you naked and bare** (v 29) (see also v 47 and the treatment of Samaria in v 10). As noted previously, this type of physical and sexual violence against a woman is a common metaphor for city destruction in prophetic texts (see Behind the Text for ch 16). In keeping with the trauma dimensions of Ezekiel's preaching, however, the descriptions here also reflect war atrocities and cruel treatment of prisoners of war attested in some ancient Near Eastern warfare accounts. While detailed accounts of Babylonian practices are lacking, Assyrian royal inscriptions preserve and even celebrate the atrocities done to victims of a conquered city. One such annal of the Assyrian king Ashurnasirpal II (883-859 B.C.) reports the following actions taken against a captured territory:

> I made a pile of their corpses. I burnt their adolescent boys (and) girls. I flayed Hulaya their city ruler (and) draped his skin over the wall . . . I captured many troops alive: I cut off some of their arms (and) hands; I cut off of others their noses, ears, (and) extremities. I gouged out the eyes of many troops. (Quoted in Block 1997, 751-52)

Ezekiel's rhetoric is disturbing in the extreme, as he not only projects these actions will come against Jerusalem but identifies Yahweh as the one ultimately responsible for the atrocities. The rhetorical move becomes more understandable, however, in the context of dealing with the trauma of destruction and exile. In the midst of an ancient context in which such a defeat could easily be understood as a sign of the failure of Judah's God, Ezekiel makes the daring assertion that even the worst atrocities of Judah's experience remain under Yahweh's own sovereignty. Such a claim is certainly disconcerting to modern readers and perhaps only functions coherently as an attempt to reinterpret disaster within ancient Judah's theological system and against the background of a trauma that threatened to dismantle that entire belief system.

After a summary statement in v 30, vv 31-35 conclude Oholibah's primary sentence with the common prophetic symbol of a divine **cup** of wrath (see Isa 51:17-22; Jer 25:15-29). Beginning with a prophetic messenger formula (Ezek 23:32), Yahweh directly addresses Oholibah and declares that she will drink the same **cup** of destruction that her **sister Samaria** drank. In keeping with the text's depiction of Jerusalem as characterized by an obsession and excess that go beyond those of Samaria, the verses paint a masochistic scene in which Jerusalem will not only drain the **cup** of wrath but go on to "gnaw its sherds" (NRSV) and **tear your breasts** (v 34). As Bowen (2010, 142) observes, this disturbing image culminates Oholibah's portrayal by turning her former "sources of pleasure" into "sources of pain."

■ **36-44** A new prophetic word formula and designation of Ezekiel as **son of man** (v 36) switches Yahweh's direct address from Jerusalem back to the prophet. Verse 36 returns to the previously used question, **Will you judge Oholah and Oholibah?** (see 20:4; 22:1), which introduces a legal judgment speech and invites Ezekiel to render a verdict based on the evidence that precedes and follows. The question also signifies another call for Ezekiel and his fellow exiles to separate from any attachment that may remain to their old capital city. The passage as a whole fits uneasily in the chapter, as it suddenly reintroduces the already destroyed **Oholah** (Samaria), giving a more detailed reprise of both sister cities' misdeeds, and contains some textually difficult and unclear verses (e.g., vv 40-44; see Greenberg 1997, 490). In describing again the sisters' behavior, vv 36-44 go over familiar ground, employing marriage/fornication imagery for political and cultic misdeeds (vv 37, 40-44) and providing a priestly interpretation that casts those misdeeds as ritually defiling acts (*tôʿēbôt*; v 36) that pollute Yahweh's sanctuary and holiness (vv 38-39).

■ **45-49** The metaphorical discourse ends with the announcement of final judgment on the two sister cities (vv 45-49). The section has the feel of a legal pronouncement. Yahweh calls forth one group to declare the sisters' guilt and a second to carry out their punishment. Some English translations render v 45 as Yahweh's call for **righteous *judges*** (so NRSV) to declare the sisters' guilt, but the NIV preserves the Hebrew's simple **righteous men** (*ʾănāšîm*). Likewise, some translations of v 46 also give a legal designation ("assembly" [NRSV]) to the group that Yahweh calls forth to carry out the sentence, but the NIV again retains a reading that fits better with the overall gendered imagery of the metaphorical discourse as a whole: **Bring a mob** [*qāhāl*] **against them** (see also v 47). These more generic, masculine images of **men** and a **mob**, combined with the personification of Samaria and Jerusalem as women, transform what appears to be a final sentence of a violent military invasion (v 47) into a disturbing picture of a mob-driven gang rape and murder of two females—a reality likely familiar to those who experienced the capture of Jerusalem by the Babylonians in Ezekiel's day. Moreover, most commentators observe that the gendered metaphor for the capital cities seems to give way in v 48 to a literal threat toward real-life women who would dare to step outside of their prescribed cultural boundaries and behaviors (see Darr 2001, 1330). Although the **all women** in v 48 may refer metaphorically to other cities, the gender-specific warning runs the risk of subverting the metaphor's overall purpose by allowing male readers to escape from seeing themselves as represented by the female capital cities (see van Dijk-Hemmes 1995).

Verse 49 concludes the discourse with the recognition formula, as Yahweh apparently addresses Ezekiel's fellow exiles and their need to acknowledge his holiness, proclaiming that through the devastation to come upon Jerusalem, **you** [pl.] **will know that I am the Sovereign LORD.**

4. The Boiling Pot (24:1-14)

Chapter 24 serves as the conclusion to the first half of the book, marking the transition from the visions, acts, and oracles dominated by the theme of judgment in chs 1—24 to the oracles against the nations in chs 25—32, after which the book turns to visions, acts, and oracles of restoration in chs 33—48. Prophetic word formulas in vv 1 and 15 divide the chapter into two main sections: the metaphor of the boiling pot for Jerusalem (vv 1-14) and the symbolic act of the death of Ezekiel's wife (vv 15-27) (with a concluding comment to Ezekiel in vv 25-27). Bowen (2010, 145) has recently tied the content of this chapter directly to the realities of trauma and the attempt to deal with them. She observes that the materials in ch 24 attempt to give coherence to the exiles' trauma by answering three primary "victim questions": (1) what happened? (2) why? and (3) why did I act as I did at that time? (see Figley 1985). In keeping with Ezekiel's emphasis on Yahweh's holiness as the interpretive category for Judah's reality, the text once again asserts that Jerusalem's destruction was Yahweh's judgment for their defiling acts.

■ **1-14** After an opening address to Ezekiel in vv 1-2, which includes the date formula that locates this oracle on the **very date** that the Babylonian siege of Jerusalem began (see Behind the Text), Yahweh (v 3) instructs the prophet to relay a **parable** (*māšāl*; see 17:2; 18:2) based on the metaphor of Jerusalem as a cooking pot. The discourse that follows features several motifs seen elsewhere in the book, thus providing a fitting conclusion to Ezekiel's judgment oracles: (1) **rebellious house** as a designation for the Judeans (v 3; see 2:3, 6, 8); (2) **city of bloodshed** for Jerusalem (vv 6, 9; see 22:2, 3, 27); (3) the people's ritual/cultic **impurities** (*ṭmʾ*; v 11; see 22:15). The form is a dispute oracle in which the divine address challenges an established perception, perhaps represented by what may have been a celebratory cooking song in 24:3-5. However, commentators regularly observe that the translation and meaning of the specific imagery are unclear, as the text is marked by a lack of coherence that suggests a complex history of editing and composition (see Zimmerli 1979, 503-6).

In general, the image presents Jerusalem as a cooking pot that must be destroyed because its contamination and filth have become too ingrained and made the pot unsalvageable. The metaphor begins with Yahweh's instructions to arrange what amounts to a sumptuous meal of the best portions of meat (vv 1-3). The two sections that follow (vv 6-8, 9-14), however, provide a host of confusing details that add up to a picture of the cooking pot (Jerusalem) being too **encrusted** with a **deposit** (v 6) of filth and **impurity** (v 13) to be able to cook the feast. The text represents the violent bloodshed for which Ezekiel has condemned Jerusalem elsewhere (see ch 22) as the literal blood of the meal's animals, carelessly sloshed about in violation of priestly purity laws (24:7).

The extreme nature of the pot's contamination (perhaps caused by misuse of the blood) dictates not only that the meal be thrown out (vv 7-8) but that the pot itself be destroyed (vv 11-12). Sweeney (2005, 150) notes that Yahweh's command for Ezekiel to prepare this meal resonates with the typical duties of the Zadokite priests in the Jerusalem temple, who prepared the sacrificial meat to be eaten by priests and worshippers (see Lev 7:28-36). Perhaps more immediately, Ezekiel's use of the cooking pot and choice meat imagery reverses the meaning this metaphor had when it appeared earlier in the book. In 11:1-13 the image of a cooking pot and choice meat was set on the lips of the leaders in Jerusalem, who used it to tout their self-perceived status as the choicest, even holiest parts of the people of Judah that remain in the sacred vessel of Jerusalem.

5. Symbolic Act: Ezekiel's Muteness (Beginning of Siege) (24:15-27)

■ **15-18** The prophet's final symbolic act (vv 15-18) has been called the "ugliest" of the book's symbolic acts because it comes out of Ezekiel's own experience at the death of his wife, using that tragedy as a symbol for how the exiles should react to the coming destruction of Jerusalem (Hals 1989, 175). Unlike most of the book's symbolic acts, this text contains all the typical elements of the genre (see Behind the Text for chs 4—7), with Yahweh giving instructions (24:16-17), Ezekiel carrying out the act (v 18), and the audience asking for an explanation (vv 19-24). In v 16, Yahweh first informs Ezekiel that he will soon **take away . . . the delight of your eyes,** and v 18 reports the death of his wife. It is unclear whether the text communicates the troubling suggestion that Yahweh causes the death of Ezekiel's wife in order to construct a sign for the exiles, or the prophet simply gives a meaning to the tragic event upon its occurrence. Either way, the point is that Yahweh tells Ezekiel not to mourn publicly at his wife's death. Commentators often interpret the actions listed in v 17 as customary mourning rituals, but there is no clear biblical evidence for this identification, and the actions may symbolize a new beginning or change of status (Odell 2005, 312). They may have connections to priestly prohibitions in which a Zadokite priest was forbidden to mourn for a deceased wife (Lev 21:4; Sweeney 2005, 151), and Bowen (2010, 150) sees here a reflection of the trauma symptom of "numbing," in which a victim is unable to be emotionally responsive in the face of a traumatic event. Whatever the specifics, Ezekiel is not to react to this death as if it is a loss.

■ **19-24** Ezekiel's actions generate a query from his fellow exiles (v 19). The language of the people's question specifically seeks how Ezekiel's behavior relates to them and their present situation (**tell us what these things have to do**

24:1-24

with us?). The prophet's response takes the form of another divine oracle (vv 20-24) in which Yahweh speaks in first person to the exiles and identifies Jerusalem's temple as the **delight of your** [masc., pl.] **eyes** (see v 16) that is about to be taken away. Yahweh's response again casts the coming destruction of Jerusalem in priestly categories, this time with Yahweh asserting that he will carry out the actions against his own temple: **I am about to desecrate** [ḥll] **my sanctuary** (v 21). Just like Ezekiel, the people are told not to mourn over the death of the city and the family members they left behind. Such an action represents Ezekiel's consistent call for the exiles to break with their past identity, letting go of their previous attachment and looking to a new future that will come through the outworking of Yahweh's holiness. As the concluding recognition formula indicates, precisely these traumatic events and their effect on the exiles' self-understanding will finally lead them to **know/*acknowledge*** Yahweh (v 24).

■ **25-27** The symbolic act of the death of Ezekiel's wife concludes with a shift back to Yahweh's direct address to Ezekiel (**And you, son of man** [v 25]) that looks ahead to the day when the news will arrive to the Babylonian exiles that the siege of Jerusalem has ended with the city's fall. Verse 27 implies that Yahweh now renders Ezekiel mute until that day. Earlier in the book (3:26-27), Yahweh told Ezekiel that he would be permitted to speak only when divinely instructed to do so, but now the prohibition on speech becomes complete. In the book's narrative chronology, Ezekiel's silence spans the duration of the Babylonian siege of Jerusalem (588-586 B.C.), the beginning of which was reported in 24:1-2. Verses 25-27 find their completion in 33:21-22, where a messenger arrives in Babylonia with a report of Jerusalem's fall and Yahweh opens Ezekiel's mouth to speak once again.

Because of this literary structure, the oracles against the nations in chs 25—32 have the appearance of an interlude, perhaps originating as an independent collection inserted into the narrative space between the beginning of the siege (and Ezekiel's muteness) and the report of Jerusalem's fall (and Ezekiel's resumption of speech) (see Behind the Text for chs 25—32). At least from a literary perspective, however, Ezekiel does not actually remain silent between chs 24 and 33, but broadens his preaching to draw other nations into the unfolding work of Yahweh's holiness. Perhaps his muteness only means that he will refrain from speaking further words of judgment concerning Judah until Jerusalem's fall. In any case, Ezekiel's silence concerning Judah and Jerusalem symbolizes the absence of the divine word/revelation as the process of judgment reaches its culmination during the Babylonian siege. Yet, readers may also see here a reflection of the struggle known to those dealing with post-traumatic stress, a struggle in which victims are often unable to bring traumatic events to expression in coherent ways, confined instead to a numb silence.

FROM THE TEXT

The metaphorical images for Jerusalem's destruction in chs 21—24, especially the extended metaphor of the faithless wives for Samaria and Jerusalem in ch 23, confront contemporary readers with the same set of interpretive challenges related to Ezekiel's portrayals of gender and sexual violence that we have encountered previously. The reflections in the From the Text section for ch 16 discussed these issues in detail, and readers should bring those reflections to bear here, as well. The close connection of the imagery in ch 23 to the actual experiences of military conquest at the siege of Jerusalem depicted elsewhere in chs 21—24 reminds readers that this is not a neutral metaphor but one that resonates with violence done to real women in contexts of war. As Darr urges, even while recognizing the truths communicated by Ezekiel's rhetoric, we must consider the impact of this imagery upon the "ancient woman who herself had experienced violence, including sexual violence, at the hands of her husband or of soldiers" and the "man who watched as his sister, wife, or daughter was stripped, raped, and then murdered" (2001, 1318). Parts of the discourse (see 23:48) even seem to turn the metaphor into a warning to real women readers/hearers, threatening them into submission to their husbands and other male power structures. We perhaps best explain the text's metaphorical rhetoric only when we see it as a product of Ezekiel's own direct and indirect experience of trauma in warfare contexts—an explanation without which our proclamation of this text runs the risk of reinscribing the gender and power structures that stand behind it (see Bowen 2010, 143).

Although there are problems that demand careful attention, Ezekiel's marriage metaphor possesses a significant theological dimension for readers from the Wesleyan tradition (see also From the Text for ch 16). *Despite the problems raised by the gendered and sexual imagery, the heart of this discourse contains an implicit call for God's people to have an undivided loyalty to God.* The text's descriptions of Samaria's and Jerusalem's reliance upon political allies symbolize the lure of other allegiances that keep the people from a fully devoted relationship with God and ultimately lead to death. Readers from the Wesleyan tradition may hear a message that is similar to John Wesley's articulation of Christian perfection and entire sanctification in the Christian life (see also commentary on ch 36), which envisions an inward surrender and outward obedience made possible by God's grace that result in all of one's life being characterized by a single motive to love God—a pure love that evicts sin and governs the heart and life (Greathouse and Dunning 1982, 88). While ch 23, with its final and thoroughgoing pictures of destruction, is hardly an evangelistic appeal to surrender the loyalties/devotions that compromise one's love for God and neighbor, Wesleyan readers may find here the heartbreaking portrayal of a life that refuses God's ultimate grace to the believer in the gift of a "single eye" and "pure heart" (Wesley 1971, 32).

In addition to gender and sexual imagery, the metaphors in chs 21—24 again confront readers of Ezekiel with the book's repeated portrayals of God who authorizes and even performs judgment actions that are by modern standards violent, ruthless, and destructive in nature (e.g., 21:3-4). These portrayals connect with another difficult interpretive issue, namely Ezekiel's repeated assertions that God directly determines everything that happens, so that bad things such as the destruction of Samaria and Jerusalem befall those who deserve it as a type of divine punishment. We have previously discussed ways that contemporary readers might think about both of these issues (see From the Text for chs 4—7), and the reader should consult those discussions again here. Most especially, the full witness of Christian scripture and the influence of tradition and experience suggest that Ezekiel's consistent interpretation of traumatic events as divine judgment does not apply in every situation, and questions of God's involvement in catastrophic events ("theodicy") do not permit only one answer. Despite the shortcomings of the prophet's rhetoric, Darr rightly notes that Ezekiel's consistent preaching of judgment is the act of one who speaks with the "courage of his convictions" (2001, 1305). As in Ezekiel's day, Christian preachers today function in an environment where it is always more popular to preach peace and prosperity—a smiling, happy gospel of personal betterment—and more demanding to engage in prophetic criticism of the social, economic, and militaristic structures that shape contemporary society and, often, the church.

The rampant violence that Ezekiel associates with Jerusalemite society (the "blood-soaked city" in ch 22) forms a powerful critique of how modern cities and societies are often marked by crime, injustice, and violence, especially against the most vulnerable persons (poor, widows, orphans, immigrants). As Odell observes, Ezekiel's preaching suggests that the "health of a society could be gauged by the availability of justice and fairness to the weaker and marginalized members of society" (2005, 283). Given Ezekiel's references to violence against women (e.g., 22:9-11), the protection that a society gives to women, especially in domestic/family settings, is an even clearer barometer of its health (Odell 2005, 292). Ezekiel's oracles, however, lay the primary responsibility for insuring such justice and protection of the vulnerable on a society's political, social, and religious leaders. Here is a call for leaders to engage actively in the creation of systems and practices that advantage the disadvantaged, and a condemnation of leaders who close their eyes to personal or systemic injustice, especially for their own power and gain (Darr 2001, 1315).

A final theological reflection on an element in the portrayal of Jerusalem's judgment in chs 21—24 may provide a more general insight into how contemporary readers may handle Ezekiel's historically, culturally, and theologically specific discourses, especially where those discourses seem problematic. Strikingly, Ezekiel's rhetoric in this section declares that there is no possibility of repentance for those about to experience judgment. This assertion conflicts with other texts where the prophet calls for repentance and affirms its possibility (e.g., 18:19-32; see Jenson 2009, 165). On the one hand, the conflicting messages regarding the possibility of repentance are a reminder that prophetic speeches are situational and specific, rather than systematic, and there is no need to harmonize the differing perspectives expressed in distinct oracles. Even so, Ezekiel leaves us with at least some texts that portray God as not allowing for the possibility of repentance.

The options for dealing with this theological issue may be instructive for handling other texts in Ezekiel that present theological and ethical problems for contemporary Christian readers or conflict in some significant way with other scriptural witnesses. One possibility, as Jenson suggests, is to find help in the historic Christian tradition's assertion that specific, especially troubling, parts of Scripture can be put in a different light when considered within the "dramatic coherence" of Scripture as a whole, seen as parts of a larger narrative of "the coming of Israel's Christ and his kingdom" (2009, 166). It may be more helpful, however, for contemporary readers to recognize and affirm that the canon of Scripture contains a diversity of theological voices, some of which stand in an unresolved, dynamic tension with one another. Accordingly, we push ourselves to seek how we may take all of these witnesses seriously, refusing to discount some of them but holding them in a creative tension in which they all help to shape our theological reflection and practice.

V. THE ORACLES AGAINST THE NATIONS (EZEKIEL 25—32)

BEHIND THE TEXT

As we have noted throughout this commentary, Ezekiel's theological responses to the trauma of exile unfold through a series of three visions of Yahweh's glory/presence (chs 1—3; 8—11; 40—48), each of which is connected to a series of prophetic acts and oracles that elaborates the vision's meaning. After reading through the symbolic acts and oracles in chs 12—24, which elaborate the vision of Yahweh's departure from the temple in chs 8—11, the reader of Ezekiel expects to move to the final sequence of acts and oracles concerning Judah that will set the stage for the climactic vision of the return of Yahweh's glory/presence to conclude the book.

Chapters 25—32, however, interrupt the expected movement with a series of oracles about various kingdoms that surrounded Judah in the sixth century B.C. As we have observed, ch 24 provides a fitting conclusion to the first half of the book's focus on judgment against Judah and the proclamation of the coming destruction of Jerusalem and further exile. That conclusion was marked by Yahweh rendering Ezekiel unable to speak for the duration of the Babylonian siege of Jerusalem (588-586 B.C.), the beginning of which was reported in 24:1. Chapter 33 will begin the second half of the book's focus on the restoration of Judah, a beginning that will be marked by the arrival of the news that Jerusalem has finally fallen to the Babylonians and Ezekiel's receiving the ability to speak once again (33:21-22). Within this literary structure, the oracles in chs 25—32 have the appearance of an interlude or hinge between the beginning and ending of the Babylonian siege of Jerusalem (24:1; 33:21-22), the event that represents the culmination of Yahweh's judgment on Judah and the prophet's transition to the preaching of restoration. On the literary level, chs 25—32 delay the report of Jerusalem's downfall, thus prolonging the suspense and giving the reader the feeling of living through Jerusalem's year and a half siege at the hands of the Babylonians. On the theological level, the oracles against the nations provide the foundation for Ezekiel's proclamation of restoration in chs 33—48, as they offer a broad vision of Yahweh's holiness and activity that places Judah's experiences into a larger conception of divine work in the world.

Due to the nature of the material in chs 25—32 and the space limitations of this commentary, the following discussion will deal with the oracles against the nations as a group, rather than providing a full analysis of each passage (see major commentaries such as Zimmerli 1983; Greenberg 1997; Darr 2001; Odell 2005). The Behind the Text and From the Text sections will discuss general interpretive issues and theological reflections that can be applied to the section as a whole.

Chapters 25—32 contain oracles addressed to seven kingdoms (and some of their rulers), with the seventh kingdom (Egypt) receiving seven oracles of its own (chs 29—32). Elsewhere in the OT, seven is a symbolic number used to represent other sets of foreign nations (e.g., Deut 7:1), and seven kingdoms also appear in the sections of oracles against the nations in Amos 1—2 and Jer 46:1—49:39. Here, the oracles begin (Ezek 25) with addresses to the kingdoms immediately surrounding Judah in southern Syria-Palestine:

A. Oracles Against Surrounding States (25:1-17)
    1. Oracle Against Ammon (25:1-7)
    2. Oracle Against Moab (25:8-11)
    3. Oracle Against Edom (25:12-14)
    4. Oracle Against Philistia (25:15-17)

The next chapters form a block devoted to the island-city of Tyre in northern Syria-Palestine, including pronouncements against the city itself and its king that alternate between oracles and lamentations. These are followed by a smaller oracle against Tyre's neighbor Sidon and an interlude devoted to Israel's future blessing, which marks the midpoint between the preceding oracles addressed to seven kingdoms and the following seven oracles against Egypt:

    B. Oracles Against Tyre (26:1—28:19)
        1. Oracle Against the City of Tyre (26:1-21)
        2. Lamentation over Tyre (27:1-36)
        3. Oracle Against the King of Tyre (28:1-10)
        4. Lamentation over the King of Tyre (28:11-19)
    C. Oracle Against Sidon (28:20-24)
    D. Future Blessing on Israel (28:25-26)

The chapters conclude with seven oracles against Egypt, also alternating between proclamations and lamentations against the kingdom and its ruler:

    E. Oracles Against Egypt (29:1—32:32)
        1. Proclamation Against Egypt (29:1-21)
        2. Lamentation over Egypt (30:1-19)
        3. Proclamation Against Pharaoh (30:20—31:18)
        4. Lamentation over Pharaoh and Egypt (32:1-16)
        5. Funeral Dirge over Egypt (32:17-32)

The literary placement discussed above suggests that chs 25—32 may represent a collection of some of Ezekiel's oracles against foreign nations (other oracles against selected nations appear outside of chs 25—32 in 21:28-32 [Ammon] and 35:1-15 [Edom]) that existed independently and has been secondarily inserted at this point in the book's presentation of Ezekiel's ministry (so Zimmerli 1983, 3). Additionally, the material in the chapters themselves reveals evidence of editing or expansion and indicates a composition and editorial process that unfolded in several stages over time (see Hals 1989, 179). Some of the oracles seem to have been updated (by Ezekiel or others) in light of the fall of Jerusalem in 586 B.C. (e.g., chs 27; 31) or may have existed as smaller collections that underwent their own stages of development (e.g., 26:1—28:19) (see Hals 1989, 178; Zimmerli 1983, 33-40; cf. Greenberg 1997, 544). Even so, the oracles are at home in Ezekiel's historical realities and thought-world, addressing some of the major political entities that shaped Judah's history in his day and further serving his aims of offering a theological interpretation of the people's trauma based in ideas about Yahweh's holiness/sovereignty.

Beyond the literary aspects, chs 25—32 represent the genre that scholars have come to designate as oracles against the nations (OAN). Such oracles occur in large sections in nearly every OT prophetic book (e.g., Isa 13—23; Jer 46—51; Joel 3:1-21; Amos 1—2; Zeph 2:4-15; Zech 9:1-8) and comprise the entirety of some (Obadiah; Nahum). Although debate continues as to whether one can speak of the OAN as a distinct, self-contained genre from the ancient world (cf. Hals 1989, 351; Block 1998, 3), the relevant prophetic texts share certain characteristics and functions. The OAN constitute a type of prophetic material in which divine judgment is proclaimed against kingdoms and rulers for misdeeds they have committed, a judgment that usually takes the form of war-like destruction. There is no clear understanding of the origins of this genre, but it is likely related to ancient rituals of warfare that included symbolic actions and curses directed against enemies in preparation for battle (Hals 1989, 179). Egyptian evidence, for example, reveals curses inscribed on clay vessels that were likely smashed to symbolize the destruction of the enemy, and some OT texts allude to prophets making pronouncements against opponents prior to battle (e.g., Num 22; 1 Kgs 20:13, 28).

Perhaps the most pressing of all the background issues for the OAN in chs 25—32 concerns their purpose and function within Ezekiel's theological worldview and discourse. Why are these nations condemned and what is significant about their actions that bring such condemnation? How do these condemnations relate to Ezekiel's historical situation in the sixth century B.C. and to his overall theological understanding of Yahweh's holiness as the key to rightly perceiving Judah's past, present, and future trauma in a coherent way? A common proposal suggests that the kingdoms mentioned in chs 25—32 were either involved in rebellious alliances or activities against Babylonia (either in concert with Judah or independently) that contributed to Judah's involvement that Ezekiel condemned as outside of Yahweh's will, or that these kingdoms participated in or at least benefitted from the violence suffered by Judah throughout the people's history and especially at the hands of the Babylonians in 597 and/or 586 B.C. (particularly in violation of treaties the neighbors may have had with Judean kings; e.g., Jer 27) (see Blenkinsopp 1990, 111). This historical explanation has produced many attempts to delineate the precise circumstances that might lie behind each of the oracles. For example, 2 Kgs 24:1-2 suggests that Ammon and Moab (25:1-7, 8-11) worked with Nebuchadnezzar against Jehoiakim of Judah leading up to Jerusalem's capture in 597 B.C., and certainly Egypt, which receives seven (the number of completeness) condemnation oracles of its own (chs 29—32), was often the primary instigator of anti-Babylonian sentiment in the region.

These historical explanations falter, however, due to a lack of evidence for the involvement of all of these kingdoms in actions against Judah during Ezekiel's time (e.g., Philistia). Additionally, Ezekiel does not explicitly condemn the nations for rebelling against Babylonia—or for any single shared activity—and, given the prophet's harsh words about Judah's foreign alliances elsewhere (e.g., chs 16; 23), it is hard to imagine him condemning these kingdoms for being unfaithful to alliances with Jerusalem that he saw as illicit (Tuell 2009, 167-68). Consequently, some commentators see only a symbolic function for the kingdoms in chs 25—32 indicated by the use of the number seven. Deuteronomy 7:1, for instance, identifies seven nations in Canaan to be destroyed before the Israelites can possess the land—a number and list that often appears to be a stock representation of enemies. Ezekiel uses the same number (but different nations), and this suggests to some that the destruction of the kingdoms functions only symbolically as preparation for the exiles' repossession of the land that will be depicted in chs 33—48 (Zimmerli 1983, 3-4).

Perhaps two additional background elements of chs 25—32 suggest a different understanding of their theological function. First, although the OAN describe the sins and judgment of foreign nations, they are not diplomatic correspondence directed to or even heard by those kingdoms. Rather, as the text's use of the prophetic word formula and messenger formula make clear (e.g., 25:1, 3), the OAN are actually messages that Yahweh gives to Ezekiel to proclaim to his fellow Babylonian exiles. The purpose, function, and message of these oracles are directed first and foremost to the Judean exiles themselves.

The other illuminating background element is the extensive appearance of date formulas in chs 25—32, which associate certain oracles with specific days, months, and years and may have been added later to the various oracles or collections thereof. The OAN section contains the highest concentration of date formulas in the book (seven out of the book's total fourteen), and six of them appear in the Egypt oracles (chs 29—32). Other than the problematic date formula in 29:17, which is the latest date in the book, even postdating the date given for the final vision in 40:1, all of the dates place the oracles during the time of the Babylonian siege of Jerusalem and its aftermath from January 587 B.C. to March 585 B.C. (the date in 29:1 ["tenth year"], however, is out of sequence with the preceding Tyre oracle date in 26:1 ["eleventh year"]). The effect of these date formulas is to link Yahweh's judgments against these kingdoms—which, together with Babylonia, represent the major geopolitical powers responsible for the chaotic events of war and destruction in Ezekiel's time—to the unfolding events in Jerusalem under siege around 586 B.C.

The Date Formulas in the Oracles Against the Nations

26:1	11th year, x month, 1st day (March/April 587-586 B.C.)
29:1	10th year, 10th month, 12th day (January 587 B.C.)
29:17	27th year, 1st month, 1st day (April 571 B.C.)
30:20	11th year, 1st month, 7th day (April 587 B.C.)
31:1	11th year, 3rd month, 1st day (June 587 B.C.)
32:1	12th year, 12th month, 1st day (March 585 B.C.)
32:17	12th year, x month (LXX: 1st month), 15th day (585 B.C.)

In light of these and other elements, Bowen has recently proposed a connection between the OAN and the lens of trauma for interpreting Ezekiel's context and theology (2010, 151-52). She suggests viewing the kingdoms condemned in chs 25—32 as "bystanders" to Judah's trauma—a category within traumatic experience that designates a third group of people (alongside victims and perpetrators) who have either direct or indirect knowledge of the violence taking place and whose help may even be sought or hoped for by the victims but do nothing in response. In this case, the oracles condemn the nations because they—like "the mother who fails to interfere when her husband sexually molests their daughter" or "Americans who fail to hold companies accountable for their treatment of workers or buy the products made in sweatshops"—neglected to help Judah in the midst of Babylonian violence and thus became complicit through inaction (intentionally or unintentionally) in the abuse and injustice (Bowen 2010, 151). Bowen links these expressions to the process of recovery from trauma by viewing the OAN as the necessary first step of dealing with the emotions toward bystanders that must precede the move to recovery from trauma expressed in the salvation oracles that follow in chs 33—48.

Bowen has rightly identified the necessity of approaching the OAN through the same lens of trauma that allows insight into Ezekiel's overall visions, acts, and oracles, yet her focus on the nations as bystanders is perhaps too narrow. While Yahweh seemingly condemns some of the kingdoms for lack of aid to Judah, he judges others for direct acts of violence against Judah, and others for actions that appear to have little to do with Judah at all. The nations in chs 25—32 are not all condemned for the same kinds of misdeeds. The neighboring peoples in ch 25 have insulted Yahweh's sovereignty by acting violently toward Judah or taking advantage of Judah's fall. Tyre (chs 26—28) faces judgment not so much for actions against Judah but for its own unjust economic practices, power, and pride. Egypt (chs 29—32) faces condemnation rooted in political affairs, as the one who most predominantly led Judah to disobey Yahweh by engaging in alliances and rebellions.

What these kingdoms share, however, is their status as the primary powers (together with Babylonia) of Ezekiel's day who were, at various times, agents in the wars and strife that Judah experienced, as well as victims themselves of the violence and destruction that Judah witnessed. In this context, the nations are symbols of the powerful forces that have enveloped Judah's world in a maelstrom of war, destruction, and displacement. Furthermore, the time in which these oracles are set—the Babylonian siege of Jerusalem in 588-586 B.C.—constituted a time of chaos, incoherence, and disorder in the people's experience. As noted earlier, such times characteristically mark traumatic events. Trauma victims are often unable to make sense out of their experience within the normal categories of their life story, so the trauma exists as a force that remains outside the recognizable narrative of life and is unable to be coherently understood or articulated—a circumstance that results in a sense of chaos, incoherence, and disorder.

Seen against this backdrop, the OAN in chs 25—32 function as another kind of response to the people's trauma. First, the language and rhetoric bring order to the chaotic events underway. We have noted, for example, the carefully structured sequence of seven kingdoms, with the seventh kingdom receiving seven oracles. Moreover, we have observed the concentration of date formulas that provide an orderliness to the very time of the siege and capture of Jerusalem—the ultimate experience of chaos, incoherence, and disorder for Ezekiel and his people.

Perhaps more significantly, however, the OAN assert that Yahweh, the God of Judah, is, in fact, sovereign over all the kingdoms of the world, judging them for their misdeeds but more importantly maintaining a moral order that locates these seemingly chaotic kingdoms and their ultimate fate within the larger working of Yahweh's divine purposes in the world. All that Judah has experienced and witnessed from these powers unfolds, Ezekiel claims, according to Yahweh's sovereign control over history and his purpose to purify Israel and restore his holiness in the world. This attempt to interpret the people's trauma may explain the lack of any oracle against Babylonia (no explicit oracle against Babylonia appears in the book, but see discussion of 21:30-32 and chs 38—39). Rather than crediting Babylonia with the destruction of these kingdoms, many of whom they did, in fact, assault at some point, Ezekiel attributes the fate of the kingdoms to Yahweh's activity alone, again transforming even the world power of Babylonia into an instrument of Yahweh's larger divine purposes. The prophet once more expresses this conviction of ultimate divine control over all the powers and their acts through the repeated use of the acknowledgment formula ("they will know/acknowledge that I am the LORD"). Hence, he renarrates the people's traumatic experiences of war and destruction into the alternative, orderly plot line of Yahweh's holiness. While these oracles do not acquit the people of the defilement of Yahweh's holiness that Ezekiel has addressed in preceding chapters, the prophet asserts that Yahweh's sovereignty has the final word, leaving his people with at least the implicit hope that there is a larger divine work unfolding in the world.

IN THE TEXT

A. Oracles Against Surrounding States (25:1-17)

The opening section of Ezekiel's OAN consists of oracles against four neighboring kingdoms of Judah, moving clockwise (eastward and southward) from Jerusalem: Ammon, Moab, and Edom (to the east and south) and Philistia (to the west) (a similar movement appears in Amos 1—2). These kingdoms stand as adjacent neighbors to Judah in southern Syria-Palestine. Additionally, the biblical texts portray the Judeans as related genealogically to Ammon, Moab, and Edom (Gen 19:30-38; 25:24-26, 30)—accounts that often cast Judah's neighbors in a negative light and depict a strained "family" relationship.

■ **1-7** Ezekiel's first oracle addresses the kingdom of Ammon, located just east of the Jordan River and north of Moab. Verses 1-3 set the tone for all of the oracles to follow, as they open with several now familiar elements that also appear in various combinations in the following passages (prophetic word formula; hostility formula [**set your face against** (v 2)], messenger formula). This opening makes clear that the OAN are not diplomatic correspondence directed to or heard by these kingdoms, but messages that Yahweh gives to Ezekiel to proclaim to his fellow Babylonian exiles. Throughout the series of oracles, virtually every chapter and subsection begins with one or both of the prophetic word formula and/or messenger formula (e.g., 25:1-2, 8, 12, 15-16; 26:1, 7, 15, 19; 27:1, 3; 28:1-2, 6, 11-12, 20-22, 25; 29:1, 3, 8, 13, 17; 30:1-2, 6, 10, 13, 20, 22; 31:1-2, 10, 15; 32:1-2, 3, 17), and many of the oracles end with the recognition formula ("you/they will know that I am the Lord"), signifying that the divine judgments will lead the exiles and the foreign kingdoms to know/acknowledge Yahweh (e.g., 25:5, 7, 11, 14, 17; 26:6; 28:23, 26; 29:9, 21; 30:8, 19, 25, 26; 32:15).

The oracle against Ammon is the only one that addresses the foreign kingdom directly in second person (see 25:3). It divides into two parallel sections (vv 3-5, 6-7), both of which begin with the messenger formula (vv 3, 6), transition to a judgment of destruction and capture by enemies with the word **therefore** (vv 4, 7), and conclude with the recognition formula (vv 5, 7). Yahweh condemns the Ammonites not for direct acts against Judah but for celebrating, perhaps with selfish gain in mind, the desecration of Yahweh's sanctuary and the tragedies that have befallen Jerusalem (vv 3, 6). Even in describing the judgment of the foreign kingdoms, Ezekiel maintains his dominant priestly perspective that casts the events not in terms of Babylonian conquest but the defilement of Yahweh's holy sanctuary and land.

■ **8-11** Ezekiel's second oracle gives Yahweh's judgment on Moab, a kingdom east of the Dead Sea and just south of Ammon. Like the preceding oracle, Yahweh does not charge the Moabites with any direct actions against Judah, but condemns them because they considered Judah to be like any other nation (v 8), thereby perhaps disparaging Yahweh's distinct sovereignty and holiness. Through the divine judgment, the text asserts that the Moabites themselves will come to know/*acknowledge* Yahweh (v 11).

■ **12-14** The third neighboring kingdom condemned by Ezekiel is Edom, located south of Moab between the Dead Sea and the Gulf of Aqaba. Various OT texts describe hostility between Judah and Edom, perhaps symbolically represented in the conflict between the brothers Jacob and Esau (Gen 25—33; see also Ps 137:7; Isa 34; Jer 49:7-22; Lam 4:21-22; Obad 1-4; Mal 1:2-5). Unlike the preceding two oracles, Edom is accused of taking hostile actions of **revenge** against Judah (Ezek 25:12). Many commentators have associated these verses with possible Edomite aggression against Judah during and after the Babylonian invasions in 597 and 586 B.C. In a unique move among the oracles in ch 25, v 14 asserts that Yahweh will exact his judgment on Edom **by the hand of my people Israel.**

■ **15-17** The final oracle against Judah's immediate neighbors is a judgment on Philistia, a group of people (rather than a single kingdom) along the coastal plain of the Mediterranean Sea to the west of Judah. The Philistines appear throughout the OT as long-standing, almost traditional, enemies of Israel and Judah, and as with the Edomites, v 15 accuses them of taking actions of **revenge** against Judah, with an **ancient hostility** ("unending hostilities" [NRSV]). Yahweh's first person declaration again asserts not only that he will act directly against the Philistines, but that as a result of the judgment, they, too, will come to know/*acknowledge* Yahweh (v 17).

B. Oracles Against Tyre (26:1—28:19)

1. Oracle Against the City of Tyre (26:1-21)

The three-chapter-long series of oracles against Tyre shows a pattern in which an initial judgment against the city (26:1-21), with an accompanying lament over the city (27:1-36), is followed by an initial judgment against the king (28:1-10), with an accompanying lament over the king (28:11-19). The section begins (26:1) with the first date formula in the OAN and the only one in the Tyre oracles (**eleventh year, on the first day of the month,** March/April 587-586 B.C.). The date, followed by Ezekiel's typical prophetic word formula, associates the following oracles with the general period of the Babylonian siege and capture of Jerusalem (the month is absent from the text). At least some available evidence plausibly indicates that around the time of the beginning of the Babylonian siege of Jerusalem (ca. 588 B.C.; see 24:1), Nebuchadnezzar's forces also initiated a siege of Tyre that would last for thirteen years but ultimately prove unsuccessful (the only reference to this siege appears in the first-century Jewish historian Josephus, who claims to rely on an earlier source; see Odell 2005, 333). As early as 604 B.C., Nebuchadnezzar, when he initially established control over Syria-Palestine, had forced Tyre to submit to Babylonian power. Subsequently, however, Tyre seems to have been involved in rebellious activities in the region (see the reference to Tyre's participation in Zedekiah's planning council in Jer 27:3), and most commentators assume that explains Nebuchadnezzar's siege (see Block 1998, 31).

Beyond the possible historical scenarios, however, it is the city's status and character that give Ezekiel's Tyre oracles their rhetorical force. Tyre was a walled city-state located on an island off the coast of southern Lebanon, a location that made the city a seemingly invulnerable fortified stronghold unmatched in the area. Even the Hebrew word for Tyre (*sôr*) is related to terms for "rock, cliff." Moreover, as one of the only cities in Syria-Palestine with natural ports, Tyre was a regional political, economic, and commercial power as a merchant city based upon and known for its thriving sea trade. Ezekiel's oracles against Tyre abound with imagery that reflects these aspects of Tyre, repeatedly picturing it metaphorically as a dazzling ship full of the best luxury items or describing it as a wealthy, commercial superpower city basking in its own prosperity. Far more than any possible historical or political activities, the divine judgments against Tyre condemn the city for theological and, even more, socioeconomic sins, especially pride, claims to divinity, materialism, unjust trade, and hoarding of wealth and resources.

■ **1-7** The first oracle in ch 26 is directed against the city itself. Yahweh's speech alternates between third person description and direct second person address to Tyre and divides into two sections (vv 1-14, 15-21). As with the earlier oracles against Ammon and Moab (25:1-11), 26:2 condemns Tyre for its response to Jerusalem's demise, apparently seeing the demise as an opportunity to expand its own fortunes. The transitional word **therefore** at the start of v 3 marks the shift to the pronouncement of the judgment to come. Throughout vv 3-14, as well as the remainder of the Tyre oracles, Ezekiel's descriptions allude to Tyre's perceived status as an invulnerable island city and maritime economy by repeating descriptions such as **in the sea** (v 5), turning the place of perceived strength into the site of destruction (see vv 17, 18; 27:2, 3). The centerpiece of the divine judgment appears in 26:7, where Yahweh asserts that he will send **Nebuchadnezzar king of Babylon** against Tyre. Although Nebuchadnezzar has been alluded to with the designation "king of Babylon" previously in the book (e.g., 17:12; 19:9; 21:19, 21; 24:2), this is the first appearance of his name (the Hebrew preserves the spelling ***Nebuchadrezzar*** [see NRSV], which reflects the Babylonian pronunciation and appears again in 29:18-19; 30:10; and throughout Jer 21—52).

■ **8-14** What follows in Ezek 26:8-14 is a detailed depiction of ancient siege warfare, portraying a full-scale siege and capture similar to the scenes preserved on Assyrian pictorial reliefs. In keeping with Ezekiel's theological emphasis on Yahweh's sovereignty, however, the conclusion in vv 13-14 shifts from a description of Nebuchadnezzar's actions to Yahweh's first person assertions that he is the one responsible for the destruction to come upon Tyre. Ezekiel's pronouncement that Tyre will be destroyed by Nebuchadnezzar has posed a difficulty for interpreters, since Nebuchadnezzar, in fact, never captured Tyre and the city apparently remained intact until the fourth century B.C. As we will see in the discussion of 29:17-21, Ezekiel (or his later editors) addressed this issue of the unfulfilled nature of the Tyre prophecy.

■ **15-21** The remainder of the first oracle against Tyre again plays upon the city's status as a maritime power whose economic and commercial ventures had given wealth and security to selected allies and partners. Verses 15-21 portray other cities and rulers—Tyre's economic partners—engaging in rituals of lamentation over Tyre's downfall and out of fear for their own continued prosperity. The section ends in vv 19-21 with Yahweh once more asserting his own control over the destruction to come. Here, Yahweh declares that he will cast Tyre down to the **pit . . . in the earth below, as in ancient ruins** (v 20). The **pit** (*bôr*) is a metaphor for the realm of the dead in OT thought, designated by the Hebrew term *Sheol*. The imagery reflects the ancient use of burial caves to house the bones of the deceased. This motif of Yahweh's casting the world's economic and military powers down to the place of the dead will return with special force in 32:17-32, serving again to underscore Yahweh's enduring sovereignty in the face of those violent forces that threaten to throw life into chaos.

Sheol, the Place of the Dead

In the OT, the Hebrew term *Sheol* (often translated as "the grave" in the NIV, although it should not be equated with the grave) is a place name designating the realm of the dead. The term occurs sixty-six times, and, as in Ezekiel, is often referred to with the metaphor of "the pit" or as the "world below" (NRSV;

see 26:19-21; 31:15-18; 32:17-32). The OT shares the notion of an underworld or abode of the dead with much ancient Near Eastern literature from Egypt and Mesopotamia. In keeping with ancient Near Eastern thought, Sheol, or the underworld, is not a place of punishment for the unrighteous but more commonly the destination for all the dead, both righteous and unrighteous.

2. Lamentation over Tyre (27:1-36)

■ **1-11, 25b-36** Following the initial pronouncement of judgment against Tyre, Yahweh instructs Ezekiel to offer a **lament** (*qînâ*; see 19:1) over the city. The chapter plays extensively on Tyre's status as an island merchant city by offering a detailed and vivid depiction of the city as an ornate cargo vessel carrying the best luxury items (27:4-9). An inclusio in vv 4-9 and 25b-36, however, provides the ironic twist that the "ship" of Tyre, so laden down with luxury goods, finds itself in rough seas and ultimately sinks under its own weight, generating further lamentation from the **mariners, seamen, kings,** and **merchants** (vv 27, 35, 36). Under Yahweh's judgment, Tyre's seemingly secure location in the midst of the seas and beneficial material wealth become the place and means of its demise. Seen in the larger context of ancient Near Eastern traditions, this depiction resonates with ancient mythological conceptions of the sea as a symbol of the powers of chaos. Against the backdrop of some ancient Near Eastern texts, as well as certain OT psalms, which depict creation as a battle won over the forces of chaos represented by the sea, ch 27 depicts Tyre as seated not simply in the sea but on the mythological waters of chaos that will eventually engulf it (Odell 2005, 344).

■ **12-25a** In between the inclusio of Tyre's depiction as an ornate cargo ship (vv 4-9) and the sinking of that ship (vv 25b-36), vv 12-25a continue the lament over Tyre by providing an inventory of the trade partners and products that constituted Tyre's commercial enterprise and provided its prosperity. The list begins and ends with **Tarshish** (vv 12, 25), a Spanish port, and in between traverses nearly a dozen regions, with **Judah and Israel** (v 17) as two of the trading partners standing near the center of the inventory. In the middle of the chapter's lamentation, these trading partners represent both those who contributed to Tyre's prosperity depicted in vv 4-11 and those who will mourn her demise in vv 26b-36.

3. Oracle Against the King of Tyre (28:1-10)

■ **1-10** In keeping with the pattern in the Tyre oracles that joins a judgment oracle with a corresponding lamentation, ch 28 shifts from a proclamation against the city in ch 27 to an oracle (vv 1-10) and lament (vv 11-19) concerning Tyre's king in particular (designated initially in v 2 in Ezekiel's typical fashion with the penultimate title ***prince*** [ruler; cf. v 12]; here with the Hebrew *nĕgîd* rather than *nāśî'*, as elsewhere in Ezekiel). The two sections depict the king in different ways, but both center on the sin of pride, with Yahweh describing how the king allowed his wisdom and prosperity to turn to arrogance and thus he will be brought low at the hands of enemies directed by Yahweh. For example, v 3, which may be read as an affirmative statement rather than a question (see NRSV), compares the king's wisdom to **Daniel** (Heb., *Dan'el*), possibly a reference to either the biblical character Daniel or the legendary wise figure "Dan'el" known from ancient Near Eastern traditions (see discussion of 14:12-20). Likewise, v 5 extols the wealth that the king gained through wisdom. In both cases, however, the king allowed his achievements to produce a proud heart, forgetting that he is **but a man, not a god** (v 9).

4. Lamentation over the King of Tyre (28:11-19)

■ **11-17** In the same way that Yahweh instructed Ezekiel to follow the judgment oracle against Tyre with a lamentation for the city (27:1-2), 28:11-19 shifts from the pronouncement of judgment on Tyre's king to a **lament** (*qînâ*; v 12; see 19:1; 27:2) over the tragedy of his exceptional beginning and ultimate fall. The lament depicts Tyre's king as the original, model human, created perfectly by God and placed **in Eden, the garden of God** (28:13), where he lived on **the holy mount of God** (v 14) until his **heart became proud** (v 17) and Yahweh drove him away.

The origins of this imagery remain debated. Ezekiel likely draws here on royal ideologies known from various ancient Near Eastern traditions that portrayed the king as a type of "Primal Human" who was created as God's special representative ("son") (see Odell 2005, 359; for sample texts, see Block 1998, 119-20). Christian readers of the OT, however, may be more immediately drawn to the stories of the first humans in Gen 2—3, which also feature an initially blameless human in the garden of Eden, who is later expelled. The Genesis stories, in fact, reflect the established royal traditions of the ancient world that depicted the ruler as the special image/son of God (see also Ps 2) and are reflected in Ezekiel's usage. In the Genesis stories, however, we find the democratization of the ancient royal traditions and thus every human being shares in both the image of God and the story of pride that leads to estrangement. In addition to ancient Near Eastern royal traditions and the biblical texts, the imagery in Ezek 28:11-19 also resonates with temple imagery so important to Ezekiel's priestly perspective (Carvalho 2010, 114). The various gems resemble the stones on the breastplate of the high priest (Exod 28:15-21), and the cherub resembles the creatures around Yahweh's chariot throne in ch 1.

■ **18-19** Perhaps the most striking dimension of Ezekiel's lament over the king, however, is the nature of the sin that brings about judgment. Verse 18 identifies the king's primary misdeeds as practices of social and economic injustice: unjust trade and commerce, violence committed through economic dealings, and related "crimes against humanity" (Odell 2005, 364). Ezekiel even brings these accusations into his priestly perspective by extending his familiar talk of how the Judeans' actions defiled Yahweh's temple in Jerusalem to assert that the unjust socioeconomic practices of Tyre's king have likewise polluted his sacred sites: **By your many sins and dishonest trade you have desecrated your sanctuaries** (v 18).

Ezekiel 28 and the Figure of Satan

Throughout the history of the Christian church, as early as the time of Origen (third century A.D.), some readers have used Ezekiel's symbolic depiction of the king of Tyre, as well as Isaiah's portrayal of the king of Babylon (Isa 14:12-21), to construct a story of the origins of the figure of Satan. By interpreting the king of Tyre allegorically, this reading sees in Ezekiel's depiction a story of an original "fall" of Satan, who supposedly began as one of the attendants in God's court and was cast out on account of pride. In spite of the popularity of this reading in some Christian circles, an interpretation that reads Ezekiel within its historical and rhetorical context raises questions about such allegorizing. Ezekiel's (and Isaiah's) words are metaphorical, but their referent and context are clearly a human king and his unjust social and economic practices. Moreover, major interpretive voices from the Christian tradition have long opposed the allegorical constructions of a satanic biography. Block notes that John Calvin, for example, while not commenting on Ezek 28, did comment emphatically on the tendency to read Isa 14:12-21 allegorically as a description of Satan: "The exposition of this passage, which some have given, as if it referred to Satan, has arisen from ignorance; for the context plainly shows that these statements must be understood in reference to the king of the Babylonians" (quoted in Block 1998, 119 n. 139). Likewise, Wesley's *Explanatory Notes upon the Old Testament* asserts that the figure in Isa 14 is merely a metaphor for the king of Babylon and that Ezek 28 is a prediction of the ruin of the king of Tyre.

C. Oracle Against Sidon (28:20-24)

■ **20-24** Two brief addenda to the series of Tyre oracles conclude ch 28. Verses 20-24 contain an oracle of judgment against Sidon. This city was another Phoenician port city located twenty-five miles north of Tyre. The two form a frequent pair, often conceived jointly as the main parts of "Phoenicia," and several prophetic texts contain oracles against Sidon linked with pronouncements against Tyre (e.g., Isa 23:1-12; Jer 25:22; Joel 3:4; Zech 9:2). Yahweh's condemnation here is generic, with no specific crimes mentioned, and Sidon is cast as yet another bystander (see Ammon and Moab in Ezek 25) to Judah's trauma. Even so, the brief oracle contains three occurrences of the acknowledgment formula, as Yahweh asserts that the destruction to come upon Sidon will cause both the Sidonians (vv 22, 23) and Judeans (v 24) to **know that I am the Sovereign L**ORD/"Lord G**OD**" (NRSV).

D. Future Blessing on Israel (28:25-26)

■ **25-26** The sequence of OAN in chs 25—32 is interrupted briefly in the final verses of ch 28 with a proclamation of future restoration for **the people of Israel** (v 25). Introduced by the messenger formula, Yahweh declares that he will gather those who have been exiled from Judah and return them to the land to dwell where Yahweh's holiness will again be manifest (**I will show myself holy among them** [v 25]). This hopeful pronouncement forms a seventh oracle in the series so far and a transition to the seven oracles against Egypt that follow in chs 29—32. More importantly for Ezekiel's theological program, however, the oracle explicitly applies all of Yahweh's judgments against the nations to the circumstances and fate of Ezekiel and his fellow Judean exiles. Ezekiel articulates a purposefulness behind Yahweh's judgments that is aimed at the exiles' understanding. Through Yahweh's judgments on the nations, Judah will again have the chance to live securely, restored to the land in which Yahweh's holy presence will once more dwell (v 26). The chapter closes with Ezekiel's declaration that the culmination of the divine actions toward the nations will be that the exiles themselves (**they**) will finally **know/ acknowledge** Yahweh (v 26).

E. Oracles Against Egypt (29:1—32:32)

After the sequence of oracles in 25:1—28:26 that address six different foreign kingdoms plus the people of Israel, Ezekiel's OAN turn to an extended focus on Egypt, with chs 29—32 containing seven oracles directed to this seventh foreign kingdom. The seven oracles (29:1-16; 29:17-21; 30:1-19; 30:20-26; 31:1-18; 32:1-16; 32:17-32) divide into two major parts (29:1—31:18; 32:1-32), with each part describing the destruction of Egypt by the Babylonians and then the descent of Pharaoh into Sheol (Block 1998, 128-29). The Egypt oracles also alternate between proclamation and lamentation against the kingdom and its ruler, concluding with an additional section in 32:17-32 that provides a climactic funeral dirge over a dead Egypt:

    E. Oracles Against Egypt (29:1—32:32)

        1. Proclamation Against Egypt (29:1-21)

        2. Lamentation over Egypt (30:1-19)

3. Proclamation Against Pharaoh (30:20—31:18)
   4. Lamentation over Pharaoh and Egypt (32:1-16)
   5. Funeral Dirge over Egypt (32:17-32)

The question of why Ezekiel devotes such extended attention to Egypt continues to be debated. A variety of references to Egypt have already appeared in Ezekiel's preaching (16:26; 17:15; 19:4; 20:5-10, 36; 23:3, 8, 19, 27), and the date formula in 29:1 (January 587 B.C.) places that oracle just after the time of Pharaoh Hophra's push into Syria-Palestine that caused the Babylonians to lift temporarily the siege of Jerusalem (see Behind the Text for ch 33). As we have seen in the preceding historical surveys of events surrounding Judah during Ezekiel's time, Egypt was the primary power in the west who was often involved, directly or indirectly, in the affairs of Judah and other Babylonian vassals in the area. Most significantly for Ezekiel's day, the victory tour of Pharaoh Psammetichus II into Syria-Palestine (ca. 592 B.C.) seems to have pushed King Zedekiah of Judah into the rebellion that Ezekiel expects to end with the final destruction of Jerusalem. However, Egypt's involvement and significance for Judah goes back much further than the events of the 590s and 580s B.C. Throughout virtually the entire period of both Assyrian and Babylonian dominance over the ancient Near East (ca. 900-539 B.C.)—and thus throughout most of the existence of the kingdoms of Israel and Judah—Egypt played a rival role to the Mesopotamian powers, often provoking the smaller kingdoms of Syria-Palestine to rebel against the Assyrians or Babylonians with promises of renewed Egyptian strength and aid. The OT depicts various Israelite and Judean kings becoming involved with Egypt in numerous ways. For example, the Israelite king Hoshea appealed for aid to "So king of Egypt" in support of his rebellion against Assyria in the 720s B.C. (2 Kgs 17:4), the Egyptian leader "Tirhaka, the Cushite" became involved in Hezekiah's rebellion against the Assyrian king Sennacherib in 701 B.C. (2 Kgs 19:9), and Pharaoh Neco II killed Josiah of Judah and placed Jehoiakim on the Judean throne around 609 B.C. (2 Kgs 23:29-35).

Alongside these historical aspects, Egypt possesses a symbolic character throughout the OT, representing the paradigm of oppressive rulers and destructive forces that arise throughout the entire course of human history. For example, while some texts mention specific rulers or events, a number of narrative and poetic texts refer only generally to Egypt or "Pharaoh," perhaps using the title to refer not merely to a specific individual, but as a symbol for oppressive rulers and regimes. The stories of Israel's exodus from Egypt (Exod 7—14), for instance, never refer to the Egyptian ruler involved by name, but designate him simply as "Pharaoh." Likewise, Ezekiel's oracles against Egypt rarely mention any specific action that Egypt took against Judah and consistently refer only to "Pharaoh." While the original rhetorical situation may have given Ezekiel's audience a clear idea about the historical person(s) involved, the language and imagery gives the oracles a symbolic and metaphorical quality that can transcend any specific historical situation and speak with relevance to any historical moment in which a pharaoh emerges to act in pride and violence. As we have noted elsewhere, such metaphorical and symbolic language is not merely decorative, but functions to reshape the audience's perceptions of the entities being described. In a context in which Egypt seems to be a dominant political force whose influence cannot be resisted, Ezekiel's oracles in chs 29—32 offer a new perception to his audience by recasting Egypt and its ruler as monsters, broken reeds, and dead persons going down to Sheol.

1. Proclamation Against Egypt (29:1-21)

■ **1-2** The initial chapter of the Egyptian oracles opens with the first of six date formulas in chs 29—32. The date (January 587 B.C.) locates the first group of proclamations just after an attempted but ultimately unsuccessful intervention into Syria-Palestine by Pharaoh Hophra that caused the Babylonians to lift temporarily the siege against Jerusalem (see Jer 37:5-8). The divine judgment that follows opens with a general statement (Ezek 29:3) and then proceeds through three sections (vv 4-9a, 9b-12, 13-16), with a supplementary oracle (marked by a new date formula) in vv 17-21. The first two main sections move from Pharaoh's sins to Yahweh's judgment, and the third contains an oracle of modest restoration for Egypt.

■ **3-16** Yahweh's accusations against Egypt center on the same sin of pride that marked the oracles against Tyre. Pharaoh is repeatedly cited as making excessive claims for his own status and accomplishments (vv 3, 9b, 15), reflecting the claims to divinity that often accompanied Egypt's rulers. The force of the divine judgment appears in Ezekiel's imagery, in particular. Much of the language and imagery throughout chs 29—32 reflects elements of Egyptian religious traditions and iconography, and ch 29 features the metaphor of Pharaoh as a **great monster** (v 3, *hatannîm*; "great dragon" [NRSV]) in the middle of the Nile river. The metaphor employs a Hebrew term that casts Pharaoh as a serpent or crocodile, but is also used in OT texts to designate mythological chaos monsters such as "Rahab" (e.g., Pss 87:4; 89:10; Isa 30:7) and "Leviathan" (e.g., Pss 74:14; 104:26; Isa 27:1). Egyptian traditions used the serpent both as a symbol of entities such as the sun god and as a creature defeated by Pharaoh himself. Additionally, the crocodile was a conventional figure in Egyptian artwork, sometimes used as a symbol for the Pharaoh himself that compares him with the god Sobek, and at other times depicted as a common animal that is hunted with hooks and captured by Pharaoh as a display of his power (Odell

2005, 371-73). Ezekiel's oracle plays satirically with these traditional images by depicting Pharaoh as a crocodile that Yahweh captures with hooks, removes from the Nile, and flings into the open field to die (29:4-5; see also 32:2-4).

Other elements that appear throughout 29:3-16 continue the indictment and sentence against Egypt. Verse 6 describes Egypt as **a staff of reed for the house of Israel** that failed to support Israel when they leaned upon it. This reference may reflect Egypt's failures to provide significant assistance to Judah in their various rebellions against Babylonia. Given Ezekiel's negative view of Judah's rebellious activities and alliances, however, the depiction may point to Egypt's role in leading Judah away from Yahweh's will and into such rebellions that would be only to their detriment. In light of these misdeeds, but, perhaps especially in view of Pharaoh's pride and claims to divinity, Yahweh's pronouncements of judgment not only declare destruction for Egypt but also assert that through the divine actions the Egyptians themselves will come to **know [*acknowledge*] that I am the** LORD (vv 6, 9, 16). Surprisingly, vv 13-16 follow this judgment with an announcement of future restoration and return for Egypt after its destruction and exile. Even here, however, Yahweh continues the judgment on Pharaoh's pride by asserting that he will restore Egypt only to a **lowly** and **weak** kingdom that **will never again exalt itself above the other nations** (vv 14-15).

■ **17-21** The initial chapter of the Egyptian oracles ends with a section that raises several questions for interpreters. Verses 17-21 read like a later supplement to Ezekiel's oracles against Tyre and Egypt. The date in v 17 (**twenty-seventh year;** 571 B.C.) is strangely outside the order and time frame of the dates in chs 29—32 and is even later than the time given for the book's final vision in 40:1 ("twenty-fifth year"; 573 B.C.). Moreover, the oracle is a divine first person statement that Yahweh will give Nebuchadnezzar the land of Egypt as compensation for the fact that he was unable to capture Tyre, a failed effort that Yahweh says the Babylonian king had undertaken **for me** (v 20). This assertion has long been recognized as a "hermeneutical dilemma" (Block 1998, 147), since Ezekiel's oracles against Tyre, set fifteen years earlier, had prophesied the total destruction of Tyre by Nebuchadnezzar (26:8-14), but the text now acknowledges that the previous prophecy did not come to pass and Yahweh has shifted to a consolation for Nebuchadnezzar. Historically, in fact, Nebuchadnezzar failed to capture Tyre (the evidence is unclear as to whether he even forced Tyre to submit) even after a fifteen-year siege, whose conclusion may coincide with the giving of this oracle.

These elements suggest that 29:17-21 are a later addition that emerged when a new situation called for an earlier oracle to be adapted (Block 1998, 147-49). From a theological perspective, however, the oracle raises the issue of unfulfilled prophecy. For some, the notion of a prophecy failing to come true and the portrayal of Yahweh adjusting his plans in response to historical contingencies are theologically problematic—a problem made more acute by the use of fulfillment as a criterion for judging a "true" prophet in Deut 18:22. Yet, oracles such as vv 17-21 remind contemporary readers that the proclamations of the OT prophets, although guided by divine direction, emerged from the insights of the prophets themselves and always retained a contingency based upon human response and divine freedom (see the prophecy of Jonah and the human and divine responses in the story). This nature of the prophetic word indicates that there are some OT prophecies—like 26:8-14—that did not come to pass, and contemporary readers need not expect them to be fulfilled in the future (at least in the form in which they were originally given).

2. Lamentation over Egypt (30:1-19)

■ **1-19** As noted above, the Egypt oracles alternate between proclamations and lamentations. Following the proclamation in ch 29, the first section of ch 30 (vv 1-19) is a lament over the destruction of Egypt. After the opening prophetic word formula, address to Ezekiel as **son of man,** and messenger formula (vv 1-2), Yahweh commands Ezekiel to **wail** (*yll*) as in mourning. What follows is a series of sayings, each introduced by the messenger formula (vv 2, 6, 10, 13). They revolve around the motif of the **day of the** LORD (v 3) as a day of judgment and share the imagery of the military conquest of Egypt. As in ch 29, Yahweh not only describes the judgment as Nebuchadnezzar's destruction of Egypt, its armies, and its allies (see vv 10-12), but also asserts that these actions will cause the Egyptians to **know that I am the** LORD (vv 8, 19).

29:17—
30:26

3. Proclamation Against Pharaoh (30:20—31:18)

■ **30:20-26** Although part of ch 30, vv 20-26 switch from lamentation to another proclamation against Pharaoh that continues through ch 31 (ch 32 switches to lamentation once again). A new date formula (April 587 B.C.) and prophetic word formula in v 20 and a concluding divine recognition formula in v 26 delineate vv 20-26 as the first part of the proclamation. The central imagery is disturbing: the text portrays Yahweh as a torturer who has already **broken the arm** (v 21) **of Pharaoh** and now **will break both** the already injured arm and the remaining good arm (vv 22, 24). The text gives this gruesome and disturbing divine portrayal the symbolic meaning commonly associated with "arm" as a symbol of strength in ancient texts and artwork: Yahweh has taken away Pharaoh's military power (sword-wielding ability) before the Babylonians (perhaps a reference to Nebuchadnezzar's recent defeat of Pharaoh Hophra's intervention into Syria-Palestine). As in the previous oracles, Yahweh proclaims that his judgment will take the form of Nebuchadnezzar's destruction and exile of Egypt (vv 24-25) and that the result of these actions will be that the Egyptians themselves will **know that I am the** LORD (vv 25, 26).

■ **31:1-14** The first fourteen verses of ch 31, although marked off by a new date formula (June 587 B.C.) and prophetic word formula in v 1, continue the proclamation against Pharaoh that began in 30:20-26. Set just two months later, the divine command in 31:2 broadens the prophet's address to include both Pharaoh and his **hordes** (*hămôn*). The Hebrew term here occurs thirteen times in the oracles against Egypt and carries a range of meanings including wealth (29:19) and armies—the likely meaning here. Yet the term also connotes the sense of "noise/tumult," symbolizing again the sense of chaos that Ezekiel attaches to all of the nations in chs 25—32. As noted above, we might understand the divine judgments proclaimed in these oracles as a message to the exiles that Yahweh exerts an orderly control over the very forces that seem to have cast their world into tumult and incoherence.

The divine oracle in 31:1-14 describes the judgment against Pharaoh and his chaos agents by means of a double comparison. Yahweh proclaims the fate of Egypt by comparing it to the former world power of **Assyria** (although the Hebrew word here could perhaps be read as simply another type of tree; see Block 1998, 184), which, in turn, he compares to **a cedar in Lebanon** (v 3). The text recounts Assyria's greatness and fall by depicting the now-defunct empire with the ancient imagery of a cosmic tree, which once stood at the center of creation in **the garden of God** among **the trees of Eden** (vv 8-9; see Dan 4:10-17). It provided nourishment to all living creatures but has now been felled and sent **down to the pit** (v 14). The force of the imagery is clear: if the former empire of Assyria—a much greater cosmic "tree" than Egypt—has suffered destruction at the hands of the Babylonians, how much more certain is the judgment to come upon Pharaoh and his armies. Although the Babylonians were responsible for Assyria's defeat and will be the agents of Egypt's, as well, Yahweh characteristically claims direct responsibility (**I handed it over to the ruler of the nations** [v 11]). The text also highlights again the sin of pride as the motivating factor for Yahweh's actions against Assyria and those who would aspire to sovereignty in its wake (vv 10, 14).

■ **15-18** As mentioned earlier, the oracles against Egypt divide into two major parts (29:1—31:18; 32:1-32), both of which end with a depiction of Pharaoh's descent into Sheol (see the similar depiction of the king of Tyre in 26:19-21 and the sidebar on Sheol there). Building upon the references to the world of the dead and the "pit" in v 14, the final verses of ch 31 conclude the first major part of the Egypt oracles by rehearsing the descent into Sheol. Verses 15-17 open with a messenger formula that establishes Yahweh as the primary agent and then continue the story of Assyria as the cosmic tree, describing its descent into **Sheol** (the grave). Verse 18 then applies the same imagery to and declares the same fate for Pharaoh and his armies, ending with Yahweh's proclamation that resembles a "here lies . . ." epitaph on Pharaoh's grave marker: **This is Pharaoh and all his hordes** (v 18).

4. Lamentation over Pharaoh and Egypt (32:1-16)

■ **1-2** The first half of ch 32 follows the pattern of the Egypt oracles in chs 29—32 and shifts from the proclamation of judgment in 30:20—31:18 to a lamentation over Pharaoh and Egypt in 32:1-16. The unit opens with a date formula (March 585 B.C.) and prophetic word formula (v 1), after which Yahweh commands Ezekiel to raise a **lament** over Pharaoh. The Hebrew term *qînâ* here again designates the genre of a mourning song, characterized by an uneven ("limping") 3:2 meter in Hebrew syllables.

■ **3-16** Ezekiel's words take on a mocking or sarcastic tone, grieving over the death of Pharaoh as if it had already happened. The first person divine speech employs similar vocabulary and imagery to the depiction of Pharaoh in 29:3-7, portraying him as a sea **monster** (*tannîm*). As noted previously, rather than simply designating a large aquatic animal, the creature to which this Hebrew term refers appears in a variety of biblical and ancient Near Eastern texts as a cosmic mythological monster that symbolized the powers of chaos defeated as a part of the divine creation of the world (e.g., Pss 74:12-14; 89:8-10; Job 40—41). As a mythological chaos symbol known to at least some of the people of Ezekiel's day, this metaphor serves to recast the exiles' perception of Pharaoh as an agent of chaos defeated by the sovereign creator God. Similar to the portrayal in ch 29, Yahweh declares that he will draw the monster Pharaoh out of the waters and fling him to his death on the land (32:3-6)—a defeat pictured in cosmic terms as effecting all creation in vv 7-8. The remainder of the lament describes several judgments to come upon Pharaoh and Egypt, including exile and captivity (v 9), death of animals (v 13), and desolation of the land (v 15). In characteristic Ezekiel style, although the text acknowledges **the king of Babylon** as the agent of destruction, the repeated first person declarations consistently emphasize that Yahweh is the sovereign force who is truly carrying out these actions (compare vv 11-12). And Yahweh once again affirms that the end result of these actions will be that **they**—either the Egyptians or perhaps the Judean exiles—**will know** [*acknowledge*] **that I am the** Lord (v 15).

5. Funeral Dirge over Egypt (32:17-32)

■ **17-19** A new date formula (585 B.C., the month is missing from the Hebrew text) and prophetic word formula in v 17 mark the beginning of the final section of Ezekiel's proclamations against Egypt. The Hebrew is obscure at points, but vv 17-32 function as a definitive "final word" on Egypt, standing apart from the sequence of two pairs that have alternated between proclamation and lamentation (29:1-21 and 30:1-19; 30:20—31:18 and 32:1-16). In v 18, Yahweh commands Ezekiel to **wail** (*nĕhēh*) over the **hordes** of Egypt (cf. the call to "lament" [*qînâ*] in 32:2). The term used here (*nĕhēh*) appears as parallel to *qînâ* ("lament") in several OT texts and seems to indicate a type of funeral dirge or "grief poem" spoken upon the physical or symbolic death of a person or entity (e.g., Jer 9:10, 19; Hals 1989, 266). Yahweh commands Ezekiel to pronounce the death of Egypt, its armies, and its allies and send them down to Sheol (see sidebar "Sheol, the Place of the Dead" above; Heb., **the world below;** the NIV obscures the reference by translating **the earth below**). Moreover, they are to be laid to rest not among the normal dead but **among the uncircumcised** (v 19), those considered ritually unclean to a Judean audience.

■ **20-21** What follows is one of the most striking metaphorical scenes in the book, and no doubt one of the most powerful messages of hope to those who suffered destruction and exile at the hands of the military "superpowers" of the ancient world. The prophet offers his war-torn audience a vivid metaphorical depiction—almost amounting to a guided tour through the world of the dead—that depicts Egypt's (and Pharaoh's) descent to Sheol (see the descent of the "king of Babylon" in Isa 14). Yahweh narrates in first person Egypt's arrival in Sheol, noting ironically that this military power who has wielded the sword against so many will now take its place as one fallen among **those killed by the sword** (v 20). To Ezekiel's Judean audience, who so often saw Egyptian influence in the affairs that led to their present situation, the text presents a counterpicture in which Pharaoh and his hordes do not receive the honorable burial of Egyptian religious practice but are cast into the sections of Sheol reserved for the unclean. Yahweh's speech offers the imaginative depiction that Egypt's violence will ultimately bring that same violence upon itself—the cycle so familiar to those who live even today in a world marked by the violent actions of nations and their armies.

■ **22-32** Yahweh's discourse then proceeds to give a haunting litany of those kingdoms that represent some of the great powers of the ancient world (vv 22-31), picturing each of them as now languishing in the depths of Sheol. Babylonia—the very world power responsible for the exiles' circumstances—is notably missing from the list, perhaps due to Ezekiel's conviction that Yahweh is using them as his instrument of judgment (but see commentary on chs 38—39). Even so, throughout the litany, there is a constant emphasis on the militaristic violence and power that characterized these kingdoms, the very acts that would have made them seemingly dominant forces in the experiences of Ezekiel and his audience. The text repeats a version of the refrain **who had spread terror in the land of the living** throughout its descriptions of each power (vv 23, 24, 25, 26, 27, 30), a phrase that resembles royal texts in which Assyrian kings describe the fear and awe that their war machine inspired in their subjects. By contrast, Yahweh's speech imaginatively recasts these seemingly unchallengeable world powers as merely penultimate pretenders that falter before Yahweh's ultimate sovereignty and end up as victims of their own violence in the recesses of Sheol. Here the prophet proclaims an ultimate leveling—as death becomes the great nullifier of even the most powerful entities. The conclusion of the speech (vv 31-32) applies this judgment directly to Pharaoh and his armies. Verse 32 is obscure, but the Hebrew preserves a first person statement by Yahweh. Whether rendered, perhaps problematically, as Yahweh claiming to be the real power behind Pharaoh's violent actions (**I had him spread terror**) or as Yahweh claiming that he, in fact, is the only one capable of generating true fear in the world (***I spread terror***), the final statement makes clear that Yahweh holds the ultimate power and sovereignty, even over those political and military forces that seem to dominate the present world.

The final dirge over Egypt in vv 17-32 is a fitting conclusion to the OAN as a whole. As noted above, Ezekiel here treats those powers that have plunged the Judeans' world into chaos, disorder, and upheaval. In order to bring a sense of order to that experience of chaos, the prophet's discourse emphasizes the sovereignty of Yahweh and provides his audience with a new imaginative and hopeful perspective in which all such powers are ultimately subdued under Yahweh's control and relegated to Sheol. This dirge becomes a statement of hope grounded in divine sovereignty and directed to those traumatized, victimized, and displaced by such seemingly unchallengeable powers. These forces of chaos and oppression are not eternal; they are only passing powers that ultimately die their own death in the face of Yahweh's triumph. This oracle's image will also contribute to the map of hope constructed throughout the rest of the book, as ch 37 will symbolically depict the exiles' future restoration as Yahweh's action to bring them up from their graves to renewed life in their land (37:12-14).

FROM THE TEXT

Although scholars continue to debate the origins of Ezekiel's OAN in chs 25—32, the reasons for the selection of these nations, and the theological function of the oracles within the book, the perspective of trauma provides a helpful window into how these difficult chapters make a bold claim for order, meaning, and divine sovereignty. The life of the people of Judah over the final decades of the kingdom's history had come to be characterized by the experience of disorder, incoherence, and chaos. True to what is now known about the experience of trauma, the people no doubt felt a loss of control and meaning, as they found themselves caught in a maelstrom of powerful kingdoms, wrong-headed political policies, and deathly war-related violence. These are precisely the kinds of happenings that produce—in the language of trauma theory—experiences that cannot be integrated in a coherent or meaningful way into the conceptual categories of the narrative of life. For Ezekiel and his audience, the sense of chaos and incoherence reached its pinnacle during the extended Babylonian siege of Jerusalem in 588-586 B.C., and it is precisely during this time frame that the book places these oracles in chs 25—32.

As noted above, although discussing the actions and fate of other nations, Ezekiel addresses these oracles as messages to his fellow Judean exiles. In contrast to the sense of disorder and incoherence, Ezekiel's oracles communicate order. The tightly structured sequence of oracles outlined above (seven kingdoms, with the seventh kingdom receiving seven oracles) and the uniquely high concentration of date formulas in chs 25—32 (seven out of the book's total fourteen) impose an orderliness onto the years of maximum disorder during Jerusalem's siege. Moreover, in contrast to a sense of meaninglessness and chaos, the oracles of divine judgment directed against the various kingdoms make a daring claim for the worldwide sovereignty and control of Judah's God over all history and its powers. Ezekiel's rhetoric reinterprets the actions and fate of these kingdoms—which stand as symbols of the chaotic forces that bring disorder and destruction—as resting within God's control (note the high number of prophetic word formulas and messenger formulas throughout the descriptions). Ezekiel introduces an alternative plot line into the story of his people that suggests that Judah's destruction and exile, as well as the actions and fate of the world's powerful kingdoms, do not constitute meaningless chaos but stand within a moral order as part of the larger working of God and God's ultimate purposes of restoration in the world. Although presented in Ezekiel's characteristically violent and totalizing language, this divine sovereignty over even international affairs provides an implicit ground for hope among those Judeans who found themselves the victims of destruction and exile.

For readers from the Wesleyan tradition, the authority of Scripture means that the biblical texts play the normative role in shaping the church's theological outlook on the world. Ezekiel's OAN in chs 25—32 provide such readers with a daring theological perspective. While we must not deny the testimony of other biblical voices that acknowledge the reality of chaos as a part of life and must resist the temptation to see direct divine causation or involvement in every event (not everything happens "for a reason"), Ezekiel's oracles allow the people of God to affirm—cautiously yet courageously—an overall working of God's redemptive purposes in the midst of the seemingly chaotic and traumatic events of our world. Additionally, the OAN that appear in Ezekiel and other prophetic books share the basic assumption that all nations—even those with no knowledge of Israel's God—are accountable to that God for their actions in the realms of social justice and military violence. The implication of these texts is that all nations have and can be held accountable to a sense of shared conventions about just social, economic, and military conduct in the world—a type of "natural revelation" that the nations can know from their own historical experiences rather than direct divine revelation. Such a conviction provides Christian readers with another daring assertion of divine sovereignty, namely, that God has established limits to the unjust exercise of power and violence that are in some way intrinsic to creation and not dependent upon particular Christian revelation. Here is the hopeful conviction that although our experience in the world may seem otherwise, a powerful, rich, and violent nation will not proceed unchecked forever but will in some time and in some way bump up against God's sovereign limits that safeguard peace, justice, and well-being. Especially in light of our short-term experience to the contrary, this conviction remains for us—as it did for Ezekiel and his fellow exiles—primarily an exercise in hope.

Even as the oracles in chs 25—32 offer a profound theological response to trauma, readers must again take account of the language of judgment, which may be offensive to modern readers because of the violence it displays, through which this response is expressed. Christian readers shaped by the revelation of God in Christ must be particularly cautious, remembering that these texts contain ancient theological formulations and recognizing the dangerous consequences of interpretations that assert that God deals with people or nations through violence and killing. Such constructions all too often result in a "divinely sanctioned model for death-dealing international 'relations'" (Darr 2001, 1399). By contrast, Bowen (2010, 159) proposes that taking account of the violence in these ancient texts can challenge contemporary readers to consider the ethical question of how to respond to violence and injustice without inflicting further violence or injustice (see, e.g., Lev 19:18; Luke 10:25-37). Additionally, those reading Ezekiel in the context of the contemporary church in the United States face a particular struggle with this violent language crafted in the experience of trauma. While we may be able to understand rightly such violent language as the trauma-shaped expression of a weak, conquered people who have no weapons or power other than words and imagery, those of us reading in today's United States approach these texts not as the conquered, but as those who live in the world's wealthiest, militarized superpower. Our reality is closer to that of the citizens in the powerful nations Ezekiel condemns than to the vulnerable, subjugated exiles of Ezekiel's audience. This observation has become increasingly poignant since the first decade of the 2000s, as the church in the United States has drawn ever closer to the mainstream of political power and influence and the nation's foreign policy has become characterized by unilateral, militaristic action, and bids for unchecked power. Ironically, then, perhaps the violence depicted in these texts serves the church with a solemn warning against becoming involved in and enraptured by the trappings of power, wealth, and war.

In a similar way, the OAN, especially those directed against Tyre in chs 26—28, provide one of the Bible's most powerful critiques of materialism, consumerism, and economic injustice. As outlined above, the text depicts Tyre as a prosperous kingdom that flourished through trade, luxury, and consumerism and provided the foundation for the international economy through its prosperity. Hence, Tyre's trading partners mourned its collapse out of fear for their own economic stability and prosperity (26:15-18). Yet, Ezekiel consistently portrays Tyre as characterized by pride and self-interest, which ultimately result in Tyre being brought down by the very economic practices from which it gained its wealth (27:25-36). The oracles against Tyre and its trading partners make clear that unjust economic and commercial practices also constitute sin that can bring divine judgment.

Several recent commentators have highlighted the troubling similarities between Ezekiel's depiction of Tyre and the materialism and commercialism that mark contemporary society in the United States at both the personal and national levels. As Odell observes, Tyre serves as a symbol that exposes and falsifies the commonly heard rhetoric that American capitalistic consumerism really benefits other nations (2005, 353-54). Just as the text depicts Tyre's wealth as initially enriching its trading partners but ultimately leading to their harm, so the accumulation of resources and the global economic practices related to American consumerism's demand for cheap goods actually lead to the injustices of cash crops, sweatshops, and exploitative corporate practices in other places. Similarly, Bowen notes that Tyre represents a nation whose international political and economic dealings are driven by the aim "to increase its bottom line at everyone else's expense" (2010, 164). This aim ultimately produces a restrictive and exploitative trade practice that often "fails to make needed resources available" to those who need them most, or produces only ideologically driven and inadequate, self-interested responses to global needs and crises such as poverty and disease in other world areas (Bowen 2010, 169). These concerns resonate in special ways with readers from the Wesleyan tradition—a perspective shaped so significantly by Wesley's concern for the poor and the proper kinds of economic practices that might allow God's people to participate in the economic structures of their context while resisting the temptation to unjust social and economic practices.

While the oracles in chs 25—32 present a litany of negative images and solemn warnings, the final scene in 32:17-32, which gives a visionary tour of Sheol and shows the end of all the powers that seemed to dominate and wreak violence in life, concludes the section with an enduring picture of hope. The final message to Ezekiel's audience is that the seemingly unconquerable forces that brought injustice, destruction, and exile are passing away. Although the vision seems unimaginable while living under the power of these forces, Ezekiel cultivates a hope in the final victory of life over death. In the end, the text asserts, the powers of death, sickness, disease, and injustice, which may cause suffering and loss in life, do not have the final word. The prophet invites his readers to look beyond the present realities and see the "end" of these chaotic forces in light of the final victory of God's peace and wholeness. Even so, for both Ezekiel's exilic audience and his contemporary Christian readers, this remains only an audacious, future hope. When the prophet spoke, many of those powers had not, in fact, passed away before God's victory. And in our world, as well, the forces of chaos and violence continue and, at times, flourish. Yet, Ezekiel's prophetic imagination calls the church to see reality differently and to live hopefully toward the peaceable kingdom that is to come (see Isa 11:6-9).

VI. PREPARATORY ORACLES OF RESTORATION: THE TRANSFORMATION OF ISRAEL (EZEKIEL 33—37)

BEHIND THE TEXT

Chapter 33 marks the major turning point in the book of Ezekiel. The chapter signifies the arrival of a new historical moment, as it narrates the long-anticipated and long-prophesied fall of Jerusalem to the Babylonians in 586 B.C. (vv 21-22). The arrival of the news of this event, which represents the culmination of the divine judgment that Ezekiel has proclaimed, inaugurates a new postdestruction era in Ezekiel's ministry that will focus on restoration and renewal.

The Behind the Text discussion for chs 12—24 outlined the course of events leading up to the beginning of the final Babylonian siege of Jerusalem, especially the events that unfolded between 592 and 588 B.C. After Zedekiah of Judah had entered into open rebellion and Nebuchadnezzar had led his forces to central Syria and established a base of operations at Riblah, he evidently divided his army and sent one contingent down the coast toward the border of Egypt and another toward Jerusalem, where they placed the city under siege sometime in late 588 B.C. (24:1). Nebuchadnezzar intended to replace the current ruling family, relocate the kingdom's capital, and rule it more directly. Various kinds of evidence indicate that Zedekiah's defensive military tactics included establishing a communication system among garrisons and commanders at key Judean strongholds such as Lachish, as well as freeing the slaves in the capital city of Jerusalem in order to add new levies for defense. At some point early in the siege, an aggressive pharaoh, Hophra or Apries, who had come to the Egyptian throne in 589 B.C., led an Egyptian force into southern Syria-Palestine and caused the Babylonians partially and temporarily to withdraw from Jerusalem. The Egyptians appear to have retreated without a confrontation, however, and the Babylonians reinstated the siege in force (see the date in 29:1, which places that Egyptian oracle in January 587 B.C., the time after Hophra's failed intervention; see also Jer 37:5-8).

Biblical texts depict increasingly dire conditions for those in Jerusalem as the siege continued, especially severe famine (see 2 Kgs 25:1-3). In part for reasons such as these, near the end of July 586 B.C., eighteen months after the siege began, the Babylonians breached the city wall on the north or west (2 Kgs 25:1-3). In the final moments, Zedekiah and a military escort attempted to flee south toward the Transjordan but were captured and brought to Nebuchadnezzar at Riblah. Probably in keeping with the stipulated punishments of his vassal treaty, Zedekiah's sons were killed in front of him, his eyes were put out, and he was sent to Babylonia blind and in chains (2 Kgs 25:7). In the weeks that followed, the Babylonians destroyed the temple, palace, and houses, broke down much or all of Jerusalem's walls, and deported a significant number of the city's population, although biblical texts contain differing numbers of deportees and the precise numbers involved remain debated (cf. 2 Kgs 25; Jer 52). While a high percentage of the population remained in the land of Judah, the Babylonians rendered Jerusalem and its immediate vicinity desolate. They established a new capital for Judah, likely now ruled as a Babylonian province, at Mizpah under the non-Davidic ruler Gedaliah (2 Kgs 25; Jer 40—41). The date formula in 33:21-22 indicates that one of the escapees from Jerusalem (likely one of those deported to Babylonia after Jerusalem's fall) arrived among Ezekiel's first group of exiles with the news of the city's destruction nearly six months after the event.

Against this historical backdrop, the announcement of Jerusalem's fall in ch 33 picks up directly from the conclusion of Ezekiel's messages of judgment in ch 24, reinforcing the impression that the oracles against the nations in chs 25—32 form a type of interlude that broadens the reader's perspective on Judah's traumatic experiences (see Behind the Text for chs 25—32). Chapter 24 signaled the beginning of the Babylonian siege of Jerusalem, and in 24:25-27 Yahweh informed Ezekiel that a refugee from Jerusalem would eventually come to report the city's fall and on that day the prophet would receive the ability to speak to the people once again. Ezekiel's words in 33:21-22 narrate the fall of Jerusalem as the precise fulfillment of Yahweh's statement. The entirety of ch 33, however, reveals that the new moment in the life of Ezekiel and his fellow exiles that begins with Jerusalem's destruction goes well beyond that event. As we will see below, ch 33 recapitulates several elements from earlier in the book that marked the inauguration of Ezekiel's ministry as one who would interpret the trauma of exile and destruction in light of the larger work of Yahweh's holiness (e.g., the prophet as "watchman" in 3:16-21 and 33:1-9). In this way, ch 33 represents a new beginning to the second part of Ezekiel's ministry among the exiles—a type of second, preparatory initiation into a work that will now focus on how the same divine holiness that explained judgment also permits the construction of a vision of hope and renewal (see Zimmerli 1983, 183; but cf. Block 1998, 234-35).

From this beginning point, the remainder of the book of Ezekiel (chs 33—48) consists of visions, acts, and oracles that proclaim restoration and renewal for the people and land of Judah within a larger vision of Yahweh's holiness. In terms of the overall structure of the book, this second part will conclude with the third and final vision of Yahweh's glory (*kābôd*), as it returns to dwell in a purified land, city, and temple (chs 40—48). Unlike the pattern we have observed with the preceding two visions of Yahweh's glory (chs 1—3; 8—11), in which each vision was followed by acts and oracles of explanation and elaboration, the acts and oracles in chs 33—39 precede and prepare for the book's final culminating vision. Within this broader section, chs 33—37 form the first of two sets of preparatory oracles of restoration, both of which set the stage for the final *kābôd* vision in chs 40—48. This first set focuses on the transformation and renewal of Israel and its land, while the second set (chs 38—39) focuses on the final vindication of Yahweh in the eyes of the nations, which entails Israel's ultimate safety from enemies. After the introductory oracle in ch 33, chs 34—37 contain five main units, with the climactic oracle of Israel's transformation (36:16-38) at the center:

A. Ending of the Siege: Ezekiel's New Commission (33:1-33)
B. Metaphorical Discourse: False and True Shepherds (34:1-31)

C. Metaphorical Discourses: Judgment on Mount Seir (Edom) and Restoration for the Mountains of Israel (35:1—36:15)
   1. Judgment on Mount Seir (Edom) (35:1-15)
   2. Restoration for the Mountains of Israel (36:1-15)
D. Oracle of Transformation for Israel (36:16-38)
E. Vision of the Valley of Bones (37:1-14)
F. Symbolic Act and Oracle of Restoration for Israel (37:15-28)

Each of these major units with the exception of 37:1-14 opens with the prophetic word formula or some other reference to the "word" of Yahweh (33:1; 33:23; 34:1; 35:1; 36:1; 36:16; 37:15). The unit in 37:1-14, the only vision report in the section, begins with a reference to "the hand of the LORD" (37:1), the common opening for the book's three major visions (see 1:3; 8:1; 40:1).

Scholars often observe that various parts of chs 33—37 show evidence of a complex history of composition and editing, with some portions likely originating as later additions. For example, the salvation oracle in 36:23*b*-38 does not appear in the best Old Greek manuscript of Ezekiel (see Block 1998, 338; Tuell 2009, 259-60). Even so, across the visions, acts, and oracles in chs 33—37 as they now stand, Ezekiel portrays an unfolding renewal of different elements of Israel's life for a new future. The prophet depicts a future transformation of these elements through Yahweh's holiness and in preparation for the return of Yahweh's glory/presence to the land and temple. Chapter 33 first reshapes Ezekiel's commission for the new historical moment and offers a renewed call for obedience in response to the hope for restoration. Chapter 34 then begins the renewal of the various elements of Israel's life by depicting the transformation of the people's leaders and the institution of new leadership. Chapter 35 follows by envisioning the reversal of the people's historic hostilities with neighboring enemies (symbolized by Judah's ancient rival Edom) and the establishment of safety, and 36:1-15 depicts the renewal of the natural world in Israel's land that had been devastated by Yahweh's judgment. The remainder of ch 36 (vv 16-38) describes the climactic purification and transformation of the people of Israel themselves, which is further symbolized by a vision (37:1-14) and symbolic act (37:15-28) that portray the people being brought back to life as a single nation living united upon their land under divinely appointed leadership. The second set of preparatory oracles of restoration in chs 38—39 will complete this progression of renewal and preparation for the return of the divine glory/presence by symbolically depicting the ultimate vindication of Yahweh and safety for Israel (portrayed either as the defeat of a cosmic, symbolic, mythical enemy representing all evil/imperial powers that threaten Yahweh's reign or as the final defeat of Babylonia that has concluded its service as Yahweh's instrument of judgment; see commentary on chs 38—39).

Seen from the perspective of traumatic experience, the progressive renewal of elements of Israel's life depicted in chs 33—37 constitutes another dimension of Ezekiel's attempt to interpret the people's trauma within an alternative plot line that provides new meaning and possibility. In the book as a whole, Ezekiel uses the notion of Yahweh's holiness to offer new interpretations of destruction and exile, as well as the possibilities for future restoration. Prior to this point, Ezekiel's words and actions have used the notion of Yahweh's holiness to explain Jerusalem's destruction and exile as the result of the people's defilement of the temple and land that caused Yahweh to withdraw his holy presence from their midst. Now, beginning in this new postdestruction moment, Ezekiel's visions, acts, and oracles turn to the task of dealing with other questions and feelings generated by traumatic experiences like those known to the Judeans—questions of survival, recovery, safety, and the possibility of new life. In the same way that we might read chs 1—24 as an attempt to give meaning and coherence to the trauma of destruction and exile, Bowen suggests that we read Ezekiel's messages of hope and restoration in chs 33—48 as "reflections of recovery from that trauma" (2010, 210).

Drawing upon trauma theory, Bowen notes that the most important element in such recovery involves reclaiming and reestablishing a "sense of self and safety" that has been shattered for the victim. This sense is precisely what is envisioned by chs 33—37 as they depict the renewal of each element of the people's life for a secure future: new leaders, safety from all enemies/hostilities, a purified and rejuvenated land, and, especially, a transformed people living obediently in relationship to Yahweh. Even more significantly, chs 33—37 return to the theme of Yahweh's holiness and integrate the people's future restoration into the larger plot line of Yahweh's holy work in the world. Although Yahweh's holiness (purity) meant that the people's defilement produced their exile, that same exile has defamed Yahweh's holiness (sovereignty) in the eyes of the nations and will lead Yahweh to resanctify his name by renewing the people and their land and once again dwelling in their midst. Having called the people to break with their old identity that had fallen under judgment, Ezekiel, in a new historical moment, calls the people to envision a future beyond their present despair and to live within that vision of Yahweh's holy work in the world.

IN THE TEXT

A. Ending of the Siege: Ezekiel's New Commission (33:1-33)

Chapter 33 is the major transition point in the book of Ezekiel, finally narrating the long-awaited judgment of Yahweh on Jerusalem and marking the establishment of a new historical moment for the people into which Ezekiel will offer pictures of hope and restoration. Yet, this chapter does not simply narrate the fall of Jerusalem nor proceed immediately to messages of renewal. Rather, Yahweh's words to Ezekiel draw together language and themes from earlier in the book, especially those connected with his initial commissioning in chs 1—3, to form what amounts to a new inauguration of Ezekiel's ministry—renewing the prophet's charge, reiterating the possibility of a new future for the people, and making an even more urgent demand for obedience in this new historical moment when judgment has come and the possibility of restoration is at hand (Zimmerli 1983, 183; cf. Block 1998, 234-35). Two uses of the prophetic word formula (33:1, 23) divide the chapter into two main sections before and after the report of Jerusalem's fall in vv 21-22. The first section (vv 1-20) further divides into two parts that mark the fresh inauguration of the prophet's ministry for the new moment by reiterating Ezekiel's commission to be a responsible "watchman" to the people (vv 1-9; cf. 3:16-21) and reaffirming the real possibility of a new future in the face of fatalism (33:10-19; cf. 18:1-32). The second section (33:23-33), which follows the news of Jerusalem's fall, does not immediately move to the proclamation of restoration but emphasizes the urgency of obedience and purity for participation in Yahweh's new future.

■ **1-9** Following the characteristic prophetic word formula and address to Ezekiel as **son of man,** Yahweh begins the commissioning for this new moment with the command for Ezekiel to **speak** (v 2; see also v 10). This command is strange in the literary context, since Yahweh apparently rendered Ezekiel mute in 24:25-27, and the text does not report that Yahweh opened the prophet's mouth until after Jerusalem's fall in 33:22 (see also 3:26-27). More significantly, Yahweh's designation of the audience for Ezekiel's message as **your countrymen** (33:2; Heb., *your people;* see also vv 12, 17, 30) identifies the focus of Ezekiel's words and ministry in this new moment as the exilic community with him in Babylonia since 597 B.C. (compare the harsh words for those in Jerusalem in vv 23-29). This designation occurred for the first time in Ezekiel's initial commissioning in 3:11 and reappears here for the first time since then, thus strengthening the impression of ch 33 as a new commissioning for a new historical moment. In both contexts, however, the designation of the exiles as **your** (Ezekiel's) people rhetorically distances Yahweh from the people. Such distance reintroduces a theme that was present at Ezekiel's initial call and will reappear throughout this chapter, especially in vv 23-33: there is no automatic inclusion in Yahweh's new future. Inclusion, even for the exiles, demands that the people heed the divine call to break with their old identity and accept a new identity within the future work of Yahweh's holiness.

After this introduction, vv 2b-9 employ the "if . . . then" scenario of case law and return to the image of the **watchman** ("sentinel" [NRSV]; Heb., *ṣōpeh*) to describe Ezekiel's responsibility to his people. The passage parallels the section of the prophet's initial commissioning in 3:16-21. As discussed previously, the image here is typically understood as one assigned to keep watch on the city walls and alert of approaching danger, although it also resonates with the priestly role of the Levitical gatekeepers who guarded the sanctuary against defilement (see 1 Chr 9:17-27; 26:1-19; Sweeney 2005, 155). At the outset of this new moment, the focus is once again on Yahweh's warning to Ezekiel that he will be held responsible for faithfully discharging his task to alert the people, regardless of their response (Ezek 33:7-8). Yet, throughout vv 2b-9 Yahweh also emphasizes the need for the people to respond in obedience if they are to be included in the new life that Yahweh is making available. This theme functions as a type of overture for the proclamations of restoration that follow in chs 33—37, establishing from the outset before any statements of hope are made that participation in Yahweh's future depends upon an obedient response in which the people submit to a new identity within Yahweh's holy work.

■ **10-20** Just as vv 1-9 revisited Ezekiel's original charge to serve as watchman and the people's need to respond, vv 10-20 continue Yahweh's recommissioning of Ezekiel for the new historical moment by revisiting an issue that surfaced in his earlier proclamations of judgment. Although the literary context would still have Ezekiel mute at this point, Yahweh's preceding instruction in v 7 that the prophet must speak whenever Yahweh gives him a "word" and the divine command in v 10 for Ezekiel to **say** places vv 10-20 as the first new "word" that Ezekiel will say to the exiles (designated again here with the broader, loaded title **house of Israel;** see commentary on 2:1-7). This word begins to frame their understanding of the new, postdestruction moment coming upon them.

What follows is a divine dispute oracle that parallels the language and issues of ch 18 (see commentary on 18:1-32; see also 11:14-21). The exiles' words in 33:10 resemble the tone and style of a lament (Block 1998, 187) and reflect the same sense of despair that they had expressed in ch 18 over how they ended up under judgment—a feeling of having been deterministically locked into a course of sinful behavior by their lineage. Unlike ch 18, the people here acknowledge for the first time their own responsibility for the destruction, exile, and trauma they have experienced (Bowen 2010, 205). Immediately, however, this acknowledgment for which Ezekiel has so long called produces another version of the fatalism seen in the exiles' words in ch 18. This fatalism finds expression in the rhetorical question that punctuates their statement: **How then can we live?** (33:10). As those who have experienced trauma and have come to the realization of their own guilt, the exiles feel themselves left in a place of despair over the very possibility of survival. For these trauma victims, the sense of hopelessness, indifference, and resignation seemingly renders them unable to believe in the possibility of Yahweh's saving ability (Bowen 2010, 209). Just as in the old moment before the destruction of Jerusalem, when the exiles saw themselves locked into a life of disobedience and punishment by their own ancestry, so now in this new moment of recognition and confession they sense themselves locked out of any participation in Yahweh's new future. Ezekiel's portraits of a new future for the exiles within Yahweh's holy work in chs 34—37 can have no force as long as this fatalism reigns.

Yahweh's rebuttal of the exiles' fatalism begins forcefully in 33:11 with a divine oath: **As surely as I live** (see 5:11; 14:16; 18:32; 20:31; 35:6) and the statement of a general principle that governs all of Yahweh's actions with his people: **I take no pleasure in the death of the wicked, but rather that they turn from their ways and live.** To spite the impression that one might gain from all of his judgment preaching, at the outset of a new ministry of restoration Ezekiel proclaims that the operative divine orientation that explains Yahweh's ways and makes a new future possible is that Yahweh ultimately prefers life over death. It is this assertion that renders the rest of v 11 intelligible, as Yahweh directs a double imperative to the people: **Turn! Turn** (šûbû šûbû). Direct calls for repentance are rare in Ezekiel's preaching, and this call contradicts some of his earlier statements that the people are incapable of obedience (e.g., chs 16; 20; 23). Moreover, the language of repentance, especially in the context of the verses that follow, seems to imply that the people could avoid the judgment, but 33:21-22 will make clear that the climactic judgment has already come. Seen against the backdrop of this new moment, however, Yahweh's call for the people to **turn** becomes a call for them to look beyond the sins of the past and submit to a new identity and place within Yahweh's future to be portrayed in the chapters that follow. To illustrate this possibility, vv 12-20 reprise the argument of ch 18 by giving hypothetical cases in which neither the **righteous** nor the **wicked** are fatalistically locked into their destiny regardless of their response to Yahweh's call. Yahweh's preference for life nullifies any fatalistic determination, yet the calls for repentance reveal that inclusion in Yahweh's restoration is not automatic. As Yahweh's concluding statement (**I will judge each of you according to his own ways** [v 20]) indicates, the people's ability to participate in Yahweh's new future depends upon their obedient response in this new postjudgment moment.

■ **21-22** The renewal of Ezekiel's commissioning to warn the people and the affirming of the real possibility of participation in a new future have prepared the way for the announcement that Jerusalem has fallen and the new postdestruction moment of the people's story has begun. The prophet's first person narration describes the moment when the news reached the exiles that Yahweh's climactic judgment on Jerusalem had come to pass (vv 21-22). Although the date given in v 21 (**twelfth year . . . tenth month . . . fifth day**) is difficult to align with other chronological reckonings of the Babylonian capture of Jerusalem (e.g., 2 Kgs 25:1-8; see Block 1998, 254; Tuell 2009, 230), it places the arrival of the news about six months after the apparent time of the capture and three years to the month after 24:1 indicated the siege began. As the Behind the Text discussion noted, Ezekiel's description in 33:21-22 connects to Yahweh's words in 24:25-27, as he reports that Yahweh opened his mouth just before a **man** (probably not an escapee but a member of the newest group of deportees from Jerusalem in 586 B.C.) arrived among the original group of exiles with news of the city's capture. Perhaps the most striking thing about 33:21-22, however, is that the text's report of Jerusalem's fall—the climactic event of the divine judgment that Ezekiel had so long proclaimed—passes with amazingly little fanfare or detail (simply, **The city has fallen**; two words in Hebrew). Such a description hints at what the remainder of ch 33 will begin to make explicit: the focus of Yahweh's actions is much broader than Jerusalem and the Judeans. The traumatic events of the people's past and the hopeful realities of their future take shape within the larger context of Yahweh's holiness/sovereignty at work in the world.

■ **23-29** The second main section of ch 33 (vv 23-33) begins in vv 23-29 with a prophetic word formula that introduces a divine oracle directed to the survivors who remain in the land of Judah after the destruction of Jerusalem. Following Ezekiel's statement in v 22 that Yahweh had again opened his mouth, the oracle represents the first "word" that Yahweh gives for Ezekiel to speak in this new postdestruction moment (but see vv 10-20). Yet, this new word that follows the long-anticipated judgment does not turn immediately to the proclamation of restoration that will consume chs 34—37. Rather, Yahweh first disputes a claim reportedly being made by those remaining in Judah, continuing the theme of Ezekiel's condemnation of those remaining in old Jerusalem that has appeared throughout the book. Verse 24 represents the dismal postdestruction situation in Judah by referring to the survivors as **living in those ruins in the land of Israel**. These people appeal to the promises of the patriarchs and matriarchs (specifically Abraham's promise of land inheritance in Gen 12:1-3) to bolster the conviction that they will now inherit the land of Judah (see similar claims made by those remaining in Jerusalem after the first capture in 597 B.C. in 11:14-21).

Yahweh's rebuttal of this claim begins in v 25 with the transitional **therefore** and messenger formula (**This is what the Sovereign LORD says**).

What follows is a list of sins that disqualify those Judean survivors from inheriting the land in Yahweh's future. In keeping with Ezekiel's identity and theological perspective (see 18:1-20; 22:1-16), most of the sins are priestly in character (e.g., **eat meat with the blood** [33:25; see Lev 17:10-14; 19:26]; **defiles his neighbor's wife** [Ezek 33:26; see Lev 18:20]), particularly describing the people's failure to follow the prohibitions of priestly laws such as the Holiness Code (Lev 17—26). To the condemnations that we have come to expect, however, Ezekiel adds a phrase that appears only here: **you rely on your sword** (Ezek 33:26). The action has priestly overtones of pollution caused by bloodshed but also expresses the people's long history of violence associated with warfare. Ezekiel asserts that the actions of warfare undertaken by the kingdom, even those presumably done in the name of self-defense, constitute the sinful practice of violence that places them on the same plane as the kingdoms condemned for such acts in the preceding oracles against the nations (chs 25—32). Despite the Judean survivors' claims, they have "less in common with Abraham than with the foreign nations" (Tuell 2009, 231). In an ironic twist, 33:27 proclaims that the people's history of violence will bring that same violence upon those who survived Jerusalem's fall and remain in the land (see Matt 26:52, "all who draw the sword will die by the sword").

33:23-29

The sins described in Ezek 33:25-27 represent acts of disobedience, but Ezekiel again labels these actions as **detestable things** (*tôʿēbôt*; ***abominations*** [v 26])—the priestly term for deeds that are not simply rebellious but defile the people and the land. It is this defilement that renders the land uninhabitable and disqualifies the survivors from inheriting the land in its postdestruction state. Verses 28-29 continue the theme of a defiled land and expand the divine judgment beyond just Jerusalem and its survivors, as Yahweh proclaims that he will **make the land a desolate waste** on account of the people's **detestable things** (***abominations***). The language here is similar to the divine devastation of nature described elsewhere in the book, and Yahweh once again identifies such devastation as the means by which those remaining in the land will **know/*acknowledge*** him (v 29) (see commentary on chs 4—7). This depiction may reflect the Holiness Code's reference to a sabbatical for the land in order to cleanse it from defilement (Lev 26:34-35), though historical and archaeological evidence reveals that Judah (outside of Jerusalem) did not become utterly desolate or uninhabited after 586 B.C. but maintained a significant population and continued to exist in many ways as it had previously (Moore and Kelle 2011, 334-95). Even so, this broader vision of destruction furthers Ezekiel's perspective that Jerusalem's fall and the people's exile should be understood as part of the larger plot line of Yahweh's response to the defilement of his holiness. Yahweh is undertaking a comprehensive judgment that goes beyond just Jerusalem as a means of reestablishing his holiness/sovereignty and creating a new future.

■ **30-33** With the transitional phrase **As for you** and another reference to **your countrymen** (Heb., *your people;* see also vv 2, 12, 17), Yahweh's speech switches focus back to the Babylonian exiles in vv 30-33. Following the condemnation of those remaining in the land for the lack of obedience that would allow them a place in Yahweh's future, one might expect a contrasting positive description of the prophet's fellow exiles, especially since they have had the benefit of Ezekiel's earlier attempts to interpret their trauma in the context of Yahweh's holiness. Yet, even this group, Yahweh says, practices the same disobedience as those remaining in Jerusalem (v 31), offering what amounts only to an outward response without truly engaging in obedience (v 32). With the return of the theme of obedience (see vv 1-9), the address to the exiles in vv 30-33 makes a fitting conclusion to the opening chapter of the book's second half. As Yahweh has renewed Ezekiel's commissioning for a new postdestruction moment (vv 1-9), emphasized the real possibility of a different future (vv 10-20), and placed the fall of Jerusalem into the context of a comprehensive judgment (vv 23-29), he now sets the stage for the oracles and visions of restoration that follow by asserting that no one—not even the original group of Babylonian exiles—will automatically participate in Yahweh's new future. This postdestruction moment requires the same obedient response to Yahweh's holiness that Ezekiel has demanded throughout the previous era, but now as the means for inclusion in Yahweh's work of renewal. At the outset of the restoration depictions that will dominate the rest of the book, Ezekiel calls his people to accept a new identity of obedience within the new work that Yahweh is about to do.

B. Metaphorical Discourse: False and True Shepherds (34:1-31)

Chapter 34 begins Ezekiel's portrayals of a new future by which he constructs a map of hope for those who suffered the trauma of destruction and exile. The chapter is the first of a series of passages that progressively depict the renewal of various elements of Israel's life for this new future (see Behind the Text), and the first element to be renewed addresses a problem that has plagued the people throughout their history, namely, the disobedient and unjust leadership by kings and others rulers that led Judah into rebellions and resulted in their destruction and exile. The first move in Ezekiel's vision of a divinely established new future is to renew the character of the people's leadership and provide them with new leaders for a new day.

The prophet's portrayal of this first renewal takes the form of a metaphorical discourse by Yahweh that draws upon the ancient Near Eastern metaphor of kings as "shepherds." Various ancient Near Eastern royal inscriptions use the metaphor to represent the king's responsibility to protect and provide for his people, as a shepherd cares for and nourishes the flock. Kings such as Hammurabi of Babylon (eighteenth century B.C.) describe themselves as the "shepherd" who must ensure justice in the land and prevent the oppression of the vulnerable (for sample ancient Near Eastern texts, see Greenberg 1997, 707). Although David is the only named Israelite king explicitly called "shepherd" in the OT (1 Sam 16:11; 17:15; 2 Sam 5:2; Ps 78:70-72), the image is connected with kingship throughout various texts (see Num 27:16-17; 1 Kgs 22:17; Jer 3:15; 10:21; 23:1-4; Mic 5:4; Zech 10:1—11:17), and the corresponding image of Israel as a "flock" appears in several places (e.g., Num 27:16-17; 1 Kgs 22:17; Pss 95:7; 100:3; Isa 40:11; Jer 31:10).

The group referred to as **the shepherds of Israel** (v 2) likely represents Israel's and Judah's own rulers and nobility (rather than foreign overlords), both in Ezekiel's day and throughout the people's history (but cf. Odell 2005, 423-24). Ezekiel has condemned the people's political and religious leaders previously (e.g., chs 13; 17; 22), and the passage here has a close parallel in Jer 23:1-4, which also uses the metaphor of shepherds and envisions Yahweh taking the role of shepherd upon himself and then raising up new rulers for the future (on Ezekiel's critiques of leaders generally, see Duguid 1994). Beginning with a condemnation of Israel's rulers as abusive (Ezek 34:1-10), the discourse builds through stages to a new vision of leadership as Yahweh takes the role of shepherd to gather the scattered flock (vv 11-16), punishes its abusers (vv 17-22), and proclaims a new future in which the people are united under one shepherd and receive protection from a divinely established covenant of peace (vv 23-31).

■ **1-10** With a new prophetic word formula, an address to Ezekiel as **son of man,** and a messenger formula in vv 1-2, Yahweh instructs the prophet to speak **against the shepherds of Israel.** The exclamation **Woe** (*hôy;* "Ah" [NRSV]), which often appears with lamentations and funeral songs, casts the text as a woe oracle that raises both condemnation and lamentation. Verses 1-6 present the indictment and use the shepherd motif to cast Judah's kings in particular (and perhaps the whole history of the people's rulers; see ch 20) as bad shepherds. The basic charge is that they have served their own interests and thus neglected and abused the sheep. Verse 2 expresses this charge with shepherding language by claiming that the rulers only *tend* (*rʿh;* **take care of**) **themselves.** Verse 4 offers a powerful list of metaphors that use the imagery of how one should care for a flock to depict what the self-serving rulers have failed to do: **You have not strengthened the weak or healed the sick or bound up the injured . . . brought back the strays or searched for the lost.** Rather, the end of v 4 asserts that the people's leaders **have ruled them harshly and brutally**. The Hebrew terminology here (*hzq; prk*) appears elsewhere in the OT to designate the ways that foreign oppressors rule over the people, specifically the ways that the Egyptians oppressed the Hebrews (Exod 1:13-14). Moreover, the Holiness Code (Lev 25:43, 46, 53) summons the memory of this Egyptian oppression to forbid the Israelites from ruling over one another in exactly such a manner (Greenberg 1997, 697). By employing these terms, Ezekiel accuses Judah's own shepherds of acting like foreign tyrants to their people. Ezekiel 34:5-6 then concludes the indictment by using shepherd imagery to give a picture of the vulnerable state in which the people have been left because of the lack of good shepherds: **So they were scattered . . . they became food for all the wild animals** (v 5).

The transitional word **therefore** in v 7 moves from the indictment to the judgment. Beginning with the force of a divine oath formula (**As surely as I live**), v 8 recaps the shepherds' bad actions and the flock's resulting dismal condition. Verses 9-10 then begin the condemnation over again with another **therefore** and add emphasis with a second command for the shepherds to hear (see v 8) and a messenger formula. Yahweh declares that he will undertake two actions: he will **remove** the bad shepherds and **rescue** the flock (v 10). Yet, Yahweh's language throughout the opening section reveals a deeper motivation for his actions that goes beyond judgment on the bad shepherds. Eight times in vv 1-10 Yahweh makes the first person claim that the people who have been scattered are **my sheep**. As we have observed throughout the book, Ezekiel, unlike Jeremiah, does not depict Yahweh as motivated by a deep compassion or connection to Israel but by concern for his own holiness. Here, however, we note the inextricable connection that will be developed in ch 36 between Yahweh's holy name/identity and his people's status and actions.

■ **11-16** Yahweh's words in vv 11-16 develop the opening woe oracle by describing how he will rescue his scattered sheep that have been neglected and abandoned. Here Yahweh's repeated emphasis that the people are **my flock** (vv 6, 8, 10, 11, 12, 15) develops into direct divine action, and a new messenger formula (v 11) shifts the focus to Yahweh. Although Israel's human shepherds have failed to act properly on the people's behalf, a dramatic grace-act of Yahweh will keep the people from being abandoned to the dismal condition described in vv 6-8. Yahweh commits to undertake the role of shepherd directly and resolves to carry out personally the task of establishing a community marked by care and justice that has been neglected by the human shepherds. The Hebrew of v 11 communicates Yahweh's resolution with heavy first person emphasis and repetition: ***Behold I, I myself will search for my sheep and seek after them.*** The image of the scattered flock resonates with the traumatic experiences of the exiles, but the royal connotations of the shepherd image also make this passage a reassertion of Yahweh's kingship in the face of rival human claims to sovereignty (recall Ezekiel's use of the terms for "prince" rather than "king" to refer to human rulers). Such use of shepherds as a metaphor for the *divine* king appears in both ancient Near Eastern and OT texts (e.g., Ps 23; Isa 40:11; Jer 23:1-4; 31:10; see also *ANET* 72a).

In Ezek 34:12-16, Yahweh repeatedly declares his intention to search for the sheep that have been scattered, bring them home to a safe pasture, and personally carry out the proper acts of shepherding care. The language casts the divine actions as a new exodus in which Yahweh will bring the people out from a place of danger and lead them into a place of safety (see Exod 3:10-12; 7:4-5; Bowen 2010, 212). With additional first person repetition and emphasis, Ezek 34:16 concludes the section by depicting Yahweh's actions as the exact reversal of the human shepherds' failures reported in v 4: **I will search for the lost and bring back the strays. I will bind up the injured and strengthen the weak . . . I will shepherd the flock with justice.**

■ **17-22** The transitional phrase **As for you** (pl.) in v 17 marks a shift in Yahweh's discourse, as he now turns from the words concerning the bad shepherds in vv 1-16 to a direct address to **my flock.** The address becomes more specific over the following verses, as Yahweh differentiates among the flock (**between one sheep and another, and between rams and goats** [v 17]; **between the fat sheep and the lean sheep** [v 20]) and focuses the indictment on one group (**you** [pl.; v 18]). As in vv 1-10, this section gives an indictment in vv 17-19, followed by the judgment in vv 20-22 (marked by the transitional **therefore** in v 20). Some recent commentators have proposed that Ezekiel here proclaims a judgment between Yahweh's flock (Israel) and other sheep, goats, and rams that have hurt the flock as foreign oppressors (Odell 2005, 428; Bowen 2010, 214). Yet, the twofold address in vv 17-18 suggests that Yahweh first shifts the focus to the entire flock of his people in v 17 and then shifts again in v 18 to a specific group *within* the larger flock.

Seen in this way, the divine discourse extends the condemnation of the shepherds/kings to include judgment upon the ruling class (**fat sheep** [v 20]) more generally (even the shepherd image refers in some texts to the nobility rather than simply kings; see Isa 56:11; Nah 3:18; Greenberg 1997, 708). In keeping with the metaphor, Yahweh accuses these sheep of not only taking the good pasture for themselves but also carelessly polluting the food and water sources by their own acts of consumption so that **my sheep** are left with only contaminated food and drink (vv 18-19). These are the nobility who have benefitted from the kings' ways, consumed the available resources, and abused the other members of the flock. The divine judgment upon the abusive sheep thus forms the next stage of Yahweh's renewal of leadership depicted by the chapter. After gathering his endangered sheep, the shepherd/king Yahweh now acts in "defense of the weak members of the flock against the strong" and provides the possibility of a safe future (Odell 2005, 423).

Fat Sheep and Ecological Stewardship

The metaphorical critique of the ruling class/nobility ("fat sheep") in 34:17-22 accuses them not only of the mistreatment of others but also of consuming, hoarding, and contaminating the resources that could provide for others. Katheryn Darr observes that this divine judgment raises the issue of "ecological stewardship" for contemporary readers of Ezekiel. The accusations against these members of Yahweh's "flock" should give pause to readers who know all too well the modern realities of "nuclear waste and chemical landfills, of cracked-open oil tankers and mountains of non-biodegradable trash" (2001, 1496). Ezekiel's words challenge the people of God to think seriously about how we fail to share available resources, benefit unfairly from overconsumption, and too recklessly pollute the good gifts that could nourish others.

■ **23-31** The stages of Yahweh's redemptive acts in ch 34 reach their climax in vv 23-31. Yahweh speaks about the scattered flock/people in third person and gives the first extended glimpse of what will be Ezekiel's most characteristic vision of the people's restored future throughout the book's final chapters: Israel will be a unified people under one Davidic ruler, living in a revitalized land and existing as Yahweh's people in safety ensured by a divine covenant of well-being.

Verses 23-24 begin this vision by returning to the shepherd metaphor. Yahweh declares that he will set over the people **one shepherd, my servant David** (v 23). Yahweh here shifts roles, stepping back from his direct activity as shepherd (vv 11-16) and envisioning a human ruler to care for the people/flock, while Yahweh assumes the role of **their God** (v 24). Ezekiel's references to David in this and other restoration oracles (e.g., 37:24-28) do not refer to the person David, but represent the Davidic dynasty, expressing the hope for a future ruler who will symbolize a legitimate royal lineage among the people. Chapter 17 previously mentioned a future restoration of the Davidic line, and the figure of an ideal Davidic ruler is a common element in prophetic texts that express hope for a restored future for Israel (so-called messianic texts; e.g., Isa 9:6-7; 11:1-9; Jer 30:8-10; 33:17-26; Hos 3:5; Amos 9:11). Such references reflect OT royal ideology that describes the Davidic king as Yahweh's son or agent who is responsible for establishing justice that is in keeping with the divine character (see Pss 2:6-11; 72:1-4, 12-14; Sweeney 2005, 156-57). Yet, the divine discourse in Ezek 34:24 incorporates this notion of a Davidic shepherd/king into Ezekiel's emphasis on Yahweh's sovereignty by once again designating the human ruler only as a **prince** (*nāśîʾ*) who functions as Yahweh's regent.

The chapter concludes in vv 25-31 with Yahweh's pronouncement that he will establish a **covenant of peace** (*běrît šālôm*) for the people that will give them a future life of blessing, harmony, and well-being. The passage resembles other prophetic texts that also describe a covenant for the people that is not so much made *with* Yahweh as guaranteed/established *by* Yahweh on their behalf (e.g., Hos 2:18), and the covenant blessings listed here are similar to those in the Holiness Code (Lev 26:4-13). The covenant in Ezek 34:25-29 entails both the rejuvenation of nature that Ezekiel has previously depicted as destroyed through divine judgment to a well-watered, fertile, and productive land (see also 36:1-15), as well as the assurance of future safety for the people in a land free from menacing animals and human oppressors. The verses provide one of the clearest pictures of the OT concept of "shalom" (peace; wholeness) as not merely the absence of strife but a full-orbed, multidimensional "well-being" that is not individualistic, but entails the wholeness and blessing of the community and the natural world. Perhaps the most significant element of this covenant for understanding the nature of Ezekiel's vision of future restoration, however, is that the prophet does not say that Yahweh's establishment of this covenant is dependent upon the people's obedience (although that might be implied by ch 33). Rather, Israel receives a new future solely on the basis of Yahweh's initiative and action (Darr 2001, 1472). Throughout his preaching, and especially in the restoration oracles in chs 33—48, Ezekiel asserts that Yahweh acts out of his own self-regard and concern to vindicate his holiness and restore his people's and land's defiled purity (see 36:16-38). The restored future received by the people is a by-product of Yahweh's actions being undertaken out of his holiness. Though perhaps troubling to contemporary readers, this perception of divine holiness provides Ezekiel and his fellow exiles with an alternative plot line within which they can reconfigure their trauma of destruction and exile as part of a larger movement of divine holiness that even extends into a new future. Accordingly, v 30 concludes with a modified divine recognition formula in which Yahweh states that the restored people not only will **know**/acknowledge him (see also v 27) but also will be able to recognize the divine presence **with them** in their land once again. Just as chs 1—24 claimed that the people could come to know/acknowledge Yahweh through the rightly interpreted experiences of traumatic destruction, ch 34 sets the stage for the remainder of the book by asserting that such knowledge/acknowledgment will now come through the experience of restoration and healing.

Ezekiel 34 and Jesus, the Good Shepherd

The metaphor of God as the true shepherd in ch 34 appears in NT texts as an image for Jesus as one who tends the flock of God's people with compassion. John 10:11-18 records Jesus' use of the shepherd image, but with a surprising addition: "I am the good shepherd . . . and I lay down my life for the sheep" (vv 14-15; see also Matt 18:10-14; Luke 15:3-7). Seen against the OT and ancient Near Eastern use of shepherd as an image of power and a representation of human or divine kings, the NT metaphor of shepherd presents Jesus in the same manner as Yahweh in Ezek 34—a different kind of sovereign, who does not simply demand for people to come to him but actively seeks after his scattered people. Yet, the description of Jesus as a shepherd who lays down his life in order to rescue his sheep goes beyond the portrayal in Ezekiel and takes on a new meaning against the royal background of the shepherd image. Rather than one who rescues by using might and force—the typical connotation of shepherd as a metaphor for a king—Jesus redefines kingship/power as the act of seeking and saving through sacrificial love. Thus, the image of Jesus as a good, self-sacrificing shepherd constitutes a powerful *political* critique that challenges modern political ideologies in which peace and provision come through strength, domination, and violence rather than sacrificial love (Odell 2005, 430-31).

C. Metaphorical Discourses: Judgment on Mount Seir (Edom) and Restoration for the Mountains of Israel (35:1—36:15)

34:23—
36:15

Although divided between two chapters in modern Bibles and possessing complex compositional histories, 35:1-15 and 36:1-15 can be read as one unit composed of two sections with contrasting images. The prophetic word formula marks the beginning of a unit in 35:1 and does not appear again until 36:16. The use of **son of man** and the messenger formula in 35:2 and 36:1-2 delineate two sections, both of which constitute metaphorical discourses using the image of mountains (**Mount Seir** and **mountains of Israel**). The discourses revolve around the questions of the status and possession of the land of Israel, yet contrast with one another, as the mountain in ch 35 symbolizes judgment and the mountains in 36:1-15 symbolize restoration.

As discussed previously (see commentary on ch 6), the phrase **the mountains of Israel** occurs seventeen times in Ezekiel but nowhere else in the OT (6:2, 3; 19:9; 33:28; 34:13, 14*a*, 14*b*; 35:12; 36:1*a*, 1*b*, 4, 8; 37:22; 38:8; 39:2, 4, 17), and the image of **mountain/mountains,** which occurred for the first time in ch 6, functions as a key metaphor throughout the book (see Casson 2004). When depicting Israel, Ezekiel often sets up a contrast between plural mountains and a singular mountain (see sidebar in commentary on ch 6), ultimately concluding with the plural mountains being displaced by the triumph of one mountain (see 40:2; 43:12). Ezekiel typically uses Israel's plural mountains as a negative image that represents the people's sin (e.g., 7:7, 16; 19:9; 20:28) or the current devastated state of the land (now promised rejuvenation in 36:1-15). In 35:1-15 and 36:1-15, mountains are used as metaphors for the land of Edom, which stands under judgment, and the land of Israel, which though currently devastated receives a promise of rejuvenation.

1. Judgment on Mount Seir (Edom) (35:1-15)

■ **1-15** The first of the two paired metaphorical discourses in 35:1-15 is a declaration of judgment and destruction against Edom. The genre resembles the other oracles against the nations (chs 25—32), which featured a brief oracle against Edom in 25:12-14. After the opening pronouncement (35:1-4), the chapter contains two oracles, both of which give an indictment of Edomite actions (marked by **because**) and a judgment of the devastation of nature and deportation of the people (marked by **therefore**) (vv 5-9, 10-15). The oracles include several elements that have appeared in other judgment passages (e.g., **set your face against** [v 2]; **I am against you** [v 3]; **As surely as I live** [vv 6, 11]). As noted above, the text uses a mountain—**Mount Seir,** located southeast of the Dead Sea in Edomite territory—as a metaphor for Edom, creating a contrasting pair with the mountains used as a metaphor for Israel in 36:1-15. The symbol reaches back to Gen 36, where the ancient writer identifies the Edomites as the ancestors of Isaac's son and Jacob's brother, Esau, and associates them with the area of Mount Seir (see also Gen 32:3-4; Num 24:18; Deut 2:4-8). Yet, it is not immediately clear why Ezekiel singles out Edom for further judgment. Perhaps the key lies in what Edom represents. As outlined previously, Ezek 33—37 as a whole depicts the progressive renewal of different elements of Israel's life, each of which undergoes transformation through Yahweh's holiness and in preparation for the return of Yahweh's glory/presence to the land and temple and a new future of blessing and safety for Israel. Following the renewal of Israel's leadership in ch 34, the oracle against Edom symbolically envisions the reversal of the people's historic hostilities and the establishment of a new safety from surrounding enemies.

Edom provides a fitting symbol for Israel's historic hostilities/enemies on two levels. On the historical level, both of the chapter's indictments (vv 5, 10) accuse the Edomites of acting against (or at least taking advantage of) Judah at the time of Jerusalem's fall (**at the time of their calamity** [v 5]—perhaps a Hebrew pun of the name "Edom"; see Greenberg 1997, 713). Other biblical texts preserve the memory of hostile Edomite actions against Judah in the days of the Babylonian siege (e.g., Ps 137:7; Obad 10-14), and some extrabiblical evidence suggests Edomite encroachment (**we will take possession** [Ezek 35:10]) on territories south of Jerusalem in the late sixth century. Edom was a local, hostile neighbor who had been a part of Israel's past experiences of **bloodshed** (v 6), **anger and . . . hatred** (v 11). On the symbolic level, however, Edom represents the prototypical enemy that symbolizes the rest of the neighboring kingdoms that have threatened Israel and Judah in various ways throughout their history. While the OT identifies Israel and Edom as "brother" nations—related descendants of Jacob and Esau, close in both geography and ethnicity—it portrays this relationship as one of long-standing hostility (an **ancient hostility** [v 5]) (see also Gen 25:22-28; 27:41-45; 32:3-21; Ps 137:7; Isa 34; Amos 1:11-12). More so than any other single nation, then, Edom symbolizes a traditional enemy that represents all those with whom Israel has lived in violent, death-dealing ways—sometimes dealing violence to them and sometimes suffering trauma at their hands. Now, however, Ezekiel envisions a new future in which Yahweh will grant safety from the enemies and violent relationships that Edom represents.

Yahweh's speech ends with a recognition formula in v 15, which has occurred in various forms throughout the chapter (vv 4, 9, 11, 12). Coming at the end of a chapter dominated by direct second person address to Edom, this final third person statement in v 15 (**they will know that I am the L**ORD) perhaps refers to the Judean exiles (but cf. the words to Edom in v 11 where the Hebrew reads **them** but the Greek reads "you" [so NRSV]). Ezekiel again asserts that the divine acts of restoration (here, the removal of ancient hostilities)—like the earlier acts of destruction—are part of the larger plot line of bringing the exiles to a new acknowledgment of Yahweh's identity and holiness.

Enemies, Violence, and the State of Israel

The part of Ezekiel's depiction of a new future that envisions the establishment of safety from neighboring enemies in ch 35 once again raises the problematic issue of the book's portrayals of violence discussed previously (see From the Text for chs 4—7, 8—11). Contemporary readers face the reality that uncritical readings of such texts have even today created a world in which people and nations seek solutions to international conflict through violence and the elimination of enemies rather than through mutual respect and collaboration (Darr 2001, 1479). Additionally, the nationalistic flavor of these texts makes it important for contemporary readers to resist reading them in terms of the modern state of Israel and using them to privilege that modern nation over its neighbors or to call for violent solutions to complex issues of land or resources. The larger Christian confession is that the group of Judean exiles to whom Yahweh promised a new future became over time an expanded people of God who cannot be identified with any one modern polity or ethnicity.

2. Restoration for the Mountains of Israel (36:1-15)

Just as ch 35 used a mountain to symbolize Edom, 36:1-15 uses **the mountains of Israel** as a metaphor for the land of Israel that has been devastated through divine judgment. The opening Hebrew word in v 1 (*wĕʾattâ*; *And you*—omitted by the NIV) signals a shift to a new instruction to Ezekiel and a new topic (see the references to **the enemy** and **Edom** in vv 2, 5), and the passage features heavy repetition of prophetic formulas that emphasize Yahweh as the speaker of these words of dramatic restoration for the devastated land (e.g., command to hear Yahweh's word in vv 1, 4; messenger formula in vv 3, 4, 5, 6, 7, 13). The text constitutes a divine oracle of restoration spoken directly to the land and its natural elements. As Odell observes, 36:1-15 extends the judgment against Edom by showing how that judgment has "salvific consequences" for Israel (2005, 440).

■ **1-7** The oracle has a similar structure to the judgment against Mount Seir, containing three sections that each combine a motivating rationale (marked by **because**) with a divine action or series of actions (marked by **therefore**) (vv 2-3*a*, 3*b*-7, 13-14), as well as a central section declaring restoration (vv 8-12). Throughout each part, Yahweh's promises of restoration explicitly reverse the descriptions of the devastation of nature and, especially, of the mountains of Israel, given in the first use of the metaphor of the mountains in ch 6 (see Bowen 2010, 218-19). Verse 1, for example, opens with language nearly identical to the oracle against the mountains of Israel in 6:2-3*a*, and the first two sections (vv 1-7) focus on the devastated state of various elements of nature in Israel's land (**mountains and hills, . . . ravines and valleys** [v 4]) and Yahweh's intent to judge those nations that have plundered and possessed.

■ **8-15** The emphatic transition, **But you** (pl.), at the start of v 8 shifts from the indictments of the land's devastation and its causes to a promise of future restoration. Verses 8-12 depict a fully revitalized fertility and fruitfulness that occurs in two steps. Yahweh first revitalizes the land, but this is a preparatory step so that Yahweh can provide the exiles—who will soon receive a transformation of their own (see 36:16-38)—a renewed land in which to live (v 12). Many commentators observe that the restoration features creation language and themes, yet Ezekiel's priestly identity highlights the text's connections with the covenant blessings in Lev 26. In keeping with Ezekiel's perspective, however, the blessings that are conditional upon obedience in Lev 26 appear here as unconditional promises based solely on Yahweh's initiative and sovereignty.

The oracle in Ezek 36:1-15 adds to preceding visions of renewed leadership (ch 34) and transformed hostilities (ch 35) by reversing the devastation of nature that accompanied Yahweh's judgment on the people's and land's defilement. We previously observed that Ezekiel placed the people's trauma into an alternative plot line by envisioning the destruction of the natural world that occurs through war and siege as a part of divine judgment and assigning the agency for that destruction to Yahweh and not to the nations who actually carried it out (see commentary on chs 4—7). Ezekiel now completes that alternative plot line for the trauma by proclaiming a future for the land itself that is different from its past. No longer will the land **devour** (v 13) or **make . . . childless** (v 14), but it will produce and provide. Ezekiel expresses here a broader ecological vision of divine redemption that goes beyond just human beings to envision redemption for all creation. Not only does Yahweh reveal a passion for the natural world ("my land" [v 5]), but the land's fate provides the motivation for divine action with the people (see Odell 2005, 435).

D. Oracle of Transformation for Israel (36:16-38)

The divine oracle that comprises the rest of ch 36 is arguably the most significant theological text in the book of Ezekiel, especially for readers within the Wesleyan tradition. Verses 16-38 contain an oracle of cleansing, transformation, and salvation for the people of Israel, a portion of which (vv 25-38) John Wesley described as one of the clearest portraits of sanctification in the OT, with v 26 yielding the picture of a "sanctified heart, in which the almighty grace of God is victorious, and turns it from all sin to God" (Wesley 1975, 2385). Within Ezekiel's depictions of the renewal of different elements of Israel's life for a new future in chs 33—37, vv 16-38 provide a type of climactic moment. The oracle stands at the center of the overall structure of chs 33—37, with two discourses on either side (see Behind the Text). Moreover, the preceding progression of renewed elements (leadership, old hostilities, rejuvenation of the land) has prepared the way to deal with the most important element in need of transformation for a new future, namely, the people themselves. In order to fulfill the vision of a purified and inhabited land, Yahweh must now deal with the cause of defilement that resulted in destruction and exile (Odell 2005, 441). Yahweh's speech in vv 16-38 addresses the exiles, who have been challenged to understand their trauma in light of Yahweh's holiness, and now offers them a promise that Yahweh will act to affect a transformation that will once again allow them to live as a holy people in the presence of a holy God.

Perhaps the most striking aspect of this divine promise of transformation, however, is the character of Yahweh's action that Ezekiel envisions. In keeping with his theological perspective that emphasizes divine sovereignty/holiness as the driving factor in Yahweh's deeds, Ezekiel describes a work whereby Yahweh solves the problem of the people's sinful acts that defile the divine holiness by permanently cleansing them from their impurity and re-creating them so that they will hereafter live obediently. Yet, Ezekiel envisions this divine work as a unilateral act motivated by Yahweh's self-regard and initiative to restore the honor of his defamed name. Ezekiel represents a different theological perspective on the divine response to Israel's exile than that expressed by his Judean contemporary Jeremiah—a perspective formed by a focus on Yahweh's sovereignty. While Jeremiah highlights Yahweh's compassion that is stirred by the people's repentance and moves him to act (see Jer 30—31), Ezekiel expresses the conviction that the people's defilement is so thoroughgoing that Yahweh acts not out of concern for them but out of concern to preserve his own holiness among the nations (see Bowen 2010, 223; Tuell 2009, 247). As Greenberg summarizes Ezekiel's perspective, "The restoration would not be a gracious divine response to human yearning for reconciliation . . . It would be an imposition on wayward Israel of a constraint necessary for saving God's reputation" (1997, 737).

Ezekiel's emphasis on divine holiness/sovereignty is apparent from the genre of vv 16-38. The passage is a salvation oracle in the style of a dispute, yet the central issue being disputed is not the people's salvation but the "reputation of Yahweh," especially as it has been defamed in the eyes of the nations by Israel's sinful acts and the destruction and deportation that they produced (Block 1998, 343). The dispute divides into four sections: a historical recital of Israel's past that explains the dishonoring of Yahweh's name among the nations (vv 16-21), an oracle of transformation that focuses on the reestablishment of Yahweh's honor (vv 22-32), and two declarations of Yahweh's intentions for Israel's future (vv 33-36, 37-38).

■ **16-21** Yahweh's climactic oracle of transformation for the people begins in vv 16-21 with an address to Ezekiel that offers a historical recital of Israel's past (see the prophetic word formula in v 16). The passage resembles the extended historical recital in ch 20 that reinterpreted Israel's history as a history of rebellion from the outset. Here, the recital interprets Israel's history in priestly terms as a history of defilement.

Verses 17-18 describe the people's misdeeds in Ezekiel's characteristic priestly language as acts that **defiled** (*tm'*) the land (v 17). This is the first reference in the book to the land itself being defiled, although elsewhere Ezekiel refers to the defilement of the temple (5:11; 9:7; 23:38) (Block 1998, 345). The text elaborates the polluting nature of the people's deeds by associating them with several images: a menstruating woman (**their conduct was like a woman's monthly uncleanness** [v 17]), the act of bloodshed, and idol worship. The simile of menstruation derives from the ritual impurity of a menstruating woman in the OT priestly system (see Lev 15:19-24). There is no question that the simile is offensive and inappropriate for contemporary readers. Yet, in the priestly worldview, contact with blood was ritually defiling because it represented the loss of life (Lev 17:11, 14) and death was seen as the ultimate source of uncleanness (Tuell 2009, 245). Thus, the priestly texts view blood flow as defiling and extend this notion to include sexual contact with a menstruating woman that defiles the man (Lev 18:19), as well as the emission of semen by a man (Lev 15:1-18). The key element in Ezekiel's use of the image is that in the priestly system impurity from a menstruating woman (or semen-emitting man) is contagious and defiles others. In the same way, the people's sins constitute acts of defilement that polluted the land where Yahweh's presence dwelled.

Even more significantly, by combining the defilement caused by menstruation with that caused by bloodshed and idols (Ezek 36:18), Ezekiel alludes to both ceremonial and moral pollution—the two main types of impurity in the priestly system (Bowen 2010, 221-22; Block 1998, 345). In the priestly order, ceremonial impurity results from routine acts or experiences (e.g., menstruation, intercourse, touching a corpse) and can be cleansed through a purification ritual. By contrast, morally defiling acts such as bloodshed and idolatry pollute the land and cannot be cleansed by a ritual but only by severe divine action such as exile to purify the land (Lev 18:25-28; Num 35:33-34). By likening the people's sins to *both* ceremonial impurity that can be cleansed and moral impurity that cannot, 36:16-38 sets up a promise of divine cleansing and transformation that will deal with *all* of Israel's uncleanness.

36:16-21

In response to the people's history of defilement, Yahweh expelled the people from the land (vv 19-20). This assertion functions as part of Ezekiel's effort to give meaning to the exiles' trauma by again reinterpreting the catastrophe of deportation not as the result of Babylonian might or as incomprehensible chaos, but as the outworking of divine sovereignty. The language here resembles Lev 18:25-28, where the land is said to "vomit [its inhabitants] out" because of defilement, yet Ezekiel places the emphasis on Yahweh's personal revulsion and action (Odell 2005, 441). Ironically, however, Yahweh's words in Ezek 36:20 acknowledge a surprising byproduct of this judgment that provides the central motivation for his new act of transformation: **wherever they went among the nations they profaned my holy name** (compare the similar charge in ch 20). As the remainder of the verse makes clear, what brought dishonor to Yahweh's name was not the behavior of the people among the nations but the very fact that Yahweh's people had been driven from his land. This statement makes sense against the background of ancient understandings in which Yahweh's holiness meant that he possesses a name, reputation, and authority that set him apart as sovereign over all human affairs. As Odell observes, the challenge of the people's exile to Yahweh in the eyes of the nations is at the level of both his character (perhaps he has treated his people unjustly) and sovereignty (perhaps he was powerless to protect his people) (2005, 442).

As a rejoinder to these possible interpretations, the statement in v 21 (**I had concern for my holy name**) represents the way Ezekiel uses Yahweh's holiness to reinterpret not only the people's destruction and exile but also their future restoration. In chs 1—24, Ezekiel used the notion of Yahweh's holiness to interpret the exile by asserting that Israel's rebellious actions of the past and present defiled the required holiness/purity of Yahweh's temple and land and forced the divine presence to withdraw from the community (see Ezek 8—11). Now, he explains the future restoration by proclaiming that the people's exile besmirched Yahweh's reputation and status among the nations and Yahweh will act to restore his holiness/sovereignty in the world. In other priestly texts (e.g., Lev 20:8; 21:8; 22:32), Yahweh promises to sanctify Israel when they have profaned his name, but here Yahweh sets the sanctification of his name as the priority. For Ezekiel, this is Yahweh's primary motivation, and the exiles' restoration is a byproduct of the larger plot line in which Yahweh acts to restore his holiness that has been diminished among the nations.

An Affected God?

The depiction in 36:16-21 of Yahweh's concern for how Israel's actions and status have profaned his name among the nations makes explicit a theme that has appeared throughout the book, namely, that human events and affairs can affect Yahweh. In ch 36, as well as in the marriage metaphors in chs 16 and 23, for example, Ezekiel portrays Yahweh as one who can feel shame and be affected and/or motivated by happenings in the world. Although some Christian readers today feel uncomfortable conceiving of a God who can be affected, perhaps these biblical texts should encourage readers to welcome such conceptions, finding in them an incarnational aspect and a truly covenantal/relational engagement among God, humanity, and the world.

■ **22-32** The transitional **therefore** in v 22 begins a divine speech (vv 22-32) that addresses the exiles directly (see the messenger formula in v 22) and describes the actions of transformation and restoration that Yahweh will take in order to make his name holy among the nations once again. The entire oracle is framed by the statement **not for your sake** in vv 22 and 32, but the climactic turning point for the exiles comes in the second half of verse 23 with two significant words: **through you** (pl.). Yahweh declares that he will rectify the problem for his holiness outlined in vv 20-21 and cause the nations to **know/ acknowledge** (v 23) his sovereignty (recognition formula) by the means of transforming and restoring the exiles. The name that was defiled through the people will be repaired through the people.

What follows in vv 24-30 is a virtual "Catalogue of Yahweh's Name-Sanctifying Actions" (Block 1998, 352)—a list of acts that will constitute the people's transformation and restoration, all of which are presented with heavy first person emphasis that identifies Yahweh as the actor and agent. The passage has a number of similarities with the rehearsal of Israel's history in ch 20, especially the times in which Yahweh claimed to have refrained from destroying the Israelites out of concern for the divine reputation, and the depictions of cleansing in the present passage reverse the thoroughgoing "defilement" (*tm'*) portrayed in ch 20 (see 20:7, 18, 26, 31; Darr 2001, 1491; Block 1997, 616). Verse 24 of ch 36 states that the first divine action will be to **gather** the people from their places of exile and bring them back to the land of Judah. Verse 25 follows this with an act of cleansing that will purify the regathered people from their defilement. The priestly term for **cleanse** (*thr*), which corresponds to the term for "defile" (*tm'*), occurs three times in v 25, and to **sprinkle clean water** reflects priestly rituals of washing for ceremonial purification (e.g., Lev 14:8-9; 15:13; Tuell 2009, 247). The primary purpose of such rituals was to render the person ritually clean so that he or she could reenter the community amid Yahweh's holy presence.

The climactic moment of Yahweh's redemptive acts begins in Ezek 36:26. This verse implicitly addresses the lingering question that haunts Yahweh's purification of the exiles and their placement back in a rejuvenated land (see 36:1-15): If this is the same Israel, how will history not repeat itself, especially since Ezekiel has so often emphasized that they have been rebellious from the start and are incapable of living faithfully before Yahweh? The divine response in v 26 is to undertake a total transformation—a re-creation—of the people that will fundamentally change their character: **I will give you a new heart and put a new spirit in you; I will remove from you your heart of stone and give you a heart of flesh.** The expressions **new heart** and **new spirit** have occurred already in 11:19 and 18:31 and, as we observed there, the **heart** in Hebrew thought represents the center of the will, decision-making, and cognition. In this context, the **heart** and **spirit** are not two separate entities but parallel terms whose meanings converge in the sense of moral will/capacity. Hence, this divine "heart transplant" amounts to a transformation of the people's character that resembles the image in Deut 30:6-8 of Yahweh circumcising the heart of the people to make them able to respond in love and obedience (see also Ps 51:10; Jer 31:31-34).

Ezekiel 36:27 continues the divine transformation with a dramatic statement that has generated differing interpretations. Seemingly in response to Ezekiel's consistent assertion that the people are rebellious by nature and incapable of living in purity before divine holiness, Yahweh asserts that the people's new spirit will give them a new future of obedience to Yahweh's commands. However, the Hebrew of v 27 is ambiguous, and the force of Yahweh's words is unclear. The difference between the NIV and NRSV translations reveals the possible nuances: **And I will . . . move you to follow;** "I will . . . make you follow" (NRSV). While the NIV understands Yahweh's statement to say that the transformation of the people's character will enable—and even inspire—them to obedience, the Hebrew (lit., *I will make [it] that you will walk in my statutes*) more directly seems to say that Yahweh will undertake a sovereign, unilateral action that will guarantee (force?) the people to be obedient so that they will indeed live in the land that Yahweh has restored without defiling Yahweh's holiness and again driving the divine presence out of their midst. From Ezekiel's priestly perspective, such an action would guarantee a new future in which Yahweh's holy name will never again be defamed in the eyes of the nations. As v 28 states, this divine action will also allow the reconstituted Israel to live faithfully in covenant terms (**you will be my people, and I will be your God**). Additionally, vv 29-30 return to the theme of the rejuvenation of nature (see 36:1-15 and the priestly blessings of covenant obedience in Lev 26), envisioning a restored fruitfulness for the land as a result of the people's new obedient life, and Ezek 36:31-32 returns to the theme that such transformation and restoration will cause the exiles to look back in shame upon their former identity and actions (see commentary on 6:8-10; 20:41-44).

How should we understand Yahweh's statement in v 27 and its related effects? Earlier in the book, Ezekiel seemingly expressed the conviction that the exiles were capable of changing their character and ways, challenging them in 18:31 to "get yourselves a new heart and a new spirit" (NRSV). So perhaps the divine statement in 36:27 represents a development in Ezekiel's thought. As the prophet observed how the people continually refused to break with their old identity and accept a new understanding of their experience even in the face of destruction and exile, he perhaps became convinced that they were, in fact, incapable of such change. By the time of Yahweh's climactic oracle of transformation, Ezekiel expresses the conviction that Yahweh will have to bring them to obedience himself (but see this sentiment already in 11:19-20). This insistence on overriding divine initiative and unilateral action fits well with Ezekiel's overall theological emphasis on Yahweh's sovereignty. Reading 36:27 in this way suggests that Ezekiel envisions Yahweh overshadowing the people's flawed humanity and changing them through divine action in a manner that guarantees their future obedient conduct. At the same time, however, the final vision of Yahweh's glory in chs 40—48 details a number of laws for the people to obey designed to safeguard the new temple (see chs 43;

46), seemingly indicating that obedience is still not automatic or guaranteed. Perhaps these texts suggest that we should understand v 27 not as a unilateral divine act that automates permanent obedience but as Ezekiel's recognition that the people's rebellious character requires that Yahweh first do a transformative work that will *make them able and inclined* to respond in obedience (so NIV)—a divine character transformation by which undivided and consistent faithfulness is not guaranteed, but without which it is impossible.

In the end, the climactic oracle of transformation may leave readers with a paradox that maintains the tension between the "call for human responsibility" (enabled by divine grace) and the "assertion that God is in complete control" (Darr 2001, 1496). Perhaps it is most important, however, to keep Ezekiel's articulation of this moral transformation, with its strong emphasis on divine sovereignty and action, in the context of the experience of trauma and the attempt to respond to it. Bowen observes that Ezekiel's response reflects a particular type of "self-blame" known among trauma victims that is often less helpful in the healing process (2010, 225). Rather than engage in "behavioral self-blame," which blames the trauma on the victim's bad behavior and sees a change of behavior as possible and beneficial, Ezekiel expresses what theorists call "characterological self-blame" in which the victim blames the trauma on some fault in his or her own person or character. Still, against the background of Ezekiel's attempt to renarrate the people's trauma into the plot line of Yahweh's holiness, the emphasis on Yahweh's sovereign action and the people's passivity reflects their experience as helpless victims of destruction and deportation. Although Ezekiel blames the trauma on the people's bad character rather than simply on their poor decisions, he also envisions an act by which Yahweh performs the crucial task of restoring agency (ability to act and gain a new future) to these trauma victims.

■ **33-38** The divine oracle of transformation in vv 16-38 ends with two declarations of Yahweh's intentions for Israel's future (vv 33-36, 37-38), each of which begins with the messenger formula and concludes with a version of the divine recognition formula. Verses 33-36 restate Yahweh's intention to rejuvenate the land with fruitfulness upon the people's return, yet the focus of this act is to change the perception not of the exiles but of **all who pass through it** (v 34). The pronoun **they** in v 35 likely refers to the inhabitants of other lands before whom Yahweh had been defamed, and it is these **nations** who will **know/***acknowledge* that Yahweh has enacted this restoration (v 36). By contrast, vv 37-38 return to the flock imagery of ch 34 and declare Yahweh's intention to provide an increased population for the new future. The pronoun **they** in the recognition formula in v 38 likely refers to the exiles' acknowledgment of Yahweh's sovereignty through this restoration.

E. Vision of the Valley of Bones (37:1-14)

Ezekiel's vision of a valley of bones in 37:1-14 is one of the book's best known passages, perhaps most widely recognized as the inspiration for the African-American spiritual "Dem Bones." The vision holds a special place in the unfolding renewal of elements of Israel's life for a new future being depicted in chs 34—37 as it reports the first words that the reader has heard from the exiles (v 11) since the beginning of Ezekiel's proclamations of restoration. Following the portrayal of the transformation of Israel's leaders (ch 34), enemies/hostilities (ch 35), land/natural world (36:1-15), and the people themselves (36:16-38), ch 37 offers two depictions of national restoration—a vision (vv 1-14) and a sign-act (vv 15-28)—that picture the return of a unified people to a renewed land, almost providing a type of visual aid for the prophet's preceding proclamations.

■ **1-10** The first section of ch 37 divides into two parts: vision (vv 1-10) and interpretation (vv 11-14). Although the passage is a vision, it is also another extended metaphorical discourse in which the elements are representations. The prophet finds himself transported by **the hand of the LORD** (see also the opening of the visions in 1:3; 8:1; 40:1) to a **valley** filled with **bones** (v 1). The **valley** evokes the place of ancient battles—no doubt conjuring images of fallen Judean soldiers from the exiles' recent traumatic experiences of war and defeat—but also links this vision of restoration back to the same setting (valley) in which Ezekiel's announcement of judgment began in 3:22. **Bones** appear throughout the psalms as a metaphor for a person's health condition, but the image of **very dry** (v 2) bones indicates a situation of long-dead remains absolutely devoid of any remaining life. By following a series of Yahweh's commands to **prophesy** (i.e., proclaim) to various elements (vv 4-10), Ezekiel witnesses the scattered bones re-form into human beings—**a vast army** (v 10). The action constitutes a new creative act that reflects the two-step process of creation in Gen 2, where Yahweh first forms the human creature and then breathes the breath of life into the creature (see Gen 2:8-10). Throughout the vision, the action revolves around the transformative force designated by the Hebrew term *rûah*, which simultaneously carries the meanings of wind, breath, and spirit (vv 1, 5, 6, 8, 9, 10, 14). Yahweh's *rûah*—the same "spirit" that Yahweh placed within the exiles for transformation in Ezek 36:27—serves as the agent that creates new life in the midst of death through the prophetic word.

■ **11-14** Verses 11-14 shift from the vision's events to Yahweh's interpretation. **These bones** represent the exiles, and v 11 ties the vision to words of hopelessness that express a real despair we can only appreciate by remembering the devastating portrayals of Yahweh's judgment earlier in the book (Bowen 2010,

227). The despair resonates with the experience of trauma, which often locks victims into hopelessness and blinds them to the possibility of newness (see ch 18). Additionally, the sense of disconnection expressed by the metaphor of scattered bones is a common symptom of traumatic events, which often break the bonds of relationships and alienate victims from a sense of order and coherence (Herman 1997, 51-52). Now, however, Yahweh instructs Ezekiel to **prophesy** to the despondent exiles the same message of re-creation and new life as that given to the bones in the vision. The metaphor changes from unburied bones to proper graves—an unexpected image for Ezekiel given the unclean status of corpses and tombs in the priestly system—but Yahweh offers an exodus-type image to declare his intention to bring the people out of their graves and reestablish them in the land of Israel. Thus, vv 1-14 describe irrational impossibilities—scattered bones returning to life as human beings and corpses coming out of graves—and thereby aim to persuade the exiles to embrace an unexpected, even absurd, hope in a new future, reconnected to their land, people, and God (see Fox 1980).

Resurrection Imagery in Ezekiel 37

How should we understand the imagery of Yahweh bringing the people out of their graves in 37:12-13? Although some early Christian interpreters used this passage to respond to the Docetism heresy and thus tried to find here a literal description of bodily resurrection, the majority of Christian interpreters from the time of Jerome (ca. A.D. 400) through the Reformation and into the modern era have understood the passage to be only a metaphor for the restoration of Israel. Evidence from throughout the OT and elsewhere indicates that ancient Israel did not have a belief in the bodily resurrection of persons, although this belief had developed in Judaism by the time of Jesus (see the earliest OT reference to such resurrection in Dan 12:1-2, commonly understood as dating to the later period in the second century B.C.; see Darr 2001, 1502). As a vision in its literary context, ch 37 deals not with the afterlife or the resurrection of individuals but with a corporate symbol of new life for a people.

37:11-28

F. Symbolic Act and Oracle of Restoration for Israel (37:15-28)

The second half of ch 37 (vv 15-28) contains the other depiction of national restoration to complement Ezekiel's preceding proclamations in chs 33—36. Beginning with a prophetic word formula in v 15, the passage is another sign-act for Ezekiel to perform (see chs 4—5). In keeping with the way sign-acts typically appear in the book, the text provides only Yahweh's instructions and not a report of the performance and reaction. Both the description of the sign-act (vv 15-19) and the explanation of its meaning (vv 20-28), however, extrapolate Yahweh's declaration at the end of the preceding vision (vv 12-13) that he will unify the people in their own land.

■ **15-19** Verses 15-19 symbolize this new future with two sticks held together as one in the prophet's hand. Significantly for Ezekiel's broader vision, the prophet's writing on the sticks indicates that they do not merely represent the formerly separate kingdoms of Israel and Judah but also all of **the Israelites associated** with each kingdom (v 16). Ezekiel offers a broad vision of future restoration that includes all those survivors and refugees that have been scattered and disconnected through the traumas of destruction and deportation. While the language of one kingdom here does not necessarily assume the existence of a previously unified state, it envisions a future that will not reflect the old political arrangements that led the people into rebellion and defilement and generated Yahweh's judgment of destruction and exile (see also the use of "Israel" with a broader meaning encompassing both former Israelites and Judeans in v 21).

■ **20-28** Verses 20-28 contain Yahweh's explanation of the meaning of the sign-act. The details closely parallel those given in 34:23-31 and 36:25-30 (see commentary on those texts) and again depict Ezekiel's characteristic vision of the restored future: Yahweh will return the people to the land (37:21), make them a unified **nation** (v 22), establish one Davidic ruler (referred to as a **king** [*melek*] in vv 22 and 24 but as a **prince** [*nāśî'*] in v 25), purify them of their defilement (note the priestly terms *tm'* [**defile**] and *ṭhr* [**cleanse**] in v 23), reestablish the covenant with Yahweh (v 23*b*), and guarantee a covenant of well-being for them (v 26). Although the text describes a national restoration with political elements such as the prominence of the king, these give way to the climax of Yahweh's restoration in vv 26*b*-27: **I will put my sanctuary among them forever. My dwelling place will be with them.** Here is Ezekiel's ultimate vision of restoration in terms of Yahweh's holiness: once the people have been cleansed and reestablished in a purified land, Yahweh's holy presence will be able to dwell in their midst in perpetuity. The text reflects the priestly legislation in Lev 26, which indicates the necessity of obedience and purity for the divine presence, reverses the imagery of Yahweh's glory (*kābôd*) being driven from the defiled temple in chs 8—11, and foreshadows the comprehensive vision of Yahweh's return to Jerusalem in chs 40—48. Yahweh's statement also articulates the broader plot line of divine holiness within which Ezekiel has attempted to find the meaning of the people's destruction and exile. The exiles' trauma has unfolded within the larger divine work to purify Israel and allow for Yahweh's holy presence to dwell in their midst. Moreover, v 28 concludes the sign-act's explanation by sounding the other theme of the broader plot line Ezekiel has articulated: Yahweh works to restore his holy presence among the Israelites so that **the nations will know/*acknowledge*** his holiness/sovereignty.

FROM THE TEXT

Perhaps the most surprising and challenging affirmation that emerges from Ezekiel's oracles of restoration in chs 33—37, coming as they do at the darkest moment of the destruction of Jerusalem and seeming collapse of the people's entire faith system, is that God's word of hope comes precisely at the point of deepest loss. As Walter Brueggemann observes, it is "the null point that is the characteristic venue in the Old Testament for the articulation of God's promises. It is in the context of *hopelessness* that *hope* receives voice" (2008, 353; italics original). This theme of hearing the word of newness at the very moment when the story has reached an end appears throughout the restoration oracles in chs 33—37. The people's sense of despair about the possibility of any new future surfaces throughout (33:10; 37:11), yet God's promises of transformation come exactly at the moments where the people are abandoned (34:5-6) or the land sits devastated (36:1-15). And one text in particular claims that there is a fundamental aspect of God's character that produces this possibility of hope in every circumstance: "I take no pleasure in the death of the wicked" (33:11). At the heart of Ezekiel's proclamations of hope is the conviction that because God is ultimately a God of life, death does not have the final word.

The exiles' experience of trauma highlights the power and challenge of the word of hope at the point of death. Far from always striving for hope, trauma victims often experience resignation or despair, finding it even more difficult to embrace the possibility of "life" than to accept "death" (Bowen 2010, 209). Likewise, Ezekiel's readers in the church today may find it surprisingly difficult to embrace the prophet's conviction of God's willingness and ability to bring new life in the midst of death. Do we really believe in the possibility of the kind of transformed future for which we pray when we ask, "Your kingdom come" (Matt 6:10)? Can we maintain the hope of a world marked by safety for all of God's creation, where a woman can live without the fear of domestic violence, a poverty-level family can live without the fear of hunger and discrimination, and the earth itself can live without the fear of harm from our ecological exploitation and overconsumption? As Darr notes, Ezekiel's oracles and visions of restoration confront contemporary readers with the same struggle shared by the Judean exiles—a struggle to move beyond cynicism and despair and "to look at our world, and at ourselves, through God's eyes" (2001, 1503). Therein lies hope.

At the heart of the prophet's restoration message is the proclamation that God will undertake an act of transformation that will make the people able to live a life of obedience, and this proclamation connects in significant ways to the perennial issue of the nature of the human person and the capacity of the moral self—an issue that has special bearing upon the Wesleyan tradition. Jacqueline Lapsley (2000) devoted a full-length study to this topic (the so-called problem of the moral self) in Ezekiel and notes that the issue typically takes the form of questions about the relationship between character and actions: do actions determine one's moral character or does one's character determine his or her actions? If we wish to change our lives, do we change our actions, or must we first have our character changed so that right actions may follow? In technical language, one can identify two views of moral selfhood behind these questions (Lapsley 2000, 4-6). "Virtuous Moral Selfhood" sees humans as capable of doing what is good, so the problem of wrongdoing lies with poor choices or a perverted will. By contrast, "Neutral Moral Selfhood" sees humans as basically incapable of knowing and acting for the good. Theological writings from the early part of the Protestant Reformation reveal significant debate about such issues, cast in the form of questions about the irresistibility of God's grace and the possibility of human cooperation in salvation, with the Calvinist tradition affirming that human salvation is a wholly divine work through election (see Odell 2005, 422).

Throughout the OT, one finds several perspectives on these questions. In the majority of texts, especially Deuteronomy and Ezekiel's own contemporary, Jeremiah, the dominant moral understanding is that human beings are capable of obedient actions and the problem of sin is simply the problem of a perverted will (see Deut 30:15-20; Jer 31:31-34). The people have the ability to live in faithfulness to God yet choose not to do so. By contrast, Ezekiel's theology of restoration expressed especially in chs 33—37 builds from his conviction that the entire history of his people was a history of sin from the beginning (ch 20) and that human beings are essentially incapable of living and acting for the good. It is not simply a matter of will; even God's own people have a flawed character and condition that make it impossible for them to live faithfully in the presence of a holy God. Ezekiel's climactic oracle of transformation in 36:16-38 offers the divine response to this situation. In order for restoration to occur and for the people to have a future with God, there must first be a transformation of the people's character that will enable them to live in holiness. In Ezekiel's language, God will remove the "heart of stone" that has made the people incapable of choosing the good and will give them a "new heart" and a "new spirit" from which right actions of holy living follow (see 11:19-20; 36:26).

Ultimately, then, Ezekiel's vision of divine salvation takes the view of humans as incapable of acting for the good and transforming their lives. Yet, Ezekiel then envisions God's initiative bringing about human salvation, as God through the spirit enables a moral self that is capable of holiness. We might read the climactic oracle not as divine action that *makes* the people obey but that which gives them a new *capacity* ("new heart") for faithful living (see commentary on 36:27). Once God has converted the people's divided heart into one that is wholly attuned to God's will, they will be able to live faithfully as those sanctified by God (see 37:28). As Lapsley notes, this divine action does not render the people incapable of further sin (see the safeguards for the new temple in chs 40—48), but the "new heart" seems to represent a changed inclination that allows the real possibility of no further rebellion by transforming a propensity to sin into a predisposition to obedience to the divine will (2000, 182-88).

Ezekiel's vision of restoration and the moral self is a special treasure for the Wesleyan-holiness tradition, as it provides scriptural resources for considering the doctrine and experience of sanctification. As noted in the introduction to 36:16-38, John Wesley himself saw in Ezekiel's language (especially 36:25-38) one of the OT's clearest portraits of sanctification that envisions God's Spirit re-creating the human heart and character in order to enable a life of undivided love and loyalty before a holy God. In the Wesleyan way of salvation, sanctification in the broadest sense refers to the ongoing, lifelong process of the restoration of the likeness of the image of God in believers. As a part of this ongoing process, the Wesleyan-holiness tradition affirms that as God's work continues in believers' lives after the first experiences of repentance and faith, they can come to an epoch in their lives in which they become free from a life of sin and marked by a pure love for God and neighbor, even as the process of transformation into the image of Christ continues. In this articulation of the Christian faith, when a believer enters into repentance and justification, he or she receives a new love for God. As that person grows in faith, however, there is an increasing realization that this love remains divided, marked by a lingering pull to self-love and sinful actions that result from that distorted/divided loyalty. Ezekiel's image of a "heart of stone" (36:26) represents well the situation of a human will that has become so "calloused by continual disobedience" that even after justification it remains bound by some degree of a lingering "commitment to rebellion" (Gowan 1985, 120). Yet, not unlike Ezekiel's depiction of a neutral moral selfhood that requires God to act upon it in an enabling way, Wesleyan theology affirms the hope that through continual consecration and the practice of spiritual disciplines, the believer can come to an epoch in life in which God drives the sinfulness of divided love out of the human heart, filling it instead with a pure love and intention for God and neighbor. This life does not entail perfection in any sense other than one's intention and love, recognizing that sinful actions may still occur as the process of full renewal into the image of God remains ongoing in the believer's life. But the message of such "entire sanctification" is the hopeful affirmation that through God's grace, a believer's life need not be *characterized* by sin (or the lingering struggle with distorted self-love) but can be *characterized* by a pure (self-emptying) love for God and neighbor. God can so transform a person that the central predisposition and driving impulse of life is no longer the power of sin but love for God and neighbor.

For Wesley, as for Ezekiel, the possibility of sin remains after God's transformative action (see the safeguards for the new temple in chs 40—48). Purity of heart (singleness of love/intention) and the new predisposition toward obedient love must be maintained through continual consecration and the practice of spiritual disciplines in cooperation with God's grace. Moreover, Ezekiel's language that Wesley saw as a primary expression of sanctification (36:16-38) is plural and corporate, not singular and individualistic (note the Hebrew text's second person plural forms throughout the passage). The text certainly envisions the transformation of human persons, but such transformation is never an end in itself—it is personal but not individualistic in nature. As we have observed, Ezekiel pictures his people's transformation as a means for God to act for the sake of the nations and even the land, establishing a community that experiences holiness in covenant relationship and thus serves as a means of God's grace to the world. The sanctification of Israel (37:28) is an element in a larger process of restoration in which this transformed people, characterized by wholehearted faithfulness, can live successfully in the land and allow the divine presence to dwell in their midst. Holiness serves God's work of redemption in the whole world, which the NT characterizes in Christian terms as God "reconciling the world to himself in Christ" (2 Cor 5:19).

VII. PREPARATORY ORACLES OF RESTORATION: THE DEFEAT OF GOG AND THE FINAL VINDICATION OF GOD (EZEKIEL 38—39)

BEHIND THE TEXT

Chapters 38—39 form the second set of preparatory oracles of restoration in chs 33—39 that prepare for the book's final vision of the return of Yahweh's glory (*kābôd*) to dwell in a purified land and temple (chs 40—48). Against the backdrop of the renewal of various elements of the people's life and land for a new future with Yahweh depicted in the first set of preparatory oracles (chs 33—37), Ezekiel's imagistic, graphic, and, at times, bizarre oracle of judgment against "Gog, of the land of Magog" in chs 38—39 is a perplexing passage. Chapter 37 ended with Yahweh's promise to reestablish his sanctuary and dwell among the people in a renewed Israel (37:28), leaving Ezekiel's hearers/readers ready to move immediately into the full depiction of that event in the book's final vision. The oracle in chs 38—39, however, introduces an entirely new scenario that jumps forward into a distant future after the Israelites have resettled in their land (see 38:8, 11, 14). The text describes a climactic battle to be waged by Yahweh (and merely witnessed by the Israelites) in which Gog, the ruler of the land of Magog, will gather allies and invade the resettled Israel. On the battleground of "the mountains of Israel" (38:8), Yahweh will defeat Gog with cosmic weapons of creation, after which the Israelites will participate in a mass burial and witness the devouring of corpses by scavenger animals. Following the climactic depictions of national restoration in ch 37, Ezekiel's exilic audience of trauma victims must have felt shock and dismay to hear the description of yet another war to come, promising the possibility of further destruction, exile, and death.

Along with questions concerning literary placement, modern readers have particularly struggled with the Gog oracle's cryptic symbolism, allusive language, and strange imagery. Due in part to these elements, chs 38—39 have played a major role in the modern phenomenon of end-times interpretation within certain fundamentalist and conservative evangelical circles (see discussion in From the Text). These interpretations, whose popularity is attested by the collections at nearly any local Christian bookstore, recast OT prophetic texts as signs of contemporary events or blueprints for future scenarios. The mysterious nature of the Gog oracle, as well as its reuse in later texts such as Rev 21—22, have provided fodder for such popular futuristic interpretations that disregard the text's historical and literary context and imbue it with meanings that serve the social and political interests of the interpreters. These uses of chs 38—39 have also found their way outside of religious circles and into American popular culture and political life. For example, Ronald Reagan, while addressing the California legislature in 1971, famously claimed that Ezekiel's "Gog" was communist Russia—a viewpoint that would shape Reagan's political perspectives and the United States' foreign policy in various ways over the next two decades.

To address these interpretive challenges, the remainder of this extended Behind the Text section will treat the basic yet determinative interpretive issues for chs 38—39, and the In the Text section will provide an abbreviated analysis of the primary exegetical features. At the most basic level, the larger context of chs 33—37, which began the preparation for the final return of Yahweh's glory to a restored temple by depicting the unfolding renewal of various elements of Israel's life for a new future (reinscribing the people's trauma into a new plot line that gives the possibility of life and meaning), provides the key for understanding Ezekiel's Gog oracle. After envisioning the renewal of Israel's leadership (ch 34), the elimination of historic, neighboring hostilities (ch 35), the rejuvenation of the devastated natural world (36:1-15), and the cleansing and transformation of the people themselves (36:16-38), with illustrations of national restoration (ch 37), this second set of preparatory oracles in chs 38—39 brings the progression of renewal for a new future to its climax by using the allusive figure of Gog and his allies to symbolize the final defeat of all potential enemies, resulting in lasting safety for Israel's future and the final vindication of Yahweh's holiness/sovereignty in the eyes of all nations. Seen in this context, Gog does not represent yet another enemy coming to bring further traumatic injury to the exiles, but the most comprehensive symbol of the lasting defeat of any and all forces that might threaten the well-being of Yahweh's people and the abiding establishment of Yahweh's lordship over all creation. Hence, the symbolic language and comprehensive picture of a worldwide threat (see commentary on 38:1-6) in this oracle go beyond the Edom oracle's (ch 35) transformation of long-standing *local* hostilities that Israel might experience from its *neighboring* nations. Chapters 38—39 depict a comprehensive safety from any and all threats. The oracle represents Ezekiel's fullest response to the lingering sense of vulnerability and fear that accompanies trauma, offering as a counterpoint the assurance that no force or threat will be able to disrupt the divine purposes for Israel's future or the ultimate establishment of Yahweh's holiness in the world.

Although this overall function seems clear, questions emerge when one tries to identify the specific way in which chs 38—39 portray the establishment of Israel's ultimate safety and Yahweh's final vindication. The Gog oracle consists of two chapters that parallel one another with two parts each, followed by a concluding coda:

A. Gog's Invasion (38:1-16)
B. Proclamation of Divine Judgment on Gog (38:17-23)
C. Gog's Destruction (39:1-10)
D. Gog's Burial (39:11-20)
E. Coda: The Final Vindication of Yahweh (39:21-29)

Taken as a whole, these parallel parts trace the movement of Gog from an attacking enemy that comes under divine judgment to a defeated foe eliminated in the land of Israel. Within this movement, however, many uncertainties remain about the oracle's authorship, editing, date, setting, and rhetoric, and these have given rise to a number of unsettled general interpretive issues. First, as noted above, the time frame for the events portrayed by the text jumps significantly forward from that envisioned by ch 37 (and that which will be again envisioned by chs 40—48), speaking now not of the coming return of the exiles but of a time in the distant future after the exiles have been successfully living back in the land of Judah. Several formulas and phrases point to this future projection: "after many days," "in future years" (38:8), "on/in that day" (38:10, 14, 18; 39:11), "at that time" (38:19), "in days to come" (38:16). The coda material in 39:21-29 returns back to the people's present reality in exile, looking forward to a future restoration to the land, but the various formulas and phrases give the preceding parts of the oracle an eschatological character of dealing with future and final acts by Yahweh. Even so, contemporary readers should note that the time frame reflected here is only the distant future *for the sixth-century* B.C. *exiles*, who currently find themselves away from the land, and not some end-times period at the conclusion of all history.

Second, we have consistently observed that many of Ezekiel's oracles show possible indications of later editing and additions, and this is even more true for the cryptic and seemingly disjointed passage in chs 38—39. The oracle contains sharp shifts in focus, disruptive formulas, and disconnected episodes (see Block 1998, 424), leading some scholars to identify the coda in 39:21-29 as an addition or to restrict the prophet's original oracle to only a few parts of both chapters (e.g., Zimmerli 1983, 296-99). Such theories remain hypothetical, however, and the oracle functions as a meaningful whole in its present literary context.

A third significant interpretive issue concerns the genre of the passage. The text's symbolic, imagistic, and cryptic elements, as well as its depiction of a future culminating defeat of evil forces, led interpreters early in the modern period to associate this oracle with a form of so-called apocalyptic literature, a genre that developed fully several centuries after Ezekiel and is represented by biblical texts such as Dan 7—12 and the book of Revelation (as well as many nonbiblical Jewish and Christian writings). This genre features several literary characteristics such as dualism (which views the world as defined by a struggle of two opposing forces), heightened eschatology (which envisions the breaking in of a new era at the end of history), and heavy use of symbolism (which recasts present social and political realities in a new light). Although chs 38—39 display some features associated with later apocalyptic literature, the oracle as a whole only minimally reflects the dominant characteristics of apocalypses, and most current interpreters resist identifying it with this genre (see Hals 1989, 284; Block 1998, 426-28; Odell 2005, 466). Contrary to the end-times readings given in some parts of popular Christianity, for example, the Gog oracle does not move to a cosmic eschatological salvation for the whole world that signifies the end of history, but remains firmly related to Israel and its experiences in the postexilic era. Hence, the genre of chs 38—39 remains unsettled, but Block observes that the heavy repetition of variations of the recognition formula ("that you/they/nations may know"), which appears seven times (38:16, 23; 39:6, 7, 22, 23, 28), suggests that the oracle is best classified as a "series of fragmentary proof sayings" joined together to form "a single powerful proof oracle" (1998, 431). This identification connects with Yahweh's first person declarations throughout the text that the ultimate goal of these events is to vindicate Yahweh's sovereignty in the eyes of Israel and the nations (e.g., 39:21-22, 27-29) and produce a new recognition of divine holiness in the world.

The fourth and most significant interpretive issue for the Gog oracle deals with the attempt to understand precisely *how* chs 38—39 symbolize Yahweh's establishment of Israel's safety and vindication of the divine holiness. This question connects to the long-standing scholarly effort to ascertain the original identity of the figure of Gog (for surveys of various proposals see Blenkinsopp 1990, 184; Block 1998, 433). Interpreters have identified Gog with all kinds of figures they perceived as evil in their settings (Muslim invaders of Europe, Mongols, Stalin, Hitler, etc.), and the speculations within end-times literature of popular Christianity (Russia, Arabs, etc.) follow in this vein. A wide variety of scholarly proposals more responsible to Ezekiel's context, however, have identified Gog as a symbol based on such things as ancient historical figures, especially Gyges of Lydia (a ruler from the century before Ezekiel known from Assyrian annals), the personification of darkness (from the Sumerian *gûg*, "darkness"), or other ancient places and powers. Such proposals vary greatly, and the precise identity of Gog ultimately remains unknown, if Ezekiel even had a specific referent in mind and not simply a legendary military figure from the past or a generic character resembling barbarians from distant lands (Darr 2001, 1512).

In current scholarly literature, however, two perspectives have emerged at the forefront that propose chs 38—39 portray the establishment of Israel's safety and the final vindication of Yahweh's holiness in one of two ways: (1) by depicting the defeat of a cosmic, symbolic, mythical enemy representing any and all evil/imperial powers that threaten Yahweh's reign, or (2) by depicting the final destruction of Babylonia that has concluded its service as Yahweh's instrument of judgment. Odell, for example, argues that Gog is not to be identified with a particular historical person but is a symbolic, nonhistorical, paradigmatic enemy that represents any evil, military, or imperial power that would endanger Yahweh's people and oppose Yahweh's reign (Odell 2005, 468-70). Much like the unnamed Pharaoh in Exod 1:8, Gog can serve as the symbol of any oppressor in any historical moment, and "Magog" may likewise be only an artificial name for the "land of Gog" ("Ma" as the Hebrew abbreviation for "place of"). Odell concludes that the text introduces Gog as one originally appointed by Yahweh to serve as a good agent who maintains order over nations for the safety of restored Israel (serving as Yahweh's "chief prince" [38:2] over the kingdoms) but is subsequently driven to attack Israel out of rebellion and greed (2005, 469-70). The depiction of Gog's defeat in chs 38—39 is a symbol of the enduring protection that Yahweh will provide for the people in new times and against new enemies.

On the other hand, Julie Galambush interprets Gog not as a generic or mythic enemy, but as a symbolic name for King Nebuchadnezzar. She sees chs 38—39 as Ezekiel's oracle of ultimate judgment upon Babylonia (Galambush 2006) that many commentators have noticed is strangely absent from the book (both Isaiah and Jeremiah include oracles against Babylon). We have observed throughout the book that Ezekiel envisions Nebuchadnezzar and his actions as Yahweh's ordained instruments of judgment against Judah, and interpreters have often seen this as the reason he does not condemn them.

Now that the judgment is completed and Nebuchadnezzar has served his purpose, however, we might read chs 38—39 as Ezekiel's final preparation for the return of Yahweh's glory to a renewed land by eliminating the last remaining threat to the people's well-being. A similar passage in Isa 10 depicts the king of Assyria first serving as Yahweh's instrument of judgment on Israel but then overstepping his role in pride and bringing divine judgment upon himself. Likewise, in Galambush's view, Ezekiel portrays Nebuchadnezzar as greedily going beyond Yahweh's purposes (38:10-12) and bringing divine destruction upon himself. This destruction represents the final necessary move in the establishment of Yahweh's unquestioned sovereignty, as it eliminates the last remaining power that could challenge his dominion. Chapters 38—39 use some of the same language that Jeremiah employs to describe Nebuchadnezzar in his oracles against Babylonia (especially Jer 50—51), and Ezekiel depicts Gog with some of the same language he uses for Nebuchadnezzar elsewhere in the book (Galambush 2006, 259-60). Additionally, the literal reading of the Hebrew description of Gog in 38:2 (***the prince of the head of Meshech and Tubal***) points to a figure who ruled over the one who was the head of these nations—perhaps a reference to Nebuchadnezzar as the ruler of a deputy who maintained peace in the region of Anatolia (Galambush 2006, 260). Read in these ways, chs 38—39 offer a coded but dramatic sign of hope to Ezekiel's victimized audience—the ultimate defeat of Babylonia and the promise of safety from the very ones who had inflicted their trauma.

Even though the interpretation of chs 38—39 as a final oracle of judgment against Babylonia has much to commend it, ultimately the identity of Gog remains wrapped in mystery. Moreover, that identity is less important than what Gog symbolizes. As the culmination of the renewal of Israel for a new future and the preparation for the return of Yahweh's holy presence to a purified land and temple, the Gog oracle symbolizes the final defeat of all potential enemies, which results in lasting safety for the people and the final vindication of Yahweh's holiness/sovereignty in the eyes of all nations. Hence, it offers a counterpoint to the sense of fear and vulnerability in the assurance that no force or threat will be able to disrupt the divine purposes for Israel's future or the ultimate establishment of Yahweh's holiness in the world.

IN THE TEXT

A. Gog's Invasion (38:1-16)

The first chapter of the Gog oracle divides into two sections: vv 1-16 constitute direct divine second person address to Gog concerning his invasion of Israel, and vv 17-23 are predominantly a divine announcement of judgment that describes Gog in third person. Both sections end with a version of the recognition formula (**the nations may know/they will know**), underscoring that the main point of the entire episode is the final vindication of Yahweh's holiness in the world.

■ **1-3** Yahweh's instructions for the prophet to proclaim judgment against Gog begin with the familiar prophetic word formula and address to Ezekiel as **son of man** (vv 1-2). The opening also features the hostility and duel formulas (**set your face against** [v 2]; **I am against you** [v 3]), which have appeared at the head of several judgment oracles (see most recently against Edom in 35:2-3). These elements recast what appears to be an attack by Gog on Israel as a confrontation between Gog and Yahweh. Verse 2 identifies Gog as **chief prince of Meshech and Tubal.** Although some translations follow the Greek Septuagint and render the Hebrew word for **chief** (*rō'š*; lit., *head*) as a place name ("prince of Rosh, Meshech, and Tubal"), the grammatical structure does not support this reading and the Hebrew more literally indicates a construct chain, *the prince of the head of Meshech and Tubal.* In either case (**chief prince** or *the prince of the head of*), the text sets up Gog as one who rules over other lands or rulers (perhaps denoting Nebuchadnezzar as the **prince** over the one who rules over Meshech and Tubal; see Behind the Text). But Ezekiel's use of **prince** rather than "king" to describe this ultimate ruler may once again serve his rhetorical purposes of subsuming this figure beneath Yahweh's authority (see commentary on ch 12).

■ **4-6** The following verses identify Gog's allies in his attack against the resettled Israel. Several of the nations (Magog, Meshech, Tubal, Gomer, Beth Togarmah) appear in the table of nations in Gen 10 as Japheth's descendants associated with the coastland areas around the Black Sea or Caspian Sea, and all of Gog's associates except Gomer appear elsewhere in Ezekiel as trading partners or political allies with Tyre or Egypt (see 27:10-14; 30:5; 32:26). Gog's homeland of Magog is unknown outside the Bible (perhaps only a symbolic name; see Behind the Text), but the remainder of the nations listed are known entities from the ancient world and not coded symbols related to the end of history (see sidebar "Gog's Allies in Ezekiel 38"). Gog first joins his directly controlled lands of Meshech and Tubal (both in the area of Anatolia or modern Turkey) with a group of three kingdoms to the east and south of Israel (v 5) and then with a group of two nations **from the far north** (v 6). Together, Gog's allies total seven, a number that symbolizes completeness (see the seven nations in the oracles against the nations in chs 25—32). This symbol of completeness combines with the geographical origins of the forces from areas both north and south of Israel to give the picture of a comprehensive attack in which the entire known world at the time comes against the restored

Israel. From the Israelites' point of view, several of these nations represented mysterious peoples from faraway places, known perhaps only through tales as wild and brutal (Block 1998, 436). And the inclusion of peoples from **the far north** resonates with the common motif of an enemy from the north that figures prominently in other prophetic texts (see especially Jer 1:13-15; 6:22; 50:41-42). Whereas Ezek 35 envisioned the transformation of Israel's local hostilities with its immediate neighbors, the proclamation of Israel's future safety that comes through the Gog oracle represents a comprehensive security from all the threats of their world.

Gog's Allies in Ezekiel 38

Contrary to the impression often given by popular end-times readings, Gog's allies in 38:1-6 are well-known entities from Ezekiel's world, attested in various ancient texts. In addition to the more recognizable Persia and Ethiopia, others include the following (see Darr 2001, 1516-17):

Meshech: attested in Assyrian texts as *Musku/Mušku* in the area of Asia Minor (modern Turkey)

Tubal: attested in Assyrian texts as *Tabal* in the area of Asia Minor (modern Turkey)

Put: the area west of Egypt near modern Libya

Gomer: likely the Cimmerians (Akkadian, *gimmiraia*), originally Indo-Europeans from the Ukraine, eventually displaced to Asia Minor during the Neo-Assyrian period, where they conquered the Phrygian king Midas (676 B.C.).

Beth Togarmah: attested in Assyrian texts as *Til-garimmu* on the eastern border of *Tabal* (Tubal) in Asia Minor.

■ **7-9** In vv 7-9, Yahweh describes the actions that Gog will take against Israel. The commands given to Gog (**get ready; be prepared** [v 7]) and the passive expression that Gog will **be called to arms** (v 8) pick up on the opening divine first person proclamation from v 4 (**I will turn you around . . . and bring you out**). Together, these statements emphasize the key point of Ezekiel's presentation of Gog's actions: Yahweh is actually the cause of Gog's deeds and he leads Gog into Israel not for judgment against Israel, as with Babylonia earlier in the book, but for the purpose of defeating Gog and thereby symbolizing the ultimate establishment of divine sovereignty. Verse 8 sets these actions into the time frame of the exiles' distant future, well after they have returned to live in the land (see Behind the Text). The description of the people as restored from war to live in safety connects Gog's attack to questions that surround the experience of recovery from trauma. After returning from exile and attempting to build a new life, the exiles remain vulnerable to a new loss of safety (see also v 11). Yet, Yahweh's sovereign control over the very symbol of a worldwide, comprehensive threat offers a word of hope and protection in the face of vulnerability and fear.

■ **10-13** In contrast to the assertion that Yahweh is the controlling force of Gog's actions, vv 10-13 present Gog's perspective. Emphasizing once again the remaining vulnerability of those recovering from the trauma of war and exile (v 11), Gog's reported thoughts turn Yahweh's purposes into an **evil scheme** (v 10) that sees the restored Israel as an easy target to **plunder and loot** (v 12). The words and imagery here parallel the description of the king of Assyria in Isa 10:5-19, as both texts picture rulers who overstep their roles as Yahweh's instruments due to greed and power (see also the depiction of the king of Tyre in ch 28). The question in v 13 likely envisions Gog being encouraged in his greed by **Sheba and Dedan and the merchants of Tarshish and all her villages** (lit., *her lions,* perhaps, *her warriors*), peoples mentioned among Tyre's trading partners in ch 27 and pictured here as potential beneficiaries of Gog's aggression.

■ **14-16** The transitional word **therefore** and a new messenger formula (v 14) mark vv 14-16 as Yahweh's response to Gog's actions and as a climactic reiteration of Yahweh's perspective that he is the purpose and power behind these events. Yahweh's first person designations of Gog's targets as **my people** and **my land** (v 16) recast Gog's actions as a direct challenge to Yahweh's own status and power. Moreover, the concluding statement in v 16 (**so that the nations may know me**) subsumes the entire scenario into Yahweh's purpose to demonstrate his holiness/sovereignty (Odell 2005, 471). Here the text provides the first explicit answer to the question of why Yahweh is bringing Gog against Israel in a mission that is already doomed to fail—a question that must have puzzled the exiles hearing this bizarre oracle (Darr 2001, 1519). The divine words to Gog specifically assert that Yahweh will establish his holiness **through you** (v 16)—the same words that Yahweh spoke to the exiles in 36:23. In Ezekiel's vision of Israel's new future, both the cleansing and the restoration of the exiles and the final defeat of those enemies who may threaten Israel's new existence will serve to establish Yahweh's holiness in the eyes of the nations.

B. Proclamation of Divine Judgment on Gog (38:17-23)

■ **17** Another messenger formula in v 17 marks the transition to the second section of ch 38 in which Yahweh turns from the description of Gog's actions to the proclamation of divine judgment. The proclamation opens with a question that Yahweh directs to Gog, asking if he is the one that **the prophets of Israel** had predicted Yahweh would bring against his people. The language sounds like the statements about Assyria or Babylonia as Yahweh's instruments that appear in other prophetic books and again emphasizes the theme of Yahweh's sovereignty over Gog's actions (**that I would bring you**). Commentators have long suspected that v 17 is a later addition to the oracle due to its distinctive style and retrospective reference to Israel's prophets. A more pressing interpretive issue, however, is whether Yahweh's question calls for a positive or negative response. Does Yahweh rhetorically imply that Gog is condemned because he is *not* Yahweh's instrument of judgment but has come against Israel on his own, or because he *is* that long-predicted instrument but will now vindicate Yahweh's holiness by suffering destruction? The NIV adds the negative to the Hebrew (**are you not?**) and slants the question toward a positive response. Scholars remain divided (cf. Block 1998, 456, and Darr 2001, 1521), but answering the question with "yes" connects well to the notion that Gog represents Nebuchadnezzar who had been Yahweh's instrument of judgment and his defeat constitutes the missing judgment against Babylonia and the removal of the last remaining challenge to Yahweh as sovereign (see Behind the Text).

■ **18-23** In v 18, Yahweh's proclamation switches from direct address to a third person description of the judgment to come against Gog. In a scene that resonates with the imagery of cosmic conflict in apocalyptic literature (see Behind the Text), vv 19-22 announce that Yahweh will defeat Gog's invasion through miraculous means, using weapons of creation and requiring no action on Israel's part. Yahweh's agents of destruction include an **earthquake** in vv 19-20, followed in Hebrew by seven weapons in vv 21-22 (**sword**, pestilence, **bloodshed, rain, hailstones,** fire, **sulfur**) that match the seven nations coming against Israel (vv 1-6) and symbolize the completeness of Yahweh's judgment (Bowen 2010, 235). Through the depiction of Yahweh fighting while Israel is passive and Gog's troops turn on each other (v 21), Ezekiel introduces an alternative vision to how the kingdoms of Israel and Judah formerly strived to have security. Rather than security through armies, alliances, and warfare, the restored Israel—like Moses and the Hebrews standing still to watch Yahweh's actions at the sea (Exod 14:14)—will receive their security from a deep trust in Yahweh's sovereignty and provision. The recognition formula and other language in Ezek 38:23 conclude this proclamation by again asserting that Gog's defeat serves the purpose of the final vindication of Yahweh's holiness/sovereignty before the nations.

The Nonviolent Defeat of Evil

In 38:17-23, the defeat of Gog, who symbolizes the evil and destructive forces in Israel's world, occurs not by the military action of God's people but through a pacifism that entrusts that defeat to God's own doing. This notion, also reflected in God's instructions for Moses and the Hebrews at the sea to remain passive and watch for God to deliver them from the Egyptians (Exod 14:14), constitutes a running theme in much of the biblical literature. Even the NT book of Revelation resists a vision of defeating evil through acting violently or in more powerful ways against it, and instead envisions evil being overcome through the suffering and sacrifice of the slaughtered lamb (see Rev 4—5). These visions fly in the face of many popular end-times and apocalyptic scenarios within contemporary Christian interpretation that envision militaristic conflicts as the culmination of God's work. Moreover, these visions challenge Christians who claim that various evils in our world (such as the practice of terrorism) must be overcome through military means. Rather than a vision of overcoming evil through superior might and force, Ezekiel, Revelation, and other texts invite their readers to ponder how evil might be overcome through a sacrificial love that absorbs violence and responds with redemptive grace.

C. Gog's Destruction (39:1-10)

■ **1-6** With a beginning marked by the transitional indicator *And you* (*wĕʾattâ;* omitted by NIV), a new command for Ezekiel to prophesy, a new messenger formula, and a new duel formula, 39:1-10 forms the third section of the oracle against Gog. The opening features repetition of Yahweh's words in 38:3-4, and 39:1-6 gives a fuller description of the divine destruction of Gog. One added dimension here is that Yahweh will disarm Gog before he even has a chance to attack (v 3). This language, which resembles Yahweh's promise to remove weapons and warfare in some psalms (e.g., Ps 46:9), once again highlights Yahweh's complete sovereignty and Israel's need only to remain passive, as Yahweh refuses to allow the battle even to take place. Ezekiel 39:6 then adds another dimension to the previous descriptions of judgment, with an ironic twist. Yahweh declares that he will not only defeat Gog and his armies but also will destroy Gog's homeland of Magog. Ironically, those who had attacked Israel when it thought itself able to live safely (38:11) will find that they themselves do not **live in safety** (39:6) in their own land. As a result of this action, the recognition formula at the end of v 6 asserts that even those who live in Magog **(they) will** come to **know/*acknowledge*** Yahweh.

■ **7-10** After the description of Gog's defeat, Yahweh's first person speech in vv 7-8 explicitly casts this event as the culminating moment in the vindication of divine holiness in the world (**This is the day I have spoken of** [v 8]). Through the defeat of this symbolic enemy, Yahweh will ensure that his holy name is no longer besmirched, and that first Israel and then the nations will acknowledge him. The use of the title **the Holy One in Israel** (v 7), which figures prominently in Isaiah's discourse to affirm Yahweh's supremacy (e.g., Isa

1:4; 5:19; 10:17), places special emphasis on the divine sovereignty to be recognized by Israel and the nations. Following this climactic statement of Gog's destruction and its meaning, vv 9-10 begin a new focus on the aftermath of the battle that will last throughout the following section in vv 11-20. The first element of that aftermath is that Israel will gather and burn the weapons left from the battle (**use the weapons for fuel** [v 9]). On one hand, this action symbolizes again that Yahweh alone defeated the enemy, as Israel is called upon only to participate in straightening up. But on a more profound level for the exiles as trauma victims in need of a new sense of safety, the burning of weapons symbolizes the end of war and its mechanisms of violence. The text once more uses the symbolic number **seven** (**seven years they will use them for fuel** [v 9]) to signify the completeness of this divine elimination of the enemy and provision of safety.

D. Gog's Burial (39:11-20)

■ **11-16** The next section of Yahweh's speech continues the description of the aftermath of Gog's defeat. Verses 9-10 describe the Israelites burning the weapons, and vv 11-16 announce that Yahweh will designate **a burial place in Israel** (v 11) for Gog and his army. But much about this scene remains unclear, especially the location envisioned by the text, if, in fact, an actual location was intended. Yahweh appoints a burial place in a valley that lies somewhere east of the Dead Sea and is referred to in Hebrew as the valley of *hā'ōběrîm*. Some scholars take the term as a place name, the **valley of the Abarim** (presumably west of northern Moab near the Dead Sea), while others read it literally as **the valley of the travelers** (although the NIV is unjustified in adding **toward the Dead Sea**). More likely, the term may have the symbolic meaning of *those who have passed on* (i.e., died) known from parallels with Ugaritic literature (Block 1998, 469). In any case, v 11 states that the valley will be renamed the **Valley of Hamon Gog** ("Valley of Gog's Horde/Army"), a name that likely plays on the Valley of Hinnom outside of Jerusalem that was associated with the practice of child sacrifice and thus ritually unclean (see 2 Kgs 23:10) (Block 1998, 469; Odell 2005, 474). Together with the reference in v 16 to a city called **Hamonah** ("chaos/tumult"), a term used elsewhere in Ezekiel to describe Jerusalem's condition that brought divine judgment (see 5:15-17), the prophet seems to envision an impure burial site that will lie somewhere outside of the newly purified Jerusalem to be described in chs 40—48.

The imagery in the burial scene is reminiscent of the piling of enemy corpses after victory in Neo-Assyrian royal inscriptions. Yahweh's statement in v 12 once again employs a symbolic number for completeness and says the Israelites will take **seven months** to bury the slain from Gog's army in a comprehensive reclamation of the land (see the seven nations in 38:1-6 and Yahweh's seven weapons in 38:21-22). Verses 13-15 of ch 39 then depict a meticulous procedure for identifying and burying the bones of the dead. Most importantly for Ezekiel's priestly perspective, however, the text repeats three times that the purpose of these burials is to **cleanse the land** (vv 12, 14, 16). In the priestly system safeguarding Yahweh's holy presence, proper burial was necessary to avoid pollution, and unburied corpses were unclean (see Lev 21:1-4, 11; Deut 21:23). By portraying this action of the people, Ezekiel envisions a future in which the same house of Israel that originally defiled the land will purify it. Moreover, this cleansing of the land's defilement prepares the way for the return of Yahweh's presence in the book's final vision.

■ **17-20** Just when the text seems ready to move to the final vision of Yahweh's return to a cleansed land, however, vv 17-20 add one more aftermath scene that seems logically out of sequence with the preceding depictions. Although vv 11-16 picture the burial of Gog's army, vv 17-20 portray a gruesome scene in which Yahweh summons scavenger creatures to come to a sacrificial feast and devour the unburied corpses of the fallen invaders. The same unusual sequence of the devouring of corpses after their apparent burial appears in Jer 7:32-33, and a later editor may be responsible for this aftermath scene. Yet, contemporary readers must be careful not to force modern notions of consistency on ancient texts (Darr 2001, 1527), and this is even more pressing for trauma literature that often relies on a series of disjointed depictions and episodes to express the experience.

39:11-20

The opening phrase, **And you** (*wĕʾattâ*; omitted by NIV; see also 39:1), and a new messenger formula (v 17) mark a shift to direct divine address to Ezekiel that instructs him to call to the animals. As Block observes, the scene portrays Ezekiel as a royal herald from the ancient world announcing an official invitation to a banquet on behalf of a host ruler (1998, 474). What follows is a priestly image in reverse: Ezekiel invites the scavenger animals to a **sacrifice** (v 17), yet not one offered to Yahweh, but one that Yahweh offers to the animals. As with Yahweh's command for Ezekiel to eat food cooked over dung in 4:12-15, the image goes against priestly mores. The scavenging animals are unclean and they engage in the defiling act of eating human flesh and blood. These elements highlight the symbolic force of the scene. Not only does the devouring of the bodies depict the utter humiliation of these invaders through mistreatment of their corpses (see also 6:4-5, 13; 29:5; 32:4-6; 35:8), but it also symbolizes the complete annihilation of Israel's enemies who might threaten them in their new future.

E. Coda: The Final Vindication of Yahweh (39:21-29)

As noted in the Behind the Text discussion, vv 21-29 constitute a type of coda on the end of the Gog oracle. Commentators often regard all or part of this section as later additions because it does not deal with Gog's invasion and defeat and contains language that has not appeared previously in the book (e.g., Yahweh's hidden face). In the final form, however, Block identifies two panels that balance each other (vv 21-24, 25-29), both moving from descriptions of Yahweh's actions and others' responses to the recognition formula and a reference to the hiding of Yahweh's face (1998, 479). The contents of these panels make the coda in its present form a fitting conclusion to the Gog oracle as a whole, and the statement made by the passage makes it one of the most important expressions of Ezekiel's overall theological message. Yahweh's discourse throughout the section directly addresses the prophet and offers the summary statement that when the nations learn of Yahweh's sovereignty through the defeat of Gog, the symbolic enemy, and the reestablishment of Israel in the land, they will come to a new interpretation of the events of Israel's exile and destruction that understands them within the larger vindication of Yahweh's holiness in the world.

■ **21-24** In the first panel (vv 21-24), Yahweh asserts that his actions with Gog and Israel will **display my glory** (v 21) in a way that serves to fully and finally establish his sovereignty to the nations. With matching recognition formulas, vv 22-23 affirm that both Israel and the nations now **will know/acknowledge** Yahweh (see also vv 7-8). Verses 23-24 in particular capture Ezekiel's overall interpretation of the trauma of destruction and exile that he has developed throughout the book. Using the prophet's characteristic priestly categories, the text declares that the nations will finally come to recognize that Israel's defeat and deportation were Yahweh's own doing as a means of dealing with **their uncleanness and their offenses** (v 24). This interpretation is the heart of Ezekiel's message—bringing the people's trauma into the alternative plot line of divine holiness whereby Yahweh had to send the people into exile in order to cleanse the defiled land and return the people from exile in order to vindicate his name/reputation in the world.

■ **25-29** Although the preceding parts of the Gog oracle have taken readers into the exiles' future well after their return to the land, the opening of the second panel of the coda (vv 25-29) abruptly takes readers back from the distant future to the exiles' present reality in Babylonia. Verse 25 opens with the transitional word **therefore**, a new messenger formula, and the temporal marker, **now**, as Yahweh declares that in order to accomplish the new understanding of his sovereignty and Israel's exile given in vv 21-24 he will begin the process of returning the people to their land. The text envisions this as an event still to come (**When I have brought them back from the nations . . . I will gather them to their own land** [vv 27-28]), and again emphasizes that it will have the effects of vindicating Yahweh's holiness and leading to the final and full acknowledgment of Yahweh's sovereignty (**I will show myself holy through them . . . Then they will know that I am the** Lord [vv 27-28]). As a part of these effects, v 26 highlights how the exiles will respond to this ultimate restoration, but the precise meaning of the Hebrew is unclear. The NIV reflects many translations and states that the exiles will finally **forget** [*wĕnāśû*] **their shame,** perhaps indicating an ultimate release from the sense of shame for their past that Ezekiel has often said would accompany the people's restoration (e.g., 16:54; 32:24-25, 30; 34:29; 36:15; 44:13). But the Hebrew word here may also be configured as meaning, ***they will bear their shame,*** and the prevalence of this idea throughout the book makes it likely here, as well (so Zimmerli 1983, 295; Block 1998, 478). In any case, by returning to the exiles' present circumstances, 39:25-29 leaves Yahweh's promises of ultimate safety from enemy threats and lasting restoration to the land not as an established reality but a hope in which the people must trust in order to envision a new future beyond their trauma.

FROM THE TEXT

In order to hear the message of Ezekiel's cryptic and sometimes bizarre oracle against Gog, contemporary readers must move beyond the futuristic end-times interpretations that have been given to this text in some conservative evangelical and, especially, "dispensationalist" circles of popular Christianity. As noted in the Behind the Text discussion, chs 38—39, and especially the mysterious figure of Gog, have fueled Christian millennialist interpretations that have produced end-times scenarios now so popular that many Christians assume they are the clear meaning of the biblical texts and the classic understanding of historic Christianity. The majority of these interpretations arose in the context of fundamentalist and evangelical movements in the United States during the nineteenth and twentieth centuries. Most notably, the particular theological movement called dispensationalism, which emerged primarily from the Calvinist Irish pastor John Nelson Darby in the 1800s, provided many of the significant roots. Dispensationalist theology operates on the notions that God deals with human beings and salvation in different ways (e.g., law, grace) in different time periods (dispensations) and that proper understanding requires a literal interpretation of the Bible.

Out of these perspectives came a scenario that revolves around seeing the power of God as a means of destroying one's heretical enemies, even if only in a final, end of time context. Darby introduced into Christian thought the idea of a secret rapture of the church, which would be followed by a tribulation period, Christ's second coming, and, finally, a millennial reign of Christ on earth. Articulations of such a scenario often envision the end times as a violent conflict between aggressors and victims in a final battle, usually imagined along racial/ethnic lines (Israel versus Russians, Arabs, Africans, etc.) (see Lieb 1998, 5-6). At the heart of these constructions, however, is a mode of biblical interpretation that is not simply literal, but makes a sharp distinction between Israel and the church in biblical texts. Dispensationalists do not see the church as the new Israel that fulfills the promises made to Israel in the OT. Rather, the church is merely a parenthesis in God's real plan for the world that remains centered on the actual, ethnic people of Israel. Hence, the OT prophets do not predict things related to the church but only Israel, and these things must be literally fulfilled by an actual people or nation of Israel. As one might expect, these interpretations accelerated after the founding of the modern state of Israel in 1948.

Variations on the perspectives associated with dispensationalism have achieved a new popularity in American Christianity through persons such as Hal Lindsey, Jerry Falwell, Tim LaHaye, and John Hagee, and through movies such as *The Omega Code* and books such as the *Left Behind* series. Consequently, many contemporary Christians may be unaware that such perspectives are a modern invention and do not reflect the mainline theology of the historic Christian church. More importantly for our purposes, however, such perspectives promote a method of biblical interpretation that views biblical texts, especially the OT prophets, as blueprints for future political and military events, containing hidden symbols and codes that reveal detailed end-times scenarios. Yet, close examination reveals that these proposed scenarios are piecemeal, inconsistent, and ever-changing, as actual realities of our world make them impossible. Ezekiel 38—39 in particular has long attracted these popular futuristic interpretations. For example, the 1917 edition of the Scofield Reference Bible, which represents dispensationalist theology, identified Gog as Russia, and this interpretation has been developed in elaborate ways by more recent popular Christian writers. Hal Lindsey's *The Late Great Planet Earth* (1970) drew the Gog oracle into an elaborate end-times scenario in which the Soviet Union gathers Arab and Chinese allies to invade Israel but is defeated through divine intervention. Writing after the fall of the Soviet Union, John Hagee adjusts the reading of the Gog oracle in his *Final Dawn over Jerusalem* (1998) so that Russia will revive itself as a superpower and lead a pan-Islamic army against Israel before being defeated by divine weaponry.

In spite of the popularity of these end-times interpretations, they are fraught with problems and dangers. At the most obvious level, they offer a flat reading of the biblical texts that does not attend to historical contexts, genres, social locations, and ideologies. The interpretations construe the prophetic literature only in terms of the political and economic realities of the modern, usually Western and European, world. Moreover, as even the history of the United States in the twentieth century has shown, the scenarios created from these perspectives have the power to influence political leaders and their approaches to public policy and foreign relations (see Behind the Text). Most pressingly, however, such interpretations lose the broader sense of what the prophets proclaimed and trade away the present speaking voice of the prophets, which calls for an alternative world of justice and righteousness, for speculative predictions of future events.

In light of the confusion surrounding chs 38—39, contemporary readers, preachers, and teachers must strive to challenge problematic interpretations while at the same time setting forth the theological message of these chapters within the context of the book of Ezekiel. Initially, we must place the Gog oracle into Ezekiel's ancient context and recognize that the text's elements were intelligible for ancient readers and not cryptic codes giving obscure predictions of the future. Nearly every nation mentioned in ch 38, for instance, is an actual kingdom known from the ancient world and not a mysterious code name for modern states. As Bowen summarizes, the depictions in the Gog oracle are "no farther in the future than any of the other passages from chapters 34—48. Nor are they particularly difficult to interpret in the context of the previous chapters, especially 36:16-38" (2010, 232). The central message of Ezekiel's oracle is to affirm God's holiness as the "unrivaled lord of human history" and God's enduring commitment to the "status and welfare" of God's people (Block 1998, 493).

Along with the affirmations of God's holiness and faithfulness, perhaps no element of chs 38—39 is as powerful for contemporary readers as God's promise of safety in a new future for God's people. As Darr observes, experience testifies to a deep longing within the human spirit for "security, for freedom from fear . . . [especially] when people know themselves to be vulnerable" (2001, 1531). Ezekiel's words respond to that human need by affirming the ultimate dependability of God's provision and protection. Now, there is no doubt that the experience of trauma, and the sense of vulnerability that accompanies it, problematize this promise of divine protection and safety. Indeed, a counselor can never guarantee a victim that he or she will not suffer again in the future

(Bowen 2010, 238). For this reason, it is crucial to note that Ezekiel's oracle remains a vision/hope/prayer for the future that is not yet realized. The message of chs 38—39 does not guarantee a future free from pain, but it offers an alternative way of viewing reality that imagines a life lived without fear through a deep trust in God's watchcare. Although remaining only at the level of hope and trust, this is the conviction expressed throughout many OT psalms, as the psalmist speaks out of a situation of danger and yet sees a God who offers safety. This is the alternative imagination that allows us to live with the sense that God breathes peace over our fears and sets tables for us in the presence of enemies. And this imagination draws us to pray trustingly as Jesus taught us, "Deliver us from evil" (Matt 6:13 KJV).

VIII. THIRD VISION OF GOD'S PRESENCE: THE RETURN TO A NEW TEMPLE, LAND, AND CITY (EZEKIEL 40—48)

BEHIND THE TEXT

Chapters 40—48 contain the third and final vision of Yahweh's glory/presence (*kābôd*) and represent the culmination of Ezekiel's theological message concerning the trauma of the exiles' past and the possibilities of their future. Throughout the book, the prophet has attempted to deal with his people's trauma of destruction and exile by interpreting it within the larger context of Yahweh's reestablishment of his holiness in the world. He has explained the exile as the result of Israel's defilement of Yahweh's land and temple, which caused Yahweh to withdraw the divine glory/presence from the midst of the people. Yet, he has proclaimed that these traumatic events are only part of a larger work in which Yahweh aims to transform the people, restore them to a rejuvenated land, and return the divine glory/presence to a purified and permanent dwelling among a holy people. The framework of this theological message has appeared in the book's three visions of Yahweh's *kābôd* ("glory/presence") in chs 1—3, 8—11, and now 40—48, which form a "connected plot line that ties the book together" (Tuell 2009, 277). Following the two sets of oracles that symbolically prepare for a vision of full restoration (chs 33—37; 38—39), chs 40—48 depict a perfectly constructed and permanently undefiled temple that can be the center of a new reality for Israel and can allow the lasting return of Yahweh's glory/presence.

In this lengthy and exquisitely detailed vision, Ezekiel depicts not simply a purified temple for Yahweh's presence, but a perfectly configured Israelite society as understood from his priestly perspective, featuring an ideal priesthood, ideal ruler ("prince"), ideal land arrangement, and ideal natural world rejuvenated by a great river flowing out of the temple. In spite of this idyllic character, the vision in chs 40—48 is difficult, if not off-putting, for contemporary readers (for three major works treating these chapters, see Levenson 1976; Tuell 1992; Stevenson 1996). The text teems with laborious and often inconsistent details of building measurements and boundary locations, as well as ancient technical language for architecture and rituals. Christian readers in particular often find the priestly sacrificial instructions and purity regulations irrelevant and anticlimactic after the oracles of transformation in chs 33—39.

Even so, the date given to this culminating vision in 40:1 marks it as particularly significant. The date is unusual within the book, as it gives a double dating (see also 1:1-2) that locates the vision both in terms of Ezekiel's exile since 597 B.C. and the more recent destruction of Jerusalem in 586 B.C.: "In the twenty-fifth year of our exile, at the beginning of the year, on the tenth of the month, in the fourteenth year after the fall of the city" (40:1). By most estimations, the chronology works out to 573 B.C. Only the apparent editorial addition in 29:17-21 (assigned to two years after 40:1) has a later date in the book, and the immediately previous date in 32:1 was the twelfth year of the exile (585 B.C.), twelve years earlier. In the story line of the book, clearly the prophet has been active in the time since the date in 32:1, especially offering oracles of transformation and restoration. Yet the date in 40:1 is laden with symbolic meaning on several levels. First, the reference to the tenth day of the first month of the year reminds the OT reader of the time set for the first Passover observance in Exod 12:2, which marked the beginning of Israel's deliverance from Egyptian bondage (Block 1998, 496). The date in 40:1 connects Ezekiel's vision of a restored temple to the exodus themes of liberation for a new beginning. Second, in priestly calculations the "twenty-fifth year" marks the halfway point to the Year of Jubilee, the period once every fifty years when priestly law calls for the cancellation of debts and the release of captives (Lev 25). Perhaps as a way of acknowledging that the audience of this culminating vision remains in exile, the date symbolically proclaims that the people are halfway to their moment of ultimate liberation. Third, and perhaps most significantly, 40:1 dates the final vision to twenty years after Ezekiel's initial vision in chs 1—3. The priestly legislation stipulates a twenty-year period of service for Levitical priests, as they are to be ordained when they are thirty and leave their duties at fifty (Num 4:47). If Ezekiel was thirty years old at the time of his commissioning (see commentary on 1:1-3), the time when, had he been in Jerusalem, he would have begun his full-time service as a priest in the temple, the date in 40:1 may indicate that he has reached the age of retirement and the vision of a new temple represents the culmination of his ministry.

Following this initial date, the remainder of chs 40—48 moves from the preparations for the return of Yahweh's presence to the effects that result from the return, yet the center part of the chapters consists of a law code woven into the vision (43:12—46:24). The vision opens (40:1—42:20) with a meticulous depiction of the new temple as a "house" (40:5), whose perfect state then allows Yahweh's presence to return permanently to the temple and Yahweh to dwell as king among the people (43:1-11). The law code at the center of the vision compliments these scenes by giving instructions for the people on how to live in the newly restored divine presence (43:12—46:24). The visionary depictions then resume with the reconfiguration and rejuvenation of the land that results from the divine presence (47:1—48:29) and the establishment of a city that provides the community with ongoing access to that presence (48:30-35). The parts divide into two parallel sections, with the law code at the center:

A. The New Temple (40:1—42:20)
B. Vision of the Return of Yahweh's Presence (43:1-11)
C. The Torah of the New Temple (43:12—46:24)
D. The New Land (47:1—48:29)
E. The New Jerusalem (48:30-35)

Although the movement of the chapters seems straightforward, a number of difficulties add to the off-putting elements noted above and create problems for interpreters. The complex transmission of the text over time has resulted in several sections, especially chs 41—42, which contain many uncertain readings and textual variants (see Block 1998, 494). The numerous footnotes in modern translations of chs 40—48 reveal the complexities. Additionally, Ezekiel's vision has extensive parallels to other OT passages, but its relationship to them is complicated. The temple description parallels the instructions for and building of the wilderness tabernacle in Exod 25—40 and Solomon's temple in 1 Kgs 6—7 and 2 Chr 3—4 (also the new Jerusalem in the book of Revelation; see commentary below). Yet the temple described in chs 40—42 does not match precisely the description of either structure, or that of the second temple built after the exile (Ezra 3—6; see Sweeney 2005, 159). Moreover, Ezekiel is simply commanded to observe and measure but never to build this temple. The law code at the center of the vision (43:12—46:24), as well as the various priestly regulations throughout, also have extensive parallels with the Torah ascribed to Moses in the Pentateuch. Within these parallels, however, are numerous differences and contradictions between Ezekiel and the priestly legislation in Exodus, Leviticus, Numbers, and Deuteronomy, giving the impression that Ezekiel is cast as a new Moses who reformulates the Torah (see Block 1998, 498-501). The relationship between chs 40—48 and the Mosaic Torah is so perennially vexing that Jewish tradition contains the story of one particular scribe so troubled by the differences that he used up three hundred barrels of oil for light until he thought he had explained away each discrepancy (see the rabbinic text *b. Shabbat* 13b).

As these parallels and differences suggest, many questions remain concerning the compositional history and editing of chs 40—48. While this commentary focuses on engaging the prophet's vision in its current form, it is worth noting that scholarly views on the unity and originality of the chapters range widely (see Block 1998, 494-95). Early in the modern period, scholars often regarded all of chs 40—48 as a later addition to the book (e.g., Cooke 1937, 426-27), while some more recent interpreters have argued oppositely for the total originality of the unit to the sixth-century prophet (see Greenberg 1983, 15). Many scholars chart a middle course, by picking up on the divergences and tensions even within parts of chs 40—48 (e.g., note the differences in the priestly status assigned to the Levites in 40:44-46 and 44:14) and concluding that there is a core of material original to Ezekiel that has been supplemented by later (priestly) additions. For example, Tuell (1992) has recently developed this notion by arguing that chs 40—48 contain an original vision of Ezekiel about the new temple and divine presence, but later priestly editors from the postexilic/Persian period in Judah have expanded the vision in a coherent way with a law code (43:10—46:24) that provides a liturgy for life in Yahweh's presence.

While these redactional theories help explain some of the complexities and inconsistencies one encounters in chs 40—48, for those seeking to engage Ezekiel's vision as it now appears, the identification of the unit's genre plays an important role. At the most basic level, the entirety of chs 40—48 is a vision report similar to chs 1—3 and 8—11 and marked by typical vision report formulas such as "the hand of the LORD" (40:1; see 1:3; 8:1) and "visions of God" (40:2; see 1:1; 8:3). Commentators also observe, however, that the genre of chs 40—48 resembles the well-known ancient Near Eastern pattern of temple or palace building accounts in which a deity or king constructs a temple or palace after a great victory (see Odell 2005, 483-84; Block 1998, 507). As noted above, the biblical parallels for this genre appear in the accounts of the building of the wilderness tabernacle in Exodus and Solomon's temple in 1 Kings, passages with which chs 40—48 share much in common. The motif of building a temple or palace is also prominent in ancient Near Eastern texts such as the Babylonian *Enuma Elish* (in which the god Marduk constructs his temple, Esagila, in Babylon after defeating Tiamat to become king of the gods; see *ANET* 68) and the Assyrian royal inscriptions of King Esarhaddon (in which he rebuilds the city of Babylon after his definitive military victories; see Odell 2005, 483-84). As Block notes, the placement of chs 40—48 immediately following Yahweh's decisive defeat of Gog in chs 38—39 allows the vision to share with this genre the function of symbolizing Yahweh's ultimate victory and established sovereignty (1998, 510). More recently, however, some scholars have given increased attention to parts of chs 40—48 that go beyond the temple building and have often been underemphasized, especially those having to do with land, boundaries, and access. In light of these elements, Stevenson (1996) proposes that Ezekiel's vision takes the form of "territorial rhetoric"—a designation drawn from the field of "human geography" that examines the ways in which societies define spaces, boundaries, and access to shape their life together. Seen in this way, Ezekiel symbolically creates a new social reality for Israel by envisioning a new territoriality with reconfigured boundaries for the community and access to the divine holiness.

The final background issue for chs 40—48 is perhaps the most pressing for theological interpretation of the vision. Throughout these chapters, Ezekiel describes a perfect temple that houses Yahweh's holy presence in the midst of the people and an ideal Israelite society that lives together in justice and purity in the midst of the divine presence. As mentioned above, however, this temple and society do not reflect any known historical realities that existed at any point in Israel's past. This disconnect raises the question of how to understand the force and meaning of Ezekiel's vision: Do these chapters describe a literal temple and society that is yet to be built (a building program for the community to enact), or only a vision that remains at the symbolic level, perhaps representing a heavenly temple built by Yahweh that Ezekiel envisions as currently in existence even while the people remain in exile? Some interpreters have argued that this vision derives from some preexilic model and constitutes a blueprint to be built (Zimmerli 1983, 412; Greenberg 1983, 15). Yet, the ideal nature of the text's depictions, as well as the lack of any commands for the prophet or people to build these structures (but only to observe and measure [40:4; 43:11]), suggests that the restored temple with the reconfigured society it generates is not a literal complex to be built but only a vision or symbol designed to reframe the exiles' imagination and lead them to envision a new reality of life before Yahweh and with each other (so also Tuell 2009, 285; Odell 2005, 488; Bowen 2010, 267; Block 1998, 505).

Even as Ezekiel and his fellow exiles remain in a foreign land, with no visible sign of hope for a new future, Yahweh shows the prophet a temple that is already complete and in existence, and can generate an entirely new picture of society. The vision imaginatively draws the exiles toward a new way of seeing not only the future but also the present—offering a picture of divine holiness and sovereignty that is already established and a glimpse of the kind of just and pure society that can emerge from life lived in the divine presence. The power of this symbol—a perfectly ordered temple and society that guarantees the purity required by the divine presence and is already in existence—addresses the trauma-related issues of the exiles, especially the need for trauma victims to feel assurance that the trauma will not happen again and to have a sense of presence and safety even in the midst of the trauma (Bowen 2010, 238). Moreover, the vision sets forth a new defining reality for the community: this is a people who, even now, live in the presence of Yahweh as he is enthroned in holiness and sovereignty. This notion of being a people among whom Yahweh dwells has the power to reshape how the community lives in holiness before their God and in right relationship with one another (see From the Text).

IN THE TEXT

A. The New Temple (40:1—42:20)

The opening section of Ezekiel's culminating vision (chs 40—42) provides a meticulously detailed description of the ideal temple that will house the newly returned presence of Yahweh (see ch 43). The scene as a whole consists of a careful measuring of various parts of a massive temple complex enclosed by a large wall. Following the double date formula that locates the vision in 573 B.C. and the typical formulas marking the vision report genre ("hand of the LORD" [v 1]; "visions of God" [v 2]) (see Behind the Text), the text depicts Ezekiel being given a guided tour that reverses his vision of the defiled Jerusalem temple in chs 8—9 by showing a pristine and pure temple, whose ongoing holiness is secured by ideally constructed buildings, gates, and walls. The temple complex is a perfect square, with each side measuring around 850 feet (42:20), and it faces east, with the complex's east gate being in line with the front of the main temple building. Ezekiel's tour begins at the eastern gate of the complex's outer wall and moves from the outer court and its gates to the inner court and its gates to the temple building itself and finally to a building behind the temple.

At work throughout the description is the view of holiness known from priestly texts in the Pentateuch (see Exod 40; Num 2), which associates certain sacred spaces with differing levels of holiness (Tuell 2009, 285-86). Not unlike the way modern churches often differentiate among the foyer, sanctuary, and altar/platform, in the priestly conception the level of holiness increases (and thus the level of public access decreases) in concentric circles as one moves closer to the sanctuary's innermost room (the "holy of holies"). Perhaps more significantly, however, the secure construction and ideal purity envisioned by the text intersect with the experiences of trauma victims seeking a new future. The complex's precisely square construction not only represents the perfection of this new reality and its alignment with the divine will (Bowen 2010, 246) but also signifies the reestablishment of a sense of order and coherence that is fractured by the experience of trauma. The temple's fortifications and careful regulations of access guarantee the protection of the divine holiness from anything that might defile, symbolically offering a new sense of safety to those trauma victims who fear the reoccurrence of their tragedy.

Drawing Ezekiel's New Temple

There has been an ongoing fascination, particularly in popular dispensationalist and end-times movements, to construct models or draw exact representations of the temple complex described in chs 40—48, often with the idea that this temple will someday exist. As noted in the Behind the Text discussion, this desire already mistakenly reads the text as a blueprint for a literal building project. Additionally, such modeling and drawing is not possible based on the text without much speculation. The chapters contain unclear and inconsistent architectural information, often featuring divergent depictions and obscure ancient terms. In spite of the meticulous detail, the text actually gives only selective dimensions, listing, for example, only the vertical measurements for the outer wall (40:5) and providing no precise locations or measurements for some of the buildings in the inner courts.

■ **40:1-4** The first four verses of ch 40 provide the overall introduction to Ezekiel's final vision. Ezekiel reports that his vision takes him to **a very high mountain** in **the land of Israel** (v 2). As we have discussed previously (see chs 6 and 35—36), mountains often function as symbols in Ezekiel, and the numerous plural mountains often associated with sinful practices here give way to the one mountain that symbolizes Yahweh's holy dwelling (Casson 2004). On this mountain, Ezekiel sees a large complex that resembles a city. The sight is not simply a set of **some buildings,** as the NIV translation suggests, but neither is it an actual city. Rather, Ezekiel encounters a walled temple complex massive enough to resemble an ancient walled city. Verse 3 introduces **a man** (Heb., *'îš*) with a shining appearance (presumably a divine figure), who will serve as Ezekiel's tour guide. As the reference to the **linen cord and a measuring rod** in the man's hand suggests, however, the primary function of this tour guide will be to measure the structure for the prophet. The only command given to Ezekiel is not to build the structure, but simply to observe carefully what he sees and then make that known to **the house of Israel** (v 4). Hence, at the outset, readers encounter a vision that does not provide a blueprint for a future building project but imagines a holy temple, already established and secure, symbolizing the presence of Yahweh that stands in the midst of the people's current reality (see Behind the Text).

■ **40:5-16** Ezekiel's guided tour of the temple commences in vv 5-16 as the man first measures **the wall** around the outside of the complex (v 5) and then proceeds to measure **the gate facing east** through which they enter the outer courtyard (vv 6-16). Although most English translations refer to the **temple area** in v 5, the Hebrew at this point and frequently throughout chs 40—48 designates the building literally as the *house* (*bayit*), emphasizing the symbolic significance of this structure as the locus of Yahweh's dwelling among the people. Verse 5 also introduces the unit of measure used throughout the vision by stating that the man's measuring rod was **six long cubits**. A normal cubit generally appears to be the length from a man's fingertips to elbow, or about eighteen inches. The word **long** does not appear in the Hebrew text, but the remainder of the phrase (**each of which was a cubit and a handbreath**) may imply the use of a special extended cubit for temple and palace construction, although evidence for this practice dates only to the Persian period (see Tuell 2009, 298). The text envisions the basic measurement of the **long cubit** as about twenty and a half inches, making the measuring rod about ten feet long and the wall ten feet high and ten feet thick.

The east gate in the outer wall (vv 6-16), as well as the north and south gates to be described in vv 20-27, resemble typical gates in Iron Age cities that were themselves large structures housing several (often six, as here) chambers within the gate. Each gate described here is very large (ca. fifty cubits long and twenty-five cubits wide), essentially comprising its own building (by comparison, Solomon's entire temple in 1 Kgs 6:2 measured sixty by twenty regular cubits). Although gates were not part of the description of Solomon's temple in 1 Kgs 6, the gates in Ezekiel's depiction relate to the aspect of traumatic experience in which victims seek future safety by symbolizing protection of the divine holiness from any kind of defilement (but cf. Odell 2005, 491).

■ **40:17-27** The description and measurement of the temple complex continues as the man guides Ezekiel through the eastern gate and into the outer courtyard with its various chambers (vv 17-19). Ezekiel then reports the measuring of the other two gates (also with six chambers each) in the complex's outer wall on the north (vv 20-23) and south (vv 24-27).

■ **40:28-47** The next leg of Ezekiel's guided tour proceeds to the description and measurement of the inner courtyard and its elements (vv 28-47). The text first describes the three gates of the inner court on the south (vv 28-31), east (vv 32-34), and north (vv 35-37), which lead into the inner courtyard through a second wall that separates the inner and outer courts. Ezekiel's guide then proceeds to show him several rooms along the wall of the inner courtyard designated for specific functions and personnel. Verses 38-43 describe chambers in which the various sacrifices and offerings for the temple altar are prepared. Verses 44-47 depict two rooms on either side of the inner court that are assigned to two different groups of priests (a distinction that will also be significant in 44:9-31). The southern room is **for the priests who have charge of the temple** and its general workings, while the northern room is **for the priests who have charge of the altar** and the actual performance of the sacrifices before Yahweh (vv 45-46).

The remainder of v 46, which identifies **the sons of Zadok** as the priests who may serve at Yahweh's altar, introduces a distinction among Levitical priests that appears in various ways throughout Ezekiel's vision (see especially 44:9-31) and remains one of the most vexing interpretive issues for chs 40—48. More will be said in the commentary on 44:9-31, but at this point we may note that Ezekiel (or his later editors) draws a significant distinction between the **Zadokite** line of Levitical priests and other Levites. The designations here derive from the stories of David's actions at the founding of Jerusalem and the uniting of his kingdom (see Tuell 2009, 288). As an act of unification, the story recounts David's establishment of two high priests in Jerusalem—Abiathar, who descended from a Levite line going back to Moses and represented the northern tribes, and Zadok, who descended from a Levite line going back to Aaron and represented the southern tribes (2 Sam 20:25; 1 Chr 15:11; 18:16; 24:6). At the time of David's death, however, Abiathar supported the rival claimant to the throne, Adonijah, instead of Solomon (1 Kgs 1:7), and 1 Kgs 2:26-27 reports that Solomon subsequently banished Abiathar and his priestly house to Anathoth (so the origin of Ezekiel's contemporary, Jeremiah, see Jer 1:1). This move made Zadok and his descendants the sole high priestly line in the Jerusalem temple until the Babylonian destruction in 586 B.C. Given Ezekiel's likely identity as a priest of the sixth-century Jerusalem temple, it is not surprising that he envisions the Zadokite line as having the sole authority over the primary priestly duty of the altar and its sacrifices.

Throughout the remainder of the vision, Ezekiel (or his later editors) continues this depiction of the Zadokites as having priority over the new temple, with the other Levites in a secondary role. Statements such as 40:46, however, raise the issue of whether Ezekiel envisions a demotion of the Levites from a higher status that they may have held prior to the return from exile. Readers should connect this passage with 44:9-31 and see the commentary there for further discussion, as the idea of a demotion of the Levites in favor of the Zadokites is often developed from 44:9-31 and read back onto the present text. At this point we may note that the NIV's **only (the only Levites who may draw near to the LORD)** in v 46 does not appear in the Hebrew, so the divine command may not be a punitive exclusion of the Levites but simply a division of duties between primary and secondary priestly groups (Tuell 2009, 299).

■ **40:48—41:26** After passing by the altar that sits outside the main temple building (40:47), Ezekiel's guide now leads him to the actual sanctuary building itself, the main concentration of holiness in the priestly view of sacred space (see above). The first section (40:48—41:4) describes the temple as having the typical ancient Near Eastern floor plan consisting of three parts: (1) the **portico** (vestibule [40:48-49]) measuring twenty by twelve cubits, (2) the **outer sanctuary** (nave/main sanctuary room [41:1-2]) measuring forty by twenty cubits, and (3) the **inner sanctuary** (most holy place/holy of holies [41:3-4]) measuring a perfect square of twenty by twenty cubits (compare the measurements given for Solomon's temple in 1 Kgs 6—7). As noted above, in the priestly conception of holiness, the degree of sanctity increases as one moves closer to the innermost room (holy of holies). The text perhaps symbolizes this conception by noting that the width of the entrances decreases as one moves further inside the temple, perhaps again reflecting the increased safeguarding of Yahweh's holiness from defilement (Bowen 2010, 242).

Following the description of the three-part sanctuary building, Ezekiel's guide measures the wall of the temple in 41:5, and then depicts and measures the side rooms (three stories in height) along the sides of the sanctuary. Verses 12-15a continue the tour by showing Ezekiel a building behind the temple (hence on the far west end of the whole complex), but the nature and function of the building remain unclear, and the guide's description returns to the interior of the sanctuary building in vv 15b-26. These verses focus on the furnishings and decorations of the interior and especially highlight the **wooden altar** in front of the most holy place (v 22).

■ **42:1-20** The final part of the first section of Ezekiel's vision (42:1-20) completes the tour of the new temple by moving back out of the main sanctuary building and describing several rooms designed for specific functions and priestly personnel (vv 1-14). The exact location and appearance of these buildings remain uncertain, however, but at least some of them are designated places in which the priests eat their share of the sacrifices offered on the altar (v 13; see Lev 1—7). Ezekiel 42:15-20 then concludes the visionary tour of the new temple, as Ezekiel's guide gives one final measurement of the whole complex (five hundred by five hundred cubits, ca. 850 feet per side—a perfect square [v 20a]). Yet, perhaps the most significant element is the final phrase of v 20 that describes the purpose of the wall around the entire complex as to separate the holy from the common (see Lev 10:10). Here the vision of the new temple connects to Ezekiel's overall explanation of the people's trauma of exile and hope of return in terms of Yahweh's holiness. In this vision of a new reality in which Yahweh's holy presence once again dwells among the people in a purified temple, the complex's architecture and wall symbolize the need to protect the divine holiness from impurity so that Yahweh's presence can dwell continually with the people in their restored land.

B. Vision of the Return of Yahweh's Presence (43:1-11)

■ **1-6** The second section of chs 40—48 constitutes arguably the climactic scene in the whole book of Ezekiel. Just as the vision in chs 8—11 portrayed the departure of Yahweh's presence from the defiled Jerusalem temple, 43:1-11 depicts the long-awaited and permanent return of Yahweh's *kābôd* (**glory/ presence**) to this new purified temple and to the midst of a now-transformed holy people. Bowen describes the power of this portrayal for those who have endured the people's trauma: "The emotional impact on the exiles of the image of YHWH's glory filling the Temple would have resembled the emotional impact of the liberation of Nazi concentration camps" (2010, 248). The **glory/ presence** returns through the east gate, the same gate through which Ezekiel had observed it depart Jerusalem in 11:23. This parallel constitutes the most direct implication that the pure temple in chs 40—48 is a new version of the defiled temple that had existed in Jerusalem before 586 B.C. Even so, the depiction of Yahweh's return in 43:1-11 is, at this point at least, only a vision of an alternative reality for those who remain in exile, although it may be designed to display a divine reality that is already in existence (see Behind the Text). Ezekiel makes this visionary character explicit in v 3 by comparing the experience of the **glory/presence** he has here with both the vision when Yahweh **came to destroy the city** (v 3; see chs 8—11) and when Yahweh had first appeared to him **by the Kebar river** (43:3; see chs 1—3). The imagery resembles that of the earlier visions (**roar of rushing waters . . . the land was radiant** [v 2]), but with particular emphasis upon Yahweh's presence. The term *kābôd* (**glory/presence**) occurs four times in vv 1-5, and the depiction as a whole parallels the ending of the book of Exodus in which Yahweh's presence inhabits the completed, pure tabernacle (Exod 40:34-38).

■ **7-11** In the context of the whole of Ezek 43, which continues into the next major section of the outline given above for chs 40—48, the opening scene in vv 1-11 gives way to a discussion of the implications of the return of Yahweh's presence for various aspects of Israel's existence in relationship to Yahweh and with one another. Yet, vv 7-9 first relate a divine speech to Ezekiel that emphatically draws the reader's focus to Yahweh's return as the culmination of all that the prophet has promised in his restoration oracles in chs 33—37 and, indeed, in his overall interpretation of the people's trauma: **I will live among the Israelites forever. The house of Israel will never again defile my holy name . . . I will live among them forever** (vv 7, 9). Ezekiel thus proclaims that Yahweh's larger aim of restoring the divine holiness in Israel and the world, which provided a way for the prophet to make sense of the trauma of destruction and exile, will come to fruition in a transformed people who will once again live in the presence of a holy God. Verses 10-11 return to Ezekiel's original charge at the start of the vision in ch 40 to describe what he has seen to his people so that they can have the full picture of this new reality. As we have seen elsewhere in the book (see commentary on 16:54, 61; 20:43; 36:31-32; 39:26-27), 43:10 states that the people's experience of this new reality will cause them to be **ashamed** of their past rebellion and trauma. In keeping with the climactic character of the passage, however, v 11 indicates that the prophet is no longer simply to leave the people in their shame. Rather, the reality of this visionary temple and what it represents of a new future in Yahweh's presence now become the answer to the people's feelings of shame: **If they are ashamed of all they have done, make known to them the design of the temple** (v 11).

C. The Torah of the New Temple (43:12—46:24)

The third major section of the final vision stands as the structural centerpiece of chs 40—48, with two sections before and after (see Behind the Text). The extended unit in 43:12—46:24 (which may contain various compositional layers added at different times) is a law code, explicitly designated as the **law of the temple** (*tôrat habāyit*; *the rule/torah of the house*) in v 12. As in 40:5, the use of the Hebrew term for **house** to designate the temple reflects Ezekiel's view that the sanctuary's central function is to be the locus of the newly restored divine presence in the midst of the people. The torah (lit., instruction) pertaining to this *house* is the only law code in the OT not presented on the lips of Moses in the Pentateuch. The statutes in these chapters contain both extensive similarities and significant differences with the Mosaic legislation in the Pentateuch, giving Ezekiel the appearance of being a new Moses and this holy mountain (43:12) a new Mount Sinai. Even so, the torah in 43:12—46:24 has been integrally woven into the overall temple vision. Throughout the unit, Ezekiel and his guide revisit several of the places mentioned in the initial tour in chs 40—42, and Ezekiel receives various elements of the torah at each location.

The law code covers a wide range of topics that can be divided in numerous ways (e.g., Tuell [2009, 306] identifies eight sections in 44:1—46:18 as the main body of the code), but the majority of them relate explicitly to elements of temple activity and worship practices connected to the divine presence. To many commentators, the legislation throughout these chapters has the apparent function of restricting access to the temple, but Odell argues that it functions in the opposite way to guarantee the ongoing availability of access to Yahweh's presence for all Israelites (2005, 500). In any case, the instructions in 43:12—46:24, following as they do the depiction of Yahweh's return to the ideal temple, spell out the *implications* of Yahweh's presence in the midst of the people on two levels: (1) the implications for how the people maintain a proper relationship *with Yahweh* (especially through worship) and (2) the implications for how the people maintain a proper relationship *with one another in the community* (especially through the practice of justice). Hence, the divine torah given to Ezekiel places the reality that Israel lives in the presence of a holy God who has been installed as their sovereign as the central defining element for how they live as a people and calls both ancient and modern readers to consider how this sense of living in the midst of the divine presence can and should lead them to recalibrate the practices of their life as a whole (see From the Text).

■ **43:12** Yahweh's statement to Ezekiel in 43:12 (**This is the law of the temple: All the surrounding area on top of the mountain will be most holy. Such is the law of the temple**) is a transitional verse. Although most English translations include it with the end of the temple tour in 43:1-11, it is a hinge that joins that vision with the laws that follow. The statement that the **area on top of the mountain** will possess the highest degree of holiness is not the **law** to which Yahweh refers, but more likely provides the basic summary statement that is explicated by all of the instructions that follow.

■ **43:13-27** The first section of instructions deals with the measurement, purification, and consecration of the **altar** that Ezekiel had quickly passed in 40:47. After giving the altar's dimensions (43:13-17), the laws stipulate the rituals of purification and consecration that are required before the altar can be used for offerings (vv 18-27). The altar occupies the same place of priority in the description of the wilderness tabernacle in Exod 20:22-26, and the instructions for purification and consecration here parallel those given in Exod 29:36-37 and Lev 8:14-15.

■ **44:1-3** Chapter 44 turns from the initial issue of how to prepare the altar to a series of instructions concerning access to the temple and the performance of its worship rituals. The first section in vv 1-3 returns Ezekiel to the east gate of the temple through which Yahweh's glory/presence had initially departed in chs 8—11 and then returned in ch 43. Ezekiel observes that the gate is now closed, and Yahweh announces that it will **remain shut** so that **no one may enter through it** (44:2). The permanent closing of the gate to through traffic will serve as a reminder and assurance that Yahweh has reentered the perfected sanctuary and will not depart again. The only partial exception to the rule is that the **prince** may enter the gate area to eat the sacrificial meal but must exit the gate without proceeding into the temple (v 3). Chapters 45—46 will provide more legislation concerning the prince and his roles in the community and its worship, but, as elsewhere, Ezekiel continues to designate the ruler of this new society as **prince** (*nāśi*) rather than "king" (*melek*), likely emphasizing his secondary status beneath Yahweh as the true sovereign (see 34:24; 37:25). Here, however, the instructions add the dimension that even the prince's political status does not give him unrestricted access to the divine presence.

■ **44:4-8** Verses 4-8 follow the legislation concerning the closed eastern gate with ordinances that expand the issue of "who may be admitted to the temple and all those who are to be excluded from the sanctuary" (v 5 NRSV; the NIV translates the Hebrew literally, **Give attention to the entrance of the temple and all the exits of the sanctuary**). The text returns to Ezekiel's characteristic priestly language of **detestable practices** (v 6; *tôʿēbôt*; ***abominations***), meaning those rebellious deeds that polluted the temple and led to the withdrawal of Yahweh's presence, but now identifies those defiling acts as the admission of foreigners into the temple and its worship practices. Odell observes that this is the same charge leveled against King Zedekiah in ch 17, where Ezekiel condemned the king for breaking his covenant with Nebuchadnezzar and engaging in rebellious alliances with Egypt (2005, 506). Hence, the charge of admitting foreigners probably does not refer to the practice of pagan rituals or the worship of other gods, but the ways in which political alliances were often symbolically consummated through joint worship between the parties. Additionally, although the command here appears to be ethnically exclusive, resulting in a vision that excludes all immigrants and foreigners, close reading reveals that the law precludes only **foreigners uncircumcised in heart and flesh** (v 7). The focus is not on ethnicity, but on safeguarding the temple from defilement by those who have not undergone a transformation of character that has produced a will oriented toward obedience to Yahweh. Another section of Yahweh's instructions in 47:21-23 will make this distinction explicit by commanding the inclusion of other foreigners as citizens who share Israel's inheritance (see also Isa 56:3-8).

■ **44:9-31** Although the NIV begins a new paragraph with v 10 (cf. NRSV), v 9 serves as a transition from the laws about foreigners to the discussion of Levites and the temple priesthood that comprises the rest of the chapter (vv 9-31). This passage begins a "comprehensive program of restoration" for the temple cult that makes up the remainder of the law of the temple in chs 44—46 and sets new instructions in place for the roles of the priests, the offerings to be made by the prince and people, and the yearly ritual calendar of holy days and festivals (Odell 2005, 506). The first section (vv 9-31) returns to the issue concerning the proper role of the Levite priestly line that was initially discussed in 40:46. The reader should refer back to the commentary there, as the present discussion assumes the former. As noted with 40:46, Ezekiel (or his later editors) draws a significant distinction between the **Zadokite** line of Levitical priests and other Levites. Just as in the previous passage, 44:9-31 depict the Zadokites as having priority over the new temple's most important function of the actual offerings on the altar, with the other Levites in a secondary role as overseers of the gates, assistants for preparation of the offerings, and basic functionaries (likewise in Num 18:1-7, 21-24).

As mentioned in the discussion of Ezek 40:46, these depictions have raised the issue of whether Ezekiel envisions a demotion of the Levites from a higher status that they may have held prior to the return from exile. The divine speech in 44:9-16, however, adds a new dimension to this question by explaining the Levites' restriction from the altar as due to the fact that they fell into apostasy and idolatry during the days of the rebelliousness of the house of Israel, becoming complicit in the people's sin, while the Zadokite priests **faithfully carried out the duties of my sanctuary when the Israelites went astray from me** (v 15). This addition gives the impression that Ezekiel indeed envisions a condemnation and demotion of the Levites, but no other evidence supports this charge and Ezekiel has previously condemned the entire Jerusalem priestly establishment (chs 8—11). So, to many commentators, 44:9-16 appears to be propaganda added by Zadokite priests in the later Second Temple period (see Tuell 2009, 308; Bowen 2010, 252). The entire issue remains heavily debated, however, as the interpretation of this passage is plagued by textual difficulties and is bound up with the complex efforts to reconstruct the history of the Israelite priesthood and the compositional history of the different literary traditions concerning priestly arrangements in the Pentateuch (see Duguid 1994, 58-90; Darr 2001, 1575-76). For example, texts from the so-called Priestly source in Num 18 establish the Levites as a secondary class of priests that serve the Aaronides, but the book of Deuteronomy describes the Levites on equal footing with full access to the sanctuary and its offerings. Scholars have, at times, suggested that Deuteronomy reflects the chronologically earlier arrangement and Ezekiel represents the demotion of the Levites that led to the later arrangement described in Numbers. Others, however, conclude that Ezekiel simply envisions a return (not demotion) to

44:9-31

pre-destruction roles as conceived in priestly circles, or even a promotion for the Levites back to a secondary role from which they had been excluded just before or during the exile (Odell 2005, 508).

Whatever the background of Ezekiel's arrangement, the rest of vv 17-31 provide instructions concerning the priests and their function in the restored Israel. The regulations here have both similarities and differences with the legislation concerning the priesthood in the Holiness Code (see Lev 21:1—22:9), but Ezek 44:23 provides the most definitive statement of the priests' overall function, again cast in terms of Ezekiel's concern with the distinction between purity and impurity for the sake of maintaining Yahweh's presence in the new temple: **They are to teach my people the difference between the holy and the common and show them how to distinguish between the unclean and the clean** (see Lev 10:10). Ezekiel 44:24-31 follows this overall statement with rules that govern the priests' tasks and status in Israel, including their role as judges for the people and overseers for the festivals (v 24), their need to maintain ritual purity in different circumstances (vv 25-27), and the provisions they are to receive from the people since they will not inherit any specific land holding (vv 28-31; see the division of the land among the tribes in 45:1-5; 48:1-29).

■ **45:1-6** The first section of ch 45 (vv 1-6) continues the theme of land inheritance introduced briefly in 44:28 and begins the visionary description of a physical map of the territory that constitutes the restored land of Israel. Prior to the presentation to the law code (43:12—46:24) still underway here, Ezekiel depicted the new temple in 40:1—43:11, and he will follow the law code with a detailed depiction of the new arrangements of Israel's restored physical territory in 47:1—48:35. At this point, 45:1-6 introduces the first part of the new territorial vision by designating a portion of land in the middle of Israel's territory as a **sacred district** where the ideal temple is located (v 1). The full description of the land in 47:13-23 and 48:1-29 will elaborate on this district, as well as the rest of Israel's new territorial divisions, and the portrayal resembles the acts of land allotment in Num 26:53-56 and Josh 14:1-5. The **sacred district is 25,000 cubits long and 20,000 cubits wide** (ca. 8 by 6.5 miles), the center of which is a square plot (500 by 500 cubits) upon which the temple sits (Ezek 45:2). Surrounding the temple within the holy district is land designated for the priests and their families (including the Levites [vv 4-5]), as well as the **city** that is not restricted to priests but **will belong to the whole house of Israel** (v 6). As we have seen in the depiction of the temple, the careful delineating and ordering of the areas around the sanctuary further serve to safeguard Yahweh's holiness from pollution that may threaten the divine presence in the restored community.

■ **45:7-9** Verses 7-9 continue the initial description of the new territorial arrangements by prescribing the allotment of the land on both sides of the sacred district to **the prince.** The designation of land for the prince outside the holy district serves to separate the prince and his political power from the temple, a separation that has been noticeably absent in eras of Israel's past, such as the days of Solomon (Bowen 2010, 256). The designation of land for the prince outside of the territories that will be allotted to the tribes in 48:1-29 also aims to discourage the political powers from unjust actions, especially the oppression of people by seizing their inherited lands for royal use and grant (45:8; see also 46:16-18). Verse 9 of ch 45 completes this thought by commanding the princes to **stop dispossessing** the people and practice justice and righteousness. The command switches to direct second person address to the princes by Yahweh, and subtly reminds Ezekiel's audience of its present time frame in which the ideal community being described remains at the level of a vision that is not yet an experienced reality.

■ **45:10-12** Although the admonitions in vv 10-12 may continue Yahweh's address to the princes, the commands seem to call for economic justice in the marketplace (**accurate scales,** consistent weights and measures) among all the people. The divine demand for economic justice echoes similar commands in the Pentateuch (e.g., Lev 19:35-36; Deut 25:13-16) and other prophets (e.g., Amos 8:5-6; Mic 6:10-11), but here it stands at the head of a lengthy section that envisions the reordering of Israel's life in light of the new reality of living in Yahweh's presence. This reordering involves not only how the people live justly in relationship with one another (Ezek 45:10-12) but also how they live in holiness before Yahweh through proper worship (45:13—46:24).

■ **45:13-25** Verses 13-25 turn from the reordering the people's relationships with one another to an extended discussion of how the people may live and worship rightly before Yahweh that will continue through the end of ch 46. The first section (45:13-17) provides instructions for the regular **grain offerings, burnt offerings and fellowship offerings (*peace/well-being offerings*).** Notable here is the text's identification of the most important **duty of the prince** in the restored community (v 17): the prince's chief task is to provide the materials needed for the people's offerings and thereby enable the community to worship rightly in holiness. This description reveals Ezekiel's perspective that the restored Israel will be a priestly/worshiping community in which the role of the political leader is virtually restricted to that of a patron who provides the resources for the proper worship of Yahweh and the ongoing holiness of the temple (Tuell 2009, 317). In this way, Ezekiel contrasts Israel's new reality with the old, in which Israel's kings/shepherds asserted their own sovereignty in unjust acts against their people and rebelliousness against Yahweh (see ch 34).

The remainder of ch 45 (vv 18-25) begins a new liturgical calendar for the restored community, the details of which continue through the end of ch 46. The entire unit moves from yearly to monthly (New Moon) to weekly (Sabbath) to daily (burnt and grain offerings) worship observances. The opening section in vv 18-25 gives instructions for the major festivals that the community will celebrate annually. The first annual festival (vv 18-20) is a new year's celebration to occur on the **first month on the first day** of each year and consists of a ritual to purify the sanctuary (v 18; note the parallel with the purification of the altar in 43:18-27). This is evidently the Day of Atonement known from Lev 16, but that festival is to take place on "the tenth day of the seventh month" (Lev 16:29-30). No other such festival on the first day of the year is known in the OT. The second annual festival (Ezek 45:21-24), which is to be held in **the first month on the fourteenth day,** is the **Passover** feast that commemorates Israel's deliverance from Egyptian bondage (v 21). The timing of this festival is the same as that given in the Pentateuch (see Exod 12:1-28; Num 28:16-25) but with different prescribed offerings (see Tuell 2009, 319). The reinstitution of the **Passover** connects the exiles' return from Babylonia with their ancestors' deliverance from Egypt (Bowen 2010, 257). Ezekiel 45:25 seems to describe a third annual festival, which goes unnamed in the text but begins in the **seventh month on the fifteenth day** and lasts for **seven days.** This is the date given for the Festival of Booths in Lev 23:34-44, but Ezekiel only mentions the prince's duty to provision various offerings. With these three festivals, the renewed liturgical calendar has both connections and disconnections with the annual worship celebrations outlined in the Pentateuch, but the Feast of Weeks (Pentecost) that occurs between Passover and the Festival of Booths (Lev 23:15-21) does not appear in Ezekiel.

■ **46:1-18** The final chapter of the law code continues the new liturgical calendar by turning to the monthly, weekly, and daily worship observances. Verses 1-12 give instructions for the monthly **New Moon** festival and weekly **Sabbath** worship (see also Num 28:9-15), with special focus on the prince's offerings to be made on these occasions. When considering this renewed calendar as a means of reordering the way the restored community will live together and before Yahweh in justice and worship, one notices a level of equality that is present. The prince has special access to the temple (Ezek 46:2, 8, 12) but also faces restrictions that bespeak of mutuality with the people. Both prince and people, for example, must enter and exit the temple together (v 10). This sense of mutuality continues in vv 13-15, which command the prince to provide the people with the resources needed for their daily offerings to be made morning by morning (see also 45:17), and in 46:16-18, which prohibit the prince from making permanent royal land grants to anyone except his sons.

■ **46:19-24** The last section of the law code resumes Ezekiel's tour of the temple, as the guide takes him back into the courtyards and shows him **sacred rooms facing north** in which the priests will properly prepare the offerings for the altar (vv 19-20) and **kitchens** in which the priests will boil the sacrifices (vv 21-24). Once again, the careful delineation of restricted places and particular processes concerning the temple worship serves symbolically to protect Yahweh's holiness from any pollution that may threaten the divine presence.

Ongoing Atonement in a Transformed Community

The repeated commands about maintaining purity, continuing concerns over sin, and provisions made for ongoing atonement in chs 43—46 may seem strange after Ezekiel has depicted the total transformation of the people's moral character in 36:16-38. Even after receiving a "new heart" and "new spirit," Ezekiel envisions the continuing need for sacrifices that provide the cleansing of sin and ensure fellowship with Yahweh. The presence of these things in the prophet's vision of a restored community suggests that the people's moral transformation, which involved the receipt of a new will/disposition oriented toward undivided loyalty to Yahweh, does not remove the possibility of moral failure or the need for ongoing forgiveness. The Wesleyan-Holiness tradition reflects this dynamic in its understanding of sanctification within the overall work of salvation. Although affirming the possibility of a moral transformation that grants the believer a pure love, an undivided will predisposed toward obedience to God, the tradition also affirms the need for ongoing moral transformation into the likeness of Christ and ongoing repentance as that process takes place. Just as Ezekiel envisions the need for continued cultic practice to shape the community after transformation, the Wesleyan-Holiness tradition celebrates the need for ongoing Christian growth after Wesley's so-called perfection of intention.

D. The New Land (47:1—48:29)

Following the law code that stands at the midpoint of chs 40—48, ch 47 marks the beginning of the last two sections that complete the overall vision (47:1—48:29; 48:30-35). These sections resume Ezekiel's visionary tour of the new temple, but the focus for the book's final two chapters broadens beyond the temple and its practices to depict the complete rejuvenation and reconfiguration of Israel's entire land. The unit portrays the rejuvenation and reconfiguration as the effects of the new divine presence and describes the life-giving resources that come from Yahweh's presence in the temple (47:1-12), the boundaries of a new land in which Israel will live (47:13-23), and the equitable division of that land among the people (48:1-29).

■ **47:1-12** The opening section of ch 47 (vv 1-12) resumes Ezekiel's visionary tour of the temple as the guide leads him **back to the entrance of the temple** (v 1). Ezekiel observes a small flow of water coming from under the temple and flowing toward the east. As the prophet and his guide follow and measure the flow out of the east gate of the temple complex and into the surrounding countryside, Ezekiel reports that the stream turns into a river, increasing in depth every one thousand cubits from **ankle-deep** to **knee-deep** to **waist**-deep to **a river that I could not cross** (vv 3-5). Moreover, as the river flows through the land, it generates life along its banks, with trees lining both sides (vv 6, 12). Verses 8-11 offer the most powerful image of this life-giving ability, as the guide proclaims that the river flows into the Dead Sea and will turn the salt water fresh, allowing people to fish along the shore. The imagery of the river here resembles several OT texts that portray Mount Zion, the location of the Jerusalem temple, as the source of life-giving rivers and streams (e.g., Ps 46:4; Zech 13:1; 14:8), and the rejuvenation of the Dead Sea employs imagery of the garden of Eden that Ezekiel has used in descriptions of Tyre (28:10-14) and Israel's restored future (36:35). The river that flows from the temple and the transformation it brings to barren and devoid areas symbolizes the life-giving character of the divine presence that has the power to breathe new life into the deathliness experienced by human persons and communities.

■ **47:13-23** The remainder of ch 47 continues the vision of the broader effects of Yahweh's presence on Israel's restored land and existence outside the temple. The messenger formula at the beginning of vv 13-23 introduces a speech in which Yahweh announces that the land is to be divided **among the twelve tribes of Israel** and describes the overall **boundaries** of the land as a whole (v 13). Combined with the preceding passage, this text represents the equitable distribution of the land as another reordering effect of Yahweh's presence in the community. Chapter 48 will detail the specific allotment to each tribe, and the number twelve is arrived at by omitting the Levites (who receive no land inheritance, see 44:28-31) and including Joseph's sons, Manasseh and Ephraim, among the tribes. Here, however, Yahweh outlines the borders of Israel's territory from north (47:15-17) to east (v 18) to south (v 19) to west (v 20). The act of allotment parallels Joshua's actions in Josh 13—21, and the boundaries bear some similarities to those given in Num 34:1-12. Yet, the precise boundaries—and the large amount of territory they enclose—do not reflect the area Israel controlled at any time in its past (although Tuell [2009, 335] suggests they reflect the borders of the later Persian satrapy of which Judah was a part in the postexilic era). Moreover, as we saw with the description of the temple in chs 40—43, the text does not provide the kind of consistent and comprehensive information that would allow a literal drawing or enactment of the territory (e.g., some geographical names mentioned are unknown or unclear).

The final words of Yahweh that follow the description of the boundaries add a significant element: the inclusion of **aliens** (*gērîm; sojourners, immigrants*) in the assignment of land inheritance: **You are to allot it as an inheritance for yourselves and for the aliens who have settled among you and who have children** (47:22). The second part of v 22 takes the equal treatment of the **aliens** to an even higher level and commands that the Israelites **consider them as native-born Israelites** (i.e., treat them equally as full members of the community). The term for **alien** here is different from that used for "foreigner" (*nēkār*) in 44:7-9, where the text described those excluded from the temple. The **alien** (*gēr*) in the ancient world was a class of immigrants or migrant workers who had left their place of origin and put themselves under the care of another society. Numerous OT texts command special care and justice for **aliens** (usually alongside widows and orphans) (e.g., Exod 22:21-24; Lev 19:33-34; Deut 24:17), but Ezek 47:21-23 extends this care to a level of equality that surpasses all other such texts.

■ **48:1-29** The first section of ch 48 (vv 1-29) completes the description of the reorganized land that began with the boundaries in 47:13-23 by detailing the land allotments given to each tribe. The use of **tribes** reflects the tradition that Israel traces its ancestry to Jacob's (Israel's) twelve sons (Gen 29:31—30:24; 32:28; 35:16-18). The most significant feature of these allotments is their equity. Each tribe receives an equal share of the restored land. The text envisions each tribe being allotted an east-west strip of land, and the tribes appear one after the other in evenly demarcated areas. The description begins with seven tribes in the north (Ezek 48:1-7), followed by the holy district in the center of the territory (vv 8-20), which contains the sanctuary, city, and priests' land, with the prince's land on either side of the center area (see the initial description of the center holy district in 45:1-8). The description concludes by listing five tribes to the south of the holy district (48:23-29).

47:13—
48:29

In spite of the seeming straightforwardness of the description, however, Ezekiel's vision of the land is a literal impossibility and functions only at the symbolic level to represent the kind of equal and just community that even includes fair sharing of land and natural resources. The vision ignores all natural geography and topography, does not provide north-south dimensions for the tribal areas, and departs from other OT listings of tribal territories. Tuell adds that the depiction of the land here could never have historically occurred for Ezekiel and his audience, since the "ancient clan-centered social system" came to end with the exile, if not before, and "by the Persian period the tribes no longer existed" (2009, 340). Yet, at the symbolic level, the text's use of the label "tribes" to describe the restored people marks this picture as a new beginning that breaks with the divisive political and nationalistic identities of "Israel" and "Judah" or "Jerusalemites" and "exiles" (Odell 2005, 521).

Ezekiel's Vision and the Book of Revelation

The writer of the book of Revelation adapts many elements of Ezekiel's vision in chs 40—48 into the vision of the new Jerusalem in Rev 21—22. Ezekiel provides many of the underlying images for Revelation's vision, yielding both similarities and differences between the two (see Bowen 2010, 266-67). Both visions feature a divine tour guide who measures a new place where God will dwell, complete with twelve gates named after the twelve tribes of Israel and a river flowing out of the structure. But Revelation reverses Ezekiel's central imagery. While Ezekiel's depiction of the new reality centers on the temple, the new Jerusalem in Rev 21—22 focuses on the city itself (as an alternative to "Babylon," i.e., Rome), and the city is distinguished by the fact that it needs no temple because God's presence is so manifest ("for its temple is the Lord God the Almighty and the Lamb" [Rev 21:22 NRSV]).

E. The New Jerusalem (48:30-35)

■ **48:30-35** The final section of Ezekiel's vision of the return of Yahweh's glory/presence shifts its focus to **the city** that has been described as standing at the center of the land in the holy district. Although located alongside the temple, previous descriptions have announced that this city, unlike the temple, is available to all Israel (see 45:6; 48:15-20). Yahweh's depiction in vv 30-35 confirms this assertion, with a special emphasis on the equal access to the city that all Israelites enjoy. The passage first describes the gates that form the **exits of the city** (v 30). Each side of the city (**north** [vv 30-31]; **east** [v 32]; **south** [v 33]; **west** [v 34]) has three gates, and Yahweh announces that the gates will each be named after one of the twelve **tribes of Israel** (v 31), symbolizing the people's solidarity and equality of access to the divine presence.

Following a final overall measurement of the city in v 35*a*, however, the vision ends with Yahweh's declaration of a special name for the new city that stands in the middle of the land and, along with the purified temple, represents the divine presence: **And the name of the city from that time on will be:** THE LORD IS THERE (v 35*b*). The name—merely two words in Hebrew, *Yahweh šāmmâ*—forms the grand climax to the entire vision in chs 40—48 that has depicted a new reality for the exiles in which Yahweh's presence dwells among them in a purified temple and holy community. The reconstitution of the land and temple and the reordering of the people's life before Yahweh and with one another have permanently fixed Yahweh's presence as the defining characteristic of this people's envisioned new life. As Odell notes, the final vision never refers to this city as Jerusalem, perhaps in order to symbolize that this is a truly new place of Yahweh's dwelling that bears no link to the old Jerusalem that was a place of defilement and destruction (2005, 525). Yet, if one reads this final vision in the context of Ezekiel's other major visions of Yahweh's glory, one sees an overall movement in which the prophet depicts Yahweh's presence withdrawing from a defiled temple, the temple being destroyed, cleansed, and restored, and Yahweh's presence returning to dwell in a purified temple and community. This larger plot line gives Ezekiel and his audience a way to renarrate their trauma of destruction and exile and understand it within the context of Yahweh's work to reestablish his holiness in the world—a work that also provides hope for a new reality beyond the trauma.

FROM THE TEXT

Throughout the preceding discussion, we have observed that Ezekiel's description of a new temple for God's presence does not provide the kind of information that would allow for it to be constructed by the people as a literal building in the future, but remains at the level of a vision of another reality to which the prophet is commanded to bear witness (see commentary on 40:1—42:20). We have also noted that unlike the description of the wilderness tabernacle in Exodus, Ezek 40—48 contains no instructions for Ezekiel or the people to build the structure being described. Hence, the theological message communicated by the meticulous details of Exod 25—40, namely, the call for careful and thorough obedience in order to be in God's presence, does not occupy the central place in Ezekiel. As noted in the Behind the Text discussion, Ezekiel's vision of a perfect temple that houses God's holy presence in the midst of the people and an ideal Israelite society that lives together in justice and purity in the midst of that divine presence is likely best understood as a symbol designed to reframe the exiles' imagination and lead them to envision a new reality of life before God and with each other.

So how would this vision have shaped the lives of the prophet and his audience who still found themselves living in exile and struggling to deal with the trauma they had experienced? *The text reveals a temple that is already complete and in existence and imaginatively draws the exiles toward a new way of seeing not only the future but also the present. It offers a picture of divine holiness and sovereignty that is already established and a glimpse of the kind of just and pure society that can emerge from participating in the divine presence.* Said differently, the theological significance of this vision is in its *immediacy*. It proclaims the existence of a present reality that awaits a future consummation but in which the people (even those in exile) can participate now. This message is particularly powerful for those living under the disorienting cloud of trauma. Even in the context of seemingly all-powerful empires, nations, and forces, the vision asserts that none of those powers can displace God's sovereignty and order. As Tuell states, "Although the earthly Zion is in ruins, the heavenly Zion—God's true home—remains pristine" (2009, 295). Ezekiel sets forth a new defining reality for the community by announcing that God's people, whatever their present circumstances, live even now in the presence of God as he is enthroned in holiness and sovereignty. In the end, however, the vision leaves God's people to live in the tension between their sometimes traumatic present reality and the conviction of God's sovereign presence into which they are even now called.

The power of Ezekiel's vision does not, of course, negate the problematic texts that seem to advocate exclusion and boundary-enforcement that results in certain persons being denied access to places of God's presence (e.g., 44:4-14). Just as these texts seem to emerge from the desire to safeguard God's presence from pollution, the concern with guarding against defilement and maintaining holiness has often resulted in the exclusion of various persons and groups from participation in the church, its sacraments, and its ministry throughout the history of Christianity (see Bowen 2010, 254). One can think here of the traditions within Christianity that have, at various times, subordinated or excluded persons of color, women, and legal or illegal immigrants, even as the church today continues to wrestle with its response to issues regarding sexual orientation. It seems that the church's desire to take seriously the present reality of God's presence and holiness will inevitably generate a tension concerning boundaries and access and call for the prayerful and graceful negotiation of that tension.

Alongside this tension, however, Ezekiel's extraordinary vision of God's presence in the community works perhaps most powerfully at the level of imagination, inviting its readers to envision a reality of God's presence and a holy community that is present now and to reimagine their current reality in light of it. The vision calls exiles of Ezekiel's day and ours to imagine a new existence with God and each other and then begin to inhabit it. Although they may first inhabit this alternative reality only in their imaginations, it does not remain a flight of fancy. When the vision has ended, the readers who have entered that alternative imagination for a time return to their "real world," but it appears different to them. When exiled readers who have experienced the imaginative power of Ezekiel's vision look again at the Kebar River (see 1:1) or a Babylonian house of worship, they cannot help but imagine the life-giving river that flows from God's presence and the new temple that brings home the divine holiness.

Within the vision's imaginative power experienced by the exiles, contemporary Christian readers in particular may hear a significant call in the book's final summary statement, **Yahweh is there** (48:35). *The affirmation is that the church lives in God's presence even now, and this notion of being people who live in God's presence has the power to reshape the way we practice each element of our relationship with God and life with others.* How would our lives before God and with others be different if we allowed the defining reality of each day to be that we live and move always in God's presence? On one level, this reality reminds us that, just as in the legislation in Ezekiel's vision, God's mercy and grace make it possible for us to come into relationship with God and be in God's holy presence even as our lives are marked by sinfulness (note the ongoing provisions for the people's atonement throughout chs 43—46). Additionally, even while the text's careful stipulation and meticulous details affirm the demanding seriousness of living a holy life in God's holy presence, imagining our lives in God's presence gives us the ability to trust in God's provision and protection and thus avoid becoming complicit in the systems and structures of our world by which we try to secure our own provision and protection through means that injure or deprive others.

On another level, the notion of living life constantly in God's presence can reframe how we live with one another in justice and righteousness. Just as Ezekiel's vision depicts a new kind of community marked by egalitarian land possession and the inclusion of outsiders (see 47:13-23), the conviction that everything we do in relation to another person is done in God's presence has the power to generate new life-giving relationships that are just and redemptive. In just two final Hebrew words (**Yahweh is there**), the lengthy book of Ezekiel concludes with what could be a defining creed: God calls God's people to imagine their world and live their lives within a deep conviction of God's abiding presence.

www.ingramcontent.com/pod-product-compliance
Lightning Source LLC
Chambersburg PA
CBHW070232240426
43673CB00044B/1766